"In this invaluable study of the central _____ _____ of _____ _____ _____ and theology of ministry and its power to fundamentally reshape our witness, Root proves once again to be the teacher we need. By story and argument, with characteristic humanity and theological insight, he bids us to repent of our culture's official optimism and to embrace the one thing genuinely needful: the good word of the cross that claims and consoles us still amid this vale of tears."

—**Philip G. Ziegler**, University of Aberdeen

"In a world marked by fleeting happiness, pervasive stress, and deepening despair, Root confronts a new set of urgent pathologies facing the church as it seeks to evangelize a secular age. Returning the church to the consoling vision of the theology of the cross, this book leads readers through these 'sad times' to a life transformed by the crucified God, calling for a reimagined evangelism—one that consoles rather than counts souls."

—**Ashley Cocksworth**, University of Roehampton

"Having read much of Root's work, I had some sense of what to expect from him on the topic of evangelism. I wasn't wrong—Root's practical theology continues to be drenched in philosophy and saturated in love for God. Still, the depth of this new conversation on the church's unique and invaluable calling to follow Jesus into sorrow stunned me. No contemporary voice of faith gives me more hope in Christ or sustenance for my ministry."

—**Rev. Katherine Willis Pershey**, co-pastor, First Congregational United Church of Christ, Appleton; author of *Very Married: Field Notes on Love and Fidelity*

"Evangelism is an area of theological inquiry that many avoid in the church and in seminaries today. Root invites us to explore evangelism anew through the lens of consolation, addressing the sorrow of this age with witness to, and participation in, the living God we know in Jesus Christ. Root's reimagining of evangelism, attending to the sacramental shape of divine-human encounter, will bless and challenge those who long for a deeper, more wholistic understanding of how best to share our Christian faith with others."

—**Ross Lockhart**, Vancouver School of Theology

"In *Evangelism in an Age of Despair*, Root piques my curiosity about the recovery of evangelism in our late-modern context. Somehow he compels me to see its surprising and miraculous usefulness for church ministry. Giving us more than a history on evangelism or another how-to program, he completely reframes it as 'the reception of care that places a person on a path of encounter with the divine.' The use of words such as *care* and *consolation* in his framing is especially resonant. It underscores a discipleship that is oriented to the human—and the relationship between the human and the divine—in such a way that the good news is an invitation to a way of being in this world that lifts up all the complexity of being human: sorrow, blessing, conflict, and the persistence of God's presence. As always, Root's work is rich and generative, and I'm eager to ponder this more."

—**Mihee Kim-Kort**, Presbyterian minister; author of *Outside the Lines: How Embracing Queerness Will Transform Your Faith*

"Root is my personal go-to when it comes to expositing the spiritual landscape in which we live. His unparalleled insight never fails to inspire compassion for my neighbors and renewed excitement about my faith. *Evangelism in an Age of Despair* is another astounding contribution in this regard, a book that dares to rehabilitate Christian evangelism in fresh and heartfelt ways, with urgency but without alarm or anxiety. I greatly needed this book (and the consolation to which it points). So too, I'd expect, does the world—to say nothing of the church. Highly, highly recommended."

—**David Zahl**, director, Mockingbird Ministries; author of *Low Anthropology*

Evangelism
in an Age
of Despair

Evangelism

in an Age

of Despair

HOPE BEYOND THE FAILED
PROMISE OF HAPPINESS

ANDREW ROOT

Ƀ
Baker Academic
a division of Baker Publishing Group
Grand Rapids, Michigan

© 2025 by Andrew Root

Published by Baker Academic
a division of Baker Publishing Group
Grand Rapids, Michigan
BakerAcademic.com

Printed in the United States of America

Library of Congress Cataloging-in-Publication Data
Names: Root, Andrew, 1974– author.
Title: Evangelism in an age of despair : hope beyond the failed promise of happiness / Andrew Root.
Description: Grand Rapids, Michigan : Baker Academic, a division of Baker Publishing Group, [2025] | Includes bibliographical references and index.
Identifiers: LCCN 2024036396 | ISBN 9781540968715 (paperback) | ISBN 9781540968722 (casebound) | ISBN 9781493449729 (ebook) | ISBN 9781493449736 (pdf)
Subjects: LCSH: Evangelistic work.
Classification: LCC BV3770 .R66 2025 | DDC 269/.2—dc23/eng/20240909
LC record available at https://lccn.loc.gov/2024036396

Baker Publishing Group publications use paper produced from sustainable forestry practices and postconsumer waste whenever possible.

25 26 27 28 29 30 31   7 6 5 4 3 2 1

To my mom, Judy,
who on the day I went to university
began praying Daniel 1:17 over me:

*"To these . . . young men God gave knowledge
and skill in every aspect of literature and wisdom;
Daniel also had insight into all visions and dreams."*

Since then, I've seen shapes and visions
of our cultural context and God's action in it.
She now prays this prayer for my children.

Contents

Preface   xi

Read before Using (Don't Skip!)   1

1. Get 'Em Healthy, Get 'Em Happy   5
   The Surprising Openness to Evangelism

2. Sad Times and a Sad (Pathetic) Church   33
   Is Evangelism's Task to Keep the Church Alive?

3. The Architecture of Our Sad Times   57
   Meeting the Positive Genealogists

4. Why All the Happiness Is Making Us Miserable   101
   Montaigne, Dead French Kings, and Immanent Contentment

5. "Not Okay"—Our Sad Times of Stress   133
   The Forgetting of Soul

6. The Math Savant and the Fire   167
   Pascal and the Promise of Our Sad Souls

7. Sisters as Pastors   203
   Leaning into Sorrow and the Promises of Consolation

8. Goodbyes That Save   221
   Great Sorrow and Consolation Evangelism

9. When Temptation Is Good   247
   And God Is Full of Sorrow

Epilogue   275
Index   281

Preface

As I was writing this book, my oldest child left for college. I was surprised at how sad it made me. I was ready for the anxiety. Months before he left, I had big, anxious questions: *Will he keep up with his work? How will he deal with homesickness? Is this school, one thousand miles away, the right fit?* And, of course, *Is it worth the money?* I knew I'd be swimming in anxiety. But it was the grief from his departure that surprised me. I was thrust into an acute sorrow. His departure was the sharp signal that our family was now different and never to be the same again. I missed him within *minutes* of him saying goodbye.

Not surprisingly, all the emotions took me back to my own freshman year. I wasn't as brave as my son. I went to school thirty minutes away from where I grew up. But the change still hit me hard. I was confused, lonely, and not sure I could do the work. I was sad. After just one week, sorrow blanketed me. I called home in tears. My mom gave me good advice. She told me to reach out to a high school classmate, someone I had known since I was young, who was at the same small university. I called her and asked if we could talk. I needed a friend. Someone to share (and hold) my fear and sorrow. I needed consolation.

She wasn't ready for that. I told her I was struggling. She told me she was mad at her boyfriend. That's all she had on her mind. Her annoyance with him dominated our conversation. There was no space for me to confess my sadness. I left our meeting lonelier than I'd entered it. I needed a minister, a consoler in my sorrow, but I found something much different.

Thirty years later, I pray that my son, amid his coming sorrows, can find someone who can give him the ministry of consolation. I pray that the ministry of consolation will deliver to him the good news of the gospel itself. That it might evangelize him, wrapping him in the message of God's own entering into sorrow, of Jesus meeting us and saving us inside our sadness.

Evangelism comes from the Greek *ev* or "good," and *angel* or "message" or "messenger." To be part of the event of evangelism is to find yourself in the angelic act of bringing or receiving the message of good news. But we late-modern Protestants aren't sure we can call evangelism *good*. "Evangelism" is a contested, even conflicted, word for late-modern Protestants. We're not sure we can still embrace it or whether we ever should have. But we also feel like we need it. With our institutions experiencing declines in numbers and resources, we wonder whether a focus on evangelism might help.

Probably not a surprise to anyone who has read my work, but I don't believe we're thinking correctly about evangelism, particularly not about its practical, theological, and cultural location. What follows in this project is a conversation on evangelism that contextualizes it in our late-modern times.

When the twentieth century ended, there arose a great swell of optimism. The twenty-first century was believed to be full of possibility. The potential has not quite come to fruition. Instead we have a society of anxious, stressed, and angry people who I believe, in the end, are sad. We are living in sad times. There are a handful of reasons for this, but ultimately I'll show that our times are so sad because, paradoxically, we are overcommitted to happiness. We seek happiness in nearly every waking moment. We want so badly to be happy that it's making us sad. To show how we have become such happiness-hunters and why this makes us so restless, and often miserable, I'll take us on a French tour. We'll meet the father of happiness hunting himself, the Renaissance French thinker Michel de Montaigne. Montaigne, we will see, is in us all.

Whatever evangelism can be for us late moderns, it will have to address our sadness. Montaigne taught us to focus on ourselves, making the self happy as the objective of life. The same French tradition that gave us happiness as our highest human goal also gave us another figure who early on saw that Montaigne's goals could never be reached. Blaise Pascal pointed out that we human beings are creatures of *soul* as much as *self*. As creatures of soul, we can never be settled and satisfied with happiness. Instead, we are the kind of creatures who require consolation, needing others to care for us in our sadness. As creatures of soul who are selves, we cannot avoid sorrow. Pascal wagers that if we can find such a minister and lean into our sorrow, we will find the very presence of Jesus Christ meeting and saving us. This becomes a dynamic form of evangelism.

In the second half of the book, I'll lead us into the pastoral theologies of five thinkers who placed consolation at the center of their thought. We'll look at Gregory of Nyssa and his sister Macrina, Jean Gerson, Johann von Staupitz, and Martin Luther. All five contend that consolation is central to our transformation, to our conversion, into the life of God. I seek in this project to construct a theology of evangelism that is a consolation theology. My hope is that doing so gives you a vision for how evangelism not only addresses our late-modern context but also gives us a practice of evangelism that escapes a market-driven consumer concern and returns us to the act of a living God. To give this all flesh, I'll again present the story of a fictional church (as in my book *Churches in the Crisis of Decline*). It's important to be concrete, and for this concreteness to reach the depth of divine action, I need to *show* more than *tell* what this looks like. I use fictional stories instead of actual field research because my goal is to shape your imagination—more than to give a scientific description of a particular context. I believe story can better carry this weight. My hope is that this story shows what it could look like for a congregation to do evangelism as a ministry of consolation.

Another way to see this project—especially as it connects to my other works—is as a presentation of evangelism born from the *theologia crucis*, the theology of the cross. I've sought to think of every part (particularly every practice) of the Christian tradition through the *theologia crucis*. My work as a whole has been a cultural philosophy in conversation with the theology of the cross. Evangelism takes center stage in this project.

Many friends have helped in this project, particularly by reading the manuscript and giving me feedback. Thanks to my colleague Alan Padgett, who is one of the best philosophical and theological minds I've known. Jessicah Duckworth and Blair Bertrand, my dear Princeton friends, again provided insightful feedback. Austin Carty, one of the best readers I know, provided wonderful insight on the manuscript as a whole and its relation to pastoral practice. Wes Ellis again provided his rich theological mind. Hank Spaulding, who's become a wonderful dialogue partner and friend, offered many helpful points to consider. Erik Leafblad was kind enough to read part of it and give some overarching comments. Mark Sampson, whose friendship and conversations around the church I value, provided unique insights at a handful of points. My work with David Wood on an Eli Lilly endowment grant continued to deepen these thoughts and my overall project. I'm honored by David's interest in what I'm trying to do.

Finally, my biggest thanks go to Kara Root for her love and talent in grounding both this project and my life.

Read before Using

(Don't Skip!)

What is this book really about?

This book is the continuation of my work on ministry as a form of action where the divine encounters the human. In this book I provide a vision of *evangelism as the practice and theology of consolation.*

But even as I write that, the syntax fails me.

In reading that phrase it's easy to put the weight on *evangelism* because it comes first. That might lead you to think that this book is primarily about evangelism, giving you a model for its shape and place in the church. If that's what you're reading for, you'll probably be disappointed. There are no models, or discussions of other models, in this book (though I do give you a picture of a church that is living out evangelism). I'm not dissecting evangelism as a practice or theology in this book. Rather, I'm exploring consolation as part of a lived theology of the cross that cannot help but make a space for evangelism.

The aim of this book, then, is *not* to endorse evangelism even in our late-modern pluralistic days. I am, however, an endorser! But instead of an endorsement, this book is more of an *apologia* (in the theological sense) for the place of evangelism inside a larger theology of ministry. It is an apology for evangelism in ministry more than it is a full-blown treatment of evangelism. What is fully treated here is a ministry of the church that is grounded in a consolation that moves us into the practice of evangelism (almost as a inevitable reflex). Through a story of one church and its laypeople alongside their pastor, this book provides a thought experiment

1

of how evangelism might be imagined inside a theology and practice of consolation that can reach those in our late-modern times—times that, as this book shows, are very sad ones.

Therefore, in the phrase "evangelism as the practice and theology of consolation," I intend to weight or underline "consolation." This book centers consolation as the practice that holds together evangelism and discipleship. The ground I'm hoping to break is not in discussing and justifying evangelism per se but in showing the ways that the divine encounters the human in consolation and therefore draws us into acts of evangelism.

My focus since my first book has been on how the divine encounters the human—how humans are transformed deeply by the act of a crucified God. Here I wish to show how consolation can bear the weight of the divine encountering the human. Through consolation, I'll show that evangelism must be imagined inside this divine-human encounter, drawing the human into Godself. That's salvation. Salvation, therefore, will be a central topic in this project but not as a point of decision—which evangelism is often reduced to. Rather, salvation and the work of evangelism will be seen as the point, the occurrence, where we turn over our sorrows to God (always with the help, with the ministry, of a community).

Evangelism and discipleship are fused. Evangelism is the invitation to receive consolation, to receive ministry. Evangelism is the reception of care that places a person on a path of encounter with the divine. Evangelism is the invitation to lean into one's sorrows to find the sacramental presence of the living God changing one's deaths into life. Walking this path, the one receiving consolation moves into discipleship as they lean into and give over their sorrows to the man of sorrows, Jesus Christ. By leaning into our sorrows, we are evangelized and therefore become Jesus's disciples. We are Jesus's disciples when, having received consolation, we go into the world to give consolation to others. This continues the unbroken circle of evangelism and discipleship, of the divine coming near to the brokenhearted, bringing life out of death and therefore saving the world.

What you're about to read is a case for how a practice and theology of consolation—which births a theology of the cross—can transform the human being so deeply, with such good news (*evangel*), that the human being is converted and claimed, made alive and saved right within all their sorrow. This project secures evangelism inside my construction of ministry as the place where the divine encounters the human. It offers a view of evangelism from the theology of the cross, one that avoids all instrumentality. It allows relationship to be for relationship (not for some other means), taking us into the divine claiming the human.

Blessed be the Lord of the cross, who raises the brokenhearted from the dead.

1

Get 'Em Healthy, Get 'Em Happy

The Surprising Openness to Evangelism

Mary Ann Hapstad has worked in human resources for twenty-five years, all but three of those with a trucking company out of San Diego County. When she started at the company, it was a small, family-owned business. By the time she left, the company had grown exponentially and had been bought by a large corporation. The company now moves over 25 percent of all industrial equipment in the California inland and Nevada.

Mary Ann fell into HR. Twenty-six years ago, she was hired as a scheduler. Her job was to keep spreadsheets tidy, drivers on time, and clients informed. It was the perfect job for her reentry into the work world. Mary Ann's youngest child had just entered first grade, and two full-time incomes had become necessary. Her affordable rural community in the foothills of the Laguna Mountains was changing fast. Companies from San Diego were pushing toward Mary Ann's once remote town, moving into newly built business complexes in the valley. Housing developers from Orange County were buying up old horse farms and turning them into high-end gated communities. The rich and the beautiful wanted out of the congested towns near the coast.

Property taxes and the overall cost of living were skyrocketing. This made it an easy decision when Bud Jr., the owner of the company and son of the founder, asked Mary Ann, just thirteen months after being hired as a scheduler, to be their first ever HR director. Bud Jr., a man of few words (but more than his father), simply said one Wednesday afternoon, "I guess they're tellin' me—the lawyers and such—that we need some kind of human resources person. I don't really know what that means. But you seem like a real organized gal, so you want it? It comes with a 10 percent raise."

That's all Mary Ann needed to hear. She'd never finished her college degree, but here was an offer with a pay level that usually came only to those with a college degree. The tensions in her marriage were high. Mary Ann and her husband fought about nearly everything. But money always seemed to be the spark that ignited the fuse. Mary Ann figured that more money would mean less tension. But that wasn't so. Just six months after starting the HR position and finding that it suited her quite well—while Mary Ann was falling in love with the job, gaining confidence and esteem as she found her way into a profession, learning so much at conferences and seminars—her marriage ended. It stung and wounded her.

Mary Ann's husband left, taking a job as a mechanic with an airline in Dallas. Her children, both under ten, were now without a father. Her oldest son particularly was shaken. It was all so painful. Keeping it all together was hard. The grief and worry were sharp and piercing. Work became her respite, the only place she felt competent. But even work couldn't completely take away her anxiety, shame, and sorrow over what was lost.

It was during that time, twenty-three years ago, that Mary Ann first connected to her church. She'd never been inside a church. Not once in childhood or adulthood. Her father had moved to California to reject polite society and all its formal beliefs—and religion was at the top of that list. The rural community in which Mary Ann grew up was made up of people like her father. They were mostly leftovers from the counterculture who migrated inland from LA and the Bay Area, as well as others who were escaping something back east. Mary Ann's wedding happened not in a church but at a park, with a justice of the peace presiding. The other two weddings she'd been to occurred outdoors as well—it was California after all. Unlike her father, Mary Ann didn't hate the church or religion broadly; she just never thought about it. She had no context, no direct experience, to either hate or care about the church and its claims.

But the separation and divorce had led her into a heavy and lonely place. Mary Ann never talked with anyone about this. Having a "stiff upper lip" was a mantra she learned from her father, and she tried to apply that to any hardship. "Never admit you're hurt," Mary Ann remembered her father saying. One day a coworker, a scheduler named Valentina, asked whether Mary Ann was okay, stating directly, "It seems like you're carrying a heavy load." Valentina's words turned on a faucet. Mary Ann began spilling her burdens. Two hours later Mary Ann felt *held* in a way she never had before. She was pretty sure this wasn't good HR practice, but she knew more than ever that she needed a friend.

From that day on, three times a week, Mary Ann and Valentina walked and conversed along an old horse trail that had been turned into a bike path. Valentina also knew loss. Her oldest son, Leonardo, had been arrested and sentenced for theft. He was stealing to feed a bad addiction. Valentina explained that at her darkest point, the people from her church sat with her in the courtroom. And as the crushing grief pinned her beneath a boulder of depression, her church fed her every night for over three weeks after the sentence. Because of that, Valentina was walking this horse trail with Mary Ann. One day Valentina said, "Our pastor says all the time, 'Followers of Jesus join sorrow.' I saw that firsthand, so now I do it. That's it. Nothing else to it really. I just follow." Mary Ann had never heard something so beautiful and true.

Twenty-three years later, Mary Ann is ending her third stint on the church council and has served as a deacon for over two decades of ministry. She loves bringing communion to homebound members. She sits with them and listens, following in the footsteps of Valentina, who followed Jesus into sorrow.

For almost two decades, Mary Ann and Valentina walked that old horse path together at least once a week. They shared so much through laughter and tears. They continued to walk until Valentina couldn't. On Valentina's sixty-second birthday, she fainted. Tests revealed that her heart was in bad shape. Eight weeks later she was dead. Mary Ann and others from the church sat with her son Leonardo for days, grieving with him, joining his sorrow.

With Valentina's death it seemed as good a time as any for Mary Ann to switch jobs. Valentina always told Mary Ann that she needed to move on. Mary Ann had watched the trucking company expand, and she even enjoyed the transition to new ownership. The changes had always kept her from truly entertaining offers from bigger companies with more people under her and better benefits. She could never make the move. She felt loyal to Bud Jr., even after he sold, and she loved seeing Valentina and talking about church. But with Valentina gone, and Bud Jr. retired to Cabo, the time seemed right.

A high-end apparel brand with a campus just miles from Mary Ann's rural community, in the valley below, was looking for a co-vice president of HR. Looking for a co-anything was appealing in itself. Mary Ann had worked mostly solo. Only in the last few years, with the arrival of new ownership, did the trucking company add another person under her to make an HR team. The apparel company promised not only a team of half a dozen people but a direct partnership at the top, with the co-VP. To make matters even better, Mary Ann had known the other half of the VP partnership for years. Mary Ann had met Garrett at conferences and seminar trainings. Garrett, about fifteen years younger than Mary Ann, considered her to be one of his mentors. Mary Ann had even written a reference when Garrett applied for the position he now held.

The transition to the apparel company was mostly smooth. Garrett and Mary Ann worked well together. But Mary Ann had to admit she found some things odd. She tried to tell herself that this was only natural. She reminded herself that a lifestyle apparel brand and a trucking company were, of course, going to be different. But it always felt strange, like being in an alternate universe, when the CEO and other executives talked. They'd often ask for reports on employee happiness. Bud Jr. never once asked about the happiness of his employees, let alone a report. Mary Ann wasn't even sure Bud Jr. truly knew the word "happiness." Cranky and curmudgeonly were more Bud Jr.'s speed. Mary Ann would always answer the executives at the apparel brand about whether the workers were satisfied and content in the work environment. Bud Jr. *had* cared about that. But that was never what they meant. The CEO, Will Winterer, stressed that he wanted them *happy*. The mission of the brand was to bring wellness to the world, to make the world a healthier and happier place. One dollar of every purchase was given to organizations and charities that brought wellness initiatives to those who were less fortunate. But the company couldn't meet this evangelistic mission of bringing wellness to the world (through expensive T-shirts, jogging shorts, and yoga pants) if its own employees weren't healthy and happy. Mary Ann picked up quickly that being healthy was the way to be happy. It shouldn't have taken her so long. There was an enormous poster in the entryway of the building with a picture of an attractive woman running and wearing a big smile, and above it in bold, red letters it said, "GET HEALTHY, GET HAPPY."

As Mary Ann and Garrett read through résumés, they agreed that Renate was overqualified to be a catalog editor. Renate had years of writing for some of New York's top publications. Her bylines included *Vogue*, the *New York Times*, *Esquire*, and *The Atlantic*. Her pieces covered fashion and lifestyle, with a few opinion pieces on celebrities. Mary Ann and Garrett decided to fly her out immediately for an interview. Mary Ann had some concerns, but Will, the CEO, was ecstatic. Having read Renate's pieces for years, he said, "Get her on a flight now!" Mary Ann and Garrett's main question and concern was, Why this position? Why go from writing journalistic pieces to writing copy for shorts and ads for underwear?

In the interview, Renate, ever polished, cited the company's mission. But in a moment of honesty, she told Mary Ann and Garrett that she was completely burned out in New York City. She wanted out of New York, and fast. It wasn't good for her health, she explained. Mary Ann sensed a great deal of discontent in Renate, but Renate never called it that; she didn't see it that way. It was the city that made her unhealthy. The only thing that made the stress of New York City livable was the wellness practices she'd found. Renate talked about wellness like it was a conversion, and she was now an evangelist. She explained that if it were not for clean and mindful eating, a seminar on sleep hygiene, CBD intakes, and hot yoga sessions, she would have burned out and faded away long ago. It was the only way to find health, and therefore happiness, in such an unhealthy environment.

Renate wanted out of New York City, but she also wanted into California, the promised land of wellness. She needed the California sun, and she saw California as the wellness capital of the world. Like a medieval village priest longing for Rome, Renate longed for California. California represented the epicenter of the wellness knowledge that had saved her. Renate told Mary Ann and Garrett that she was ready to leave New York City behind and be truly healthy. This, she knew, could make her happy. She was putting wellness above career, she explained. It was time to put her happiness first by putting her health first. She'd tried to get to happiness through career, but that only made her unhealthy. Sensing that this statement could be misunderstood and might not show the best tact for an interview, Renate added, "If my career can't allow me to be healthy, then I'll never be happy. That's what I love about this company, the way health and happiness are connected. For someone like me who was saved by self-care and wellness, this company is heaven." Renate laughed. She was hired before the end of the day.

The first six to nine months were great. Renate seemed to be excelling, and the executives loved her. She returned from almost every weekend with tales of a wellness retreat or new product she'd found. The latest was her charcoal-infused pillow and a session she'd attended on a mushroom-only cleanse. There was always a cleanse.

But then everything changed. Renate's carefree and upbeat attitude was gone, and her work was not getting done. Will, who was Renate's direct report, became frustrated. He asked Mary Ann to talk with Renate and offer her the company's personal perks. The personal perks process never felt quite right to Mary Ann, but it was common practice for Garrett and it came from the top. When an employee voiced stress or any form of unhappiness, the company would respond by offering the employee services and access to mindfulness sessions and decompression techniques, even free months at a high-end gym. It fit perfectly with the ethos of the company. If an employee was unhappy, it was because they were unhealthy. To get happy, get healthy. The actions of the worker, more than the work environment itself, needed reforming toward health. None of this was at Mary Ann's speed (and she knew Bud Jr. would think it completely bogus). But she wasn't doing HR for Bud Jr. anymore. And good HR always serves the mission of the company. So she met with Renate.

"How are you feeling about work?" Mary Ann asked. Renate assured her it was good. Mary Ann explained that her supervisor was concerned that things were not getting done in a timely manner. Renate agreed and mentioned some stress she'd been under. Mary Ann could tell. Per the practice of the company, Mary Ann offered Renate access to mindfulness breaks and a certificate to a touchless spa in La Jolla. Renate could only muster a small nod and a half smile. The offer seemed to land as if it were more weight added to an invisible load Renate was already carrying. Mary Ann, staying on script, asked, "Are those options something you'd like to take advantage of?" Renate seemed more burdened than anything; exhaling, she seemed to concede in a near whisper, "Yes, sure."

It was then that Mary Ann heard it. It was coming from within her but somehow outside her as well. She heard herself say the same words that

Valentina had said to her over twenty years earlier. Words far outside the HR handbook of the apparel company. Mary Ann said, "It seems like you're carrying quite a load." This recognition of sadness was the first step of following Jesus into sorrow. Renate's head dropped, her hands moving to her brow, and she pushed back her hair. She then said with glossy eyes, "I know this isn't suited for work. I know it shouldn't affect my work, but my father died two weeks ago."

For all the wellness and self-care, all the cleanses and charcoal-infused pillows that Renate embraced for the health that would produce happiness, none of it helped her with this sorrow. There was no optimizing her grief, no new superfood to cure it, no yoga teacher to visit her with a meal. She was alone. The California sun now just burned with the heat of loneliness. She was away from her father when he died, unable to get home. Now feeling guilty for that, she bore his absence acutely. Renate's father was dead, and she had no idea how to grieve him. She'd moved to California to be healthy, but now she was alone.

Mary Ann was pretty sure this wasn't good HR practice, but she knew Renate needed a friend. Mary Ann found herself asking Renate, "Do you know that old horse trail that's now a bike path off Highway 17? Meet me there at six. Wear good shoes."

All the Conversions

It may not be obvious at first, but the story above contains multiple conversions. Both Mary Ann and Renate are converted (and maybe more than once). Mary Ann's conversion is bound to classic religious forms. Mary Ann's portion of the story mentions a church, a pastor, and a community joining in grief. Renate, too, is converted. She too finds new meaning and purpose inside a call to a distinct way of life. Renate gives herself over to an overarching goal—an aim, a horizon—that she names as happiness through health. This horizon, this reaching for the ultimate pursuit of happiness, calls her to take on distinct and morally infused ways of being healthy. These moral ways of being are bound to distinct forms of knowledge, which she often shares with others, trying to convert them to this way of being through this knowledge (or perhaps it's better to call it information). Renate is on a constant search to uncover which toxins need to be avoided or which superfoods can lead to a breakthrough in health.

She listens intently to the wisdom of her gurus and those in the know, ready to pass on what she learns to whomever will listen. Renate must live this certain way because of what she has come to know, and what she knows can lead her to the salvation of happiness.[1]

Returning to Mary Ann, her conversion takes a classic religious form. Unlike Renate, there is a church, a pastor, and a community of people. Even so, her experience is missing some of the stereotypical marks of modern understandings and practices of conversion. There is no sense that Mary Ann responded to an altar call. Nor did she embrace the meaning, purpose, and practices of Christianity in order to escape the ledger of hell and secure a seat in heaven. And yet Mary Ann is converted. She is made into a Christian. But the work of this *making* happened outside the model that has been called "conversionism"[2]—a kind of obsession with getting people to decide, as if it were in their own power to do so, for heaven instead of hell. Mary Ann's conversion is different and yet no less bound in the Christian tradition.

Mary Ann is transformed into participating in the very life of Christ. This participation—being conformed to Jesus Christ (Gal. 2:20)—happens not through her decision as much as through her surrender to follow Jesus into sorrow. It's not as much about rational belief and consent for Mary Ann as it is about following. Mary Ann follows Valentina (making Valentina a saint) into following the living Jesus Christ through the sorrow of the cross.[3] This kind of following requires, and therefore takes on, a distinct

1. Rina Raphael provides a helpful explanation: "Perhaps Gwyneth Paltrow explained this endless quest for self-improvement best when she exclaimed on her Netflix series, the *Goop Lab*, 'It's all laddering up to one thing: optimization of self: We're here one time, one life. How can we milk the shit out of this?' And hence we need fitness trainers, gadgets, and strenuous workouts to reach this magically hidden but tappable perfection. Our enhanced self is all there, simmering under the surface, just waiting for us to unlock it." Raphael, *The Gospel of Wellness: Gyms, Gurus, Goop, and the False Promise of Self-Care* (New York: Holt, 2022), 232.

2. Richard Osmer says, "I will call this evangelism as conversionism. This particular understanding of evangelism emerged after the Reformation of the sixteenth century among the renewal movements and new churches that followed the Reformation." Osmer, *The Invitation: A Theology of Evangelism* (Grand Rapids: Eerdmans, 2021), 7. Bryan Stone adds, "I argue that the practice of evangelism is not guided by the aim of conversion, where conversion is conceived of as a good external to that practice and something to be secured through various tactics (even if one might show how those tactics are ethical). It is instead guided by the aim of faithful witness. The ethics of evangelism is concerned more with the character and beauty of our witness than whether that witness yields 'results' measured in terms of conversions." Stone, *Evangelism after Pluralism: The Ethics of Christian Witness* (Grand Rapids: Baker Academic, 2018), 17.

3. Echoing Dietrich Bonhoeffer's *Discipleship* (Minneapolis: Fortress, 2001).

form of knowledge. But this knowledge is not mere information, as it is for Renate and for many Christian forms of conversionism.[4] Such knowledge, rather, is bound inside an encounter that calls to Mary Ann. The knowledge that Mary Ann receives is interconnected with (even inseparable from) the event of encountering the person of Jesus Christ through the personhood of Valentina and the church community itself, which joins together in sorrow.

What we shouldn't miss, up to this point, is that both Mary Ann and Renate have conversion experiences, though the experience is different for each. They both turn, or find themselves turning, toward new ways of living. These new ways are infused with what they believe are deep senses of meaning and fulfillment. Each comes to know or experience something that gives her purpose and direction. As this project unfolds, I'll return to this story to more fully articulate and examine these conversion experiences. As with my other projects, this story will be a red thread running through this book. I'll use this fictional account to illustrate the perils and possibilities of conversion in our late-modern context. The story of Mary Ann and Renate will help us examine conversion from cultural and theological perspectives, all with a deep interest in how our perspective on conversion shapes the practice of ministry and the life of the church. But this project is meant to do more than just examine conversion.[5] This project wants to take the next step, which takes us back to Paul.

From Conversion to Evangelism

Unless you're the apostle Paul, all conversion experiences seem to include an act of transfer. A conversion experience rarely comes without the words or acts of other sinful human beings who call you to change or turn your direction, to ultimately find a different way of rescue or salvation that they

4. Osmer discusses the importance of knowledge: "To encounter Jesus and begin fellowship . . . with him is to begin to know him. How can we know who Jesus is and what he means to us and our world unless he is described, narrated, talked about, read about, and related to the specific circumstances of our lives? Knowledge shared through words in evangelization is knowledge of a person, not a set of ideas or laws. In this sense, evangelization might be described as facilitating an encounter with Jesus. It is a personal meeting on the basis of words." Osmer, *Invitation*, 156.

5. I've already discussed transformation as a dynamic form of conversion in Andrew Root, *The Church in an Age of Secular Mysticisms* (Grand Rapids: Baker Academic, 2023).

themselves have already discovered. Paul, however, seems to tell the Galatians that his gospel came directly from Jesus Christ himself (Gal. 1:11–12), unmediated, without any transfer or passing on from another person. But even Paul would admit that Ananias played an important part in his own conversion, sitting and praying with him at his bedside in Judas's house on the street called Straight (Acts 9). Ananias followed the leading of the Spirit into Paul's sorrow, which was central to Paul's conversion. Faith, Paul would therefore agree, is always passed on, even for him—after all, that's his mission as he travels far and long across the Mediterranean. Paul's point, even to the Galatians, is *not* that a conversion experience can happen without a passing-on but only that *the message* Paul passes on, and the one that he has passed to the Galatians themselves, came to him directly from Jesus himself, as it did for Peter and James as well.

It so happens that the Galatians have been visited by some representatives from the Jerusalem church who are claiming that Paul's message isn't quite right. There is this little missing detail about male converts needing to be circumcised. The Galatians are told that their conversion is incomplete because of this missing detail. What's been passed on to them is therefore not *completely* true. Paul's point to the Galatians is that even though he didn't walk the dusty Galilean roads with Jesus, Paul's gospel—the one that converted them without any need for cosmetic surgery—nevertheless came directly from Jesus too. It's a flex, a résumé battle, and an important one—especially if you're a male member of the Galatian church. Yikes! Paul wants his readers to see that the gospel passed on to the Galatians, the one that converted them, was circumcision-free and true and beautiful. He wants them to see that the message he received was also passed on to him: it was transferred to him right from Jesus himself.

I bring up Paul because this project seeks to directly explore evangelism. It's at the heart of what follows. The story of Mary Ann and Renate is about not only conversion experiences but ultimately evangelism. It's about what converts people, shifting them to shape their lives around a certain *take* or *position* or *explanation* that helps give their lives meaning, direction, and order. This ultimately is crucial to the transformation of their very selves. Mary Ann and Renate are evangelized by messages that direct them to new visions of the good life and new senses of ultimacy. They are converted because each comes to embrace a message passed on to her as good. Those messages are so good that they call them to change core elements of their lives and shift their vision for the future (even their senses of the future of the world). Their ways of being are transformed by others sharing messages. The messages redirect their lives. They save them.

And yet, at the point we've left the story of Mary Ann and Renate, they have much different visions of what is good and what this goodness is centered on. For Renate, goodness is centered on happiness, and for Mary Ann goodness is centered on sorrow. Those are quite different. As in diametrically opposed! To fully grasp this difference, below I will provide further nuance and depth. For now, it seems fair to say that the good news (the *evangel*) that converts each of them is not only different and oppositional but also contested. Yet we late moderns, even those of us still committed to religion and the life of the church, feel much more comfortable with Renate's good news of happiness than the necessary invitation into sorrow. We are uncomfortable with the very fact that sorrow is unavoidable for us all. The reason has much to do with the air we breathe, with what it means to be citizens of this late-modern world. Much more on that to come.

Now, before we go any further, we need to ask, Should we even be talking about conversion and evangelism? Isn't "evangelism" a bad word now? In these times in which we're rightly sensitive to difference and appropriation, historic traumas, and hidden, colonial chauvinisms, can we even talk about such things? Ultimately, isn't this cultural moment allergic to evangelism?

Surprisingly, no. But it's complicated. Of course, in this moment of late modernity, in the first half of the early twenty-first century, what *isn't* complicated?

The Odd Acceptance of Evangelism

Fraught complication is just the air we breathe. We have a good sense that this air is polluted but inescapable. We're all inhaling plumes of debris from the countless explosions of our culture war. Inside this culture war, hardly anything is straightforward and almost nothing is uncontested. Confusing times make for odd bedfellows. Seemingly opposed ideas, concepts, and perspectives often somehow nestle together between the sheets, knee-to-knee. Just when you're sure *this* or *that* will be either hated or loved by a certain group, you find the opposite.

Evangelism is an example.

American Protestantism is undoubtedly in the throes of a shake-up. Some even call it a "reckoning." Particularly, the children of conservative Protestants have been pushing back, many even exiting the churches of their youth. And not quietly. They name regressive social stances; a lack of acceptance or openness to pluralism, difference, and gender; and an overall capitulation to partisan politics (they're particularly disturbed by one party's perceived regressive social stances) as their reasons for leaving.

Mainline liberal Protestants have, quietly, found all of this delicious. For decades—closer to a century—mainline Protestantism has championed the openness, pluralism, and political progressivism that the exiles from conservative Protestantism are now seeking. This should be the heyday for mainline Protestantism. Church participation and the institutional resources for such denominational congregations and institutions should be skyrocketing. This should be a moment of hockey-stick growth. There should be 10 to 14 percent gain, instead of the continued (more than three decades long) 10 to 14 percent decline.[6] But the decline persists, and this decline for mainline Protestants is a seemingly incurable condition.

Inside this moment of reckoning, it would be plausible to assume that evangelism is out, even reviled. With the abounding of identity openness, social tolerance, celebrated pluralism, and progressive views of freedom, it seems logical that Protestantism would lock away evangelism in a dusty backyard shed as an embarrassing old tool, or throw it out completely in the dumpster labeled "regressive historical artifacts of torture," heaving it on top of hairshirts and other accoutrements of penance. But even with all our talk of colonialism and cultural appropriation, this hasn't happened. Neither mainliners nor exiled conservative Protestants, not to mention (unsurprisingly) conservative Protestants proper, have been ready to completely disparage and discard evangelism. Most agree that evangelism is risky and potentially dangerous, and that it is rarely done well, even tipping into abusive at times. But nevertheless, across the Protestant spectrum there seems to be a soft or weak desire to hold on to evangelism.

6. For more on the statistics of decline, see Ryan P. Burge, "Mainline Protestants Are Still Declining, But That's Not Good News for Evangelicals," *Christianity Today*, July 13, 2021, https://www.christianitytoday.com/news/2021/july/mainline-protestant-evangelical-decline-survey-us-nones.html.

Mainliners, at least those leading congregations or supporting those who do, remain open to evangelism. The rash of decline opens them to the necessity of some kind of evangelism. Maybe a focus on evangelism, they reason, will help us kick this infection of decline and get more people here. Maybe, particularly now that so many exiled young evangelicals hold mainline social views, these young people will come and decline will end! Focusing on evangelism, it's assumed, will get the word out and bring these exiles and their disaffiliated friends through the door. But the difference between this so-called evangelism and plain marketing is hard to discern. In the end, these efforts are reduced to propaganda. Overall, mainliners are not completely clear on how evangelism should be understood and shaped. They tie themselves in knots, wishing for people to come but remaining uncomfortable with making any bold statements as to *why*. They contend that evangelism needs to demand a conversation or change that can lead to commitment, but not in any aggressive or exclusivist way. It needs to be an evangelism without judgment, even an evangelism without an apologetic or a case being made (or else the apologetic must avoid all metaphysics and just be social and affirming). There remains a soft openness to evangelism, but not much appetite to think about what evangelism is and what it demands. Too much thinking beyond "letting people know that we're loving and accepting" could lead to issues.

For different reasons, the exiles too are not opposed to the idea of evangelism. They've come from a classic conservative Protestantism, which in the late twentieth century encased itself in an ethos of consumer capitalism. Consumer capitalism, especially after the arrival of lifestyle branding, sees itself as a form of (secular) evangelism. Starting in the late 1960s, to get people to buy, you needed to convert them to a new way of life.[7] Instead of products being pitched on the merit of their function and use (this soap works better or faster), products were sold for their meaning and feeling (this product, this soap, communicates that you're a certain kind of person). In this context, marketing became evangelistic. By the early 1970s, people, particularly young ones, were converted from Coke

7. See Thomas Frank, *The Conquest of Cool: Business Culture, Counterculture, and the Rise of Hip Consumerism* (Chicago: University of Chicago Press, 1998). The whole book is a discussion on this transformation in marketing and its impact on our culture. I've drawn more extensively from his work in part one of *Faith Formation in a Secular Age* (Grand Rapids: Baker Academic, 2017). For more, particularly on Christian faith, see Mara Einstein, *Brands of Faith: Marketing Religion in a Commercial Age* (London: Routledge, 2008), chaps. 1–3 and 5.

to Pepsi, from Ford to VW, by the force of lifestyle. Marlboro went from a woman's cigarette to a manly cowboy's smoke. They were beckoned by ads that were calls to convert. They were evangelized to new brands.

Those brands are now passé. But living in an environment where consumer patterns bear the weight of conversion is not. This has become even more significant in a digital age of social media. You could even argue that in this digital age products are overshadowed by lifestyles. It's now possible (even normal) through social media to be advertising *yourself*. On social media sites you sell yourself for the sake of winning attention and affirmation for the lifestyle you embrace and broadcast. The new superproduct is the *self* and the performance of its chosen lifestyle. If you're successful enough at selling or performing yourself, you can monetize this by selling products as enhancers of your lifestyle.

The goal of marketing, even digital marketing of yourself, is to convert consumers to a lifestyle that includes, as its anchor, certain brands and products that you sell. This is how an influencer is created, and it's what makes an influencer so influential. An influencer is a master of lifestyle who has been converted to this lifestyle and won a lot of attention, and now they can evangelize others by the testimony of how a product improved their life by adding to their lifestyle. They advertise a lifestyle that you wish you could have with all its attention, reach, and free stuff. You can start having it, at least to a degree, by taking the influencer's knowledge and applying it. It all starts by using the brands and products they do.

Renate is an example of such a conversion, though with a slight difference. Because Renate's focus is on happiness through health (and health seems to point beyond just the science of medicine to the hopes of true healing), her conversion carries more gravitas than that of an influencer who testifies to their love for a certain lip balm. But similarly, for both Renate and the influencer, a lifestyle shift wins you happiness ("wins" being an important word in late-capitalist neoliberalism).[8]

Conservative Protestants in the last decades of the twentieth century copied how brands convert people: meeting their felt needs and advertising

---

8. Andreas Reckwitz states, "The late-modern subject culture is radically economized in the fundamental sense that it is competitive to an extent that goes beyond mere commercialization. Subjects are now almost universally within constellations of competition, both as 'consumers' of other subjects and objects that compete for attention and as 'self-entrepreneurs' who compete with others for the attention of third parties." Reckwitz and Hartmut Rosa, *Late Modernity in Crisis: Why We Need a Theory of Society* (Malden, MA: Polity, 2023), 67.

a lifestyle. Conservative Protestantism offered people programs as products and branded their local congregations, all as a way of converting people's interests. This version of evangelism is bound in a consumer logic that holds to a tacit theological anthropology that believes people *are* most fundamentally what they are individually interested in.[9] Having come of age inside a conservative Protestantism bound in consumer capitalism, and being natives of digital influencer-based marketing, these young exiles are predisposed to accept evangelism. It's part of the consumer zeitgeist, and even the word "evangelism" is something ordinary from their past. As long as evangelism isn't harsh, abusive, or repressive to identity openness (ignoring its link to late consumer capitalism), it's fine. It's even normal and assumed to be part of faith practice. These exiles have not escaped this consumer evangelistic ethos. They've just shifted it to an open lifestyle and a new brand of religion that refuses and resists the old brand of classic conservative Protestantism.

One powerful way to get attention is by calling out the repressive religion of your past. Most disaffiliating exiles, therefore, never really think to join a mainline church because its lifestyle appears too passé and irrelevant. Its brand is too bland. They adopt instead this more progressive Christianity not by joining a community but by changing their digital consumer patterns—following different people on Instagram and updating their podcast feeds. They do what they've been taught to do by this consumer secular evangelism. They broadcast their departure and change in lifestyle loudly on social media, winning more attention.

What's Missing

We find ourselves in a moment where evangelism is *not* completely hated and thus discarded and canceled. But nevertheless, evangelism is confused and mostly unwanted. Evangelism has become American Protestantism's schmole. In the parlance of slang, a "schmole" is a friend, or core part of your group or crew, who is an obnoxious downer who you don't really want around. But the schmole comes with the group. The group has not figured out how to rid itself of the obnoxious and embarrassing schmole.

9. I explore an anthropology of interest versus relations in Andrew Root, *The Relational Pastor: Sharing in Christ by Sharing Ourselves* (Downers Grove, IL: InterVarsity, 2015).

The group knows or senses that, in the end, it needs the schmole—maybe for the schmole's energy but more so for the schmole's car or access to the pool.

Evangelism is the schmole of American Protestantism. Evangelism is assumed to be a bit obnoxious and annoying and more than a little embarrassing—even a potentially dangerous downer if we're not careful. Mainline and exiled evangelical Protestants worry that if they give evangelism too much focus, evangelism will potentially ruin things, violating ethical and cultural sensibilities. But these Protestants, while mostly uncomfortable with and wanting to ignore evangelism, sense that they *need* evangelism. Evangelism can't just be kicked out of the crew! Hence, American Protestantism's soft openness to evangelism.

Yet even with this soft openness to evangelism, most would agree that evangelism has little traction in the discussions, let alone practices, of American Protestants. Evangelism is the schmole, after all. Evangelism is kept around, though banished to the fringes, because we think we might need evangelism, even if we're embarrassed by it. After all, evangelism might be necessary in helping us beat back decline and the need for lifestyle marketing. Evangelism is justified for its instrumental function. It's a tool (and to add another layer of slang, a schmole is always a tool).

This (tacit) assumption shows that our conceptions of evangelism have been almost completely hollowed out. Evangelism has become shrouded in immanence, or stuck in the tangible, because evangelism is assumed to be a *tool to gain things that can be counted*. Mainline and exiled evangelicals may not count souls converted, as classic conservative Protestants do, but they nonetheless *count*. They're not counting who is praying the sinner's prayer, but they count how much their soft evangelism wins them reach, quantified by the number of new members and the amount of likes (which is a direct sign of brand uptake).

Focusing on the immanent and quantifiable affords little to no sacramental sense to our visions and practices of evangelism. There is little grasp of how evangelism witnesses to, and joins, the infinite's participation in the finite. Little concern with how evangelism testifies to a reality—to a world as a whole—that is sacramental in nature. Our lives in the world are the very place where God comes to and shares in. Theologians call this "sacramental ontology." The sacraments themselves, such as bread and wine, witness that the infinite God shares in our finite bodies in the world, joining us in finite elements. The world is a place where the infinite and finite commune.[10]

How evangelism invites others into this event of communion has not much been explored. The shell that remains of evangelism is almost completely immanent, with little to no inbreaking transcendent quality. Evangelism's value contributes only to the finite plane (more people will come, giving will go up, relevance will increase, institutional fragility will be reversed).

But there are risks that come with getting free from being locked solely on this finite plane and placing evangelism on the ground of a sacramental ontology. Inside this more mystical (or even liturgical) spirituality of divine and human—infinite and finite—union, evangelism risks becoming abstract and disconnected from the concrete lives of people like Mary Ann and Renate. Trying to place evangelism on the ground of a sacramental ontology—onto a place where the divine truly encounters the human—runs the danger of losing the practical nature of evangelism, which is the only thing keeping the schmole in the crew. If this abstract anti-practicality prevails, what's the point of keeping evangelism around at all? This danger of abstraction from our concrete lives casts suspicion on an evangelism that is bound in something other than the immanent and instrumental.

But this shouldn't be. Attending to the sacramental shape of divine and human encounter in evangelism should not lead us away from the concrete and practical lives of Mary Ann and Renate. Nor should focusing on the practical turn evangelism into a schmoley tool for crass gains. But how do we keep this two-headed monster of a problem from chomping? How do we imagine evangelism as sacramental without losing evangelism's practicality and concreteness?

The answer is by joining sorrow.

Theologians of Consolation and Their Blessing

The remainder of this book explores how evangelism invites participation in the life of God. We participate in the life of God through the work of the Spirit. The Spirit leads us to hear the voice of the living Christ calling

---

10. Hans Boersma is the contemporary theologian who has most directly named this sacramental ontology. See Boersma, *Nouvelle Théologie and Sacramental Ontology: A Return to Mystery* (Oxford: Oxford University Press, 2009).

us to follow. This following takes us into sacramental participation as the concrete invitation to join another's sorrow. Where Jesus calls us to follow is to the cross (Matt. 16:24–25), which is to concretely enter the sorrow of our neighbor and give the ministry of consolation.[11] This, I'll show, is both to do evangelism and to be evangelized.[12]

Ultimately, we'll see in the chapters that follow how this sacramental sense of evangelism is bound to consolation.[13] Evangelism as consolation not only rests on a sacramental ontology but, in turn, avoids the triumphalism of some Protestant forms of evangelism, and it altogether avoids instrumentalization (a sense that all our relationships and connections must produce means and values that are more than the relationship itself). Evangelism shaped by consolation as a true sharing in the sorrow of our neighbor cannot be instrumentalized, and thereby it keeps its integrity. To enter sorrow (even the sorrows of joy, as we'll explore) as the sacramental embodying of the good news is to release our grip of control (instrumentalization is always a form of control).[14] Evangelism, seen through consolation, is not bound in *what we do* but in *who we can be* for our neighbor and how we can be with them. Period. To console is never to control another but instead to share in their sorrow, contending that sharing is enough. Sharing itself is the place where the infinite encounters

11. Michael Ignatieff helpfully says, "Console. It's from the Latin *consolor*, to find solace together. Consolation is what we do, or try to do, when we share each other's suffering or seek to bear our own. What we are searching for is how to go on, how to keep going, how to recover the belief that life is worth living." Ignatieff, *On Consolation: Finding Solace in Dark Times* (New York: Metropolitan, 2021), 1. He continues, "Consolation is an act of solidarity in space—keeping company with the bereaved, helping a friend through a difficult moment; but it is also an act of solidarity in time—reaching back to the dead and drawing meaning from the words they left behind" (5).

12. Bonhoeffer essentially sees discipleship as following the call of Jesus Christ to the cross, entering obediently into the life of our neighbor. This entering is itself an event that allows our neighbor to hear the call of Jesus to them. We can see how evangelism and discipleship are fused inside this attention to consolation.

13. Sylvia Walsh, drawing from Søren Kierkegaard, says powerfully, "Christian strivers are not to seek consolation for their own suffering but, like Christ, should seek to console others in theirs. Yet it is precisely in comforting others that one finds consolation for one's own sorrows. . . . In this way suffering reaches its highest point but also its limit. . . . The sufferer becomes the comforter and finds his own consolation through this act." Walsh, *Living Christianly: Kierkegaard's Dialectic of Christian Existence* (Happy Valley: Penn State University Press, 2005), 143.

14. Pointing to Hartmut Rosa's *The Uncontrollability of the World* (London: Polity, 2020). Rosa's point is essential. He claims that the only way to avoid instrumentalization and therefore alienation is to participate in a form of action that lets go of control. Uncontrollability is a core dynamic to Rosa's articulation of resonance. For more on resonance, see Rosa, *Resonance: A Sociology of Our Relationship to the World* (Cambridge: Polity, 2019).

the finite.[15] The great temptation of evangelism is control, imagining that evangelism is the way to get control of decline or lost relevance (or new land or political power). To turn to consolation as the shape of evangelism is to let go of all seeking for control and instead to embrace encounter.

If we look, we can spot the centrality of consolation in theologians throughout the tradition. Not surprisingly, the theologians who recognize the centrality of consolation (entering another's sorrow) as the gift of inviting another into the divine life have been pastors as much as theologians (or their pastoral concerns turned them into groundbreaking theologians).

We'll see a concern for consolation—an entering into sorrow as an evangelistic practice—in the Cappadocian patristic bishop Gregory of Nyssa (ca. 335–94) and his sister Macrina (ca. 327–79), the Parisian medieval mystic Jean Gerson (1363–1429), the Augustinian prior Johann von Staupitz (1460–1524), and the Wittenberg Reformer and preacher Martin Luther (1483–1546). For each, consolation—walking into and joining sorrow—is the deepest witness to the beautiful truth that God sacramentally enters death to bring life. We receive the *evangel* (the good news) of God's redemption of the finite in the life of the infinite by concretely and practically consoling our neighbor in their sorrow. (Consider that the greatest novels, paintings, songs, and poems—those that really move us—have sorrow at their center. There is a sacramental reality that can only be touched through sorrow.) Walking into sorrow is the evangelistic shape of a church that is inviting its neighbors to share in the place where the divine shares in the human, turning death into life, bringing the world back together.[16]

15. Not surprising to people who have read my other works, this project rests on both Luther's and Bonhoeffer's conceptions of *Stellvertretung*. I've defined Bonhoeffer's use of *Stellvertretung* as place-sharing. What Bonhoeffer particularly means by this word is that Jesus Christ and we, in following Jesus Christ, take the place of our neighbor, joining them and becoming present in the middle of their life. Bonhoeffer always uses *Mitte* ("middle") with *Stellvertretung*. In a sense, this project is an exploration of evangelism as *Stellvertretung*. To echo Isaiah Berlin's metaphor that thinkers are either foxes (who know many things and work on many ideas) or hedgehogs (who know just one big thing and have one big idea), I am a hedgehog. All my writings seek to explore the depth and possibility of *Stellvertretung* for a theology of ministry that attends to God acting in the concrete.

16. "When we seek consolation, we are seeking more than just a way to feel better. Serious losses cause us to question the larger design of our existence: the fact that time flows inexorably in one direction, and that while we can still hope for the future, we cannot unlive the past. Serious reversals cause us to reckon with the fact that the world is not fair and that, in the larger domain of politics and the smaller world of our private lives, justice can remain cruelly out of

Sorrow and the Sacramental

Musician and poet Ben Howard touches on this sacramental nature of consolation in his song "I Will Be Blessed." Howard, who is in no way an apologist for Christian belief, touches on something incredibly profound (poets tend to do that). The heart of evangelism is to bless the world; the good news that the church shares is that God through Jesus Christ has blessed all of creation. Evangelism invites another to receive a blessing, and therefore the evangelizer is blessed by blessing others in their sorrow. Howard (again, intending no Christian apologetic) ends his song by repeating, "If you're there when the world comes to gather me in," then he will be blessed. Howard has told us earlier in the song that "heaven is the arms that hold us." These "arms" could be interpreted as reductive, flattening reality and eliminating inbreaking transcendence. Howard might be saying that there is no real place called heaven, nothing beyond us, but nevertheless we experience something grand or full in the arms of a lover. We *might* call that heaven. That's one read. That would be a nice rationalistic and disenchanted interpretation, spiced with a pinch of romantic sensibility. Or, and I think more beautifully, we could interpret his line as sacramental. That heaven itself (the place where the infinite and finite join) is encountered when death is shared through consolation.

In these arms of consolation, heaven is near because these arms minister new life out of death. These arms proleptically witness to the time when all sorrow will be so consoled that sorrow itself will be no more. This is heaven. Howard then witnesses, whether intentionally or not, that we experience the infinite in the finite by the concrete acts of consolation—by being held. This sharing in sorrow is eschatological and apocalyptic. Consolation participates in, and yet awaits, the world coming together to gather us in. The world is renewed in small but true ways in these arms that console. Gathering us together in shared sorrow is the proclamation that soon all will again be renewed and that all that is lost and grieved will be given back. We await this great act by sacramentally sharing in its actuality, by being held by and holding one another. Being held by and holding others is a true taste of heaven. We await this great gathering by

---

reach. To be consoled is to make peace with the order of the world without renouncing our hopes for justice." Ignatieff, *On Consolation*, 7.

living with and before the God who acts to turn all sorrow into joy, blessing the world, through its sorrow, with new life.

Evangelism, if we can see it through consolation as sacramental, invites others to receive a blessing. It is to invite others to be blessed by the ministry of the Christian, of the church, of the living God who is ontologically a minister. God enters all sorrows for the sake of redemption and participation in God's infinite life (that's what heaven is). Ben Howard's song is a prelude that points us to the depth that Macrina, Gregory of Nyssa, Jean Gerson, Johann von Staupitz, and Martin Luther will take us into in the second half of this book.

But These Dudes and Their Sisters Are Too Old and Our Days Are Too Sad

Before we examine these pastors' theological thoughts on consolation, we must wrestle with the question, Why now? Ben Howard's poetic song is one thing, but we must admit that Macrina and her brother Gregory of Nyssa, Gerson of Paris, Staupitz of Munich, and Luther of Wittenberg are *old*. They have no sense of our context. And context is what keeps evangelism from sliding into abstraction. Asking questions about worldviews, new digital realities, psychology, consumer patterns, work and leisure spaces, and all sorts of contemporary forms of meaning-making seems to ground evangelism in context. Focusing on context often keeps evangelism in the practical departments of seminaries and colleges (often, for good or ill, making the content of evangelism in the classroom the findings of the sociology of religion). Evangelism is always context bound. Looking back at our theologians, Luther is the young pup of the group, and he's been dead for almost five hundred years. All these pastors of consolation are premodern. What could they possibly teach us about evangelism today here in late modernity?

All are concerned with consolation and sorrow because they are first and foremost pastors, doing their theological work from the place of ministry. As ministers, all write in sad times. The context of their distinct ministries was filled with plagues, short lifespans, social instability, religious failures, famine, and many more losses. Sure, these ministers were living in much different times from our own. But if we look closely, we can see that they're not as different as we might think. We too have come to know plagues, and we have ministered in the middle of social upheaval, religious failure, and, for the first time in the modern world, declining lifespans, at least in America.[17]

But it seems more right to say that, like them, we too are living in sad times. Ours may not be the sad times of physical distress, as in the time of Gregory, Gerson, and even Luther. Let's thank God for penicillin and vaccines! But ours is a time of deep emotional sadness. We, like them, are in an epoch of great anxiety. Our times are filled with material possibility but overwhelming amounts of depression and disconnection—seen most starkly in our adolescent children. Painfully, people in late modernity are lonely and isolated. Even with (or because of) all our technological connections, we are as alone as ever in bearing our own burdens. In this late-capitalist secular age of all-out competition, people find few who are available or willing to give consolation. In an age of capitalist winners and losers, consolation is for losers (think of a consolation prize or a consolation game). Everyone wants to avoid being a "loser." There are few who will walk into sorrow who are not paid to do so.[18] There are few who will proclaim inside sorrow that there is a deeper meaning, that there is a communion that saves and redeems all—that, indeed, there are arms to hold and bless.

A blessing is never earned. Often, as with Jacob, it is given after a defeat, as a consolation to sorrow that moves the one cared for into a new reality (Gen. 32), from being Jacob to being Israel. The one who blesses proclaims to the one consoled that the world starts coming together in these arms that now—literally or figuratively—hold you. For these arms are a witness, even a sacrament, to the very ministry of God, who in Jesus Christ, the man of sorrows, is bringing the world together through the

17. For a book-length discussion of this reality, see Anne Case and Angus Deaton, *Deaths of Despair and the Future of Capitalism* (Princeton: Princeton University Press, 2020).

18. For all the good that the therapeutic does in our time, we should not ignore that therapy is big business. Apps like BetterHelp are tapping into a major market. The market exists because people are so lonely and disconnected, having no one to console them other than those they pay. The question is whether paid consolation is really consolation. Arlie Russell Hochschild argues that we now pay for everything, seeking to pay others to do our most basic things. Paying for consolation seems to be one. See Hochschild, *The Outsourced Self: Intimate Life in Market Times* (New York: Metropolitan, 2012). Again, I'm not against therapy—for some, a therapist is needed just as much as any other doctor—but it cannot replace the acts of ministry. Therapy will always be tangled up with consumer-provided services.

Spirit of joy.[19] This God made known in Jesus Christ is blessing the world in its loss. For the church, to evangelize the world is to bless the world by joining the world's sorrow, which is the true sacrament of God's promise to bring back what's lost (Luke 15).

Ultimately, and ironically, we are in sad times in the early twenty-first century because we're a society obsessed with happiness. We are sad because we've made happiness our highest aim and goal. We are so depressed and anxious because we so deeply just want to be happy. Being happy seems so simple and basic. But it's anything but that. Happiness appears easily available but disappears quickly. We pursue happiness, always elusive and beckoning, even taunting, but never graspable. We're lonely, finding so few to join our sorrow, because others too are busy with their all-out pursuit of happiness. There is no time to join sorrow, no payoff to giving consolation. Most people assume that too much secondhand sorrow will taint their own reservoirs of happiness. Let's keep it all positive.[20] Thus, a return to consolation could not be more contextually important than in this time of sad and lonely happiness-seekers.

A French Infusion

To fully develop evangelism as consolation, and to clarify our contextual challenges, I'll need to explore how happiness became our aim. Few living in the time of Macrina, Gregory, Gerson, Staupitz, or Luther would have imagined that being happy, as we conceive it, was the best way to live. And yet this assertion is almost entirely unchallenged in our late-modern times. How did we get here? Without knowing how we got here and how happiness functions, we'll struggle to see the importance

19. Ronald K. Rittgers discusses how in medieval thought Jesus is understood as the man of sorrows: "Scholars agree that a key factor in the rise of Passion devotion was the emergence of an alternative image of Christ as the Man of Sorrows rather than as Pantokrator or Judge. Christ could certainly still be depicted as the impassible Lord, but from Anselm forward, there was a new emphasis on his passible humanity. This is especially true in art, where Christians displayed a sometimes morbid fascination with the wounded and broken body of the Savior." Rittgers, *The Reformation of Suffering: Pastoral Theology and Lay Piety in Late Medieval and Early Modern Germany* (New York: Oxford University Press, 2012), 69.

20. Byung-Chul Han has warned us of a society obsessed with positivity. See Han, *Saving Beauty* (London: Polity, 2020). For a further discussion, see Andrew Root, *The Church in an Age of Secular Mysticisms* (Grand Rapids: Baker Academic, 2023), chap. 7.

of consolation, particularly consolation to failed happiness-seekers like Renate.

The American project has turned to an all-out pursuit of happiness. America is the land where the pursuit of happiness has been most formalized and intensely chased. America places the pursuit of happiness both in its structures (institutional shape) and its agency (way people act). But the pursuit of happiness as the best way to live is *not* an American invention. Rather, it is from the French, particularly Michel de Montaigne (1533–92), who, through his extremely popular essays, invented the self as a free person who seeks happiness. Thomas Jefferson (1743–1826) adored Montaigne and his essays, as did many of the Founding Fathers. Including the "pursuit of happiness" in the Declaration of Independence was a call to make America a land of freedom where people like Montaigne would be at home and happy. Therefore, to get a handle on our unhappiness, we'll need to explore the life and thought of the founder of happiness, Monsieur Montaigne.

But there is another dimension to my interest in Montaigne and his late-Renaissance and early-modern French world. Though the French created the pursuit of happiness, Paris was also home to one of modernity's greatest critics of a Montaigne-shaped pursuit of happiness. This young Parisian man, walking the same streets that Jean Gerson walked five hundred years earlier, also became one of the most well-known converts of our modern era, which makes him doubly relevant to us and our conversation on evangelism. This young man is Blaise Pascal (1623–62). Pascal, a brilliant young polymath, through the consolation of his sisters, came to find Montaigne's position counterfeit and misleading. Pascal discovered, through a direct encounter with the acting God, that it was not in happiness that we meet the living God of Abraham, Isaac, and Jacob but in loss, in sorrow, inside impossibility. It is in the dark that God comes to us as more than an intellectual theorem or idea but as a person, who in fire redeems and renews all.

To develop evangelism as consolation we'll need to examine Montaigne to understand our context and prepare us to glean directly from Pascal, the modern exemplar of one who has been evangelized. Examining both the French founder of happiness and the great French dissenter will allow us to have an insightful and constructive dialogue with Macrina, Gregory of Nyssa, Jean Gerson, Johann von Staupitz, and Martin

Luther for our own sad times. Montaigne and Pascal create a bridge to the others.

The Bridge from France to Us

But could this *still* be a bridge too far? A great distance remains between Montaigne's château and Mary Ann's human resources office, between Pascal's arrondissement of fiery confession and Renate's wellness cleanses. Therefore, it will be helpful to have one more bridge to span the gap. This bridge will help us understand how it is that someone like Montaigne, who is largely unknown to us, could be our cultural parent. It's a good possibility there would be neither HR offices nor wellness cleanses without Montaigne. Montaigne never thought to do yoga or keep a gratitude journal, but without him centering things on happiness, such practices and pursuits would likely have little importance to us. If those of us born and living in the West did a paternity test on our social imaginary, a good amount of its DNA would be Montaigne's. He's the founding father of happiness, and therefore we can understand our sad times only in relation to him.

What will come next is this paternity test of sorts. There is a branch of philosophy, called genealogy, that conducts such cultural paternity tests. Philosophy has been doing such genealogies since the nineteenth century.[21] As the twentieth century came to an end, two British-educated philosophers (one at Cambridge, the other Oxford), who spent most of their careers writing and teaching in North America, offered their own genealogies. Both genealogies are built around Montaigne.

In 1991, Stephen Toulmin, who was educated at Cambridge under the twentieth-century polymath Ludwig Wittgenstein, published *Cosmopolis: The Hidden Agenda of Modernity*. While Toulmin was finishing a career teaching at a handful of America's elite universities and publishing *Cosmopolis*, the Oxford-trained Montreal philosopher Charles Taylor was offering lectures titled "The Malaise of Modernity." In 1991, these lectures were published (in the US) as *The Ethics of Authenticity*. Both Toulmin's and Taylor's works draw from Montaigne and arrive

21. The great father of philosophical genealogy is Friedrich Nietzsche. See his *On the Genealogy of Morality: A Polemic* (1887).

at the dawn of the twenty-first century. In the light of the coming new century, both works, though quite different, are optimistic (though, as we'll see, Taylor starts with some concerns). Neither philosopher sees the clouds of sad times coming in the early decades of the twenty-first century.

And why would they? The iron curtain had fallen, and conditions were ripe for the flush economic markets of the Clinton era. The 1990s (stretching even into the early 2000s), at least in the West, may have been the last days where happiness seemed to be outrunning sadness. Little did anyone know—other than hip-hop artists from South Central Los Angeles and grunge rockers from Seattle—that the 1990s would not be the fulfillment of our happy days, that a major sadness was gathering. From the belly of the happy 1990s came the worrying, anxious times of the 2010s and the very sad days of the 2020s. Raging loneliness, depression, and anxiety, mixed with misinformation and deep cynicism, typify the third decade of the new century. These are days of pandemic, social upheaval, religious failure, climate vulnerability, and deep-seated divisions.[22] Our happiness has turned rotten and bitter because inside the failure of our happiness we've found little else to live for, so little that no one seems to stop and question happiness itself. Searching for happiness is making us miserable, but the only solution to our misery is to drive harder toward happiness. We keep worrying about why we aren't happy—angry with others and even ourselves that we've failed to procure our happiness.

Now, just because Toulmin and Taylor are optimistic does not mean there isn't much to learn from them. Neither may have seen or anticipated our sad and divisive times, but both astutely help us understand the DNA that makes up the context in which we examine evangelism. They help us understand the world that Mary Ann and Renate live within.

Therefore, as our next step, we will examine these two genealogies. Doing so will lead us into the lap of Montaigne, who will carry us to Pascal, who will point us to the pastors of sorrows who constructed sacramental theologies of consolation. The effort of this journey, as we meet such strange people as Montaigne, Pascal, Macrina, Gregory, Gerson, Staupitz, and Luther, will help us reimagine evangelism in our late-modern secular age as consolation.

---

22. For an insightful examination of the cultural realities of our climate crisis, see Bruno Latour, *Down to Earth: Politics in the New Climatic Regime* (Malden, MA: Polity, 2019).

■ ■ ■ ■

Mary Ann pulled off Highway 17 into the parking lot of the trail just a minute or two before 6 p.m. She wanted to be waiting for Renate when she arrived. Mary Ann figured that if she left her house at 5:45 p.m., she'd arrive first. She never imagined Renate wouldn't show at all.

2

Sad Times and a Sad (Pathetic) Church

Is Evangelism's Task to Keep the Church Alive?

Mary Ann leaned against her car waiting for Renate for almost thirty minutes. After ten minutes, she thought about texting Renate, but she wasn't sure it was appropriate. Renate never specifically gave Mary Ann her number. Mary Ann had Renate's number only because she had access to all employee information. She wasn't sure it was right to use this information outside of work. She wasn't even sure that this invitation to meet was appropriate at all. Mary Ann answered her own conscience, saying out loud as a defense to her inner inquisitor, "It may not be the right HR thing to do, but it's the right human thing to do. And 'human' is in human resources, isn't it?"

Mary Ann resisted texting. But after ten minutes turned into twenty-five, she decided she needed to. She worried that Renate had been in an accident or that some other emergency had occurred. Renate had been in a bad place when Mary Ann last saw her. Added to this, Mary Ann reasoned that she needed to leave by 7 p.m. to get to a church meeting at 8 p.m. She couldn't wait much longer, and she didn't want Renate to come late and not find her here.

Mary Ann texted Renate: "This is MA, u ok? I'm at the trail off 17, need to leave by 7. Can still walk if ur close. Let me know."

Mary Ann sent the message and waited. The three dots appeared. Renate was responding, maybe she was close. But that thought quickly faded. The dots disappeared and didn't reappear. At 7 p.m. Mary Ann left, her shoes never hitting the trail.

Mary Ann made it to the church meeting a few minutes early. It was a denominational gathering of congregations in the region, a quarterly meeting. Attending was one of the responsibilities that came with Mary Ann's position as deacon and elder in her congregation. People, particularly the pastors, complained about the meetings. They felt like the meetings sucked energy and time, and added little value. But Mary Ann liked them. She noticed the political maneuvering and passive-aggressive positioning, but it was nothing compared to the corporate world. This association, like so many other synods, districts, and presbyteries, was conflicted. People feigned a breezy peace, while distrust and deep anger lay under the surface. But she somehow still enjoyed the gatherings. She liked talking about church stuff. It seemed to matter much more than her nine-to-five discussions on running shorts and mindfulness sessions. "People disagree, but at least they care," Mary Ann thought to herself.

Earlier in the day, Mary Ann had told her fellow elders from her congregation that she'd be late. But with Renate's no-show, Mary Ann beat them to the meeting. Everyone was pleasantly surprised to see Mary Ann already there saving them seats. The meetings always began with announcements. The announcements were supposed to last only a few minutes. But over the last few years they'd taken up more and more time. People began using the announcement period to make pitches for their pet projects or political and theological perspectives. They remained guised as announcements, but there was no mistake that these "announcements" were minisermons or lectures seeking to sway the assembly in one direction or the other. In the agenda the announcements were now taking over thirty minutes (in actuality, going closer to forty). When Mary Ann had first started attending, the agenda listed announcements as ten minutes.

On this night, as someone was going on about inclusiveness training and the importance of radical, complete acceptance and how the church had failed at this and lost opportunities to grow because of it, Mary Ann's phone vibrated. As she read the text from Renate, a new announcement followed on Bible memorization and the need to return to believing in the Bible because so many churches had lost people because they'd lost the Bible. The text read, "I'm so sorry." Mary Ann waited, thinking more was coming. But no dots appeared. Nothing. Tentatively Mary Ann wrote back, "No worries. I hope ur okay." Dots appeared and then disappeared. Appeared again and then vanished.

Mary Ann didn't know what to make of it. But she quickly found herself forgetting all about the text as she slid her phone into her purse. She was transfixed now. The final announcement grabbed her attention completely. It seemed to grab everyone's attention. A special group was being formed. They would hear more about it at the next quarter's meeting. The group's job was to meet with a consultant and conduct a district-wide study. The consultant was going to take the group through a process called "Grow or Die." "The church in America, and the district with it, is on a precipice," the gray-haired man explained to the gathering. "If we don't get things together and find ways of reaching people fast, then, in a generation, there will be *no church at all in America*." He paused, looking intensely at the gathering, continuing, "No time to waste!"

These dire words stirred up anxiety in Mary Ann. She'd never once heard her pastor talk like this. And while her congregation was fragile financially, steady but plateauing in membership, she never felt they were on any precipice. Maybe they were, but they hadn't noticed. Was this true? Mary Ann recognized the anxiety. It reminded her of the biannual calls with the board of directors at work. Mary Ann's nine-to-five was all about growing fast, though growth in health and happiness. The founder, Will Winterer, and his executives kept reminding the board that a mission of health and happiness promises growth. "Healthy things grow, and growth brings happiness," they repeated. Mary Ann was now hearing this same logic inside the church.

Just as Mary Ann was thinking about how this all sounded so similar to work, and perhaps rightfully so if the church in America could just die out, her phone vibrated in her purse. Renate had responded. Mary Ann had forgotten all about Renate in these few minutes of lightheadedness on the precipice. Teetering on the edge, even if only in her mind, had a way of making her forget certain things and certain people. Renate's text read:

Again, sorry, I really wanted to and needed to walk with you. But I was going to my car and remembered I didn't have my sunglasses. The sun was bright and beautiful as it reflected off the ocean. I had the thought that my dad would love this. And then I remembered a line from a movie or poem or song or somewhere that said "We're under the same sun" and I realized that wasn't true anymore with me and my dad. I've never been under this sun without him. Even when I was living so far away from him, we were still under the same sun. But not now. He's gone. Realizing that made me a mess. A real mess. I just couldn't make it being such a mess. It wouldn't be fair for you to deal with that. Again sorry. Figured it was better to deal and not make you deal, you know. Sorry if this is all just TMI. Again, I'm a mess.

Preparing for the Genealogies, or Why Our Times Are So Sad

The Modern Pursuit of Fulfillment

As Mary Ann sits in the district meeting, moving between announcements and text messages, experiencing both Renate's individual sadness and the sorry, sad institutional state of the church, she's exposed to something completely modern. Her exposure to this modern reality preludes our exploration of the 1990s genealogies of Toulmin and Taylor, and it represents a step toward the sixteenth-century château of Monsieur Michel de Montaigne. We won't get directly to those genealogies until the next chapter, but here we will start to introduce them along with Monsieur Montaigne. The completely modern reality that Mary Ann experiences rests at the center of Charles Taylor's explorations in *The Ethics of Authenticity* and is so fundamentally modern it's hard to even spot. Like certain fish against the reef, it's camouflaged by our assumptions. We can't spot it because it's the water we swim in. What Mary Ann is exposed to is the deep aspiration and drive for *self-fulfillment*. Taylor begins his lecture there. Mary Ann witnesses that at the heart of our conception, for institutions and individuals alike, is a striving for hope or ambition, to reach something we name as fulfillment. Taylor reminds us that this striving, in itself, is not modern. This striving and moving toward a hope or ambition, this deep desire for fulfillment—to live fully—is core to our humanity. We've always engaged the world, evaluating what is good to do and what next to aim for that will be full.[1] We've always been moral evaluators in this way. We can't escape that. Human beings have always

---

1. Charles Taylor calls this "fullness." See Taylor, *A Secular Age* (Cambridge, MA: Belknap, 2007), 5–15.

been moral animals.[2] But it's a modern condition that our moral evaluations assume that our fulfillment is never outside *our own* reach and power to achieve.

What makes us modern is having a deep sense, which holds its own moral weight, that the responsibility for our fulfillment is almost completely in our own hands. This fulfillment we seek comes not from above (heaven, the church, the crown) but from within us. It comes from our own effort, genius, and creativity. We all have our own sense of fullness. As moderns, we assume that we need no permission or even direction (though we could all use a little advice) to seek our own fulfillment. We know this fulfillment because it is inside us. Fulfillment is born within, not without. We just need to get clear on what we want. Then we'll know or quickly figure out how to get it.

Those in the medieval period, for example, would not have assumed that this sense of fulfillment could be in their own hands. They couldn't believe this. It's unlikely that anybody in the medieval period thought their own fulfillment was self-imposed, self-created, self-achieved. The future was not a blank canvas onto which any institution or individual could paint their own fulfillment. Only in the modern epoch do we assume that every institution or individual can and should seek their own self-fulfillment, painting their own fulfilling portrait. You need modernity to contend that the world itself is open and available to chase your own fulfillment.

For example, in the medieval period neither the church nor the crown pursued fulfillment; it was bestowed. The church and the crown existed and persisted not because of their own ambitions and will but because of God's. Those who represented the crown, for instance, didn't achieve their station but were given it by heaven. And not "given" like a consumer is given a free sample at Costco. Rather, their fulfillment was given as their right coming from the very order of heaven itself, reflected directly in nature. Fulfillment was given to them by birthright, by blood.

One great house fought another for the throne not because they were compelled by self-fulfillment. Not because they were like Uber trying to

---

2. "Animals" is not a reductive description but embodied, bound in a lifetime, encompassing life and death. The moral-believing aspect reveals that there is something fundamentally spiritual about the human creature. We must live inside stories that aim toward some level of ultimacy. For more on this, see Christian Smith, *Moral, Believing Animals: Human Personhood and Culture* (Oxford: Oxford University Press, 2003).

maim Lyft and fulfill its ambitions of complete market dominance. The game of thrones was embedded not necessarily in self-ambition but in the right of nature and heaven. One house fought another house for the throne because it was their right by blood. The other house was seen as opposing not the pursuits of self-fulfillment but the order of creation—they were therefore God's enemies. Civil war was ignited when one house believed it was by *their* blood, not another's, that they were given the right to thrones and lands. The houses fought not over competing projects of self-fulfillment but over what, by nature and God's design, was their destiny.

What makes us modern in major part is that we don't believe honor and privilege are based solely on nature or blood but on the will of individuals or institutions to seek and achieve their own self-fulfillment. We contend that institutions and individuals can make their own worlds by the force of their own capacities and aptitudes. What makes us modern is that we assume that we ourselves, or the institutions we choose to be part of, are free to make and chase our own fulfillment. And it's a fulfillment that does not fall from heaven but one *we* create.

The "self" in self-fulfillment does not necessarily signal the performative drives toward singularity as it will in late modernity.[3] This sense of the self can't happen until the ideas of Jean-Jacques Rousseau meet the neoliberalism of late capitalism and our entrepreneurial ways of working. And to clear the ground for his own ideas, Rousseau himself needs Montaigne, who writes two hundred years before Rousseau stumbles his way into Paris.

What the "self" in self-fulfillment refers to is that both institutions and individuals must make their own worlds. In their own worlds, institutions and individuals must, through their own will and ambition, create their own fulfillment. Once it's imagined that we can make our world from our own ambitions, acting to fulfill this world by our own powers, happiness enters the scene in a different way.

Happiness and Sad Individuals

Happiness becomes the feeling of being near to or actually achieving my own self-fulfillment. Happiness becomes so important for us late

---

3. I've sketched this history in Andrew Root, *The Church after Innovation* (Grand Rapids: Baker Academic, 2022), chaps. 2–6.

moderns because it is the test or gauge of how near I am to realizing my own self-fulfillment. If I'm happy, I'm close to, or have even arrived at, my self-fulfillment. Happiness is the confirmation of self-fulfillment. Because happiness is tied to self-fulfillment, happiness follows self-fulfillment in step. As with fulfillment, modern people think happiness is achieved, not bestowed. Happiness comes from within, by my seeking it, not as a gift or surprise given by the gods.

In ancient Greece, people wanted to be happy; they just imagined that it often only occurred right before a person died. And only if they'd lived well by seeking not self-fulfillment (not by being concerned with happiness itself) but virtue. Happiness was nice but nothing to live for, nothing that promised a life lived well. Happiness was not glued to fulfillment, as it is for us. For the ancients, *destiny* and fulfillment were glued together, not *happiness* and fulfillment. When fulfillment becomes self-created, happiness must bear the weight of signaling my nearness to fulfillment.

As late moderns, we crave happiness because it's the only way for us to know if we're aimed toward, and therefore near, fulfillment. For late-modern people, happiness is the (only) sign or signal that we've achieved our fulfillment. One horrifying nightmare for late-modern people is to achieve the feat that they believed would win them self-fulfillment—a successful business, a certain car, fame, even a lover—only to discover that they are still not happy. This unhappiness means that, though they have what they want, they're not fulfilled. How despairing! Because they don't feel happy, they have no self-fulfillment, even with a shiny Mercedes in the driveway. They should be self-fulfilled, but they're not happy.

It gets worse. If unhappiness clicks over into sadness, we have a real problem. To be sad is not only to *not* be happy. We assume that sadness is an emotion that attacks, like cancer, our remaining happy cells (as we'll see, I think this is deeply untrue but nevertheless something we seem to believe). To be sad, which often takes the form of despondency in late modernity, is to be "a mess," as Renate says. What being a mess ultimately means is to be *completely unable to accomplish the pursuits of self-fulfillment*. This causes Renate's sadness to feel so heavy, so much like a failure.

Late-modern people seek to avoid sadness like the plague. We may not be happy right now, but at least we are still intently pursuing self-fulfillment. If sadness comes, we'll be tripped up, even stopped completely, from our pursuits. We'll be a mess, someone who can't get it together and keep going toward the pursuit of self-fulfillment. Sadness, then, has the power to keep us bound and unable to chase self-fulfillment, which blocks us from happiness. And without this ability to chase, what is life? We need to avoid sadness at all costs.

Yet, ultimately, it's impossible to avoid sadness. Tragically, once we've invited happiness to be the measure of self-fulfillment, we cannot keep sadness at bay. Sadness and happiness are conflicted twins, like Jacob and Esau, fighting since the womb. Sadness and happiness are emotions that roll together. To feel happy is to also open yourself up to feeling sad. But we late moderns have tried to avoid this reality. We've come to believe that we can have happiness without sadness, because happiness is so glued to self-fulfillment.

We are in sad times because we've asked happiness to bear the weight of signaling our self-fulfillment.[4] Inside this uniting of happiness and self-fulfillment, sadness is assumed to come as a nightmare, a horrible reaper. We tacitly suppose that to be sad is to be lost on the self-imposed route to fulfillment. Sadness, in this logic, has no beauty, nothing to teach. It only seeks to condemn. When self-fulfillment is distant and confused and when happiness is absent, sadness has no other task than to convict us of our failure to find self-fulfillment. Sadness, then, can never be welcomed and must always be feared. Forebodingly, we sense that sadness is always crouching at the door ready to pounce, and we're terrified of it. We're all working so hard not to be a mess so that sadness won't lunge for the neck of our self-created fulfillment.

The Founder of Self-Fulfillment

Montaigne is the father of this shift toward visions of self-fulfillment. This shift creates the possibility for our obsession with happiness and our paranoia about sadness. It's Montaigne and his *Essays* that pull the lever. Montaigne gives us the first reflections on fulfillment resting in an

4. For an empirical example of these sad times, Anne Case and Angus Deaton say, "Deaths of despair among white men and women aged forty-five to fifty-four rose from thirty per one hundred thousand in 1990 to ninety-two per one hundred thousand in 2017. In every US state, suicide mortality rates for whites aged forty-five to fifty-four increased between 1999–2000 and 2016–17. In all but two states, mortality rates from alcoholic liver disease rose. And in every state, drug overdose mortality rates increased." Case and Deaton, *Deaths of Despair and the Future of Capitalism* (Princeton, NJ: Princeton University Press, 2020), 40.

open future made by the ambitions of a self, rather than fulfillment being embedded in the rights and blood of the crown (or church) and the orders of the domain.

In 1570–71, after years as a noble by the king's side, winning honors in battles for the king, Montaigne chooses, for the sake of his own fulfillment, to leave court and return to his château. In Montaigne's mind, his château was no longer a noble stronghold, the purpose of which was first and foremost to fortify the king's rule of the land. Instead, Montaigne now imagined his château as a warm, humanist habitat where he could be most fulfilled. Montaigne's home was made by him, by the warm air of learning and reflection. It was *not made* by blood, ritual, and symbol. Montaigne contends that fulfillment is closer in the château than in the king's court. At the very end of the medieval period, that's a shockingly different way to live. Montaigne believed this because home was a place where he could write, search his own heart, and lovingly teach his daughters. The château, more than the court, upheld the humanist spirit. Now that his château was no longer tied so tightly to the crown's will and the church's demands, Montaigne could make it a place to discover the self's own fulfillment. Montaigne could paint his own picture of what fulfilled. And paint it he did in the *Essays*. Montaigne was no revolutionary, not necessarily, but in his château, surrounded by a humanist ethos, he was free to reach for his own fulfillment as he saw it, no longer dependent on the whims of a king and his divine rights. In his château he was happy; he'd found self-fulfillment.

Montaigne's early DNA on self-fulfillment can be found in almost all late-modern institutions and individuals. Both institutions and individuals are assumed to make their own fulfillment. Thanks to Montaigne, we suppose that this fulfillment is always self-made and self-dependent. In that way we are all humanists. But now, as we'll see in the next chapter through the teaching of Charles Taylor, our humanism bears a heavy burden of authenticity. Before we get there, though, we shouldn't forget that in modernity this drive for self-fulfillment is not only an individual project but an institutional one. This is worth pausing to take in. It leads us to wonder how institutions, like individuals, can be sad.

The Institutional Drive

Our unthought assumption as modern people is that not only do individuals aspire to some sense of self-fulfillment, seeking to fulfill their own aims and goals and therefore become something, but so do institutions. The stability and life of institutions also comes from their capacity to reach a sense of fulfillment from within the institution's own ambitions. But this is where things get a little heavier and why the threats of the church's disappearance pierce those in the assembly, Mary Ann included (the church's disappearance is *not* something any medieval person, noble or not, ever could have imagined).

An institution must achieve its pursuits to justify its existence. Unlike persons, modern institutions have no inherent value outside their ability to achieve their own self-fulfillment and therefore self-perpetuation. However, as a parenthetical and pointing to our deeply sad times, we may be at a moment where individual people also assume that their existence is contingent on their individually achieved self-fulfillment. Maybe this is a reason our young people are so depressed and suicidal. Our cultural way of being has communicated that if you can't reach your own self-fulfillment and be happy, there is no real justification to exist. Sadness is just too heavy and devoid of anything good. And in turn, it's assumed that people who oppose your chosen self-fulfillment (e.g., identity) hate you because they don't want you to be happy, and therefore they wish you not to exist, blocking you from any self-fulfillment. Yet, if individuals can't meet the burden of creating their own self-fulfillment, we often think they just have to keep trying and never give up (this is the only thing that will keep sadness at bay). They must find the energy and will to keep reaching for self-fulfillment. (This is why burnout is an existential crisis.)

But if institutions fail to meet their self-fulfillment, and no road to achieving this goal is uncovered, they must be put down. They must stop existing, no matter their history or impact. If an institution can't achieve its self-fulfillment, then it is a sad (i.e., pathetic) institution. It should disappear and die out completely—particularly before it wastes resources other institutions could use for their own self-fulfilling missions.

In our fictional story, the denominational church in that district gathering is aspiring for self-fulfillment, as much as Renate is. And fascinatingly, both the institution and the individual are mutually, though differently, thrust into crisis, into being sad, when this self-fulfillment seems blocked, lost, or squandered. Renate is pushed into deep unhappiness, which signals that she is lost and far from fullness. She is shamefully a mess. The institution is compelled into contemplating or conceding to its own extinction.

Maybe they're too sad and pathetic to exist. The announcement concedes that unless something is done fast, the church, even Christianity itself, will have no future.

These are the heavy contexts and pressures that evangelism meets. These pressures of lost self-fulfillment produce a sense of crisis that both institutions and individuals face. It makes for a sadness that creates environments of anxiety. Evangelism is pinched between these institutional and individual senses of crisis. Evangelism, in mainline denominations at least, is asked to give individuals purpose and meaning, showing how the Christian story can fulfill them, buffering all sadness. Evangelism is also meant to win the institution resources that can free the church from being so sad (i.e., pathetic). Evangelism is asked to give both individuals and institutions a future.

When Darth Vader Enters the Château

When Montaigne in his château gives fulfillment its early orientation toward the self, our relation to time becomes shifted. Self-fulfillment is always a future orientation. It needs little from the past. Montaigne begins this by unhooking us from the crown and the cosmic order of divine rule. Now, in our own little châteaus, inside our own lives, we (our own selves) are our own rulers. We seek, first and foremost, fulfillment of our own selves as much as or more than of the crown or some outside authority. This changes our way of being in the world, but it doesn't yet make us obsessed with the future. That obsession occurs when Montaigne's self-fulfillment is mixed with another French component. This second French component is an ingredient added to the modern batter that Stephen Toulmin, our other genealogist of the 1990s, believes sours the whole recipe.

In the genealogy that Toulmin presents in *Cosmopolis* (which we will explore in the next chapter), Montaigne is the hero, and René Descartes is Darth Vader. Like Vader with Obi-Wan, Descartes learns some essential things from Montaigne, only to corrupt them completely. Montaigne, Toulmin believes, is the last true humanist, the last man of the Renaissance. Montaigne holds that line in France until the rationalist-empiricist takeover in the seventeenth century. It's Montaigne's show until Descartes and his mathematical obsessions overrun humanism and ruin the Renaissance spirit. Toulmin is no fan of Descartes.

Descartes is also concerned with the self. He picks that up from Montaigne.[5] But Descartes's self is no longer in the château, reflecting on itself and its past, artistically examining all parts of human life and one's own longings. Instead, Descartes's self is doing hardcore math. The self is thinking and calculating, coming to know laws and theorems.[6] The self is not inside the château but inside the code of the Matrix. Toulmin contends that the rationalist Cartesians overtake Montaigne's humanism (turning it to the dark side). This ends the Renaissance desire to recover wisdom from the past and instead makes everything (even the fulfillment of the self) completely future-oriented. Our chins are now turned completely to the future, leading us to scorn what has been. We are encouraged to forget all about the past and just focus on the math. The past has nothing for us. What we need to be self-fulfilled, particularly institutionally, is the discoveries of the future. Without those discoveries, which only math can produce, we have no future.

The Church Has No Future

Inside this rationalist logic, Western modernity invents its narratives of progress. From this rationalist assumption, we tend to see history as always moving forward, becoming more and more advanced. We're drawn like moths to the light of the future. We know that the world is not necessarily becoming a better place, though many Western thinkers assumed so in the nineteenth century. For instance, Hegel believed that the *Geist* (spirit)

5. Thomas Hibbs says, "If Socrates and his notion of philosophy as care of the self permeate the texts of Montaigne, that ancient philosophical authority and his wisdom would appear wholly irrelevant to the writings of Descartes, who seems to reverse the famous Socratic turn from natural philosophy and mathematics to human things. The pursuit of certitude and utility replaces the love of wisdom and the cultivation of the virtues constitutive of happiness. And yet the questions of happiness and the life are not absent from Descartes' writings. In a letter to Princess Elizabeth, Descartes writes, 'Beatitude, it seems to me, consists in perfect contentment of spirit and interior satisfaction.'" Hibbs, *Wagering on an Ironic God: Pascal on Faith and Philosophy* (Waco: Baylor University Press, 2017). He continues, "Meeting Montaigne on his terms and deploying genres of writing that engage the style of Montaigne's essays, Descartes fashions a narrative whose telos is the transcendence of narrative. More than Montaigne, Descartes is a reformer, whose task is to improve nature, to move it from what it is now to what it might become if it were rendered docile to rational, methodic control" (77).

6. Isaac Newton was doing something similar. Newton in a sense would become the new Montaigne—but in a much different way. Newton has his own château. He has his great breakthrough on gravity while on his family estate, escaping the plague. But in so doing Newton fits a different paradigm. He is a self on his estate, in reflection, but what he is reflecting on is hidden mathematical orders, not the art of living well.

of history was bringing more and more freedom to all people. Freedom was progressing with each passing minute. The twentieth century, starting in 1914, shook us loose from these progressive dreams of the world becoming a better and better place. Still, even in the twenty-first century, we assume that our technology is making the world, if not better, more advanced. This is just how mathematical discoveries work. Every year that the earth circles the sun, we assume the human societies living on the earth become more technologically evolved (the exponential increase in computer microprocessing power, called Moore's law, will make you think, whether true or not, that advancement is unstoppable). What is exciting to us is what's next. The future has *all* our attention. The future is the plane where self-fulfillment is chased and procured.

It's hard for us to get our minds around the fact that this wasn't always the case, not even for Montaigne. For instance, before modernity, it was assumed that some societies of antiquity had methods for building or medicine or artistic abilities that were far advanced from what those living possessed. In both antiquity and the medieval period, people often looked back, not forward. What was exciting for people before the modern era was what had been. They attended to the past because they assumed or knew that there were lost civilizations that had technologies, know-how, and wisdom they did not. The Renaissance itself is the rediscovery of the art of antiquity, where the beauty of the human form was central. Plato's fictional story of Atlantis is another example from antiquity of this imagination. Atlantis, long lost but somehow still throbbing with wisdom and meaning, was far more advanced in every way than any Greek city-state and therefore any civilization known on earth. If only Plato's readers could see through the shadows of the past, they could gain wisdom. Atlantis had not so much disappeared as been buried by time. To live well, it was assumed, people needed to sink their hands deep into the soil of the past.

But we care little about the past now. And we find such backward looking to be a waste. We wish only to see through the opaqueness that shields us from knowing the future. We want to peer into the future so that we can best invest our energy and capital to reach self-fulfillment. We can justify exploring the past only as an instrument for not messing up the future and wasting the capital that could win self-fulfillment. We say ominous things like, "We must know the past so we don't repeat it." This is a loaded statement that contends that the past is mainly filled with mistakes that we need to avoid in order to have a future of self-fulfillment.[7] The wisdom of the past is almost completely obsolete, other than its instrumental warnings of what *not* to do. We are obsessed not with what was but what will be. Therefore, it's been a live question throughout modernity: Will the church and Christianity itself have a future? Is there any reason for it to exist? In a world focused on what will be, can the church be anything but sad and pathetic?

Those sitting in the district gathering feel this anxiety as they are taken to the height of the precipice and feel its dizzying disequilibrium. Everyone sitting in the gathering thinks it plausible that the church (even Christianity itself) could just disappear. Therefore, they'll need to really listen up at the next quarter's meeting and respond to the action plans of the committee.

But as we explore evangelism, finding a way to imagine it beyond the double pinch of individual and institutional self-fulfillment, we need to ask ourselves, Is it possible for the church and the Christian (even Christianity itself) to disappear? What could destroy Christianity, pulling the church into dissolution? Clearly not an earthquake, like what took Atlantis, or an evil that brings divine judgment and a word of destruction like the fourteenth-century reformers heralded against the pope in Avignon. Our vision of dissolution is much more banal and flat. Here in late modernity, we assume that what could take down the church is its own inability, as an institution, to reach self-fulfillment. The church and Christianity might fail to procure the resources and relevance the institution needs to have a future. We actually believe that if we're not careful, the church could just disappear without even a notice, and by extension all Christians with it (and not in the *Left Behind* way but in the Blockbuster Video way). The church could sadly become like Kmart, just a foggy memory. There'd be no gnashing of teeth, no falling steeples, no shaking and cracking earth below, just a whimpering disappearance, death by a thousand paper cuts of irrelevance. Self-fulfillment is such a powerful structure shaping our imaginations that we think that without it even the church will be vaporized by the future. Without the ability to produce its own self-fulfillment, the church and Christianity will have no future.

7. Such reflections on the past and history fit the methods of science and find a home in the university. There is assumed to be no value for history in itself, but it has some value if, like a technology or a hard science, it can help us in the future.

But is this possible? Could the church and Christianity just *disappear*? Is evangelism tasked with keeping Christianity from becoming bankrupt by making more Christians?

Eugen Rosenstock-Huessy thinks not.

Rosenstock-Huessy

If anyone should think the church could just disappear and Christianity could have no future, it's Eugen Rosenstock-Huessy.[8] Rosenstock-Huessy wrestled with the question of the future of Christianity in a time when many of the literal steeples and spires had recently fallen to the ground in flames and blood soaked the earth, crying out to God. He is of the generation that lived in Germany during the First and Second World Wars. Right before WWI, he had converted to Christianity. His cousin, Franz Rosenzweig, was going to follow in his footsteps. Franz admired Eugen greatly. After an all-night discussion (the *Leipzigspractnach*) on the place and future of Christianity, Rosenzweig, convinced by Rosenstock-Huessy's proclamation of the work of God and the place of Christianity, decided to remain a Jew instead of casting off his religion altogether. Rosenstock-Huessy's vision of the gospel was so faithful, and his commitment to Jesus Christ so sure, that it turned Rosenzweig back to the faith of Israel. That's a unique kind of evangelism. It's an evangelism that is far from obsessed with rescuing Christianity from the crisis of self-fulfillment.

In the aftermath of World War II, with the West coming to grips with such overwhelming devastation and evil, Rosenstock-Huessy published *The Christian Future* in 1946. The book looked to address two questions. Was the church in peril? If so, what was Christianity's future? The assumption was clear and one that today many of us share. If we answer in the affirmative that the church is in peril, then clearly Christianity has a troubling, even bleak and sad, future. The logic goes like this: if the church is in jeopardy, Christianity needs saving. These two questions are inseparably correlated in a direct sequential logic. Because the church is endangered, its own self-fulfillment is unreached and therefore its institutional existence is in question. Christianity itself faces a clear and

8. After he was married he hyphenated his name, making his full name Eugen Rosenstock-Huessy.

present danger. These are indeed sad, even devastating, times in which Christianity needs saving.

Just pause and think about that for a second. The confession of faith in Jesus Christ is the claim that his life, death, resurrection, and ascension save the world. His life frees the cosmos from death by him dying, then overcoming death with life. Christianity is the cleaving to the body of Jesus Christ, who does this cosmic saving. And yet here in late modernity we think we must save Jesus Christ, giving Christianity a future—the hubris is intense.

Rosenstock-Huessy's book was released in 1946, but these are the same questions, with the same presumed logic, that drive the district to remind the gathering that they are on a dangerous edge and need a consultant quickly to give them a future. But what if Eugen Rosenstock-Huessy was that consultant? What would Rosenstock-Huessy say to the denominational gathering? He would tell the district the same thing he told his readers just months after the end of WWII. He'd tell them that "'saving' Christianity is unnecessary, undesirable, impossible, because it is anti-Christian. Christianity says that he who tries to save his soul shall lose it."[9] Any individual or institution that seeks to flee sad times for its own self-fulfillment will, like Peter (Mark 14; Luke 22; Matt. 26), deny Jesus Christ. Anyone who thinks that they can wield a sword, again like Peter (John 18), and save the Savior, chopping off ears through impassioned effort, is deeply confused.

In the 1946 book, Rosenstock-Huessy does something amazing that no consultant, or even practical theologian, would dare. He breaks the sequential logic. Remember the questions Rosenstock-Huessy addresses. The first: Is the church in peril? He answers yes; in the dark shadow cast by the A-bombs and concentration camps in relation to a Christian Germany, indeed it is. In our own time, the church is nearing or at bankruptcy. It cannot cash in its resources to reach its own self-fulfillment.

Then comes the second question: Does this impoverished peril—this bankruptcy of resources—mean that Christianity has no future? If the church is in peril, is Christianity refuted and pathetic? Following the sequential logic, it appears that the answer to this second question is clear. If the church is in peril, Christianity is too, right?

9. Eugen Rosenstock-Huessy, *The Christian Future: Or the Modern Mind Outrun* (New York: Harper Torchbooks, 1946), 61.

But, shockingly, Rosenstock-Huessy breaks completely with the sequential logic. He denies a sequential logic for a sacramental one. He answers no to this second question. He insists it is quite the opposite, telling his readers, "Yes, Christianity is bankrupt today. But not refuted. Christianity has repeatedly been bankrupt. When it goes bankrupt, it begins over again; therein rests its power."[10] Therein lies the church's conformity to the body of Jesus Christ. Therein lies the sacramental logic of the infinite entering into the finite, finding union in opposites. When Christianity faces death, it lives.

Shockingly, Rosenstock-Huessy believes that bankruptcy is the sign that assures Christianity of its future. Let that sink in. It's bad math, but Rosenstock-Huessy is drawing more from Jesus's parables of the kingdom being built on bad economic mathematics (the shepherd leaves the ninety-nine sheep to find the one, the $1 > 99$ of Matt. 18) than he is drawing on Descartes's mathematical decoding. But even with this backward kingdom math, Christianity is not a madness that shouts irrational things into the wind, like $2 + 2 =$ pineapple. Rather, Christianity believes in this interrupted sequential logic not because it is mad but because the church has been renewed by the Holy Spirit again and again out of its bankruptcy. The church holds to this sacramental logic, evident when Jesus breaks bread and pours out wine as his body and blood before his arrest (Matt. 26). The bankruptcy that saves is manifest on Holy Saturday and then in Jerusalem before the coming of the Spirit in Acts 2. Being bankrupt, embracing poverty, is where the church finds its renewal. The church's beginning comes from the renewal that emerges from the bankruptcy of the loss and confusion of the cross. Rosenstock-Huessy believes that ending and restarting is the very blessing that Christianity brings to the world. This blessing can happen only by letting go and entering the dark, waiting on God's renewing life of light.

Rosenstock-Huessy believes that the confession of faith in Jesus Christ is a way of experiencing the light in the dark; this is his sacramental nature. The mission of the church is to be present at the end of cycles of death, participating in the redemption of the world by ministering to the world. Renewal is found not in the innovation of new resources but

10. Rosenstock-Huessy, *Christian Future*, 89.

in dying for the sake of others. New life is in the confession that dying itself is infused with God's ministering presence. Evangelism is central to Christianity, but *only if it wears these marks of a sacramental dying for the sake of others*. The life of Christianity is found not in the prospects of its own self-fulfillment but rather in its willingness to confess its brokenness (bankruptcy) and in faith anticipate its renewal. The faithful know that this renewal comes not from our effort but as a gift bound to our confession of bankruptcy.

The renewal happens when the church stops thinking about itself and seeks to love the world, treating this encounter with the world as an encounter with the person of Jesus Christ. Rosenstock-Huessy says, "Christianity is the power to open and to close cycles; hence it is not cyclical itself, but is able to contain many cycles, and periods, spirals and lines."[11] The church is always present at the end of these cycles, periods, spirals, and lines, helping birth a new time, not by trying to produce a new epoch but by ministering to others in love and suffering. This redemptive work of loving the world changes the world.[12] Christianity, Rosenstock-Huessy believes, is a source of redemption when it abandons its own self-fulfillment and seeks to enter death to minister to others. When Christianity does this, it renews its life (by giving its life away, Matt. 16:25) and opens up new cycles in history. Christianity renews the world by living as a sacrament in the world, loving the world more than the life of its own institutions, more than its own self-fulfillment.[13]

11. Rosenstock-Huessy, *Christian Future*, 84.

12. You can spot how Rosenstock-Huessy influenced his cousin's work, Franz Rosenzweig, *The Star of Redemption* (South Bend, IN: University of Notre Dame Press, 1970). Rosenstock-Huessy convinced Rosenzweig that Christianity had a mission of redemption in the world and that it was Judaism's essential job to remind Christianity to never depart or hate the world. This convinced Rosenzweig that he should remain a Jew. Paula Fredriksen supports Rosenstock-Huessy's position: "The only firm evidence we have for such a mission [that never departs from the world but seeks to participate in the redemption of the world] is that of Paul's apostolic opponents, mid-first century, in Galatia. In singular instance, the motives for that mission stemmed from dynamics internal to the Jesus movement itself. The mission does not reflect a standard and widespread Jewish behavior." Fredriksen, *Paul: The Pagan's Apostle* (New Haven: Yale University Press, 2017), 76.

13. Jacques Ellul adds to this: "For Christianity to have an entry point into the world today, it is ultimately less important to have an economic or political theory, or even political and economic positions, than to create a new way of living. It is quite evident that the first effort occurs through faithfulness to revelation, but this faithfulness to revelation can be embodied only in this creation. And here is the 'missing link.' There was a medieval way of living; there was a Reformed way of living in the sixteenth century, and it is indeed quite

This kind of redemptive work is the church's mission. This is the shape of evangelism. Rosenstock-Huessy, in many ways, is the original missional theologian.[14] He believes the church, from head to toe, must be missional. Evangelism is always central. Christianity itself cannot be faithful without being missional. The church cannot be faithful to the Christian confession without moving out into the world, bearing the world's cycles, redeeming and shifting them. Evangelism, therefore, is not an investment to secure the church's resources but is an act of giving away by entering into a shared sacramental life. This is salvation. Evangelism is the mission of sharing in the life of the world, suffering in the world. Christianity's central evangelistic thrust is an act of renewal. Sharing in the suffering of the world is what connects the evangelistic and the sacramental.

But the centrality of mission can be kept from corruption only if the sequential logic of the questions that Rosenstock-Huessy's book addresses is decoupled and their dialectical and sacramental nature embraced.[15] Mission and evangelism become destructive rather than redemptive when the church fears its bankruptcy. Evangelism becomes warped when we believe that the church must procure its own self-fulfillment for Christianity to have a future. Only when the church confesses its brokenness and opens its hands to give and receive—knowing that this confession of brokenness is its only source of renewal—can its evangelistic mission participate in redemption. Only when the church confesses both that it is bankrupt and that its future is secure can its mission be shaped by the cross.

---

interesting to consider it in contrast to the Renaissance way of living. There was a bourgeois way of living, which no longer has any spiritual quality. There is a communist way of living. There is no longer a Christian way of living." Ellul, *Presence in the Modern World* (Eugene, OR: Cascade, 2016), 96.

14. Lesslie Newbigin is often considered to hold that place as the original missional theologian. Rosenstock-Huessy has been overlooked because his perspective is too contrary to church growth and resources. However, someone would do well to connect Rosenstock-Huessy and the missional theology conversation that started with Newbigin. There is also an interesting connection between Rosenstock-Huessy and Andrew Walls's *The Missionary Movement in Christian History: Studies in the Transmission of Faith* (Maryknoll, NY: Orbis Books, 2009). Walls, well known as a missional theologian, also thinks Christianity finds itself at points of cycle interruption and that Christianity's incarnational nature means it can embed itself in many different times and places.

15. By "dialectic" I mean the seemingly opposed ideas that the church is bankrupt and yet still secure. It's only in leaning into this seeming incongruity that we can find a deep truth.

Renewal in the Three Millennia

Rosenstock-Huessy sees this renewal out of bankruptcy happening in each of the three millennia of the church's life. Evangelism itself, he believes, is shaped as Jesus's own life. Evangelism entails dying to the world as the way of loving, and therefore participating in and redeeming, the world and renewing the church.

In the first millennium, the dying occurred in the church's refusal to worship false gods and demons. Martyrs and hermits renewed the church out of its bankruptcy. The martyr has everything taken from them, life itself and even the dignity of a good death. The hermit renounces all forms of living other than the bankrupt life of poverty in the desert, where nothing grows and self-sustaining is nearly impossible. Both the martyr and the hermit deny any fulfillment that would come from the gods of Caesar. This frees the world from the capricious rage of the cacophony of the pantheon of gods and their blood sacrifices. The blood of the martyr forever ends the river of ritual blood sacrifice.[16] The church, by embracing this bankruptcy of the life of the martyr and the hermit, is renewed, and the world is transformed.[17]

In the second millennium, the Caesars come from within. Rulers and kings, with a decree and cavalry, convert whole lands and tribes. The church swells overnight. Its coffers are full, but its spirit is bankrupt. The leaders are too corrupted by power, the laity too easily sliding back into

16. Constantine, the first Christian emperor, ends blood sacrifice in the fourth century. For a book that warrants further consideration, see Peter Leithart, *Defending Constantine: The Twilight of an Empire and the Dawn of Christendom* (Downers Grove, IL: IVP Academic, 2010). Leithart takes important strides to complicate and, at times, refute the John Howard Yoder–inspired claims of the Constantinian captivity of the church. This assumption has been central to missional church conversations, and Leithart shows us it is not right. Rosenstock-Huessy would stand more with Leithart (who quotes Rosenstock-Huessy a few times) than with Yoder. In relation to this point of the blood of the martyrs ending the blood of sacrifice, when Constantine ruled that blood sacrifice was no longer allowed, he stood on the veneration of martyrs, further pushing the cult away from this practice in the direction of this honoring of their sacrifice.

17. Here is a taste of this argument in Rosenstock-Huessy's own words: "But though the meaning of mission and conversion is ever the same, they have taken on different forms with the course of time. In the Church of the first thousand years—still preserved in the East—men died to the world of false gods and demons. The supreme exemplars of this form of mission were martyrs and monks or hermits. A martyr, as the name itself indicates, was a witness; by his refusal to worship Caesar's statue or shout the equivalent of 'Heil Hitler,' he testified to the Living God against the idols of the marketplace." Rosenstock-Huessy, *Christian Future*, 119.

paganism. In the second millennium, the Western church becomes aware of the bankruptcy of its disobedience. Starting in the eleventh century the martyr and hermit are replaced by the reforming monks. The core practice for the monk and laity alike is to walk, becoming a pilgrim. The church is renewed as pilgrims aim themselves toward the holy and abandon all else to seek it. The pilgrim prepares to die, giving his last will and testament, and then joins the trail, often walking barefoot, toward a holy place. Along the way the pilgrim relies on the kindness of others, blessing those met with prayers. The pilgrim's paths knit the world together, concretely making those of different lands, once of warring tribes, into companions. The church is renewed, and the world is blessed, when the church embraces the bankruptcy of the pilgrim's way as the shape of its evangelism. The pilgrim and reformer, the reformer as the pilgrim, is the renewing mission of the second millennium.

Rosenstock-Huessy is not yet in the third millennium when he writes his book. But he's close enough to see the shape of mission and the place of renewal. He says, "Mission and conversion will continue as long as the soul loses her path and needs regeneration. . . . The temptations of our time do not arise from heavenly demonism [as in the first millennium] or earthly provincialism [as in the second millennium]. *They come from soul erosion.* Our life is haunted by boredom and neurosis; it is disintegrated. . . . We are tempted to worship crude vitality, sensationalism, life at any price."[18] Shockingly, the pressure of our all-out pursuit of happiness as the measure of self-fulfillment has eroded our souls.

Rosenstock-Huessy is prophesying now. These realities leaked through the cracks of life in the second half of the twentieth century. But, for the most part, the soul erosion of boredom, neurosis, and disintegration was held at bay. Even in the 1990s, it could be assumed that the dam walls would hold. But they didn't. Now in the third decade of the third millennium, soul erosion is everywhere, and yet we still, with even more force, seek happiness and self-fulfillment. We are now fully embedded in sad times. Our very ways of seeking self-fulfillment measured by happiness have tempted us, as Rosenstock-Huessy foresaw, into worshiping crude vitality and sensationalisms in all sorts of digital spaces: social media sites,

18. Rosenstock-Huessy, *Christian Future*, 121 (emphasis added).

Pornhub, Amazon, and more. We've also entered a time where a politics that matches *my life*, *my identity* must be fought for at any price—even the cost of decency, honesty, kindness, mercy, and humanity. It's a way of life fueled by fear and hate. Though we all are seeking so badly to be happy and sure of our own self-fulfillment, we're compelled to fear and hate those who put at risk our own self-fulfillment. We are so sad (and anxious and angry because of it) that we rarely stop to spot the depth of erosion in our soul. We know, at one level, that our soul is eroding, but we ultimately feel powerless to stop it.

It is into this bankruptcy that the church is called. Christianity's renewal is possible only inside embracing and joining this poverty, for this is what leads us to the cross. Renewal is always contingent on the embrace of poverty (not creativity and genius). Renewal is dependent on a mission and evangelism of martyrdom, or pilgrimage, or—as we'll see and develop—consolation. The church will always be tempted to seek its own self-fulfillment and fear its own bankruptcy or brokenness. But as Rosenstock-Huessy has pointed out, only by losing itself in an evangelism that joins these sad times will the church find the Spirit generating renewal through the redemptive work of bringing life out of death.

■ ■ ■ ■

When Mary Ann made it back to the office there was a message. It was from Will, the founder and CEO of the company. It read: "When you're in, come see me ASAP!!!" The three exclamation points gave Mary Ann pause and an uneasy feeling. Will was mainly good to work with. He was more than twenty years younger than Mary Ann and always high energy. The verve of that energy was primarily positive. But when it turned, and when frustration became anger, he was a striking viper.

When Mary Ann walked into Will's spacious and meticulously clean corner office, with its spectacular view of the mountains, Will was staring at the door. His face was frozen. Recognizing the frustration on his face, Mary Ann braced herself. The viper was loose in the room.

Will sighed dramatically and struck with venom, "Took you long enough."

Mary Ann held her ground. She'd learned never to turn her back on the viper. Hands folded in front of her, she said, "I'm just back from vacation," and stared back.

Will gathered himself by looking out the window. Sighing again, he struck once more, "I want her gone. Fired. Now." The words were as jaded in tone as the orange mountain rocks out the window.

Mary Ann was confused.

"Who?" she asked back.

"Renate. Do it now. She's done."

3

The Architecture of Our Sad Times
Meeting the Positive Genealogists

Mary Ann was shocked. Even disturbed. But she didn't react. No sudden moves when the viper is loose.

She knew that, in this mood, Will could not be reasoned with. He spoke often of collaboration, insisting, in the good times at least, that people not think of him as the boss or CEO but just one of them. He was always careful, however, to never downgrade "founder." He'd say, "Don't call me boss or think of me as CEO," but he would never renounce the title founder. In good or bad times, Will was always spouting, and wanting others to remember, that he was the founder of the company. Calling Will the founder made him continually, even in those good times, "*first* among equals." But when times were bad or frustration high, first among equals disappeared, replaced by fits of fierce control and assertions of authority. As founder he was magnanimously *first* among equals, but this also let him justify aggressively taking back the reins and barking commands when deemed necessary. "I founded this company after all," he'd say to validate his demands.

Mary Ann's shock froze her. She had so many questions and even more concerns. Not the least about Renate and her personal situation. But she knew those questions wouldn't be welcomed.

■ ■ ■ ■

After Renate's no-show to the walk and Mary Ann's experience at the district assembly, Mary Ann went on a two-week vacation. She'd wanted to go on a cruise her whole life. When she was young, her dad often took her to the harbor to watch the cruise ships leaving and returning. Mary Ann and her dad would eat ice cream and watch people streaming on and off the boats, either filled with anticipation or sunburned and satisfied. She and her dad could never afford to be one of those passengers coming or going, but they could dream. Her dad particularly loved ending their time by joining the crowds, pretending to rush into the parking lot looking for a cab. He'd grab Mary Ann's hand and say loudly as they walked through the mass of busy people, "Wasn't that great, honey? I loved it! The water was so blue and food so good. I couldn't eat another piece of cake or drink another free Corona." He'd then wink at her and smile.

In the car they'd laugh. It was the only memory Mary Ann had of him laughing, the only times he'd ever called her "honey" or winked. To be honest, it was the only times he was even sweet at all. When she thought about a cruise, Mary Ann didn't know what warmed her more: Was it the thought of being someone who could afford such a trip? Or was it how the make-believe with her dad made him someone who held her hand and called her "honey"? Even if he could only role-play this warmth, it was a taste of heaven, a glimpse of everything being right and solid and sure. All the ice in their relationship thawed to a warm, flowering spring inside this game of pretend cruising.

Whatever it was, Mary Ann treasured the thought of going on a cruise. This is why, even when she had the money, she didn't go. She was afraid that none of it would meet her expectations and longings. Deep down she knew that the cruise was too linked to her father. Mary Ann worried that, in actuality, the cruise wouldn't be the heaven she had imagined it would be since she was nine years old. She knew boarding that boat from that same harbor parking lot would only make her both miss and resent her dad. She didn't want to face that. She'd be forced to miss something that she never really had. It would force her to face why he could be so sweet in the dreams of a cruise but never outside them.

Mary Ann had never really consciously thought about any of this. It lived inside her, but she never really connected it all together. She never allowed herself to feel it. She just knew she both craved and feared cruises.

It wasn't until a Bible study at church that Mary Ann made the connection. Pastor Manta was taking the group through a discussion on 1 Corinthians 13. When they came to verse 11, where Paul says, "When I was a child . . . I thought like a child," Pastor Manta invited them to tell a story from their childhood. He asked them, "What was a childhood dream you had that you can still remember?" People said things like playing in the major leagues or owning a farm filled with ponies or being able to fly or to be invisible. Mary Ann found herself saying, almost as a reflex, "Going on a cruise." When she said it out loud, it didn't feel on par with flying or having some other superpower. Pastor Manta invited her to say more. Mary Ann did, and the group held her story, holding her. It was a blessing.

Pastor Manta asked Mary Ann, "How long since your dad passed?"

Mary Ann thought about it, and then with a bit of shock said, "Twenty years next month. Wow. Twenty years since that old bat has been gone."

Walking to her car, Hazel Curran said, "You know who else loved cruises? Valentina."

"That's right!" Mary Ann responded.

"And the end of next month will be four years without her," Hazel added.

"It will, won't it?" Mary Ann answered, with a slight shake of her head.

"You know what we should do?" Hazel said. "We should go on a cruise to remember your dad and Valentina. My nephew works for one of the big companies. He can get us a discount. What do you think?"

And so Mary Ann, Hazel, and two other women from church decided to go on a two-week cruise down Mexico's Pacific coast. It was a journey of friendship but also an act of remembrance. Together they remembered a friend who had always stood with them in painful moments. These friends also stood with Mary Ann as she grieved and embraced her father. Mary Ann went on the cruise her dad never got to take with the daughter he never really knew.

On the cruise, remembering her father, Mary Ann thought about (even prayed for) Renate. This cruise put Mary Ann more in touch with Renate's burden than she had been before. The cruise reminded Mary Ann of those first weeks and months of her own father's passing, and the regret and anger that met her. She always knew that Valentina had helped her through her divorce, but now Mary Ann remembered that Valentina was there too when her father passed. Mary Ann texted Renate twice, and even called once from the ship, but never heard anything back.

■ ■ ■ ■

Now, just a day and a half back from the cruise, and not even an hour back to work, Mary Ann was told to fire Renate. How could she? She knew, at least broadly, the darkness that Renate was experiencing. Mary Ann wanted to shout "No! Why?" But she knew that was no way to handle the viper. As HR, Mary Ann worked at the pleasure of the CEO. All Mary Ann could do was nod. Gathering herself, she said, "Okay. I'll get on this. But legal will need to know why. Is there cause?" This was the best Mary Ann could do to push back.

"Hell yes, there is!" Will shouted. "She's dragging her whole team down. There is no energy anymore. Not only are pieces coming in late, they're lifeless. We hired someone creative and there is no creativity. But . . . BUT . . . what really pisses me off is that she reused some of her writing. A few of the descriptions in her fashion pieces for the *New York Times* were submitted as fresh descriptions of this season's catalog. And then . . . AND THEN . . . I come to notice that the design of the catalog is pretty much a rip-off of one of our major competitors! Like she just copied it, or at least was majorly inspired by it. That sucks! We're about originality here. She was hired because of her freshness, and it's all gone. I can't have that. No authenticity, no job. It's that simple."

"Okay," Mary Ann responded. "So you want me to fire her for a violation of authenticity? I get it—I do, Will—but I'm not sure legal will say we're protected."

"No, don't say it like that!" Will shot back with frustration. "She's being fired because she's working against the mission of the company. Our mission is to make the world happier by making it healthier. She doesn't fit that. I thought she did. I thought she epitomized it, but she doesn't. Her 'lack of authenticity,'" and here Will made exaggerated air quotes, "makes her an enemy to happiness. As someone who oversees our brand, her 'lack of authenticity' makes the whole company unhealthy. I'm firing her to protect us all."

Will always found a way to be the hero.

Mary Ann sighed and repeated, "Will, I can't say that. Legal will not allow us to fire someone for that. We'll be open to a false termination lawsuit." Mary Ann was thinking that she'd even tell Renate to sue if this was the reason.

"Crap," Will responded. "Then there is this."

He pulled up a screen on his computer. It was numbers and graphs.

Will pointed to the screen and said, "Since she's been writing for us, and particularly in the last six weeks, our click-throughs are way, *way* down. Our algorithm shows that her marketing has been the worst in the company's existence. Think about that! Numbers don't lie, Mary Ann. I mean, I'm so peeved because I had such high hopes for her! I loved her writing before she came, and I loved her first few pieces. But this sucks. She scores the worst on all our analytics. And those are only external. Look at the numbers related to her team. We survey people every week. That was Garrett's pet project. Her team is down twenty-five points in happiness, ten in creative energy, and up fifteen points in stress. These numbers are awful."

Will paused, allowing it all to sink in. Then, looking intensely at Mary Ann, he said sarcastically with a dramatic shout, "Is that justification enough?!" Pausing again, he continued, wide-eyed, "Fire her in the next hour. Call legal, clear it. And get her out of here. Got it?!"

Mary Ann could only nod defeatedly and start the process.

Welcome to the 1990s: Genealogy One

In 1991 Charles Taylor gave the Canadian Broadcasting Company's (CBC) Massey Lectures. They were titled "The Malaise of Modernity," and when published as a book, they took the title (at least in the US) *The Ethics of Authenticity*. The title of the lectures and the title of the book seem somewhat juxtaposed. The title of the lectures—"The Malaise of Modernity"— seems ominous and negative. *The Ethics of Authenticity*, on the other hand, seems, if not overtly positive, at least sanguine. Are we dealing with a *malaise* or with *ethics*? And how are *modernity* and *authenticity* connected? Or we could ask it this way: Why would Will think a lack of authenticity is a fireable offense? Why would authenticity's absence seem to ignite a raging flame of righteous indignation within him? Will is sure that what Renate has done (or not done) by being inauthentic is a moral violation. Why?

Like a movie that gets its name from the first scene, the whole of Taylor's lecture series gets its title from the topic of the first lecture. Taylor takes us right into the malaise. He wants to name three worries that bubble up from within modernity. He believes these concerns are inseparable from the modern project. The worries are a kind of sickness or bellyache that comes from the developments, progress, or advancement (discussed in the previous chapter) of modernity. Inside this sense that modernity is pulling us toward development and growth, we fear we're losing something. As modernity pushes us forward (speeding us from what was to what will be), making the future and its development our aim, we find ourselves missing something we maybe never had. Taylor diagnoses it as a malaise. It's a kind of illness we can't quite name or source. Taylor spends the rest of the first lecture naming and discussing the three malaises.

Just as it's no surprise for a kindergartner to get a runny nose and cough in the winter, so none of the three malaises will surprise us late moderns. Inside modernity, these three malaises are as common as a cold. Taylor says, "No one needs to be reminded of them; they are discussed, bemoaned, challenged, and argued against all the time in all sorts of media."[1] Everyone feels these three malaises. We adopt all sorts of home remedies to eliminate their sources and symptoms. But like a cold, while so ordinary, we're often confused about the virology of the strain and where we picked it up from. Our home remedies are often more placebos than medication. Taylor explains that we talk about these three malaises often, but because we do, we are confused by them. We don't really understand the sickness we have. Taylor says, "I believe that this great familiarity hides bewilderment, that we don't really understand these changes that worry us."[2]

These three malaises brought on by our modern developments are the worries of (1) individualism, (2) instrumental reasoning, and (3) the loss of freedom. All three are a result of our development. For instance, modernity values the individual. Inside the modern project, "in principle, people are no longer sacrificed to the demands of supposedly sacred orders that transcend them."[3] Now, we follow what speaks to us. In theory, everyone's life is important and, in some sense, equal.[4] Everyone has their own life to

---

1. Charles Taylor, *The Ethics of Authenticity* (Cambridge, MA: Harvard University Press, 1991), 2.

2. Taylor, *Ethics of Authenticity*, 2.

3. Taylor, *Ethics of Authenticity*, 2.

4. Francis Fukuyama says, "Individuals throughout human history have found themselves at odds with their societies. But only in modern times has the view taken hold that the authentic

live, their own self-fulfillment to seek. This development of centering the individual, however, leads us to worry that it may tumble (or has already tumbled) over into individualism. People no longer see themselves as part of something larger. They (we usually don't include ourselves, which just perpetuates the individualism) feel little obligation to care about anything that isn't directly about them and their own self-fulfillment. This is our first malaise.

Our second malaise is our worry that our developments in technology and science, like the focus on the individual, will turn on us. "The fear is that things that ought to be determined by other criteria will be decided in terms of efficiency or 'cost-benefit' analysis." We come to worry that "our lives will be eclipsed by the demand to maximize output."[5] We fear that we are just tools. Or now, in the third decade of the twenty-first century, just data. We worry that our most common and central human interactions are instrumentalized. We are not human beings with stories but just numbers. We sense that we're free to be individuals, and yet we are frustrated because we're supposed to express our individuality in an environment that makes the world only a flat object, something very hard to encounter.[6] This instrumental reasoning works against our individuality or makes our individuality an object for someone else's profit. We fear that, because of this instrumentality, we are uninhibited individuals but living in a deadened landscape.

These two malaises coalesce to create the third: what Taylor calls "the loss of freedom." He means it at the location of our political lives. Inside societies where instrumental reasoning and individualism run loose, freedom is slowly but surely eroded. To give a somewhat benign example, instrumental reasoning means that even on our own property we must conform to building standards. We sense that there are all sorts of regulations and patterns that make little difference but are in place for some instrumental purpose. When we have too many of these experiences, we

---

inner self is intrinsically valuable, and the outer society systematically wrong and unfair in its valuation of the former. It is not the inner self that has to be made to conform to society's rules, but society itself that needs to change." Fukuyama, *Identity: Contemporary Identity Politics and the Struggle for Recognition* (New York: Profile Books, 2019), 10.

5. Taylor, *Ethics of Authenticity*, 5.

6. The whole of Hartmut Rosa's project is to both describe and address this reality. See Rosa, *Social Acceleration: A New Theory of Modernity* (New York: Columbia University Press, 2015); and Rosa, *Resonance: A Sociology of Our Relationship to the World* (Cambridge: Polity, 2019).

quickly feel like our freedom is being lost in procedures and paperwork. Or to give a less benign example, we know that spending any time on the internet erodes our privacy. But we're willing to give up our privacy for the expressive and entertaining opportunities our digital actions give us.

Similarly, and somewhat in tandem (especially in digital spaces), individualism pushes us into the loss of freedom. Individualism has the effect, as Alexis de Tocqueville saw in the early nineteenth century, of turning us in on ourselves to such an extent that we find little reason or patience to participate in the processes of citizenship and self-government. We "prefer to stay at home and enjoy the satisfactions of private life,"[7] to stay home to doomscroll the internet.

These two realities have the potential effect of bringing about something that was only hypothetical for Taylor in the 1990s. Following Tocqueville, Taylor says that this instrumentalism and individualism *could* lead to a soft despotism (oppressive authority exerted by the government). Taylor explains, "It will not be a tyranny of terror and oppression as in the old days. The government will be mild and paternalistic. It may even keep democratic forms, with periodic elections. But in fact, everything will be run [in a way that] . . . people will have little control."[8] If only!

What Taylor couldn't imagine in the 1990s is that this soft despotism would move from potential to actual and become not so soft.[9] In the twenty-first century despotism has not (yet) become as hard as granite, as with Mussolini and Franco in the early twentieth century. But it is present and much firmer than the Taylor of the 1990s could imagine. In the 1990s, with the Berlin Wall having just fallen, Taylor couldn't have imagined that

---

7. Taylor, *Ethics of Authenticity*, 9.

8. Taylor, *Ethics of Authenticity*, 9.

9. Jacob Hacker and Paul Pierson add, "Plutocratic populism is rather new; the political dilemma that gives rise to it is very old. For as long as the idea of democracy has existed, thoughtful observers—both those who supported democracy and those who opposed it—have asked a fundamental question: What happens when an economic system that concentrates wealth in the hands of the few coexists with a political system that gives the ballot to the many?" Hacker and Pierson, *Let Them Eat Tweets: How the Right Rules in an Age of Extreme Inequality* (New York: Liveright, 2020), 18. They continue, "The historical record reveals a clear pattern. Whenever economic elites have grossly disproportionate power and come to see their economic interests as opposed to those of ordinary citizens, they are likely to promote social divisions. They are also likely to come to fear a fair democratic process in which those citizens have significant clout. These elite responses to extreme inequality enter into politics mainly through conservative parties, which must navigate the tension between unequal influence and democratic competition. The Conservative Dilemma is not a problem of a particular moment. It is a problem inherent in democratic politics in contexts of extreme inequality" (39).

in the third decade of the twenty-first century, something more than soft despotism would be pumping through the veins of countries like Hungary, Sweden, Italy, Turkey, the Netherlands, and the United States of America.[10] And he further couldn't have imagined how religion itself would be used as an instrumental tonic, mixed in the water of a hyperpopulist individualism, to produce and then solidify this despotism. It would surprise the 1990s Taylor that this thick despotism would take the shape again of the "strong man" on the far right. But it would blow his mind that the left would lead in attacking free speech in relation to language use and identity policing.[11] The Taylor of the 1990s would be stunned that a more-than-soft despotism is present on the right *and* the left in the sad times of the twenty-first century.[12]

Looking closely, we can see that these three malaises—individualism, instrumental reasoning, and a soft despotism—have contaminated Protestant conceptions and practices of evangelism like microplastics in our bodies. It's hard for us to imagine evangelism outside or beyond

10. Pippa Norris and Ronald Inglehart give us more texture: "For many populist leaders, ranging from Donald Trump and France's Marine Le Pen, Hungary's Viktor Orban, Venezuela's Nicolas Maduras, and the Philippines' Rodrigo Duterte, behind the populist facade, a more disturbing set of authoritarian values and policies can be identified. Not all populists endorse authoritarianism, and authoritarian rulers do not necessarily adopt populist appeals, but the combination often occurs. Logical connections tie the two together: populism tends to undermine the legitimacy of democratic checks on executive powers, opening the door for soft authoritarian leaders. And the steady erosion of democratic norms and political freedoms over a sustained period of time leads toward the consolidation of authoritarian regimes, such as Venezuela, which outlast particular leaders." Norris and Inglehart, *Cultural Backlash: Trump, Brexit, and Authoritarian Populism* (New York: Cambridge University Press, 2019), 69.

11. For an example of this, see Robby Soave, *Panic Attack: Young Radicals in the Age of Trump* (New York: All Points, 2019). For a more scholarly and philosophical take, see Susan Neiman, *Left Is Not Woke* (London: Polity, 2023). She argues that the far left actually isn't left; they have become despots as they've thrown off liberal values. The feminist sociologist Eva Illouz agrees, saying, "The political language of victimhood is now entering a new phase of its history: having been appropriated by the right in order to incriminate the old left as an oppressor, it can no longer be effectively used by liberals. *Ressentiment* becomes a weapon in an internecine war between elites, one representing business and neo-liberalism, the other representing the culture vanguard." Illouz, *The Emotional Life of Populism* (Malden, MA: Polity, 2023), 123.

12. Colin Campbell draws this deeper, saying, "A crucial feature of this process is an inherent tendency towards despotism. Since pleasure can only be successfully assessed subjectively yet is a function of the sensations arising from objects and events in the environment, the pleasure-seeker will naturally be pushed towards acquiring greater and greater control over all that surrounds him. Such control is not merely a question of ensuring that others submit to his will, but is more a matter of possessing complete power over all sources of sensations so that the continuous adjustments can be made which ensure prolonged pleasure." Campbell, *The Romantic Ethic and the Spirit of Modern Consumerism* (Cham, Switzerland: Palgrave Macmillan, 2018), 116.

an individual person "making a decision" (individualism), through a strategy or by a tool like a tract (instrumental reasoning), where the one evangelizing speaks with a kind of paternalistic authority about the benefits of conversion (soft despotism). The pastors who've been lauded for evangelizing many in late modernity, growing huge churches, too often function as more-than-soft despots and near fascists. Allowing evangelism to be molded by individualism, instrumentality, and soft despotism not only exorcises humility from the practice but, even more, removes the sacramental. Such evangelism tries to offer good news to people coping with these malaises such that it just doubles down on the malaises. It's like saying that the best way to deal with a head cold is to get the stomach flu. Ultimately, conforming evangelism to the very shape of our malaises has meant that evangelism has struggled to address our sad times.

To summarize, it was hard for Taylor to imagine in the 1990s that this individualism could produce such loneliness, this instrumentalism create such angry alienation, and this loss of freedom spawn such outlets for political revenge that our times would become sad ones. But here we are. While Taylor couldn't quite spot how these three malaises would produce a disease of sadness, he did believe that we weren't thinking rightly about our time and its malaises. This lack of understanding may have allowed the malaises to turn into our disease.

Homing In on One Malaise

Taylor ends the first lecture in the book by telling us that all three malaises need to be reexamined. He believes there are dimensions and elements to each that we often misunderstand. Yet unfortunately (or maybe it's to our fortune), he doesn't have the time or space to do so. Taylor's gift is not brevity,[13] and to look at all three of these malaises would mean another five-to-seven-hundred-page book.[14] It would mean more lectures than any

13. I see the irony (or better hypocrisy) of this statement. Maybe it's because I'm taken by Taylor's thought, but I too do not possess the gift of brevity. I not only don't have the gift but rather have a problem as a three-volume series becomes six and still I'm working at it.

14. When Taylor gave these lectures, he had just published the six-hundred-page *Sources of the Self*, and *A Secular Age* was on the horizon. His book *Hegel* was published in 1975, which is a long treatise as well.

listener has patience for. Therefore, Taylor explains that going forward, he'll leave malaises two (instrumental reasoning) and three (loss of freedom) behind and focus only on malaise one, individualism.

Focusing only on malaise one will suffice because Taylor's objective is to show that we're not quite thinking rightly about any of the malaises that modernity has thrust upon us. The rest of the lectures dive deep into individualism.[15] This deep dive will show that there is indeed an ethic that drives toward authenticity in modernity (hence the shift from *The Malaise of Modernity* to *The Ethics of Authenticity*). As we'll see, Taylor wants to show us that our times are not individualistic in a completely hedonistic way. There is an ethic at play. This ethic, at least in the 1990s, is often missed due to our hand-wringing over concerns about individualism. But we must also wonder, now in the twenty-first century, whether 1990s Taylor recognizes how deep our loneliness could become. We need to consider his ethics of authenticity but also wonder whether this ethic creates further conditions for isolation or even division. In other words, was Taylor too positive?

For our purposes, exploring at least the next lecture of Taylor's series will help us see the texture of our sad times. But we can't get a full grip on these sad times unless we go where Taylor can't. We must at least dip our toe into the other two malaises to be able to construct our sacramental evangelism born of consolation—an evangelism that can address failing happiness-seekers and escape the destructive contaminants of our malaises.

Following a discussion of Taylor on individualism, we'll explore Toulmin on instrumental reasoning. More than individualism, Toulmin's genealogy tells the story of how modernity has been tempted to follow in the footsteps of one of its parents over the other. Modernity has been too taken with the parent of rationalistic instrumental reasoning, forsaking the parent of Renaissance humanism.[16] A discussion of Toulmin's genealogy will allow us to explore not only instrumentalism but also the loss of freedom by meeting Michel de Montaigne more directly.

15. "By, at the latest, the final decade of the nineteenth century, many were diagnosing a deep malaise in western culture, which expressed itself in various forms of individual and social disorientation." Raymond Geuss, *A World without Why* (Princeton: Princeton University Press, 2014), 91.

16. At times, to add Isaiah Berlin to Toulmin, modernity has followed its brother of Romanticism, which is linked to the Renaissance humanism that Toulmin lauds.

As we've seen, for Montaigne, happiness is the freedom of the tower of the château. While this longing is in our cultural DNA, we've given up some of our freedom for the sake of a happiness that is both instrumental and individual. Both Taylor and Toulmin are big fans of Montaigne. After looking at their two distinct genealogies, we'll be in a position to see why. But we'll also notice that both of these genealogists end things quite positively. They both believe, for different reasons, that the 1990s have gotten us back on the right track. They both seem to succumb to the process of development that Taylor names in lecture one. Standing in the third decade of the twenty-first century, we'll wonder whether our sad times don't make French polymath Blaise Pascal a more important companion than Monsieur Montaigne. We'll take steps, then, toward the tortured boy genius Pascal, who experiences the infinite encounter with the finite as a consoling fiery light in darkness.

But first to individualism.

Exploring Malaise One

It's not hard for us to believe that we're thinking wrongly about our sickness. We moderns are easily convinced that our reasoning around what ails us is off—why else would Goop or even WebMD exist? We wonder if perhaps there isn't another source or treatment for our illness or itching uneasiness. Maybe what's afflicting us isn't what we think. As late-modern individuals drawn to instrumental reasoning about freedom, we're happy to entertain this possibility (it's big business). But we'll need an example of someone who's got it wrong. Better, we'll need a contrasting position. Taylor doesn't disappoint. In the first sentence of lecture two Taylor gives us a foil: political theorist Allan Bloom.

In 1987 Allan Bloom published a bestseller titled *The Closing of the American Mind*. Bloom explains in his book that he'd been teaching at elite American universities for thirty years. His main responsibility was taking students through great books courses. The way this new generation was reading books greatly disturbed him. Bloom's teaching career stretched from the mid-1950s into the late 1980s; basically, the same time span as the movie *Back to the Future*. Bloom saw a huge difference between the mid-1950s and mid-1980s. These two periods, only thirty years apart, for all intents and purposes were different worlds.

And Bloom doesn't much care for the new world. It isn't the changes in technology, music, or consumer choice—which Robert Zemeckis's movie highlights—that bothered Bloom. I'm sure Bloom is fine with skateboards and puffer vests, maybe even with plutonium and DeLoreans in mall parking lots. What bothers Bloom (a lot!) is a change in thinking. What he's worried about is a new way of reasoning that is fully and finally about the individual. Bloom believes he's seeing the arrival of a facile relativism.

This relativism, Bloom believes, is birthed from the womb of the turbulent late 1960s. But there is a difference (he thinks the Boomers did it right and Gen Xers not so much). Students of the late 1960s entertained a (soft) relativism as a way of protest. It was a way of opening their minds to new ideas, perspectives, and ways of being. They came to realize that their forms of socialization at home and school needed to be broadened and deepened. The next generation, however, Bloom contends, has wrapped itself in a relativism for the sake of closing their minds. They've done so in hopes of narrowing and flattening the demands on their minds. They're slackers! They've closed their minds for the sake of pacifying and pleasing their individual selves. The relativism of the students of the 1980s is used as a cop-out, as a form of narcissism.[17] This relativism frees students from having any demands to reason about anything beyond their own tastes and choice. Bloom contends that, for this generation, anything outside individual taste and choice is unwelcomed, rejected, shut out, and closed off. They just are so very individualistic!

Taylor cannot abide Bloom's thesis. Taylor follows Bloom a long way. He agrees with Bloom's descriptions and concerns about individualism all the way up until the end. But in the end, Taylor thinks Bloom's thesis is in error. He finds it a poor way of conceiving of how human beings act in the world. But even so, Taylor and Bloom agree on a certain starting point, which keeps Bloom's thesis from unfairly becoming a straw man to use as a punching bag. Taylor and Bloom agree that fulfillment is now self-located (discussed in the previous chapter). The individual is the locus of fulfillment. But here Taylor departs. Bloom thinks this self-location is de facto hedonistic and destructive. The self-location of fulfillment

---

17. Taylor mentions Christopher Lasch's book *The Culture of Narcissism: American Life in an Age of Diminishing Expectations* (New York: Warner Books, 1979). Bloom is following Lasch's lead in his own argumentation.

produces a lazy relativism and a desert of critical thinking that destroys the minds of a generation.

Bloom thinks this self-location of fulfillment creates the possibility only of a stiff and closed-off individualism. Bloom is an example of what Taylor calls a "knocker" (or what we might call today a "hater") of modernity. What Bloom is knocking is the self-location of fulfillment. But Taylor has gone far enough with Bloom to not be his complete opposite. Taylor is not what he calls a "booster," someone who only celebrates and sees no problems with the self-location of fulfillment. Taylor is trying to thread a needle; he isn't a knocker or a booster. Rather, Taylor believes that this self-location of fulfillment just means we're modern (remember, Taylor loves Montaigne; my guess is that Bloom does not). With Bloom, and unlike the boosters, Taylor thinks individualism is a concern. But unlike Bloom and other knockers, Taylor believes that just because fulfillment is self-located doesn't mean it's hedonistic or relativistic or flat or closed off. He believes the contrary.

Ethics now eclipses *malaise* in Taylor's lectures. The self-location of fulfillment means that "being yourself" takes on moral weight. The drive to be yourself, to see everything through the goal of being true to yourself, isn't just crass rejection or lazy relativism. It's an ethical construction. Taylor believes it further reinforces, even here in late modernity, that we are fundamentally moral creatures. Even individualism (with its problems and dangers) cannot help but be moral. The kids aren't relativists—giving up on ethics—Taylor contends. Rather, their ethic is one of authenticity. Being yourself is not a degradation into some primal libido state. It is the construction of a rich moral vision that demands that each individual have a right to define for themselves what it means for them to be human. What is right and what is wrong is what allows or keeps someone from being their truest self. The self-location of fulfillment remains moral.

Taylor contends that modernity isn't a hedonistic hellscape of narcissistic individualists. Modernity is made up of individuals seeking fulfillment by being their truest selves inside an ethic of authenticity. The problem with Bloom and his knocking ilk is that they ignore this moral reality. Taylor says it like this: "The force of terms like 'narcissism' (Lasch's word), or 'hedonism' (Bloom's description), is to imply that there is no moral ideal at work here; or if there is, on the surface, that it should rather be seen as a screen for self-indulgence."[18] Without recognizing the moral quality embedded inside individualism, there can be no redeeming quality or even possibility within it.

Taylor holds that as long as this ethic is operational—as long as we're moved by some moral ideal giving us something better and higher to desire—there is the possibility that we'll escape a flat and narrowing existence. If the moral ideal is still beating, even in the heart of individualism, it bears the possibility of opening us to others and directing us to a good that is beyond us. While Bloom accuses the 1980s generation of giving into relativism, Taylor believes they instead operate out of a distinct ethic of authenticity. Their outrage at systems and structures that keep people from being their selves shows this. Individualism may have its dangers. The drive to be yourself may be fraught. But it is far from hedonistic. The fact that there remains a moral ideal means, for Taylor, that there is the potential to open up and reach for the good, for the better and higher. Taylor says, "Authenticity is not the enemy of demands that emanate from beyond the self; it supposes such demands."[19] For Taylor, even individualism remains human. Individualism may make us sick, but it's not completely diseased. The fact that individualism has a moral ideal (authenticity) is its immune system that fights off deadly infection.

Does this tip Taylor over into the booster category? How can Taylor be sure that this moral ideal to "be yourself," to be authentic, takes us out of ourselves, escaping a closed individualism and leading us to reach for the "better" and "higher"?

To thread this needle between booster and knocker, Taylor stands on the shoulders of others. He makes his unique contribution by drawing several thoughts together. Drawing these thoughts together, he believes, allows authenticity to be ethical and allows self-fulfillment to rest on beliefs (not relativism) and moral ideals (not hedonism and narcissism).

On the Broad Shoulders

Taylor has the time and space to discuss only the malaise of individualism. Choosing individualism isn't random but strategic. Individualism is the most visceral of the malaises, connecting most directly to the listener

18. Taylor, *Ethics of Authenticity*, 16.
19. Taylor, *Ethics of Authenticity*, 41.

and reader (Bloom's bestseller is proof). But wrestling with individualism also allows Taylor to hint at how to combat the other two malaises.

To see how, we need to notice the shoulders that Taylor is standing on.
Taylor is an expert on Hegel, publishing a lengthy book on the German
philosopher in 1975. We also must remember that in the 1950s Taylor
broke with the Oxford establishment of analytical philosophy by turning
to the work of Maurice Merleau-Ponty and Martin Heidegger. Heidegger
contends that our modern problem is the loss of being. For example,
technology disconnects us from authentic ways of being in the world.
There is just too much stiff instrumentalism for Heidegger. This stiff
instrumentalism strips us of our *Dasein*, our authentic way of being.
Authenticity opposes this instrumentality. While Taylor is not able to
wrestle directly with instrumental reasoning, by borrowing and recasting
authenticity for his own use (even inside a discussion of individualism),
Taylor nevertheless addresses instrumentality. Taylor assumes that an
ethic of authenticity—being true to yourself as an ideal—cannot stomach,
in a Heideggerian vein, an overreach of instrumentality. Taylor is using
authenticity to subtly critique instrumental reasoning in a Heideggerian
tone. Authenticity moves out from the self to encounter a world, shaping
this world. The authentic, in this Heideggerian way, stands between the
knocker and booster perspectives.

More than a hundred years before Heidegger, Hegel centered his philosophical project on freedom. In the early nineteenth century Hegel did his
part to expand our imagination of freedom. Hegel believes that freedom
is progressive and expanding. But for this expansion to continue uninterrupted we need recognition (Taylor discusses recognition in lecture five).
Freedom and recognition are interconnected. Authenticity demands, at
some level, recognition. You need others, even the systems and structures
of society, to recognize your unique (or free) ways of being yourself.

The need for recognition allows the ideal of being yourself and the
drive for self-fulfillment to have a moral horizon and to escape a closed
individualism. The need for recognition demands that authenticity and
self-imposed fulfillment be conversational. Recognition necessitates a desire for the self to reach out to something or someone in conversation.
Authenticity's need for recognition makes it extrinsic. Recognition gives
authenticity a desire for what is beyond or outside what the self alone
possesses. The need for recognition keeps even individualism open.

In Taylor's mind, this need for recognition means that the ethic of authenticity will create a politics of recognition.[20] It will get people talking to each other across their own ideals of being their true selves. The politics of recognition will demand discussions of freedom and even protections against despotism (because one's unique way of being human will be expressed, producing an open and generative pluralism that will need to be protected). Taylor is hopeful that giving people space and therefore freedom to express their authenticity—and have that authenticity recognized—will create livable democratic spaces of distinct yet collective freedom.

In 1991, Taylor proves to be quite positive.[21] He sees great hope in the ethics of authenticity. He's not a gleeful booster. He's doesn't shy away from naming the malaises. He refuses, like the boosters, to call the malaises imaginary or even misunderstood goods. Rather, Taylor contends that there are real dark sources to our malaises. Even if we struggle to name the sources of the malaises, the malaises are real. But unlike the knockers, Taylor thinks the ideal of being yourself (and the self-location of fulfillment) produces an ethics that *can* allow for true conversation, connection, and fortifications of freedom (even the growth of democracy).[22]

But Taylor concedes that his thesis all depends on three certain beliefs, as all moral ideas do.[23] Taylor never wavers from contending that we humans are always moral-believing creatures. Taylor can be positive in the 1990s because, for the most part, these three beliefs held. *We, however, cannot.* I think it's fair to say that, here in the third decade of the twenty-first century, these beliefs that safeguard the ethic of authenticity are severely

20. See Charles Taylor, *Multiculturalism*, ed. Amy Gutmann (Princeton: Princeton University Press, 1994).

21. The truth is that Taylor is always positive. This is part of his personality. He's never naive but always positive.

22. Taylor explains, "In the light of this developing understanding of recognition over the last two centuries, we can see why the culture of authenticity has come to give precedence to the two modes of living together I mentioned earlier: (1) on the social level, the crucial principle is that of fairness, which demands equal chances for everyone to develop their own identity, which include—as we can now understand more clearly—the universal recognition of difference, in whatever modes this is relevant to identity, be it gender, racial, cultural, or to do with sexual orientation; and (2) in the intimate sphere, the identity forming love relationship has a crucial importance." Taylor, *Ethics of Authenticity*, 50.

23. This focus on belief reveals the hermeneutical core to Taylor's project. This core is always consistent with him. This hermeneutical center also keeps him from embracing the knocker or booster perspectives.

endangered, if not maimed and bleeding out. Taylor explains that "being true to yourself" can produce a moral ideal only if we believe the following:

1. That authenticity is a valid ideal [for everyone];
2. That you can argue [and] reason about ideals and about the conformity of practices to these ideals;
3. That these arguments can make a difference.[24]

The Three Beliefs Are No More

Building off the work of Susan Neiman, a philosopher of significant clout herself, I believe it's fair to say that we no longer believe these three things. We've come to refuse each of them. *But we need to be careful here; we need to understand this intricate but powerful change* before we can draw directly from Neiman and understand what has replaced these three beliefs. Surprisingly, the refusal of these three beliefs has not ended the ethics of authenticity but *intensified it* by reshaping it.

Taylor imagined that if we lost these three beliefs, authenticity would be downgraded, shaking loose its ethical propensities to a sea of apathy. It's not hard to spot here the assumed propensities of the slacker Gen X (*Reality Bites* was just a few years from theatrical release). What I don't think Taylor imagined was that these three beliefs could end and that the ethical impulse of authenticity would not dissolve along with them but instead intensify tenfold. Taylor saw authenticity as requiring these three beliefs, and so he couldn't imagine that authenticity could remain without them, let alone turn into a gremlin with a racing pulse. But it's happened. Losing these three beliefs has expanded and intensified authenticity exponentially. Oddly, the refusal of these beliefs *has not* ended the moral drive to be yourself but turned it into a no-holds-barred fight. Discarding the three beliefs that (1) authenticity is a valid idea, (2) it can be reasoned and argued over, and (3) arguing can make a difference has allowed the ethics of authenticity to evolve into a blunt object. Authenticity is now used even by new late-modern despots.[25]

---

24. Taylor, *Ethics of Authenticity*, 23.

25. Whether in the US, Hungry, Poland, or Russia, the despots win ground by pushing back against those who keep pushing further and further for the recognition of their drives to be their selves. These despots not only fight back but often use racist and sexist acts to uphold

The need for recognition has been the entry point for this new, intensified authenticity. Authenticity has accumulated both defensive and offensive weaponry because recognition (while good and necessary for consolation) has also turned into an all-out battle, and individual happiness has become everything (making so many of us feel like we're teetering on the knife's edge of mental illness). Recognition for being yourself has intensified into a fight, becoming a hypercompetitive war. This has happened because the three beliefs have not held, allowing authenticity to take a shape Taylor couldn't imagine back when *The Fresh Prince of Bel-Air* was premiering on national television. The loss of these three beliefs has made authenticity ground zero of our culture war.

This is where Susan Neiman comes in. Neiman is an American Jewish philosopher who spent her student days in the civil rights movement and teaching career in Israel and Germany. She's wrestled both practically and philosophically with issues like evil, totalitarianism, and racism. Even more than Taylor, Neiman sees herself as a liberal or a supporter of the left. Yet she senses that something is deeply wrong. The new left,[26] or what she calls the "woke left," has abandoned the essential ideals of the project of liberty and therefore operates much more like far-right despots, using their same tactics.[27] Neiman lays this out vividly in her book *Left Is Not Woke*, where she describes three lost ideals of liberalism. Neiman never mentions Taylor, but her three lost ideals map perfectly onto the three beliefs that Taylor in the early 1990s thought were essential for the ethic of authenticity to hold. Naming her three lost ideals, Neiman shows, stunningly, that Taylor's three beliefs have indeed been abandoned.

Taylor told us that for "being true to yourself" to be a legitimate moral horizon, you first (1) need to believe that authenticity is a valid ideal. What

---

white or dominant-culture identity. They push back against the drive to be yourself with their claim that white nationalists, too, are just trying to be themselves.

26. Not to be confused with the old new left from the 1960s, which shaped the Democratic Party for decades. By "new" I mean the identity-politics left that Mark Lilla and others discuss. See Mark Lilla, *The Once and Future Liberal: After Identity Politics* (New York: Harper, 2017).

27. Doug Rossinow adds, "The centrality of the search for authenticity in the new left is what recent work on this movement has neglected to appreciate or explore, and this accounts in large measure for the failure to assimilate the new left fully to the main lines of historical development in twentieth-century America. In the future, rather than asking why a left-wing movement became so pre-occupied with authenticity, we might do better to ask how it was that one branch of a broad-ranging youth existentialist movement, a search for authenticity, turned leftist." Rossinow, *The Politics of Authenticity: Liberalism, Christianity, and the New Left in America* (New York: Columbia University Press, 1998), 8.

Taylor means is that you need to believe that *everyone* universally has the right to seek their own authentic way of being. That means everyone. This belief must rest on the acceptance of a common, shared humanity that sees difference but claims universality. While our differences are real, there nevertheless is a shared, even universal, human journey or experience. Therefore, everyone has a right to speak and to be recognized. This right rests in our universal humanity, on universal human rights.[28]

Neiman thinks we've lost the ideal of universalism, replacing it with tribalism. The right for recognition is now assumed to be reserved only for those who deserve it. Recognition, therefore, becomes bound in something other than our universal humanity. Only victimhood gives a person a voice now. Neiman says, "Victimhood should be a source of legitimation for claims to restitution, but once we begin to view victimhood *per se* as the currency of recognition, we are on the road to divorcing recognition, and legitimacy, from virtue altogether."[29] Taylor did not foresee this divorce in the 1990s. But here it is starkly in our own time.

Inside recognition's divorce from virtue, what has arisen is tribes of warring victims. Who is victim and who is victimizer becomes contested ground, causing a division that keeps us from claims of a common humanity. Inside victim-based tribalism, it becomes essential that the world be divided between groups (a strategy of the far right that, Neiman grieves, the new left is using). Only those whom your group perceives as victims are allowed the ideal of authenticity.[30] Only victimhood is authentic. Those who get to be recognized for their authenticity are those who are highest on the claim of victimhood. But who is the victim is contested and ultimately determined by your tribal affiliation. We must, then, constantly battle, even within our own tribes, for platforming and deplatforming.

28. Neiman discusses how far-right thinker Carl Schmitt argued heatedly against this in the Nazi era. She shows how this thinking has been picked up by the new left. The new left, of course, doesn't name Schmitt, but their perspectives are in union with his. See Neiman, *Left Is Not Woke* (London: Polity, 2023), chaps. 1 and 2. For more on Schmitt, see Reinhard Mehring, *Carl Schmitt: A Biography* (Malden, MA: Polity, 2022).

29. Neiman, *Left Is Not Woke*, 17.

30. Andreas Reckwitz adds insightfully, "Struggles for recognition, in which social groups seek recognition as victims, seem to be just as typical of this phase of modernity as the loss of political utopias. A proactive attitude toward progress has clearly been replaced by a defensive orientation toward prevention, resilience, and the minimalization of loss." Reckwitz and Hartmut Rosa, *Late Modernity in Crisis* (Malden, MA: Polity, 2023), 69.

Neiman believes that inside the fight for recognition of identities, universalism has been eclipsed by a tribalism built on victimhood. Taylor's first belief, that authenticity is a valid ideal for everyone, no longer holds. With the loss of a universal humanity, we no longer believe that authenticity is a valid ideal for all. Some people of a certain kind of privilege can never be authentic, and therefore should never have a right to express their authenticity, unless they can provide some level of victimhood (my son was told this very thing at his high school). The nonvictims need to be eliminated from the conversation, their fulfillment no longer mattering. The only recognition nonvictims can receive is negative. Inside the victim-victimizer dialectic there is a ranked order of more to less (to no) authenticity.[31]

Taylor's second belief is that you can argue and reason about ideals and about the conformity of practices to these ideals. Taylor contends that inside each person's authentic stating of what it means for them to be true to themselves, there can be debate, disagreement, and even persuasion. We can come to agreements and even work to make the world a more just place through our own expressions of authenticity.

But *not* if we lose the universal inside the tribal. If a common humanity is lost and the world is divided between victim and victimizers, I can never accept another argument or form of reasoning. I will hate the other's practices. I must. Despising their way of life is the only way for me to be authentic and receive the recognition I need. Inside this victim-victimizer dialectic, why should I listen to them? None of their points or practices can lead to justice. There is no justice for them, just power. The other has been corrupted completely by power, or they are pawns in someone else's power game. Justice is simply the victims getting power.

Neiman's second lost ideal is that justice has been eclipsed by power, at least in practice. We are still giving lip service to justice, but for many the

---

31. French intellectual Élisabeth Roudinesco adds, "In a work . . . devoted to the identitarian left [*The Once and Future Liberal*], Mark Lilla pointed out that the adjective 'identitarian' initially brought to mind protesters with shaved heads, dressed in black leather, tossing pigs' heads at mosques or hunting down migrants while brandishing banners decorated with fleurs-de-lis. . . . From one political extreme to another, 'identitarianism' is present: identity versus identity. Since the fall of the Berlin Wall and the global triumph of liberalized capitalism based on the cult of the individual, left-wing movements linked to identity politics are in search of a new model for society, one that would be respectful of differences, attentive to equality, well-being, and care." Roudinesco, *The Sovereign Self: Pitfalls of Identity Politics* (Malden, MA: Polity, 2022), 136.

cry for justice is a smoke screen, a power move to push our agenda. In our time, the ethic of authenticity is not used to make the world more just for *all*. This has been lost to the assumption that all of our human interactions, every single one (even the debates and disagreements that Taylor believes are essential for democracy), are only contests of power. Because for the new left (and far right) there is no justice but only power. Despotic dreams now threaten democracy from both the far right and the new left.

Justice demands a vision of the good that reaches outside the self. Justice embraces some universal vision. Even Jacques Derrida once said, "Justice cannot be deconstructed."[32] Power makes only one thing good: the recognition of one's tribe of selves winning over another.[33] When we see the world bound totally and completely in power, and justice having no universal vision (like the *imago Dei* or the inalienable rights of equality), then recognition loses any impulse for alterity. Recognition does not open us to otherness but becomes a or *the* source of power. It becomes the way to win. Win what? More recognition, because in a digital age where attention is currency, recognition is gold. Enemies need to be deplatformed and canceled; winners are rewarded with more recognition for being most authentic. The winners achieve power, not encounters of discourse that produce justice.

Taylor's third belief is that these arguments—these ways of hearing and engaging others' articulations of their authentic ways of being true to themselves—can make a difference. They can lead us toward justice. Hearing and engaging with others can make the world a better place. For this belief to hold, we must resist, Taylor continues, "accounts of modernity

32. Jacques Derrida, *Force de loi* (Paris: Galilée, 2005), 6.

33. For Neiman this is the victory of Foucault. Neiman, *Left Is Not Woke*, chap. 3. Here is Foucault in his own words about power: "[Both liberal and Marxist positions have a] common feature [that] is what I will call 'economism' in the theory of power. What I mean to say is this: In the case of the classic juridical theory of power, power is regarded as a right which can be possessed in the way one possesses a commodity, and which can therefore be transferred or alienated, either completely or partly, through a juridical act or an act that founds a right—it does not matter which, for the moment—thanks to the surrender of something or thanks to a contract. Power is the concrete power that any individual can hold, and which he can surrender, either as a whole or in part, so as to constitute a power or a political sovereignty. In the body of theory to which I am referring, the constitution of political power is therefore constituted by this series, or is modeled on a juridical operation similar to an exchange of contracts. There is therefore an obvious analogy, and it runs through all these theories, between power and commodities, between power and wealth." Foucault, *Society Must Be Defended: Lectures at the Collège de France, 1975–76* (New York: Picador, 1997), 13.

that see us as imprisoned in modern culture by the 'system,' whether this is defined as capitalism, industrial society, or bureaucracy."[34] There must be a sense that our agency makes the future better.

Neiman thinks this ideal too has been lost by the new left and the right. Inside the victim-victimizer dialectic of tribalism, and the sense that power is everything (always, all the way down), progress is not possible. The future is doomed. Any changes in the system itself are equivalent to rearranging deck chairs on the *Titanic*. You can win more recognition, and therefore power for yourself and your tribe, by heralding that nothing ever really gets better, can't get better. We can't admit that progress is being made if the power of recognition is built around victimhood. If our goals are actually accomplished and the world becomes better, groups become less victimized and therefore have less power (see how justice is eclipsed by power?). They therefore lose the impetus for more recognition. Oddly, if the world were to improve, it would make people much less happy and less fulfilled. Better to live in a constant state of doom, cuddling up with the anxiety, refusing to celebrate or even see the gains that self-expression has achieved. Just stay fixated on the doom; that's better than allowing yourself to feel sad. We must always be wrestling with never-abating catastrophe, and always use statements to that effect, to keep the sadness from overtaking us.[35]

Neiman is amazed at how the new left refuses to see the real change that has taken place in racial equity and gender rights. She's lived through these struggles and fought these battles. She knows there is still a *long way* to go, but there has been important change. The South and the boardroom of the 1960s are not the South and the boardroom of the 2020s. Yet, in this battle for authenticity, admitting progress is a problem because one slip, even in celebration, could lead to the loss of power and recognition. Inside the firm victim-victimizer dialectic there can be no progress, only the shifting of

34. Taylor, *Ethics of Authenticity*, 23.
35. Walter A. Davis adds, "The deepest lesson anxiety teaches us is not that we exist, but that we must act. This is the secret Heidegger cunningly kept from himself. One always has to take action in the face of anxiety—even if that action be only flight—because anxiety reveals the self as action through and through. Deprived of any contemplative stance toward either itself or its possibilities, the subject is driven into the world in a way that makes action the source and the locus of whatever qualities of character the subject wants to give itself." Davis, *Inwardness and Existence: Subjectivity in/and Hegel, Heidegger, Marx, and Freud* (Madison: University of Wisconsin Press, 1989), 131.

power and the trading off of who is victim and who is victimizer. You must stay always on point. You better always keep the doomsday clock at 11:59.

Why Our Times Are So Sad

Taylor's ethic of authenticity still holds. We remain authenticity seekers, even more intensely. Our ethic is one of authenticity. Our fulfillment is self-located. This means we put a great deal of weight on being happy; we're even willing to see and present ourselves as victims to receive a recognition that will produce fulfillment for our self. Evangelism will have to avoid the malaises we named above (individualism, instrumentalism, and the loss of freedom). But evangelism can do so only if it embraces and even takes the shape of authenticity. I know that might seem counterintuitive. But remember that authenticity is the way to keep individualism from imploding on itself. It will be a very tricky game. As we've seen, embracing authenticity has its own dangers. Authenticity has taken on ideals that have stripped it of its universalism, justice, and visions of hope. Without these ideals, recognition (the extrinsic organ of authenticity), instead of being a proclamation of our need for consolation, becomes the ground for a battle.

Therefore, we can't be as positive and as upbeat as Taylor was in the 1990s. Taylor feared that if we lost the three beliefs, we'd slide into individualistic shells of apathy. He feared that a generation of narcissistic slackers would proliferate (and then, sadly, Bloom would be right). The three beliefs *have* failed, and *yet* this has not happened. The three beliefs are denied, and what's come instead is a hot culture war of victim-based tribes on the right and left who worship power and believe that systems, structures, and institutions are irretrievably and irrevocably corrupt.

What is demanded inside this flavor of authenticity, or what happens after Taylor's three beliefs are lost, is not apathy but shrieking anxiety. This deep anxiety can even grab hold of fourth graders. Living inside a war zone tends to lock people between anxiety and depression. The new ideal of victimhood, the exchanging of justice for power, and the constancy of doom make our times sad and violent. They make our authenticity heavy.

Inside this ethic of authenticity, the headwinds that evangelism meets are not relativism or religious apathy (as hand-wringing Protestants thought in the late 1990s and early 2000s, worrying about nebulous "postmodernism").

The ethic of authenticity no longer makes relativism and a laissez-faire sense of identity the major issue. Inside the lost beliefs and shifted ideals, the larger issue Protestant forms of evangelism must face is how, and whether, the Christian confession can bring peace by bringing a vision of universal humanity, justice, and hope. How can this vision comfort (console) a weary soul like Renate's? The practice of consoling weary souls is both the necessary coherence with, and prophetic stance toward, authenticity.

We must embrace authenticity, but at the fork in the road we must follow the trail leading into sadness rather than performance. We need to embrace authenticity through events of sorrow, which interrupts the violent competition and recasts recognition itself. When we join sorrow, we discover that the reference point of recognition changes completely. What is recognized as authenticity is not performances of victimhood but the universality of loss and finitude and the human need and longing for someone to bring consolation. What is yearned for is not power but peace born out of the justice of cohumanity. What is possible is new life coming through a shared suffering that makes even tribal enemies into friends.

Renate is exhausted from chasing authenticity on the battleground of competitive recognition. She's fatigued by the need to win recognition. Renate isn't apathetic but exhausted and lost in her own sadness. Her sorrow and grief push her deep into loneliness. Her sadness seems to have no value or, better, veracity. Instead, her sorrow is a threat to her ability to access her creativity to win recognition and be considered authentic. This is exactly what Will believes. What value could Renate's sadness have inside tribal ideals of victimhood, power, and doom?

For Renate's sadness to have any value, it would need to be instrumentalized. Her sadness would need to be used to position herself as a victim to win power. But the loss of her father feels too sacred for her to do that. Though losing her father is one of the most poignant experiences Renate has ever had, it appears to have no direct place, no point of leverage, inside the ideals of victimhood, power, and doom. It feels almost inauthentic. Renate is embarrassed for feeling so sad. Will can give her flowers, even a day or two at a spa, if that will return Renate to happiness and creativity. But it doesn't. It all tastes so sour next to her sorrow. This makes Will acutely annoyed. "Get your stuff together and get over it," Will mutters in frustration. Renate is lost, alone to bear her sadness.

Will has spiking righteous indignation. He knows he's being harsh, but he can't help it. It feels like something moral has been violated. That something isn't necessarily Renate's sorrow. What really angers Will is that Renate can't meet the measure of creativity that creates authenticity. Recognition, when losing the three beliefs, has no time for noninstrumental sadness. Recognition is a battlefield filled with trenches, barbed wire, and exploding bombs. To Will's anger, Renate is no longer someone to have with you in a foxhole. The company is losing in the war of recognition, as demonstrated directly in its lack of creativity. It becomes a fireable offense, in Will's mind, because the company is in a war. If Renate can't access her authenticity and win recognition, the self-fulfillment of the company is in peril. If she can't generate the energy to be something other than basic, the company has no hope of winning more market share in a creative economy.

The fact that Renate can't be authentic means she's violated something deeply moral. It won't hold up with an independent employment arbitrator, but it nevertheless feels like a deep offense. To Will, Renate's inability to be authentic is deviously deceptive. Will simply doesn't have the time for, or the interest in, Renate's experience because of his own and the company's drives toward self-fulfillment. Renate's perceived lack of authenticity enrages him. Will starts to even wonder whether Renate is really as sad as she says she is. Because of his location in the war for recognition, he even ponders whether Renate is using her father's death to win her own recognition through sympathy. In his anger Will says, "I honestly wonder if her dad even died. We get it, now get over it."

Will is moving right on the fault line of the first malaise. Renate's value comes from the creativity of her individual abilities to bring self-located fulfillment to the company. Her lack of authenticity, her inability to access her unique creativity, is a threat. But if that's not a fireable offense in itself, Will places his other foot on the fault line of the second malaise and turns to the numbers.

This takes us to our second 1990s genealogy and the work of Stephen Toulmin.

Exploring Malaise Two: Modernity's Paternity

Charles Taylor is trying to thread a needle in his lectures. He is neither a knocker nor a booster of modernity. There are real malaises, even sicknesses, in modernity. Even so, Taylor believes, human beings engage their world morally, giving us the possibility (even, at times, the actuality) of knitting together a society of people with well-lived lives. Stephen Toulmin is interested in paternity tests. He's not looking for a third way of understanding modernity and its discontents; he's sleuthing modernity's origins. He thinks getting clear on modernity's origins exposes and redirects our misconceptions. Ultimately, Toulmin's book is in the genre of a paternity whodunit (do those exist?). He believes that the one who everyone thinks is modernity's baby daddy is not modernity's baby daddy.

This confused paternity, Toulmin contends, has major ramifications. Like Taylor, Toulmin is interested in how we imagine a good society. Our society gets its moral shape in and through its stories. Therefore, how we tell modernity's origin—who we claim is modernity's parent—matters greatly. The title of Toulmin's book, *Cosmopolis*, refers to a society that is rationally ordered on firm natural laws. When modernity operates as a cosmopolis, it's sure its daddy is Isaac Newton, or that weird René Descartes (more on this in a bit). A cosmopolis is a society that glorifies reason and reason's ability to create structures of efficacy. This kind of reason is determined by, and in turn shapes, our own deepest human longings. Our deepest human longings need to be instrumentalized and ordered reasonably. A cosmopolis, then, is a society built on and for instrumental reasoning. But Toulmin is not sure that this is really our daddy. Therefore, the cosmopolis, and its malaise-filled air, is not the house we should be living in.

Toulmin's paternity work addresses the second of our malaises: instrumental reasoning. Interestingly, Toulmin doesn't once name, let alone discuss, individualism. In his quest for paternity, he's got his eyes set squarely and solely on the malaise of instrumental reasoning.

The Paternity Test in Thirty-Year Segments

Toulmin begins this paternity test by sketching his own intellectual heritage. As with Taylor's foil Allan Bloom (who sketched a difference between the 1950s and 1980s), thirty years also plays a role here. There is something about thirty years. More than even ten or twenty, thirty causes us to reflect. Thirty years has the weight of being a long time, particularly in relation to a human lifespan. Most of us get two or three of these thirty-year points of reflection in a lifetime. My bet (and it's just a hunch) is that if you looked back at the age of those who buy vintage toys or open an Ancestry.com account or Facebook-stalk past friends, they are clustered around the ages of thirty and sixty, or they happen around some thirty-year anniversary, like a thirty-year high school reunion. Looking back thirty years is intoxicating. There is something compelling about reflecting on the way things used to be.

Toulmin is making his own thirty-year assessment. He contends that his own thirty-year reflections encapsulate in miniature the last three hundred years of the modern project. Toulmin contends that the 1930s to 1990s—these two thirty-year spans—are a small model of what's been happening for more than three hundred years. As we'll see, there is a kind of Woodstock logic running through Toulmin's imagination. But that's getting ahead of ourselves. Let's start in the 1930s.

Toulmin tells us that in the 1930s he was studying mathematics and physics at Cambridge. To this day, when you walk the streets of Cambridge you can still sense the ghost of Isaac Newton. Like a time portal, the seventeenth century seems eternal in Cambridge. Newton and the rationality that forged the cosmopolis hovers over the colleges that make up the university. The seventeenth century and Newton's ghost are so haunting that you can feel yourself being pulled back to those lofty days of reason, even if you're following the GPS on your smartphone to a Lime scooter by the train station.

At Cambridge in the 1930s, Toulmin was taught that Newton and Descartes were the grand architects of modernity. They were our daddies. It was our daddy's architecture, like a great dam or impressive bridge, that saved the West from being washed out in irrationality. The cosmopolis that resulted from their discoveries saved us from the superstitions of the arcane and the ignorance of the *ancien régime* (i.e., the world of kings, queens, and knights). We were modern because of these seventeenth-century giants and their theorems and numbers. When these theorems and numbers that made up the laws of the universe were infused into the orders and laws of society, the cosmopolis was born.

On the lap of our mathematical daddies in the cosmopolis, we became attracted to reasoning. We grew out of the dark ages and into the Enlightenment. It seemed to be the knowledge that saved us. We had become modern because of reason. This instrumental reason was manifest in the numbers of the cosmos. Reason was in the laws that governed motion. If you could *know* these laws, you could order all things correctly—at least it was assumed. But to know these laws, and particularly to gain from them, you needed instruments, like Galileo's telescope. Every part of life, in fact, needed not only to bow to reason but also to be instrumentalized so gains could be produced. The cosmopolis was imagined to be a nonstop societal machine of gains and growth won by instrumental reasoning.

The conventional story goes that this shift toward reason all started in the seventeenth century, and it's what made us modern. Reason may make for a cold, uptight, and erudite society, but that's better than the crazy superstitions of the *ancien régime*. Our daddy may be unemotional and distant, but he protects us from irrationalities. It was *this* calculating daddy who bravely saved us from superstition, or it was no daddy at all. That was the tale. Toulmin was a true believer of that tale. Until thirty years later.

In the late 1960s, Toulmin, with the whole of Western culture, started to question the saving power of rationality. Or perhaps it's better to say that in the late 1960s, the cosmopolis was doubted and even turned against. The counterculture kids felt compelled to both refuse and resist the cosmopolis. The 1950s and '60s were high seventeenth-century times. Technical rationality and instrumental thinking were thrust deep into the structures of our societies. The late 1960s, however, revealed just how instrumental and inhumane this seventeenth-century-inspired cosmopolis could be. Our abode was exposed as a house of horrors. As firehoses were turned on African Americans in the South and bombs were littered across the landscape of North Vietnam, the cosmopolis showed itself to prefer its instruments and growth over humanity. Young people found themselves doubting that the rationally constructed cosmopolis was fundamentally good.

Toulmin concurred. The kids rejected their daddy, making late modernity an emancipated orphan. (Late modernity was always more post-seventeenth-century cosmopolis than postmodern, but as we'll see, this too didn't quite stick.) Inside the vacuum of this orphaning, the kids headed to The Haight to tune out and to the streets of Chicago to protest.[36] Toulmin traded in the narrow, Newtonian-haunted streets of seventeenth-centuryesque Cambridge for the South Side of Chicago and one of the great mid-twentieth-century schools, the University of Chicago.

36. I'm thinking here of the demonstrations that exploded into violence during the 1968 Democratic National Convention.

Cambridge and UChicago are much different places. While the kids flooded the streets of America's great second city in protest, Toulmin returned to the library to run paternity tests. Like the plot from the Pearl Jam song "Alive" ("what you thought was your daddy was nothing but a . . . I'm still alive"), Toulmin discovered that modernity might have *two* daddies. And both might still be alive.

There is no doubt that modernity was raised in a seventeenth-century house. But its paternal father may be more Renaissance than Enlightenment, more literary than mathematical, more humanist than rationalist, more expressive than instrumental. As the kids traveled to Woodstock, New York, to find something human in the mud and rhythms, Toulmin saw that modernity's birth certificate was wrong. Modernity was born not in the seventeenth but the sixteenth century. As the kids threw themselves into the unquantifiable at Woodstock, seeking free love and artistic expression, Toulmin recognized that it wasn't Newton or Descartes who was modernity's daddy but our pal Monsieur Montaigne. Woodstock was not antimodern but truly modern. Woodstock symbolized a rejection of its seventeenth-century home for a return to modernity's biological Renaissance daddy. Toulmin states it like this:

> Here we may therefore ask if the modern world and modern culture did not have two distinct origins, rather than one single origin, the first (literary or humanistic phase) being a century before the second. If we follow this suggestion, and carry the origins of Modernity back to the late Renaissance authors of Northern Europe in the sixteenth century, we shall find the second, scientific and philosophical phase, from 1630 on, leading many Europeans to turn their backs on the most powerful themes of the first, the literary or humanistic phase.[37]

Renaissance Bacteria

The seventeenth-century parent was such a domineering adoptive daddy that modernity completely forgot its biological sixteenth-century parent. This had its costs. The cosmopolis, with all its instrumental reasoning, was supposed to save us from the savagery of the rights of blood and the

37. Stephen Toulmin, *Cosmopolis: The Hidden Agenda of Modernity* (Chicago: University of Chicago Press, 1990), 23.

mysteries of the priestly power of the *ancien régime*. But in so doing, Toulmin believes, we lost a humanist impulse. The cosmopolis and its instrumental rationality, to switch our analogy, was such a strong antibiotic that it not only killed our supposed irrational disease but also decimated our good Renaissance bacteria.

There are four strains of good Renaissance bacteria that were obliterated by the rationalist antibiotic, making our instrumental cosmopolis possible. Without these four good Renaissance bacteria, Toulmin believes, practical reasoning is overtaken by the instrumental and we enter a malaise. Thanks to instrumental reasoning we get technological developments but lose Renaissance ideals.

The first good Renaissance strain that is lost is (1) *rhetoric*. Toulmin believes that rhetoric is overtaken by the antibiotic of formal logic. The Renaissance conceives the modern era as an act of retrieval. Greek philosophy and art of the classical period inspired Renaissance thinkers. Like the ancients, the Renaissance thinkers brought science and beauty together through art—think Leonardo da Vinci.

For Renaissance thinkers, philosophy is an art. Philosophy addresses how we directly live. Philosophy's access to truth is in its speaking. Montaigne optimizes this approach. It is through rhetoric that the philosopher not only shares their thoughts but persuades others to see the world in a certain way. There is always an *audience* to engage and interact with. The job of the philosopher is to use the art of rhetoric to persuade an audience—this is why Socrates was considered such a danger to the youth of Athens and was forced to take a shot of hemlock. There are people to connect with and convince, shaping their practical lives.

But this strain is wiped out, Toulmin believes, by the seventeenth-century rationalists. Rhetoric is too irrational, too contingent on feelings. In the house of the seventeenth century, rhetoric is out, formal proof is in. There is no audience to persuade; there are only impersonal and abstract laws to discover. Who cares about a public that often can't understand these proofs? These proofs can shape a cosmopolis, and that's more important than the public understanding them. The goal of the philosopher, then, is not to say something beautiful that might address our practical lives. Instead, the philosopher seeks to find the logical string through proofs that prove something. Proof, not persuasion, matters. It's not hard to see the origins of instrumentalism in this switch from persuasion to proof.

Three other losses follow this first one. To continue our analogy, these are losses of the good bacteria of the Renaissance that protect against instrumentalism. When proof of logic, not persuasion of rhetoric, is what matters, (2) *abstract axioms* are honored more than *concrete diversity*. For instance, Descartes "taught that philosophical understanding never comes from accumulating experience of particular individuals and specific cases. The demands of rationality impose on philosophy a need to seek out abstract, general ideas and principles, by which particulars can be connected together."[38] Your experience, or anyone else's, gets in the way. You need to think outside your experience. The proofs you seek are not bound in any experience. After all, the laws of motion, for example, don't care about your experience. When it comes to the earth moving around the sun, your experience fools you. The cosmopolis of instrumentalism must be built on something other than the diverse experiences of the populace. It must be grounded in abstract axioms based on the numbers.

This development means that (3) *general principles* are weighted more than *particular cases* in the cosmopolis. Your unique experience, or even that of a certain group, should not weigh more than the general commitment and principles that order a rational society. We must each conform to these principles, doing our duty not to a king or a lord but to the general principles themselves. We are governed by principles, not personalities. The general is always preeminent over the local. Sure, the individual matters inside the cosmopolis—each individual is responsible for themselves—but general principles order society.

Building off this, (4) the *permanent* or *timeless* is more important than the *timely*. "From Descartes' time on, attention was focused on timeless principles that hold good at all times equally."[39] Because philosophy had little concern for the practical and the particular, instead seeking proofs that were beyond feelings or even experience, what mattered was *not* what was timely in the moment but what was firmly permanent. Toulmin sums this up: "From 1630 on, the focus of philosophical inquiries has ignored the particular, concrete, timely and local details of everyday human affairs: instead, it has shifted to a higher, stratospheric plane,

38. Toulmin, *Cosmopolis*, 33.
39. Toulmin, *Cosmopolis*, 34.

on which nature and ethics conform to abstract, timeless, general, and universal theories."[40]

These losses have produced a cosmopolis of developments through an instrumentalism. Therefore, we've come to worry, to feel sick with malaise, not just about individualism but about instrumentalism as well. We sense that all these societal developments minimize the particular, concrete, timely, and local. All our deepest experiences are either ignored or used for the cosmopolis's drives for growth and advancement.

It's right here that we see a similarity between Taylor and Toulmin. Each has focused on one of the three malaises, Taylor on individualism, Toulmin on instrumentalism. And while both see real concerns in relation to individualism and instrumentalism, standing in the early days of the 1990s, they both believe the decade promises an escape from these concerns and dangers. Toulmin thinks the 1990s promise to be the fulfillment of the 1960s. This takes us back to his thirty-year sequencing.

The Hope of the 1990s: Here Comes the Positivity

In the 1930s Toulmin was a student in Cambridge being taught that modernity's daddy was the seventeenth-century rationalists. In 1960s Chicago, as the city burned in protest, Toulmin ran some paternity tests. He came to see that modernity's real daddy was not the seventeenth-century rationalists but the Renaissance thinkers of the sixteenth century (particularly our man Monsieur Montaigne). In the 1990s, Toulmin was in Southern California, believing that the legacy of the 1960s and its revived Renaissance humanism was about to burst into bloom.

Toulmin contended that the 1960s put to doubt the cosmopolis (a society that is instrumentally ordered like the firm laws of Newton's universe).[41] But the Woodstock kids of the 1960s, whom Toulmin admired, couldn't end the illness of instrumentalism. Though the cosmopolis was injured in the late 1960s, it was still breathing, even healing itself in Thatcher's UK and Reagan's US. But the 1990s, Toulmin believed, would be the decade where the promises of the 1960s were fulfilled. Toulmin was not alone in seeing this parallel and possibility—that thirty-year thing is powerful. Even

40. Toulmin, *Cosmopolis*, 35.
41. The 1960s were a time of relativity in an Einsteinian sense. Though Einstein died in 1955, he is a man of the 1960s, lauded and made a celebrity in 1960s, because he was a forerunner to the age.

the music and fashion of the early 1990s pointed back to the 1960s.[42] The Black Crowes topped the rock charts in 1990 with a very sixties-sounding album called *Shake Your Money Maker*. Everyone, even Charles Taylor, was hopeful for the 1990s.

It's true that Renaissance ideals did indeed return and bloom as the 1990s went on. But what bloomed was not all flowers. The kids of the 1990s were not flower children. We were too latchkeyed and raised by MTV for that. Instead, a lot of poison ivy came with this bloom, causing an intense itch of rage. The persuasion, the diversity, the audience, the concrete, the timely, and the local all became more and more intensified as the 1990s unfolded. But this didn't seem to release us from the cosmopolis's instrumentality. It only gave instrumentality a new shape. Instrumentality, I'd imagine to Toulmin's shock, was able to take on the flavor of Renaissance ideals while never losing its aim for growth and optimization. These Renaissance ideals were used to sell us more products and, eventually, to turn us into data itself. Oddly, as the 1990s unfolded and these Renaissance ideals became common, anger grew as each part of our lives was made into a performance of particular (unique) individuals compelled to use their time well to win the attention of any audience. The 1990s, even with these blooming Renaissance ideals, produced not the peace envisioned at the first Woodstock but the violent anger that pulsed through the veins of the 1990s Woodstock.

By the end of the decade, to usher in the fulfillment of the 1960s in the 1990s, Woodstock was on the calendar again. It was supposed to be the crowning coronation of the idealism of the late 1960s at the end of the 1990s, taking these Renaissance ideals into the new millennium. The 1969 Woodstock seemed to somehow avoid all malaises of modernity. Individualism overcome in a single voice of song, instrumentality enveloped by a spirit of expressive togetherness, and freedom expanding as love gave no space to despots.

Instead, in the 1990s all the malaises, like a flock of sick chickens, came home to roost. Besides the location, the only similarity between the 1969 Woodstock and the 1999 Woodstock was the mud. The consumer cosmopolis that took the shape of these Renaissance ideals reared its head in price gouging and then crumbled in chaos. Blood, rape, and fires of vandalistic

42. For more on this, see Chuck Klosterman, *The Nineties: A Book* (New York: Penguin, 2022), 5–29.

rage lit up the hills that in the 1960s were filled with ease, communion, and togetherness. The hills were wild with the raging outgrowth of the three malaises. The 1990s would end and the new millennium begin with no 1960s fulfillment. All the blooms withered, and now the cosmopolis was fully expressivist, wrapping its instrumental impulses in Renaissance garb. The 1999 Woodstock was a sign that sad and violent times were on the horizon. There was no coronation.

The Woodstock of mud, rape, fire, and blood took place nine years after Toulmin's *Cosmopolis* was released. Toulmin's book was released the same year as Taylor's lectures. Just as Taylor couldn't imagine how authenticity would hold and his three beliefs be lost to tribal victimhood, power, and doom, so Toulmin couldn't imagine that the Renaissance ideals of persuasion, the audience, the timely, and the local could come and nevertheless bring with them rage and violence as instrumentalism took on the form of art. Toulmin couldn't imagine that into the third decade of the twenty-first century these Renaissance ideals would spell the death of expertise. He couldn't believe that these very values would make societal responses to crises like a global pandemic deeply fraught at best and impossible at worse.

But so it is. Tom Nichols vividly reveals this development in his book *The Death of Expertise*.[43] If Neiman has critical words to say about the left, Nichols has them about the right. He shows that things have become so particular, so concrete, so local, and so intended for persuasion of an audience that everyone is an expert now. Experts themselves are doubted (even fodder for cannon fire). The expert's knowledge, it is assumed, makes them too general and too abstract. With the internet, everyone is their own expert, doing their own research. Even if this self-expertise conflicts with the expertise of others, who cares, because things are so local, timely, and intended for a niche audience that nothing matters beyond that audience. Unless, of course, you're in the middle of a pandemic and need to get people to understand the abstract, the global, and the overall interactions of findings and people. Then experts *are* important. But inside these radicalized Renaissance ideals, experts are doubted. People came to hate Anthony Fauci and wanted him locked up, even killed. This reality has led to great amounts of anger and fighting. Why wouldn't it?

43. Tom Nichols, *The Death of Expertise: The Campaign against Established Knowledge and Why It Matters* (New York: Oxford University Press, 2017).

Everyone is an expert, leading to conflicts at every level as people fight for an audience. There is nothing objective but persuasion itself. On who you should listen to or not, persuasion rules, that core Renaissance ideal Toulmin wanted us to return to. It's not credentials but followers that matter. Now we hear statements like, "He might have a lot of book smarts, but I just don't like him, and I think he's hiding something." Our discourse becomes edgy and harsh, and anger is right under the surface. Violence is always before us. To arm a late-modern society that is so sad it is prone to rage is a very bad idea. All our mass shootings are proof.

These are indeed sad times.

Back to Renate and Will

Charles Taylor couldn't imagine that the three beliefs (authenticity is for all, we can discuss and debate perspectives and practices, and we can make a difference) could disappear and authenticity remain, making recognition not the place of connection and understanding but a zone for aggressive competition. Toulmin couldn't imagine that the Renaissance ideals could come to full bloom and yet an instrumentalism be recast within them, producing rage and inviting violent fantasies of revenge. But this is just how Will responds to Renate.

Will comes back to the numbers. When Will can't fire Renate for being inauthentic, he can fire her for bad stats. The bad stats are proof of bad—that is, inauthentic—performance. Bad performance is fireable. The cosmopolis now takes a different form. Instrumentalism is not used to discover the hidden orders of creation. It doesn't create buttoned-up bureaucrats with pocket protectors and calculators. Instead, instrumentalism is used to measure the reach to an audience and the overall impact of one's persuasion. It creates people like Will, goal-driven number hunters, counting their reach toward influence and impact. The numbers are used to instrumentalize the Renaissance ideals that Toulmin wrongly thought could avoid instrumentalization.

The cosmopolis is no longer headquartered in Washington, DC, or even New York City. Instead, Northern California is the new mecca. The cosmopolis is reworked into an expressivist Renaissance form, with beanbags and baristas. Silicon Valley leaders wear not suits but hoodies. But these leaders, who embrace the Renaissance ideals, keep the instrumentality even as they welcome persuasion, the timely, the local, and the practical. It's here in Silicon Valley that the Renaissance ideals are mixed seamlessly with the ultimate instrument: the algorithm.

Renate's value is measured by her reach of persuasion and by the growth of her won audience. When her authenticity cannot win gains in these measures, she is discarded. Will is so angry because of the ethic of authenticity. Renate's lack of reach is a violation of an ethic—it's wrong. Will is justified in firing her, however, because of the instrumentality of the numbers. These two, authenticity and instrumentality, are held together by Renaissance ideals of persuasion, audience, and the timely. Just as it's shocking that authenticity's recognition could house the victimhood of tribalism, cutting off discourse and an overall openness to justice and progress, it is shocking in turn that these Renaissance ideals could be used to double down on instrumentality, making stats and algorithms seem expressive, even artistic.[44]

To turn to evangelism, we can understand why it's hard for evangelism to be imagined sacramentally. Connected to this, evangelism remains tentatively, but surely, welcomed by all forms of Protestantism. Evangelism is welcomed because as late-modern people it's very hard for us to shake the instrumentality of it. We wonder, oddly, if the illness is what can save us. Could instrumentality, used to our benefit, become good? We sense that we need reach and therefore need to grow our persuasion and audience by being more timely and local. Evangelism becomes the instrument by which to win this reach. Thus evangelism loses any sacramental imagination. The decline narratives produce so much anxiety that we are happy to contaminate ourselves further by taking in the germs of instrumentality, assuming the malaise is necessary. Protestantism is fooled by the Silicon Valley recast, assuming that this instrumentality is actually artistic and therefore authentic.

But the sacramental can *never* (*ever*) abide the instrumental. The sacramental, as we'll see in later chapters, cannot be mixed with instrumentality. A sacrament is a doorway into an encounter that gives ontological participation in the infinite rather than gains and reach. As we'll see,

---

44. Byung-Chul Han reminds us, "The algorithmic processing of big data aims to capture and include the whole population. Dataists would even claim that artificial intelligence is a better listener than a human being." Han, *Infocracy: Digitization and the Crisis of Democracy* (London: Polity, 2022), 35.

joining sorrow in consolation brings judgment to all forms of human action that seek recognition as competition and instrumentality as a way toward growth. Joining sorrow in consolation breaks these malaises, not by effort or genius but by suffering bound to the cross and Jesus's body broken.

The Third Malaise

Charles Taylor taught us in his first 1991 CBC lecture that modernity produces three malaises. These malaises come from our exposure to modern developments and advancements. As things develop inside modernity, we worry—feel a stomachache of concern—that we're losing or becoming something we shouldn't. With the rest of his lectures, Taylor focused on the malaise of individualism. Taylor didn't have the space to explore the other two malaises. We turned to Stephen Toulmin and his 1990 book *Cosmopolis* to examine the second malaise, instrumental reasoning. Both projects provided rich alternatives, even solutions, to the malaise they addressed. Taylor contended that while individualism is worrisome, embracing authenticity and offering recognition could produce an eccentric ethic and therefore real connections between people. Toulmin believed that if we get clear on the origins of modernity and embrace Renaissance ideals more than rationalist ones, we can escape instrumentalism and create a world beyond the cosmopolis.

Both Taylor and Toulmin believed that the 1990s dawned with great potential to meet and overcome these malaises. The dawn of the 1990s was not a sad time but an optimistic one. Yet, as I've hoped to show, this optimism didn't pan out (hip-hop from the coasts and rock from the Seattle scene were trying to tell us this all along). Instead, these malaises have only grown into a grave sickness as we've moved into the first three decades of the twenty-first century. Oddly, the malaises have deepened not because we've resisted authenticity and Renaissance ideals but because we have fully accepted them. Individualism and instrumentalism have adapted, changing their viral gene sequences, attaching themselves to authenticity and its recognition and to Renaissance ideals. This makes our times nauseous with sadness. We live in a time where individualism and instrumentalism are radicalized as they take the shape of the ethics of authenticity and persuasion, the audience, the local, and the timely. Our times are as dizzying and confusing as they are sad.

But what about the third malaise? Taylor calls this third malaise the loss of freedom and the birth of soft despotism. Above I explored the despotic elements of this malaise, claiming that in the third decade of the twenty-first century, the despotism is not as soft as Taylor imagined in the early 1990s. The growth of populism across the globe has made this much more than spongy.[45] We've even seen how Will, as founder and CEO, can easily function as a despot inside his company. He always wants to be first among equals until he needs to take control, at which point he feels no hesitation in dictating the work lives (even inner emotional lives) of each employee. What I had less to say about above, however, was freedom. Like the other two malaises, there is a paradox here as well.

As if with sea walls, we *seemed* to be protected from the excesses of individualism by authenticity, shielded from instrumentalism by the ideals of persuasion, audience, and the timely. Like the other two malaises, freedom is also assumed to be fortified by the pursuit of happiness. Being happiness-seekers, as individuals and as a society, will mean that our individual and institutional self-fulfillment will (supposedly) honor freedom. Freedom will be safeguarded by happiness (my point is that into the new millennium the safeguards and sea walls didn't hold).

The Jeffersonian logic that rests at the center of the American project is that this pursuit of happiness is what makes America the land of the free (though Alexis de Tocqueville, as well as Black intellectuals, saw from the beginning that this pursuit of happiness had its concerns and problems). The assumption is that we are free because we seek happiness. Happiness protects us and even advances freedom. We will always defend freedom, being on the side of freedom, because of our near apotheosizing of happiness. If fulfillment is self-located, then happiness will be the (almost complete) measure of reaching fulfillment. In turn, freedom will have to be expanded so that all selves can seek a fulfillment that speaks to them. Liberty is the free pursuit of happiness.

45. Pippa Norris and Ronald Inglehart explain further, "Populism is understood . . . as a style of rhetoric reflecting first-order principles about who should rule, claiming that legitimate power rests with 'the people' not the elites. It remains silent about second-order principles, concerning what should be done, what policies should be followed, what decisions should be made. The discourse has quality which can adapt flexibly to a variety of substantive ideological values and principles, such as socialist or conservative populism, authoritarian or progressive populism, and so on." Norris and Inglehart, *Cultural Backlash*, 4.

But into the twenty-first century, this too didn't hold. Inside a neoliberalism of all-out competition, happiness became comparative. Like everything else, happiness became a commodity that grew in value as a person had more of it than others. Happiness, even more than freedom, became our *summum bonum* (our highest good or deepest longing).

As a result, something strange happened in the sad decades of the twenty-first century. We've become willing to give up freedoms—particularly as they relate to privacy and performance—for the sake of a happiness that is molded more by individualism and consumer and digital instrumentalism. Therefore, happiness has been slowly but surely unhooked from freedom. This safeguard has failed as well, allowing the obsessive need for happiness to wash through our lives, making for a generation who needs to hide from the world, frightened by what they meet that could keep them from being happy. Mental health issues are spiking, and we speak frequently of resilience and grit because there is so little of it. We've become so centered on needing to be happy that we are primed to see threats to it everywhere, which we interpret as a threat to our very existence (because why exist if you can't be happy?). We come to even imagine that if someone else exercises their freedom in a way that makes us unhappy, they wish us not to exist. Those are harsh and sad assertions, and they demand that freedom be tempered and even tamped out at times. Yet, wrongly, we don't imagine our discontent is with happiness itself but with those other people who don't support our individual pursuits of happiness. We're willing to abandon freedom because we'd be happier if they, those haters, lost their liberty so that we could be safe enough to be happy.

It's much easier to blame others for our unhappiness than to put happiness itself under examination. But when we do reflect on happiness, we begin to wonder whether happiness can really make us happy—or, better, fulfilled. Is happiness the best way to find self-fulfillment? In these sad times, we're not sure, which makes us even sadder. We see no other way to seek fulfillment, speak of fulfillment, or be shaped by fulfillment other than to center it all on happiness. But again, happiness seems elusive and unfulfilling. When we get it, we're not sure we really have it or whether happiness can truly sustain us. The chasing of elusive happiness, giving up freedoms to run after happiness faster and more safely, has produced high levels of burnout and depression. The all-out chasing of happiness is making us unhappy. But we see little or no way out of this cycle. Better to blame others, stripping away freedoms so we can be safe and they can be punished.

Our need for happiness has made us sad. Happiness has become so singularly important that the quest for it has freed itself from larger moral visions like freedom. Most of us would rather be happy than free. We no longer see how one begets the other. Both individualism and instrumentalism can never be eliminated or even controlled—their nauseous malaise can never be medicated—because we are so anxious to be happy. Happiness disconnected from freedom (or some other deep moral vision) drives us deeper into individualism (it's about me) and leads us to accept all sorts of instrumentalization (I need pills and therapeutic strategies to fix me). Yet, in the end, we become sad that we're not as happy as we'd like to be.

There are few places for grief and other forms of sorrow in a late modernity that has divinized happiness. Experiences of sorrow that can't be instrumentalized and that demand something more than individualism will leave us at a loss. This is just what Renate is experiencing. She is lost in her grief, alone to face it, unable to parlay it into instrumental value. Thrust into sorrow, she finds no consolation, no sense that there is a good that can meet her in her sorrow. Renate finds no one to walk with her. Wellness gurus can help you seek happiness by health, but because of the way they imagine happiness next to individualism and instrumentality, they have no desire to walk with you in your sorrow.[46] They all—including Renate's friends—walk away (even run away) from her sorrow, not into it. Of course, if Renate's sorrow could have produced unique and authentic pieces for the website, upping her numbers and making her more interesting, even more positive and happy, it would

---

46. Tara Burton offers texture to this: "The language of energy, toxins, adaptogens, and neuron velocity—so much of it rooted in flawed or outright fallacious science—is also providing us with a sense of meaning, of order. There is an implicit theology to wellness culture, even if it more closely resembles the Force of Star Wars than any more concretely developed system. Energy—something that is at once spiritual, metaphorical, and scientifically concrete—runs through us all. We can tap into its primal and mystical properties to achieve concrete, real-world results." Burton, *Strange Rites: New Religions for a Godless World* (New York: Public Affairs, 2020), 98. She continues, "Implicit in the wellness ideology of energy is that the world is inherently meaningful, even orderly. 'Positive' feelings, like love or happiness, are concretely and measurably different from 'negative' feelings like fear. We tap into and improve our personal energy, we'll have a more fulfilling life; not just because we'll feel better, but because (by some metaphysical law) better things will happen to us" (99).

have had value. People would notice and follow her. But Renate's sorrow does the opposite. It is too heavy to instrumentalize. It makes her only sad and broken. Therefore, her sorrow becomes only a problem that isolates. Renate's sorrow can't be instrumentalized, and so her individual pursuit of happiness can't be fulfilled. When Renate can't do this, she is alone and lost.

If our sad times that produce isolation are tied to our obsessions with happiness, and if our obsessions with happiness make consolation in sorrow often absent, we need to look further at happiness itself. How did happiness become so important? As we'll see, it became important by its link with the very freedom it has now become untethered from. It was our pal Monsieur Montaigne who first linked happiness and freedom. Jefferson was inspired by Montaigne. Toulmin thinks that Montaigne is modernity's true daddy. Taylor, too, is a big fan of Montaigne. To get a sense of how happiness could become so important, and why evangelism will need to take the shape of consolation in a society of sadness, we need to spend some time in the château of Michel de Montaigne, entering his tower. We'll have to see whether our daddy has given us a good inheritance by taking stock of his château of happiness and freedom.

■ ■ ■ ■

Mary Ann sat at her desk not sure what to do. She knew she had no choice; there was no way of saving Renate's job. Mary Ann knew that losing her job would further isolate Renate. But she didn't know what to do. None of this sat well with her. She'd been there; she knew just what Renate was going through. If Mary Ann hadn't had Valentina, who joined her sorrow, she'd have been lost.

Before calling legal and starting the process, Mary Ann thought about Valentina. "What would she do?" Mary Ann thought. "Pray and be there," came shooting into Mary Ann's mind. That's what her church does; it shows up. So she prayed, texted Hazel, her friend from the cruise, to pray as well, called legal, and walked to Renate's office. Usually, all terminations happened in the HR boardroom. While the person was being fired in the boardroom, IT wiped their computer and security took all company property from their office. Mary Ann wouldn't do it this way. Not with Renate. The least she could do was tell Renate in her space, her office.

When Mary Ann walked into her office, Renate was staring down at her desk. Looking up and seeing Mary Ann, Renate said in bewilderment, "What's going on? No one will look at me. Everyone is cold. Will's door and shades are shut, and everyone else looks away when I come near. What is happening?"

4

Why All the Happiness Is Making Us Miserable

Montaigne, Dead French Kings, and Immanent Contentment

"You're being let go," Mary Ann said.

Renate's jaw dropped. She was blindsided completely. She was stunned. Letting it hit her for two beats, Renate said, "I know my work hasn't been its best these last few weeks. But my gosh! I mean, my dad just died! What the hell? And you're firing me?!"

Renate's eyes were filled with both the fire of anger and tears. "Really? Really?" she repeated, her voice raising. "Well, that's great," she said as she threw her hands down on her desk.

The fire left her eyes, extinguished by tears. Now her eyes were only sad. "Just one more thing on top of another," Renate said through quivering lips.

There was so much more Mary Ann wanted to say. She wanted to relay that none of this sat well with her. That she too thought it was unfair. That she thought Will was being a jerk. That corporate America was soul crushing. Ultimately, Mary Ann wanted to hug Renate and tell her she cared. That she was there for Renate.

Aware that she'd already broken protocol and that legal was not to be messed with, Mary Ann could only muster, "I'm sorry." She was about to say more, maybe even all those things she wanted to, when legal and security showed up at Renate's door.

"We have to escort her out now," said a middle-aged security guard.

"Right now," added Roman from legal, who was holding an empty box.

Renate took five minutes to fill the box with her stuff and was walked out of the office to the building's front door. Mary Ann never made this walk with other terminations, but this time she did. The security guard opened the door to the building and planned to walk Renate to her car. But Mary Ann assured him that she could take it from here.

Mary Ann held the box as Renate got in her car. Handing the box to Renate, Mary Ann said, "I am sorry about this." Renate gave a hurt but affirming nod. "And hey," Mary Ann continued, "that invitation to walk is still open. I walk every Monday, Wednesday, and Friday at 6 p.m. I hope you'll join me sometime."

Renate stared back, seeming a bit stunned. Mary Ann couldn't read her. Mary Ann's invitation seemed to both touch her and annoy her. Giving into the rage and getting her revenge, Renate chose the darker route, saying as she pulled the door shut, "Why? So you can finish me off and bury me in the woods? Screw. You."

Renate slammed the door.

■ ■ ■ ■

It wasn't the first time, nor would it be the last time, that Mary Ann was lashed out at. She assumed it would be the last time she saw Renate. Mary Ann figured that's why it took so long to recognize Renate the next week. Exactly one week after Renate's termination, Mary Ann was finishing her walk with Hazel when she noticed someone leaning against her car looking at their phone. Mary Ann was a bit nervous and somewhat annoyed. "What's that person doing by my car?" she said to Hazel with frustration. Hazel had heard all about Renate. It was Hazel who suggested that Renate be put on the Wednesday night Bible study prayer list. The whole group had been praying for Renate the last few weeks.

Mary Ann and Hazel walked slowly to the car. Mary Ann said, "Can I help you? That's my car you're leaning against." As she said this, the person looked up and Mary Ann realized it was Renate. "Renate?" Mary Ann said with surprise.

"This is *the* Renate?" Hazel asked. "Wow, I've heard so much about you."

Renate was warmed by Hazel's response. She'd felt so alone these last few weeks. The idea that she'd been thought about moved her. The realization that she'd been thought about, not because of her writing or other performance but because she was struggling, almost made Renate cry with gratitude. But Renate had to hold it together. She was here for a purpose. Renate looked Mary Ann in the eyes and said, "I came here to say I'm sorry. You didn't deserve me yelling at you. I feel really bad about that. You were the only one at that place—really the only person I know—who seemed to care about the loss of my dad. I wish I hadn't said that to you. I'm sorry."

Mary Ann, now further shocked, just nodded her head and smiled back. Silence came upon the three standing in the parking lot. Finally, Hazel broke it. "You know, Renate, you should walk with us on Friday. We need someone younger to help pick up our pace. You should come."

And Renate did. On Friday the three women walked and talked. They mainly discussed the highlights of the cruise Mary Ann and Hazel had just gone on. That was it. Renate told a friend it was the first time in a long time that she had smiled and not had a throb in her head that repeated, "Your dad is dead, your dad is dead."

On Monday they walked again. About halfway through the walk, Mary Ann asked Renate, "How are you doing?" Renate knew just what she meant. She wasn't doing well. She felt so alone, so much sadness. She'd promised herself she wouldn't sob all over these women, so she stuck with the details and facts, steering clear of emotions. "Well, I'm stressed. Actually, really stressed. My dad's house needs to be cleared out. We need to sell it. But he lived there for over forty years, and I don't think the man ever threw anything away. It's a big, terrible job. And my brother and sister won't help. They're too mad at him. His relationship wasn't at a good place with any of us. I could just hire someone to do it, but that doesn't feel right. Most of the stuff is junk, but some of it was important to him. And I think maybe to me."

Renate paused, breaking her own rule for just a second, and continuing, "It's not just the monumental amount of work; it's the thought that being around his stuff may break me. It may help me feel closer to him, but that might be too painful for me to handle."

"You know what you need?" Hazel interjected with her usual energy.

"What?"

"You need our church's Swedish Death Cleaning Team."[1]

It made Renate chuckle.

"I'm serious," Hazel bellowed. "We first did it at our church. Some of our closets hadn't been touched since 1977. But we started doing it for a few people and their houses after they lost someone. We do that kind of stuff. It's part of who we are. We follow Jesus into sorrow, as our pastor always says."

Renate was confused. Not because she didn't understand but because she couldn't imagine people doing this.

"How much do you charge?" Renate asked, intrigued.

"Oh, nothing," Hazel returned. "Like I said, it's just our way. I'll ask our Bible study about it."

"But he lives in Phoenix! That's a long way from San Diego County," Renate said.

"Don't worry, I'll talk to them," Hazel said with a brush of her hand, communicating that distance was no deterrent.

A week and half later, Edith Meinhard, AC Williamson, and Myrtle Halverson were with Renate in Phoenix cleaning out her father's house. Mary Ann was a day and half behind them, taking Friday off to drive the five hours and help over the weekend. When Mary Ann arrived, two dumpsters were filled in the driveway, and Renate seemed both exhausted and exorcised.

From Swedish Death Cleaning to the Château

If you've sat down to write an essay for a class, you can thank (or curse!) Michel de Montaigne. Someone must be the first. When it comes to the invention of the essay, that honor goes to Monsieur Montaigne. The French have given us chivalry, the baguette, fashion week, *frites* or french fries, and the essay. *Vive la France!*

Like so many other creations, the essay was birthed by mistake. Michel de Montaigne never intended to create anything. He intended to just retire. Montaigne was the inheritor of new money—he was sixteenth-century *nouveau riche*. Or, better than *nouveau riche*, he was *nouveau noble*. His

---

1. This is gleaned from Kara Root and the Swedish Death Cleaning Team of Lake Nokomis Presbyterian Church.

father, as a soldier, had won the prestigious "de." This little mark placed in the family name signaled nobility. Montaigne's father used this mark to procure lands that a generation earlier were not available to people like him. French serfdom was giving way to something new, and the elder Montaigne took advantage.

In this new order, a new educated class of public professionals was becoming esteemed. The young Michel was groomed for just this place in society, receiving a classical and humanist education from the age of six. To make this education as successful as possible, the elder Montaigne took pains to make sure that his son spoke perfect Latin. The elder Montaigne even hired a German tutor who knew no French and demanded that only Latin be spoken in the home (a tough gig for the cooks and maids). From the earliest days, Michel was bathed in the Renaissance return to the classical.

It worked. As a young man, Michel found himself in an esteemed profession as an important public servant. It was the young Montaigne's job to prepare documents for the judge. He'd spend his days reviewing the disputes of conflicting parties. It wasn't a profession Michel loved, but as it did for Albert Einstein long after him, such work became formative. It's amazing that modernity had its start and its greatest scientific insights thanks to office work. As a patent clerk Einstein was exposed to the earliest uses of electricity. This exposure ignited his mind to think differently about light and time and space. From this paper-shuffling job that Einstein tolerated came the greatest rapid outburst of scientific breakthroughs ever (his renowned five papers from 1905).

Two hundred and fifty years earlier, something similar happened to Montaigne. Preparing legal documents for the judge meant that Montaigne had to stand fully on the side of each disputing combatant, seeing things from each party's perspective. From this exercise Montaigne began to see that what we know is so bound up in our subjective experience that if we ever stand outside of it, even for a second, we come to realize that we actually know very little. Preparing these documents led Montaigne to stand back and ask, "What do I really know?" This question would eventually frame his *Essays* and make him the father of modern skepticism.

The one thing Montaigne did know was that Étienne de La Boétie was a true friend. This is right where the Einstein-Montaigne similarities break down. Einstein shuffled papers as a lower-middle-class clerk. Einstein was *petit bourgeois*.[2] Montaigne was anything but. Montaigne may have also been shuffling papers, but serving in the Bordeaux Parlement was a position for a true noble. This position offered the privilege of rubbing shoulders with France's most important and interesting people. It granted him entry into the king's court. Étienne de La Boétie was unequivocally one of these very interesting people. La Boétie was a true Renaissance man. He was a poet, conversationalist, and controversial political theorist. He was fascinating in every way, and Montaigne was infatuated. They quickly became the closest of friends. They were the truest of bros. Montaigne and La Boétie discussed everything all the time. They were inseparable. That is, until La Boétie became a casualty of the plague. Montaigne watched as La Boétie painfully died the good death, reflecting on his experience until his last breath.

With La Boétie dead and Montaigne deeply grieved, Montaigne saw no reason to continue in the Bordeaux Parlement, no sense in being connected to the court. There was no reason to rub shoulders with the powerful and profound. After all, no one was as impressive and interesting as La Boétie. Once you've known the best, who cares about the rest?

Retiring to the château at just thirty-eight was the only option Montaigne saw. The problem was that the conversations with La Boétie weren't finished—they had just started—and yet La Boétie was gone. La Boétie had opened a tap in Montaigne's mind but was no longer present to receive what was flowing. Montaigne had so many more discussions and so many more topics that he wanted to explore with La Boétie. With his great conversation partner gone, Montaigne's only choice was to continue the conversation with himself. That's what La Boétie would want. And so, the essay was accidently born.

If La Boétie had lived, it's possible you'd never have written countless essays in college. More importantly, to follow Toulmin, it's possible modernity may have missed its moment of conception. It's the *Essays* that birthed modernity, linking fulfillment to self-reflection, turning us into happiness-hunters.

But how?

2. Through his bohemianism he resisted some of this, which helped make up part of his lore. But the job was a conventional middle-class position, which—to echo the lore—could not hold the genius of the great Einstein.

Essays, Religious Conflicts, and a Lot of Dead Kings

Students are asked to write essays because an essay is a test—of a certain kind. Montaigne retreated to the tower of his château to reflect and therefore test himself through his reflections. That's what "essay" means, *to enter a test of reflection.*[3] There had been many who had written disputations laying out arguments. The whole medieval scholastic system had followed Aristotle's lead in this. But no one before Montaigne had decided to put down on paper their internal reflections on such wide-ranging topics. The essay is not necessarily about proving a point but about learning to reflect and think. The essay draws out what one really thinks, somewhat like a deep conversation with a friend. The essay is not a friend, as every student knows. But it is the record of the reflector's thoughts, something a friend shares in. Therefore, to read an essay, especially as Montaigne writes them, is to become Montaigne's friend. The reader cannot become La Boétie to Montaigne. Montaigne is tragically left alone in his tower. But in reading the *Essays*, we the readers are gifted with becoming La Boétie by receiving Montaigne's unfiltered reflections.[4]

In the *Essays* Montaigne's mind flows freely, like a late-night conversation with a friend. The topics are broad and far reaching. He discusses smells, why sons are like their fathers, sadness and emotions, the New World, thumbs, and even, most famously, cannibalism. These are reflections he might have had with La Boétie. But La Boétie is gone. Montaigne plans to publish these reflections alongside La Boétie's famous treatise on authority. The plan is for La Boétie's treatise to rest at the center, with each essay surrounding it. But it can't happen. La Boétie's piece is

3. As an example, Colin Campbell says, "In emphasizing that the book was intended as an essay I did not just mean that it was intended to be a short piece of writing (in fact some reviewers considered it to be quite long), but rather, as stated above, that it was intended to represent an attempt or an effort, one aimed at exploring a new way of looking at familiar phenomena and in the process resolving certain intriguing problems." Campbell, *The Romantic Ethic and the Spirit of Modern Consumerism* (Cham, Switzerland: Palgrave Macmillan, 2018), 6.

4. Donald Frame adds, "There is much to show that the *Essays* themselves are—among other things—a compensation for the loss of La Boétie. Montaigne's need for communication is deep. . . . He has missed a congenial friend on his travels to share his experiences with." Frame, *Montaigne: A Biography* (San Francisco: North Point Press, 1984), 81. Frame continues, "Montaigne's loneliness led him to write; the lack of his friend, leaving him no one to address in letters, made him seek a form of his own that would be both a testimony to his life and a means of communication which might bring him another good friend and thus fill the void in his heart" (83).

too controversial, too antiauthoritarian. La Boétie claims that all rulers, all the time, become self-serving. We should never trust them. La Boétie is one of the first anarchists. His treatise becomes "indexed," or censored, by the Catholic Church, and then banned. But La Boétie must remain at the center of the *Essays*. Montaigne writes these essays only because La Boétie is gone, and so he replaces the controversial treatise with La Boétie's poems.

Ultimately, what Montaigne discovers in his essays is that the more he reflects on any topic, the less he knows. For instance, the more Montaigne thought about even something like cannibalism—even meeting some cannibals brought to France by the Spanish[5]—the more skeptical he became of his position. Standing inside the rituals and practices of that society, truly reflecting on cannibalism as a person living on those islands, made it seem far less strange. In turn, imaginatively standing inside rituals of those Caribbean tribes caused European practices to seem very odd. For instance, Montaigne saw how cruel and unusual it must appear that European rulers don't *eat* human flesh but *torture* it—often severely. Which is crueler? Montaigne wonders.

Ultimately, the more he reflects, the less he knows. The more he knows, the more he needs to tolerate, and even accept, those who see and therefore live differently. This kind of skepticism that moves the reflector to stand inside another's experience was unheard of inside the religious conflicts that were ripping France to pieces. The conflicts between Catholics and Protestants were raging across France. The religious wars were alternately cold and hot. But the conflict was always present, weighing on all parts and in all corners of France.

These wars reached their apex when the spirit of Reformation created turbulent times for the crown. Henry II was second son of Francis I and part of the Valois dynasty, a deeply Catholic house. Young Henry II was given the Florentine Catherine, from the powerful Medici family, as his wife. Catherine, only a young teenager, who tragically lost her parents,

---

5. It is more than likely accurate that tribes in the Caribbean were cannibals. Particularly Columbus used their cannibalism as a reason to disobey Queen Isabel's command to not subjugate any person he met in the New World. Isabel, out of deep Christianity piety, believed that all human beings met in the New World were under her responsibility and thus needed to be treated as dear and valued. This clashed with Columbus's deeply held Christian belief of conquest. Cannibalism became Columbus's justification for his commitments over Isabel's. Montaigne is unmasking this in his skepticism.

was given in marriage by her uncle, Pope Clement VII.[6] Nothing could be more Catholic than to marry the young Henry II to the pope's niece. When they were married, Henry II was not the heir apparent, but he would ascend to the throne when his brother and father died. But his reign was short-lived. Tragically, Henry II died from injuries in a jousting tournament. Luckily for house Valois, Henry II and Catherine had three sons. But a pox was on the house. Catherine lived to see not only her husband die but her three sons as well, each crowned king, one after the other.[7]

Each son came to the throne relatively young and unfit for the position. Francis II was sickly and only fifteen when his father died of jousting wounds. Francis II would be dead from illness a year later. His brother, Catherine's second son, Charles IX, was only ten. Charles was on the throne for fourteen years but did not rule so much as he was the puppet of his mother and uncles. His mother and uncles were at times partners and other times the deepest of enemies. Catherine's objective was to keep her boys alive and the family enthroned. The objective of the uncles, the Guise brothers (Henry I Duke of Guise and Cardinal Louis de Guise), was to keep France Catholic, extinguishing the flames of Protestant fervor.[8] The uncles did this by controlling and empowering the Catholic League and oppressing the Huguenots (Protestants) wherever possible. Under Charles IX's puppet rule there were three bloody wars between Catholics and Protestants.

And then came the red wedding!

6. For much more on Catherine, see the wonderful biography by Leonie Frieda, *Catherine de Medici: Renaissance Queen of France* (New York: Harper Perennial, 2003).

7. Robert Knecht gives us more detail: "The untimely death of King Henry II in July 1559 plunged his kingdom into a major political crisis, for his eldest son, Francis II, was only fifteen years old and in precarious health. Officially, he was old enough to rule, but he lacked political experience. Effective power inevitably passed into the hands of his mother, Catherine de' Medici, who, from now until her death in 1589, became the dominant figure in French political life. Three of her sons, Francis II, Charles IX and Henry III, became successively kings of France; another, François, duke of Alençon, is mainly remembered as a troublemaker. None, with the possible exception of Henry III who did strike out on his own, was as politically significant as Catherine." Knecht, *The Valois: Kings of France 1328–1589* (London: Continuum, 2007), 193.

8. Knecht tells us more: "Yet many Frenchmen regarded the Guises as foreigners, for their origins lay in the duchy of Lorraine, which was still part of the Holy Roman Empire. They failed to see by what right the Guises controlled the government instead of Antoine de Bourbon, first prince of the blood. But Antoine was in Guyenne when Henry II died and took so long to reach the court that, when eventually he arrived, he was admitted to the king's council but excluded from the inner circle of ministers who decided policy." Knecht, *The Valois*, 196.

The Real Red Wedding

As Charles IX moved into adulthood, he was able to cut a *few* of the strings connecting him to his mother and uncles. He did this by taking counsel from someone outside their circle—even outside Catholicism. Admiral Gaspard de Coligny had been the military leader of the Huguenots. As Charles negotiated peace with Coligny, he came to admire him, which made Catherine uneasy and enraged the Guise brothers. Charles's mother believed it could bring France too close to Protestant nations such as England and Holland. The uncles believed Coligny had killed their father in the siege of Orléans. Both mother and uncles agreed that Coligny needed to go. The perfect opportunity was in Paris, during the wedding celebrations of Marguerite (Charles's sister and Catherine's daughter) and another Henry—Henry of Navarre (the future King Henry IV). Henry of Navarre was a Protestant from the House of Bourbon. Charles IX imagined that marrying his sister to a Bourbon would be a good political move, cooling the religious tensions. The plan backfired.

On St. Bartholomew's Day, with Paris filled with both Catholics and Protestants—all of them to see a Protestant prince marry a Catholic princess—the Guise brothers had Coligny killed. But the uncles went a step further. They not only killed Coligny but had his body thrown into the street to be mutilated. With the blood of Coligny running on the streets, Parisian Catholics, stoked by the Catholic League, lit aflame with violence. Mobs went on a five-day massacre, killing ten thousand Protestants. The streets of Paris ran red. Henry of Navarre himself was cornered and escaped with his life only by denouncing his Protestantism. A red wedding indeed.[9]

9. "On 22 August, however, as Admiral Coligny was walking back to his residence from the Louvre, he was hit by a bullet fired from an upstairs window of a house. The assailant has been identified with the seigneur de Maurevert, a client of the Guises. The admiral was only wounded, but his companions called on the king to take appropriate action. Writing to his ambassador in England, Charles blamed the Guises for the crime: 'This wicked deed,' he wrote, 'has come from the enmity between the houses of Guise and Chatillon.' The attempt on Coligny's life was followed two days later by the Massacre of St. Bartholomew's Day in which thousands of Huguenots in Paris were slaughtered in cold blood by a mob. The government, it seems, was partly responsible. The failed attempt on Coligny's life had caused panic at court. On 23 August the king and his council had decided that a renewal of civil war was inevitable. They thought 'it preferable to win a battle in Paris, where all the leaders were, than to risk one in the field and to fall into a dangerous and uncertain war.' Coligny was among the first victims of the massacre, which was soon repeated in a number of provincial towns." Knecht, *The Valois*, 208.

The shock of the whole thing killed Charles IX. Actually, it was tuber-culosis that killed him, but he died without peace. As he slipped away, he equally cried out to God for forgiveness and blamed his mother. The un-cles, who orchestrated the murder of Coligny, somehow escaped Charles's deathbed laments. But they would soon be in the crosshairs.

To confuse matters further, another Henry enters the scene: Henry III. He's the third son of Catherine (and Henry II, who died in the jousting accident). Henry III ascended the throne after the death of his brother. He was the last of the Valois kings, but not the last King Henry. The Guise brothers figured that Henry III, like the other two boy-kings, would be their puppet. And he was for a while. But he had also ruled as king in Poland and therefore knew a world outside the Guise brothers' influence. Eventually Henry III could no longer stomach his uncles. In 1588 he moved to have them killed, and killed they were.[10] In retalia-tion, in 1589 a fanatical monk named Jacques Clément assassinated Henry III.[11] All of which foreshadows more assassins and more murdered Henrys to come.

The Friend of Montaigne: The New Henry and the Move to Happiness

With all the Valois boys dead and Catherine without sons, Henry of Na-varre, from House of Bourbon, the groom forced to convert or die (talk about evangelism!), became king. Henry of Navarre had to prove again that his commitment to Catholicism was strong and sure. His statement seems anything but strong and sure. Henry of Navarre declared, *Paris vaut bien une messe*. "Paris is well worth a Mass." Basically, if the price

10. Knecht gives us more insight: "Henry suspected that they were being manipulated by the League. He also saw the hand of Guise in a recent invasion of the marquisate of Saluzzo by the duke of Savoy. He accordingly decided that the time had come to assert his authority. On 23 October Guise was lured into the king's chamber at the château of Blois and hacked to death by the 'Forty-five,' Henry's personal bodyguard. Next day, the duke's brother, the cardinal of Guise, was also murdered." Knecht, *The Valois*, 224.

11. "On 1 August the friar made his way to the king's camp, claiming that he carried a mes-sage from some of Henry's friends in the capital. He was admitted to the royal presence, even though Henry was sitting on his close stool at the time. He invited Clément to come nearer, whereupon the friar stabbed him in the abdomen. A few hours later, Henry died. He was the first king of France to die at the hands of one of his own subjects and his death may be taken as a sign that the mystique of monarchy had collapsed. Yet the institution itself survived. It was the Valois dynasty which stood discredited in the eyes of most Frenchmen. News of Henry III's assassination caused wild rejoicing in Paris." Knecht, *The Valois*, 226.

of Paris is going to Mass, it is worth paying. It's a cynical statement with a kind of "say whatever you need to" logic.

But another way to understand it takes us back to Montaigne. *Paris vaut bien une messe* is both practical and skeptical. It is practical in that Henry of Navarre knows very well that without accepting the Mass, he can bring no peace to France. What he wants far more than doctrinal purity is the practicality of peace. If it means he must go to Mass, so be it.

Paris vaut bien une messe is also a skeptical statement, but not in the sense of believing nothing. Rather, it recognizes that standing inside your own life—as a Catholic or a Protestant—you see things much differently. Henry of Navarre was not trying to wipe away all difference in unanimity. He was trying to create a way for diverse and distinct ways of life and worship to coexist in one unified country. This had not been done before in the West, not even across the channel in Protestant England.[12] While England seemed less volatile than France, diverse worship practices did not coexist there. King James's men sought to violently weed out all Catholic worshipers. In retaliation, while Henry of Navarre was ruling in France, a group of English Catholics tried to use gunpowder to blow up King James—in the famous but failed Gunpowder Plot, which oddly is still celebrated in England every November. Never had the West found a way to allow for diverse and distinct worshipers to coexist. But Henry of Navarre was going to try it. (This commitment to coexistence and tolerance would become a staple of liberalism, particularly the kind of political order that Charles Taylor wants to affirm and bolster, as we'll see at the end of this section.)

From the beginning of his reign, Henry of Navarre worked on this reshaping, leading to his greatest accomplishment, the Edict of Nantes. The edict secured tolerance and therefore peace between Catholics and Huguenots across France. It unified France, at least for a time, under two distinct forms of worship.

12. G. M. Trevelyan explains further, "The analogy of France was also before the King's eyes in the matter of Toleration. France was still, nominally, the land of the Edict of Nantes. For a few years longer she was still distinguished among the States of Europe as a place where the rights of Dissent were acknowledged in theory, though her practice was beginning to be very different. In the past at any rate, the royal power and the Catholic power had grown up by the alliance of the House of Bourbon with the principle of Toleration: and now the happy result had been reached that the tolerated were too weak to insist upon their privileges. The recent history of his own realm also pointed the would-be despot of England in the same direction." Trevelyan, *England under the Stuarts* (London: Methuen, 1965), 352.

But Henry of Navarre did not do this on his own. His friend Michel de Montaigne supported him. Montaigne knew these conflicts from the inside. Montaigne remained Catholic, but his brother was Protestant. Skepticism (as the ground of tolerance) proved to offer a way forward beyond the religious wars.[13] Skepticism provided a way to respect fellow citizens and make a world of coexistence—after all, even in your worship, what do you really know? Henry of Navarre learned much of this from Montaigne. Henry of Navarre went so far as to send his friend on diplomatic missions for this cause. Montaigne became the diplomat of tolerance, negotiating with both Protestant and Catholic leaders, even going to Rome and kissing the pope's slippers—which the pope didn't like much. The documentation on Montaigne's level of involvement is hard to trace. Montaigne died of kidney stones just three years into Henry of Navarre's reign. But it's clear that Henry of Navarre and Montaigne shared a perspective. "They may even have been members of the same secret society."[14] It was secret, so it's hard to know! Henry of Navarre knew and was shaped by Montaigne long before Henry took the throne.

Toulmin lauds Montaigne, seeing him as the true father of modernity because of his ability, through Renaissance commitments, to create ways of tolerance and acceptance of distinct and different ways of life. Montaigne gives us practicality and skepticism as the means by which to create a happy society. Practicality and skepticism create a happy society because they produce free citizens, able to worship however it is that makes them happy. (As we'll see, this is all built on Montaigne's own way of being and reflecting.) Henry of Navarre was the prince who lived this out. Toulmin adds, "Henri's skepticism (like Montaigne's) was no 'negative dogmatism,' which systematically refuses to accept whatever is not

---

13. Biancamaria Fontana says, "Montaigne was twenty-nine years old when the first religious troubles broke out in 1562; when he died, thirty years later, in 1592, the conflict was only just approaching its conclusion; it would still take several years before the new king, Henry IV, achieved a complete pacification of the country, while the marks of destruction across French territory would remain visible for decades afterwards. The protracted character of the French crisis—with civil war becoming a permanent and almost 'normal' state of affairs—should be kept in mind, since it helps to explain how people in Montaigne's generation tried to shape their lives both away from and around public events, alternating moments of intense participation with intervals of disaffection and despair, falling in and out of the projects and initiatives that were subsequently hatched to provide a political solution." Fontana, *Montaigne's Politics: Authority and Governance in the Essais* (Princeton: Princeton University Press, 2008), 5.

14. Stephen Toulmin, *Cosmopolis: The Hidden Agenda of Modernity* (Chicago: University of Chicago Press, 1990), 50.

totally certain. Rather, it was the modest skepticism of those who respect everyone's right to opinions arrived at by honest reflection on first-hand experience."[15] This "right [or freedom] to . . . honest reflection on first-hand experience" is what Montaigne gave to the West and what Henry of Navarre embraced.

This "right to . . . honest reflection on first-hand experience" is exactly what Charles Taylor affirms and seeks with his own project (he even thinks that authenticity can carry this weight in late modernity). Taylor, like Toulmin, also greatly admires Montaigne. Taylor's whole project seeks to help Western democracies not lose these Montaignian commitments inside late modernity. His work pushes for late-modern political philosophies to hold to the "right to . . . honest reflection on first-hand experience."

Taylor accordingly opposes how the French *laïcité*—separation of church and state—has been used to restrict Muslim women from wearing symbols of their religion in public. Taylor worked hard in the 1980s and 1990s for this expression of *laïcité* to not come to Quebec. He considered it a violation of the Western moral commitment to the right to honest reflection. Taylor believes that the twenty-first-century French *laïcité*, which became more restrictive in 2010, violates one of France's heroes, Montaigne. Taylor contends that holding and bolstering this right to honest reflection creates free, pluralistic societies that honor all forms of human fullness and worship.[16] "Taylor is keen to endorse the balanced approach that comes through Montaigne's self-reflection, the avoidance of extremes and ultimate ideals, and our self-acceptance of limitation."[17] Taylor believes that life is dialogical and best lived in an openness of conversations that hear and reflect on our firsthand experiences of goodness and fullness.

In *Sources of the Self*, Taylor explains that Montaigne helps us all accept "what we are," with its limits, desires, and specific practices.[18] Montaigne prepared us to engage in conversation by confessing, "What do we really know?" This honest confession opens us to both the expressions and

15. Toulmin, *Cosmopolis*, 50.
16. Taylor is not shy in thinking that worship is important. His secular project comes from the commitment that firsthand experience matters, that worshipers must be respected and heard, that worshipers know a fullness that must be examined. Taylor knows this from his own firsthand experience.
17. Stephen Loxton, *Dialogic Life: Charles Taylor and the Ethics of Authenticity* (London: New Generation, 2022), 36.
18. See Charles Taylor, *Sources of the Self: The Making of Modern Identity* (Cambridge, MA: Harvard University Press, 1989), 181.

encounters of our neighbor's reflections on their firsthand experience. This acceptance of who we are, our limits, becomes a central theme of modern culture. It even frames our sense of freedom as our pursuit of happiness. To be free and to be happy is to be who we truly are. Freedom and happiness become linked, Montaigne putting them together in the skepticism of his *Essays*. We'll explore this much more deeply in the next section, but what must be pointed out now is how Montaigne's practicality and skepticism makes him not only the father of modernity but the cipher that brings the pursuit of happiness to the fore of the Western good life.

The skepticism of the *Essays*, with La Boétie's poems in the middle, inspires Thomas Jefferson as he writes the Declaration of Independence. All people (the "all" that Jefferson can imagine: white, landowning males) have inalienable rights to honestly reflect on their firsthand experience of being who they are and worshiping as they wish, free from the coercion of any crown or governmental power.[19] All have the right to live a quiet life in their own château. Thomas Jefferson, as the third president, purchased Louisiana from the French. With this purchase, Jefferson made New Orleans and its Bourbon Street—named after Henry of Navarre's family line—part of the United States. The United States would come to see itself as the land of the free who most vigorously pursue happiness. Bourbon Street in New Orleans is now one of the core places Americans go to be happy (and drunk!), pursuing their pleasures.

Welcome to the World of Contented Happiness

Inside the context of all the dead kings, vindictive uncles, plotting mothers, and wedding massacres, we can understand why Montaigne decided to retire to his château tower. With La Boétie dead, there was no reason to remain in proximity to the chaos. It would take Henry of Navarre—a man after Montaigne's own heart—for Montaigne to dip his toe again

19. Ann Hartle adds, "The clearest expression of Montaigne's preference for the private life and its relation to freedom is found in 'Of vanity': 'I love a private life because it is by my own choice that I love it, not because of unfitness for public life, which is perhaps just as well suited to my nature. I serve my prince the more gaily because I do so by the free choice of my judgment and my reason.' Montaigne does not need the public arena of politics in order to be (or to become) what he is. The sphere of the private allows him sufficient scope for his actions." Hartle, *Michel de Montaigne: Accidental Philosopher* (New York: Cambridge University Press, 2003), 184.

into the scalding hot waters of the game of thrones. Being a diplomatic envoy for Henry of Navarre, at the end of his life, was worth it. Henry of Navarre was looking to reshape France in the image of the *Essays*.

In the *Essays* Montaigne discovers something profound in this skepticism that will forever change us all. Inside honest reflection on firsthand experience, Montaigne discovers that the point of life is not to know things or even to heroically shape the world (look where that got all those Valois boys!). The point of life, he concludes, is to enjoy the reflective leisure of friendship. The essay, as the work of a friend looking for a friend, is primarily a self-located process.[20] The essay mines the self for what fulfills the self.[21] Montaigne's *Essays* will give his readers new concerns and dimensions of the self.[22]

What truly matters, Montaigne believes, is peace with yourself—contentment. The height of life, the fullness of existence, is found not in arcane religious pursuits or even in the power of conquest—look where that got France!—but in the contentment of self-reflective happiness.[23] This discovery of Montaigne's has become lodged deeply in our own imaginations. Jefferson even built a nation around it. Montaigne is the first (at least outside Greece and on the other side of the medieval period) to

20. Byung-Chul Han says, "For Montaigne, a friend is a 'second self.' Such a friendship of fusion doubles the I. The 'we' is an 'I in twos.' The individuals are no longer separate, but they are still deeply entangled in inwardness. In order to get to original friendship, it is necessary to cut all ties with inwardness." Han, *The Philosophy of Zen Buddhism* (Malden, MA: Polity, 2023), 90.

21. There would be no Jean-Jacques Rousseau without Montaigne.

22. M. A. Screech adds, "Of Montaigne's originalities none was greater than his decision to write about himself, to make himself the central subject of a constantly expanding book. The idea did not come to him all at once. Originally the *Essays* were conceived on a much more modest scale. At first, he was content to write down his reactions to particular pieces of conventional wisdom or controverted assertion. Soon he was so disturbed by strange fancies that he decided to write them down too. Later, he thought he would leave behind a portrait of himself in words for his family to remember him by. (Self-portraiture was a feature of some Renaissance painters: Montaigne was probably influenced by their example.) His last step was to believe that by studying himself he could find out what the nature of mankind really was and so how he, or anyone else, should wisely live and wisely die, in accordance with Nature's leadership alone." Screech, *Montaigne and Melancholy: The Wisdom of the Essays* (New York: Penguin, 1991), 6.

23. Henry Spaulding in conversation with Hannah Arendt points to this château escape that is central to Montaigne: "Here we pause to clarify the form of the modern self Arendt describes. She argues that humans in modernity turn to the self and away from the world. Such a construction of the self is what I call the attempt to create self-sufficient, privately interested humans. When the individual rejects the world, thereby alienating oneself from it, then the self relies on something else as its source of being." Spaulding, *The Just and Loving Gaze of God with Us: Paul's Apocalyptic Political Theology* (Eugene, OR: Wipf & Stock, 2019), 27.

claim that contentment as happiness should be our *summum bonum*, our highest good. Montaigne is the first to lift up happiness bound in a self as the pursuit and measure of fulfillment. The point is "to 'loyally enjoy' the human condition."[24] Montaigne famously says, "When I dance, I dance. When I sleep, I sleep."[25] The point being that he contentedly enjoys life, seeking happiness.

Montaigne creates the conditions to combine freedom and happiness. Montaigne has few new thoughts about freedom or happiness. Other philosophers, stretching back to the classical period, contributed important thoughts on both. But Montaigne dipped one into the other, marrying freedom and happiness in a way that we'd never again be able to separate in our imaginations. Montaigne saw that happiness was the freedom of contentment in ordinary life—to loyally enjoy life and dance when you dance and sleep when you sleep. Live in happy leisure with the self.[26]

This talk of freedom and happiness and the self all rings so beautifully in our own ears. To us late moderns, it sounds like really living. But it's only because of Montaigne and his reflections on contented happiness that this could sound so good to us. Because of Montaigne's sense of contented happiness, Will could start an apparel company of leisure wear, Renate could become obsessed with the ordinary secrets of wellness, and even Mary Ann could dream of going on a cruise of stress-relieving relaxation. These modern pursuits exist only after Montaigne and his *Essays*, only after Montaigne "finds his happiness by disdaining no aspect of the

24. Benjamin Storey and Jenna Silber Storey, *Why We Are Restless: On the Modern Quest for Contentment* (Princeton: Princeton University Press, 2021), 2, quoting Montaigne's *Essays*.

25. See Montaigne, *Essays*, trans. Donald M. Frame (New York: Everyman's Library, 2003), 3.13.1105–15.

26. Philippe Desan gives us texture to Montaigne the person, bringing the self into view further: "Beyond his political activities and the book to which he devoted part of his time, in the 1570s Montaigne also had children, five of them in seven years, all girls, only one of whom survived him. He recorded in his almanac the names of those who died in infancy; without a son, he had to find a way to perpetuate his name. The name 'Montaigne' begins and ends with Montaigne! What a paradox for a man who constantly demonstrated that he had a noble spirit and sought to construct a renown for posterity, without any concern for his descendants. Ultimately, his marriage to the muses produced his sole male child—the *Essais*—which bore his name and allowed him to foresee a new kind of posterity. It might even be argued that the success of his first *Essais* of 1580 allowed Montaigne to glimpse the possibility of an illustrious fame without putting him at the mercy of hypothetical descendants or the unforeseeable vicissitudes of the battlefield." Desan, *Montaigne: A Life* (Princeton: Princeton University Press, 2017), 253.

human condition but partaking joyfully of all of it—books and horses, travel and love, food and art, talking with his daughter, playing with his cat, tending to the cabbages of his unfinished garden."[27]

Dying Well Means Dying Happy

There is another element that we need to explore, an element that Montaigne learned from La Boétie. Montaigne invents the essay because La Boétie died. The *Essays* are written to honor not only La Boétie's life but also his death. Montaigne believes that La Boétie died well. La Boétie dies loyally living. On his deathbed, he reflected on each moment that made up the experience of dying. La Boétie's mind did not veer to the next life. No, he was interested in sucking out the marrow of this life. In dying, La Boétie reflected loudly on the experience of dying, embracing it as one would embrace a dance.

Montaigne finds this beautiful. Therefore, the *Essays* intend to sustain the reflections that started with La Boétie. But they also teach Montaigne, and of course his readers, to die well—just as La Boétie did. Montaigne wants his readers to really dance when they dance, and really die when they die.

Montaigne is clear that learning to die a good death entails forgetting about the next life. A person who dies well concerns themselves only with this life. The immanent over the transcendent, even in death, must be embraced completely. Montaigne has little to nothing to say about a next world or anything transcendent for that matter. The contented happiness that Montaigne seeks is completely and fully of and in this world.

That doesn't mean Montaigne will not think about death. He's living too close to death to avoid it. His dear La Boétie died, as did four of his five daughters, whom he greatly loved. Montaigne is not a late modern who denies death by distracting himself from death. He's not like us in that manner. Montaigne thinks about death often. The *Essays* are filled with such reflections. He comes to see that the path to a good death avoids all temptations to go seeking for something beyond us.[28]

27. Storey and Storey, *Why We Are Restless*, 3.
28. I personally cannot go too far with Montaigne because of his spurning of the beyond. He is in me, and my imagination is shaped by him. But this lack of the beyond, I believe, presents a

Montaigne thinks it is always a problem to be propelled beyond.[29] When pushed beyond the self, we too easily lose our handle on the contentment that produces happiness. (See how Montaigne is our father! Toulmin's paternity test seems to pan out.) Montaigne "criticizes not only the Christian concern with eternity but every movement of the restless human soul that takes us beyond ourselves: the love of knowledge, the love of honor, even the love of virtue."[30] Montaigne willingly discards them all if they take us away from the contentment of being happy with our self.

Montaigne believes that resisting anything that would take us beyond the self is the secret to living. That's how we stay true to the self: by never escaping the self. This will make us happy and content. Such an approach frees us for just this kind of contented happiness inside our ordinary lives. Bedamned extraordinary life of royal and holy duty where there is no time for reflection and no friends to reflect with and where dying is escaping! Montaigne discovers that we are most free, as La Boétie wanted us to be, when engaging the world as a friend in reflection, freely searching ourselves, happily being ourselves, dying well with no illusions of what may come. Montaigne is *all* about *this* life, forming us to be. Montaigne "challenges us to stay *chez nous* ["with us"], to learn to be at home within ourselves and within our world, and to cease measuring our lives against any transcendent goal or standard. He challenges us to practice the art . . . that transforms the soul into the self."[31]

---

problem for the human soul, which I discuss in Andrew Root, *The Church in an Age of Secular Mysticisms* (Grand Rapids: Baker Academic, 2023). I believe this rejection of the beyond by Protestants who are trying to find a safe harbor in late modernity has had a deeply negative effect. See *Church in an Age of Secular Mysticisms*, chap. 5.

29. Thomas Hibbs explains Montaigne's turn away from the beyond: "Montaigne states directly, 'I rarely repent and . . . my conscience is happy with itself.' Before Nietzsche's proclamation of eternal return, Montaigne says of his whole life, 'If I had to live again, I would live as I have done; I neither regret the past nor fear the future.' Or again, 'My doings are ruled by what I am and are in harmony with how I was made. I cannot do better: and the act of repenting does not properly touch what is not in our power—that is touched by regretting.' Montaigne can conceive of a kind of repentance or regret that arises from a desire for one's life to be quite different from what has been or currently is, but he finds himself unable to treat that as a rational desire." Hibbs, *Wagering on an Ironic God: Pascal on Faith and Philosophy* (Waco: Baylor University Press, 2017), 59.

30. Storey and Storey, *Why We Are Restless*, 13.

31. Storey and Storey, *Why We Are Restless*, 13.

Sincerity in Its Nonchalant and Chalant Forms

Benjamin Storey and Jenna Silber Storey have called this Montaignian way of being "immanent contentment."[32] They believe we all have, in one way or another, followed Montaigne's legacy, becoming ferocious happiness-seekers. But ironically, our ferocious happiness seeking takes the shape, again thanks to Montaigne, of seeking the freedom for immanent contentment.

It is my contention that this desire for immanent contentment not only turns us into happiness-seekers but also makes us—even more ironically—so miserable. Our times are sad because more than ever we are committed to immanent contentment (we Western late moderns of the twenty-first century are the deeply loyal and fretful achieving-minded children of Montaigne). What makes our times more committed to immanent contentment than, say, those in the 1990s is that we share a trait with our daddy Montaigne that those in the 1990s did not.

This trait is untainted sincerity. As Storey and Storey say, "Montaigne, who never claims to be wise, heroic, or holy, does claim to be sincere."[33] Montaigne is sincere even in his dancing and sleeping. Even his gardening, which he's bad at, *must* be done sincerely.[34] Montaigne wants without exception to live sincerely, even to die sincerely in reflection. Life is lived best by being sincere.[35] Therefore, Montaigne has not a moment—not even a beat—to remove himself from the sincerity for this life to think about the next one. He won't admit, as the author of Ecclesiastes does,

32. Storey and Storey, *Why We Are Restless*, 3–33.

33. Storey and Storey, *Why We Are Restless*, 27.

34. I'm tempted to say that Montaigne is a sort of Wes Anderson character. Wes Anderson writes and directs movies where the comic engine is in the character's utter sincerity. We see this particularly in his early films. Our times still contain humor, but it is more Michael Scott or David Brent (even Ted Lasso) humor. All three characters, who are quite different, are 100 percent sincere. Brent at least is such a buffoon that the tragic and ironic seep from every scene. But it may be that David Brent is the last far-reaching ironic comedy character.

35. The eminent Lionel Trilling offers these thoughts: "On his preeminence in sincerity Rousseau is uncompromising. The claims of his likeliest rival are dismissed out of hand—his expressions of scorn for the show of sincerity made by Montaigne are recurrent and unqualified. 'I have always been amused,' he says grandly, 'at Montaigne's false ingenuousness and at his pretense of confessing his faults while taking good care to admit only likeable ones; whereas I, who believe, and always have believed, that I am on the whole the best of men, felt that there is no human breast, however pure, that does not conceal some odious vice. About his own truth telling he says no more than the truth. He does not shrink from injuring himself in the world's eyes." Trilling, *Sincerity and Authenticity* (Cambridge, MA: Harvard University Press, 1972), 59.

that even the joys of dancing and sleeping are folly. For life is but a blink, and all our living is just meaningless dust.

There is no irony or tragedy in Montaigne (Montaigne can't be confused for Søren Kierkegaard, who puts both irony and tragedy at the center of his imagination). Montaigne refuses to put tragedy and irony anywhere near his thought because he knows too much of it. He knows intimately how Catholics are killing Protestants and Protestants killing Catholics. He knows that the shoes of Parisians are literally soaked in blood. And that kings, uncles, and mothers plot and murder. And that even in the château, beloved daughters die. To counter all this tragedy, Montaigne takes on a completely untainted sincerity. This is the way, he believes, to live with the tragedy that floats on the air of France. Untainted sincerity is the way to keep the tragic at bay.[36]

For those who came after Montaigne and before us, it seemed impossible to keep out the tragic (spoiler alert, even Henry of Navarre is killed). Therefore, irony was always needed. Immanent contentment could never be uninterrupted. The twentieth century was filled with ironic opposition to suburban sincerity—think of the beat poets, Jack Kerouac, Lenny Bruce, SNL, heavy metal, Andy Kaufman, and Kurt Cobain. Yet, as the novelist David Foster Wallace has explained, the ironic tropes of the late twentieth century needed to be met by the sincerity of the new century.[37] This, Wallace believed, could offer a way beyond the vapid consumerism of the second half of the twentieth century. Wallace couldn't believe that commercial America was using irony to sell cereal. The countercultural

36. Frame shows us that Montaigne knew much tragedy: "The earliest essays are not gay; their author seems quite different from the hedonistic young friend of La Boétie and the smiling sage of the third book. This is not wholly surprising; for when he retired, his last ten years had been full of the pain and death of those dearest to him. In 1561 his father, without warning, had fallen ill of the kidney stone, which killed him after seven painful years. Two years later his beloved La Boétie, not yet thirty-three, had been stricken with dysentery and soon died. A tennis ball had killed his brother Arnaud in his twenties. His long-awaited first child had lived only two months; though the second, Leonor, survived, he lost a third in 1573, and later the fourth, the fifth, and the sixth, all as infants. August 1572 brought the terrible Massacre of Saint Bartholomew's Day, which was almost as bad in Bordeaux as in Paris. Montaigne himself, from a mere peaceful collision on horseback, had for a while been taken for dead by himself and others." Frame, *Montaigne*, 151.

37. I've more intricately sketched this out in Root, *Church in an Age of Secular Mysticisms*, chap. 6. Wallace discusses this in interviews with Charlie Rose in 1996 and 1997, available at https://youtu.be/J3qjCvkQWvs and https://youtu.be/GopJ1x7vK2Q.

elements of the ironic were tainted, meaning that a return to untainted sincerity was needed.

But what Wallace did not live to see is that sincerity would be taken so far to achieve immanent contentment[38] that the tragic and the ironic would be perceived not as banal but as abusive. Wallace would not likely have supported happiness being contingent on one's own and others' acceptance of one's chosen identity, such that someone's pursuit of happiness could never be questioned. The unquestionableness of a person's pursuit of happiness (which Neiman finds unliberal) has made the tragic and ironic out of bounds. In the white-knuckle pursuit of an identity bound inside immanent contentment, the tragic and the ironic are strangled. Only untainted sincerity (from family, friends, society, institutions, even religion—from everything!) is allowed to exist. Our untainted sincerity turns into such deep earnestness that the ironic becomes a form of abuse.

Montaigne sought sincerity as a warm oasis in the frozen tundra of tragedy. We, on the other hand, have tried to construct such insulated walls that the chill of tragedy is never felt. Following the sincerity of immanent contentment, we've turned up the dial of its heat to eleven. The first three decades of the twenty-first century have dried up all irony and tragedy (even humor at times). We are the most sincere of Montaigne's children, more untaintedly sincere than our father Montaigne himself. Montaigne sought unflinching sincerity as a way through the tragedy that he experienced. We, on the other hand, want to obliterate tragedy and irony, claiming that the ironic and tragic is an attack on the self, keeping us from the happiness of contentment. Without the ability to be happily content, confronting those who question our self, we come to perceive that they want to obliterate *us*—"wishing us not to exist," as young people say today.

A great burden accompanies our contentment, forcing contentment to carry a heavy ontological weight. We must live without the antibodies of the tragic and ironic. What we've failed to see, because we're so concerned about the threat to our expressed identities, is that tragedy and irony are like vaccines to sadness. Though they contain sadness, they are a prepared dose that helps us deal with the impossibilities and limits of being human. (Neoliberalism has convinced us that impossibilities and limits are unreal

---

38. Wallace himself doubted that immanent contentment could be good, because for him it turned into watching hours and hours of television.

and only exist in our mind, having no connection to our creatureliness.[39])
Irony and tragedy help us find ways of seeing, even embracing, our sadness.
They help us not take ourselves too seriously. Irony and tragedy teach our
immune systems to recognize and cope with sadness—mostly by calling
others to join us in our sadness. Irony and tragedy call for the camarade-
rie of friendship, inviting others to journey with us. Untainted sincerity
settles for fans, admirers, therapists, coaches, and others who are paid or
prodded to care for us. Untainted sincerity fails to deal with sadness and
ultimately makes us lonely, bearing the burden of taking ourselves (our
self) too seriously.

We are a particularly sad society in the first three decades of the twenty-
first century because we so deeply believe that the happiness of immanent
contentment is contingent on untainted sincerity. Put simply, we can no
longer laugh at ourselves (at our *self*). We no longer recognize that the
uneasiness of being playfully teased may also be the ground that births
a communion of real commitment, a gift to laugh and to love our self.

There is one trait in Montaigne's sincerity that we children of the
twenty-first century cannot match: Montaigne's sincerity is untainted but
also *nonchalant*. There is still a hint (not enough to taint) of the tragic and
the ironic in Montaigne's sincerity. This gives Montaigne some humor,
allowing him to accept the lack and limitations of his life. Montaigne's
commitment to the nonchalant makes him one of the first to see that
being laid back is good. In this sense Montaigne is the inventor of cool.

We can match Montaigne's untainted sincerity but *not* his nonchalant
nature. Our sincerity is anything but nonchalant or cool. We still use the
slang "cool" but rarely as a descriptor of a person who is admired for their
nonchalance. We use "cool" for a product, experience, or even a person we
desire. We use "cool" for something that is titillating or alluring. Overall,
the twenty-first century is *not* a nonchalant time—even the admirably desired things or people we consider to be "cool" are high-strung (Gawker's
list of most annoying celebrities of the year interestingly often matched
the list of the most influential).

39. Tara Burton adds, "It's Headspace's blithely capitalistic ads—'I meditate to crush it,'
one subway-plastered client testimony reads; 'I meditate to have the edge,' says another—that
have made it a particular target of media coverage and, at times, suspicion. Meditation, in
Headspace's rhetoric, is a kind of self-optimization: encouraging users to focus on themselves—
their thoughts, their needs, their desires—in order to, as in New Thought, improve their sur-
roundings." Burton, *Strange Rites*, 108.

We even "outsincere" Montaigne. Instead of being seekers of nonchalant sincerity, we go for *chalant* sincerity. Unfortunately, "chalant" isn't a word. It's been lost in translation from the Old French to English. "Nonchalant" comes from *non* ("not") and the Old French *chaloir* ("concern")—to not concern. We late-modern middle-class people have made concern our sport. Just talk with upwardly mobile parents about their anxious parenting style of ambition and control. Worrying about their children is their (competitive) sport.

Montaigne believes that living happily in this immanent contentment requires being sincerely nonchalant. Don't concern yourself with too much. Be free to just dance and sleep, garden and read. Just be. But we can't do this. We want to, but we can't. We buy $100 shorts and read all of Renate's wellness articles. But those shorts and articles oddly just make us feel like we're not measuring up, not doing the dancing and sleeping rightly (because no one seems to be recognizing it as excellent). Our untainted sincerity has been poisoned because we've been convinced by late-stage capitalism that there are winners and losers in the game of achieving the happiness of immanent contentment. We are so untaintedly sincere because we're in the middle of intensely vicious competition. How can you be nonchalant inside the hypercompetitive environment of a neoliberal late capitalism and its countless battles for identity? We can't hold to the nonchalance of sincerity when every minute is about sincerely performing our self so that we can win immanent contentment.

Because our sincerity is so chalant, our sadness is all-encompassing. Because we're inside a competition, our sadness is a sign that we've lost, that we are losers, unable to lift high the trophy of immanent contentment. We therefore demand that the few friends we have (outside of social media) carry the weight of our losses. We ask them to recognize our sadness as a way to win their attention. But they have their own sadness to carry with their own chalant sincerity. They are intently seeking to hold on to their own happiness as immanent contentment and therefore cannot abide our sadness—not if it becomes a burden to their own selves. Such friendship is exhausting. If friendship cannot be the source of contentment, it is stressed to the point of evaporation. We quickly find that there is no one who is able or willing to bear our burdens. Our only options are to pay professionals or make overexposing rants on social media. We are all alone with our sorrow, fearing that our burdens are eating permanent holes in our contentment. We are too turned in on ourselves, too stressed and exhausted from the burdens of our own chalant sincerity, to find any real consolation.

The Implications of Immanent Contentment, and Back to Renate

Being Montaigne's children, we late moderns of the early twenty-first century cannot stomach any interruption in our immanent contentment. The truth is that we experience these interruptions all the time, and the interruptions stress us out. Most of us live wishing we could just feel more contentment with our lives and therefore really be happy. But it never feels as easy as it was for Montaigne. When we dance, we put it on Instagram and wonder whether (a lot of) people will like it—making it a "good" dance. When we sleep, we can't sleep. We're too stressed to sleep. There is too much to finish or accomplish so that we can finally earn our contentment. We feel guilty that we're not good enough dancers and don't get enough sleep. We need to take dance classes and sleeping pills.[40] We want to loyally enjoy life as Montaigne tells us to do. We believe deeply in the freedom of immanent contentment and the happiness it produces, but it's always slipping away or just around the next corner.[41]

Immanent contentment even shapes our presumptions about identity, justice, politics, and religion. We come to believe that anything that keeps us from immanent contentment is an existential terror (which just so happens to be what gives terrorists their psychological power). We cannot *be* without being happy. We cannot be a self without complete acceptance of our self—which is the direct outgrowth of immanent contentment. We're willing to ignore one lesson from our daddy, Montaigne, and do our best to never think about dying. Most late moderns will say with exasperation, "I just want to be happy," meaning "I just want the freedom of uninterrupted immanent contentment." But immanent contentment—so linked to feelings of happiness—is first and foremost a psychological reality.[42]

---

40. Jonathan Crary argues that a society with a sleep problem is a society with moral existential issues. See his provocative book 24/7: *Late Capitalism and the Ends of Sleep* (New York: Verso, 2013).

41. This echoes Hartmut Rosa's descriptive work of modernity and its acceleration. See Rosa, *Social Acceleration: A New Theory of Modernity* (New York: Columbia University Press, 2015).

42. Daniel Haybron offers prophetic words: "The difficulty of pursuing happiness is no reason to think happiness a mainly biological or temperamental affair, unchangeable and

And we've convinced ourselves that it is attainable with the right attitude or hack. No wonder that our age has become a therapeutic one, filled with online therapists and podcasters who talk about mental health challenges.[43] What we're mostly anxious or depressed about is that we can't win our way back to immanent contentment; we just can't be happy. The anxiety upends the contentment. The depression attacks the ability to feel happy.[44]

In a news story on hate crimes against Asian Americans, an expert reports on the real discrimination that is rising in American society against those of Asian descent.[45] But when it comes to the necessary moral assertions on why this discrimination is wrong, there is no claim of universal humanity, no sense of the goods that all human beings deserve, no statement on hate being an unacceptable evil. Rather, the reporter claims that the reason such discrimination and hate is wrong is its mental health impact. Mental health—understood as the blocking of happiness and immanent contentment—becomes the only measure of justice because it is the only shape of the good life. If you can't reach immanent contentment, it's because you're stressed; and if you're stressed, it's because you can't achieve your identity; and if you can't achieve your identity, it's because someone is hating; and if someone is hating, you can't be happy; and if you can't be happy, you face injustice—taking us full circle—because, at the very base, you're kept from immanent contentment.[46]

---

unconnected with the conditions of our lives. Consider the way that depression has skyrocketed in decades. How should we explain this trend? It could be due to some environmental contaminant burning up our neurotransmitters. Or perhaps there is something wrong with the way many of us are living." Haybron, *The Pursuit of Unhappiness: The Elusive Psychology of Well-Being* (New York: Oxford University Press, 2010), 126.

43. "The causes of mental health problems are obviously complex and do not lie simply in the economy any more than they do in brain chemistry. But it is the way in which these problems manifest themselves in the workplace, threatening productivity as they do, that has placed them amongst the greatest problems confronting capitalism today." Haybron, *Pursuit of Unhappiness*, 107.

44. See Philip Rieff, *The Triumph of the Therapeutic: Uses of Faith after Freud* (Wilmington, DE: ISI Books, 2005).

45. Amna Nawaz and Courtney Norris, "Survey of Asian Americans Paints Sobering Picture of Fears about Violence," *PBS News*, May 15, 2023, https://www.pbs.org/newshour/show/survey-of-asian-americans-paints-sobering-picture-of-fears-about-violence.

46. Rowan Williams says powerfully, "Combine this—especially in the USA—with a culture often deeply preoccupied with rights, and the fragmentation is even more acute. My position or my interest group's position needs protecting and reinforcing from the tribunals of public order: practical politics thus rapidly becomes a matter of how these tribunals are to be persuaded to acknowledge and enforce claims. It is certainly true that this sort of concern arises from the acute vulnerability of some groups, minority and otherwise disadvantaged groups, in a diverse and increasingly mistrustful environment. But the effect of a policy of arguing claims

Trauma has been stretched and expanded to encompass the experience of direct blockage to immanent contentment. *Everyone* is traumatized now. Maybe we are. But if so—if we all are traumatized—it's because we've tacitly put so much weight on the happiness of immanent contentment.[47] We *all* feel traumatized, because to be blocked from the happiness of immanent contentment is to be made captive, with no escape from our sorrow (except perhaps with a psychological hack to cope with the stress). There is no bigger horizon. Montaigne's immanence, embedded in happiness, will not allow it. The centrality of contentment allows us no possibility or reality (like the sacramental one I explore below) to meet something bigger and fuller *inside* our sorrow. Sorrow becomes flattened to unhappiness. Sorrow has no efficacy—not while you're inside it at least. We come to disdain and fear sorrow because it cannot coexist with immanent contentment. Immanent contentment—at least in its late-modern form—wants to make sorrow extinct. But trying to make sorrow extinct will only make for more sorrow, because our sincerity is too heavily chalant and our drives for happiness are too performative and competitive. What's more, the immanence of it all will keep sorrow from having any deeper meaning and purpose than simply blocking you from being happy and content as your magnificent self.

Poor Renate. She was a boss of immanent contentment, an exemplar and influencer. She was a real winner. But the sorrow of the loss of her father cruelly interrupted her immanent contentment. Her own and others' untainted sincerity are now cold comfort. There is no *immanent* contentment in the grief.[48] Now she doesn't know how to go forward. All the practices of immanent contentment she'd used and mastered—yoga, mindfulness, oatmeal and asparagus infusions, lavender—cannot return her to happiness.[49] They are no match for her sorrow. She's been fired

---

in this way is ultimately to aggravate both the suspicions that originally prompted the search for protection and the sense that the social order in its public and comprehensive form of legality is essentially something alien." Williams, *Lost Icons: Reflections on Cultural Bereavement* (Harrisburg, PA: Morehouse, 2000), 85.

47. And because the victim narratives are so powerful—again taking us back to Neiman.

48. People who lose someone often grab hold of some spirituality or religion that has a transcendent quality to it. Many people contend that their loved one is in a better place. Our grief and sorrow reach for something outside of us.

49. Andreas Reckwitz adds, "For systematic reasons, in fact, a form of life that ties happiness to individual self-growth and the demonstration of singular success—demanding that we all

because Will needs performance, a performance that must serve immanent contentment. When Renate can't get back to happiness, she becomes a detriment. Out of his untainted sincerity—which is deeply and aggressively chalant, with no place for tragedy or irony—Will fires Renate. Her sorrow has no value. Will initially treats it as a mental health issue, looking to fix it quickly. But when "quickly" doesn't come, Will cannot abide the tragic drag on immanent contentment (they don't mix). Will is in a battle. He's competing to help his customers and employees—and of course his own self—win the happiness of uninterrupted immanent contentment. They are all fighting to sincerely seek health so they can be happy. When they dance, they dance to burn calories, and when they sleep, they sleep to live longer and more successfully (it's all about brain optimization!). They do it all to secure their immanent contentment.[50] Being healthy is being happy because you can never be content without being secure in your health, so says the immanent frame of mind (no wonder the wellness industry is a $4.3 billion consumer sector).[51]

---

live an 'interesting life'—has proven to be prone to disappointment." Reckwitz and Hartmut Rosa, *Late Modernity in Crisis* (Malden, MA: Polity, 2023), 76.

50. Michael Thompson says powerfully, "In this sense, perhaps the most insidious change in the structure of the self has been the transformation of desire away from objects that enhance our experience and freedom and toward the objects of the system itself. Indeed, it is perhaps more correct to say that genuine desire itself has been subverted; capitalism in its current phase of the commodification of everything, preempts desire. Each time I feel a need, a restlessness with my aloneness, I reach for a device to connect me with the prepackaged experience of the commodified world. With this erosion of desire, so, too, goes the very energy for political transformation and the capacity to think capitalism's alternative." Thompson, *Twilight of the Self: The Decline of the Individual in Late Capitalism* (Stanford, CA: Stanford University Press, 2022), 11.

51. Rina Raphael says, "The wellness industry stepped in to fill a void created by the unreasonable expectations that torment us. Self-care promised salvation, deliverance from the evils of stress. But if it's a toxic workplace, a meditation program isn't going to fix it. A fitness app won't solve the uneven distribution of housework within your marriage; CBD gummies will not enforce better childcare policies; bath salts won't stop late-night work emails. Buy whatever makes you feel good, but realize that these are short-term mental Band-Aids that do not ensure long-term redemption. Wellness remedies help, but the problem is that they're sold to the public as miraculous cure-alls." Raphael, *The Gospel of Wellness: Gyms, Gurus, Goop, and the False Promise of Self-Care* (New York: Holt, 2022), 36. She continues, "The wellness industry has succeeded in convincing consumers they can master their life—and solving the problem of isolation was no exception. Over the last two decades, boutique fitness studios marketed their intimate social settings, spurring rapid expansion over the last decade. Some studios host book clubs, holiday parties, even weekend retreats. These gym societies draw millennials with the allure of meeting new people. Instructors ask participants to high-five their neighbors and to hang out at post-class happy hours. Planet Fitness throws pizza parties where members socialize over a free slice and bodybuilding tips" (108).

Evangelism

What we've talked about so far has done important work for our recon-
ceiving of evangelism—particularly for our ability to ground evangelism
in the sacramental. Too often evangelism—out of the good intention to be
contextual—has embraced the pursuit of happiness by means of immanent
contentment. Look no further than the light and heavy prosperity gospel
of the right and the ramped-up claims of acceptance and affirmation on
the left. Both sides (and many more in less extreme forms) claim that the
gospel is in tune with, adding musical texture to, the happiness seeking
that is grounded in immanent contentment. The gospel becomes another
(the best!) tool to find real happiness. The gospel becomes the best device
to finally find the true blessing of immanent contentment. Salvation is
assumed to be happiness, and peace is seen as contentment.

It is assumed that the gospel can find a way to grow in this soil of immanent contentment. We have believed that evangelism itself must embrace
immanent contentment to persuade happiness-seekers that the gospel can
enhance or fulfill the contentment that produces happiness. Salvation itself
has been molded in the form of immanent contentment. We've even proclaimed that Jesus Christ can make you happy! Even though his crucified
body and call to follow him to the cross says something much different
(Matt. 16:24–26).

When evangelism shapes itself for immanent contentment, it risks losing the sacramental (the sense that the infinite participates in the finite)
and therefore the very dynamic that can transform. It definitely loses the
cross. Paul becomes all things to all people (1 Cor. 9:22) only so that he
can proclaim Christ and him crucified (2:2). Paul becomes the man of sorrows so that Jews and Greeks can encounter the God of the cross.[52] The
enclosed world of contented happiness cannot stomach the centrality of

---

52. Kierkegaard says, "Yea, he learned obedience by the things which he suffered when he,
who is the Lord of bliss, was as a curse for everyone approaching him, and for everyone who
fled him a sorrow while he lived; a sorrow for those few who loved him, since he must draw
them out with him into the most dread decisions, since for a mother he must be the sword to
pierce her heart, for his disciples, love crucified; a sorrow for the hesitating who, deep down,
in the impenetrable secret of desire, understood perhaps that his words were true, but dared
not join themselves to him, wherefore also they retained in their souls a goad, an inner discord,
the painful evidence of being his contemporaries; a sorrow for the wicked, since by his purity
and holiness he must reveal their hearts' thought to them, making them guiltier than before,
Oh, grievous suffering, that as the Saviour of the world he must become a stumbling-stone!"
Kierkegaard, *Gospel of Suffering* (Cambridge: James Clarke, 2015), 54.

suffering and the embodied but transcendent kingdom it brings. Jesus is not coming to make people happy; rather, he reminds them that he is to be found where consolation is needed and brokenness is operative. He is present in places of hunger and imprisonment (Matt. 25:31–46), where son turns from father (Matt. 10:34–39), where the sword is wielded. Jesus comes not to bring happiness as immanent contentment; he comes to bring the apocalyptic. He is found in sorrow. But Jesus takes this sorrow and, in sacramental fashion, makes it the very place where God is active, ministering life out of death, saving the world.

Enclosed in the happiness of immanent contentment, sorrow cannot possibly be the ground of such transformation. Rather, sorrow is seen as a problem to be fixed, even a sickness to be solved. Sorrow has zero efficacy. Immanent contentment gives us no invitation inside sorrow to find something transcendent and full, something true and beautiful. Inside immanent contentment, sorrow only interrupts you from securing your own self's happiness.

Evangelism will need to be the judgment of immanent contentment, because the gospel of Jesus Christ is this too. This judgment will be embodied not by standing over against happiness-seekers but by sharing tenderly in their inevitable grief and sorrow, allowing friendship to be the sacrament of God's salvation. Just as the church was built by entering the sorrow of the plagues in the first and second centuries,[53] so Protestantism will be renewed in the West by the church entering the sorrow that plagues happiness-seekers with the sacrament of (noninstrumental) friendship.[54] Just as the church added to its number by not fleeing the plague but nursing the sick, so Protestantism will be renewed by giving consolation to the grieved, burdened, and broken happiness-seekers like Renate.

■ ■ ■ ■

Since Renate was in middle school, she had always thought of herself as someone with many friends. When she lived in the city, her calendar was chock-full of lunches and brunches. Her networks were thick. She was admired for them. When Renate moved to Southern California, her calendar and her networks expanded.

53. See Rodney Stark, *The Rise of Christianity* (New York: HarperCollins, 1996).
54. It must be noninstrumental if it is to be sacramental. More on this in the chapters to come.

But when her father died, she was alone. When Renate posted on her socials that her dad had died, there were many—many—sad faces and almost a hundred comments of "sorry" and "that sucks." But no one called. No one. Almost no one texted. No one came to sit with her. She was alone. She'd never felt more alone.

Even her siblings weren't present. They disappeared inside their own anger. Her brother brazenly told her that he was glad their dad was dead. "He was a real jerk, Renate. Good riddance," he said the day after he died. When she asked for help cleaning out his house, her sister said, "Burn it all down. He would like that since he's burning in hell now."

The loneliness stung. But at a woeful and forlorn level, Renate understood it. She had no recollection of ever reaching out to anyone who was in grief. She remembered seeing posts of lost jobs, broken marriages, and dead loved ones. Never once did she do more than click a sad-face emoji. She never even thought about visiting and sitting with the person. She was frightened of entering another person's sorrow. She even skipped her old editor's funeral, telling a friend at lunch, "It would just be so awkward. And a downer. I'm kind of just too stressed for it. I'll take a minute of silence and have a glass of wine for him. He'd like that. The funeral would just be too much."

Renate thought about those words when her dad died. She decided not to have a funeral for her dad. She knew no one would come, not even her siblings. She couldn't do it alone. She was already so alone. She just wanted to be okay. And she was sure that a funeral wouldn't help.

Before the Swedish Death Cleaning Team arrived, Renate picked up the ashes at the funeral home. They sat in a box in the back seat of her car. At the end of the first day of cleaning, AC Williamson found them when he was putting two keepsakes in Renate's car.

"Whatcha gonna do with his remains?" AC asked Renate.

5

"Not Okay"—Our Sad Times of Stress

The Forgetting of Soul

To her surprise, Renate hadn't thought about what to do with her dad's ashes. She just wasn't okay enough to know. Thinking about it was too stressful.

"Nothing. Bringing them home, I guess," she told AC.

"He didn't have no special place or nothin'?" AC asked.

Renate just shook her head. All she could think of was the living room where he watched all the Cardinals games.

"Because I saw a lot of pictures of lakes and stuff," AC added.

"Oh, those are pictures of the Finger Lakes in upstate New York. My dad grew up there before moving to Phoenix. He went back every summer to fish. Usually alone."

It made Renate sad to think of him there all by himself. He was such a miserable man, she thought. But thinking of him alone in his boat made her miss him, causing a stab of grief for the life he lost long before he died.

"Did he say he wanted his remains scattered there?" AC probed.

"He didn't say anything. We never talked about it. We didn't talk much."

"What'd he say about his funeral?" AC asked, looking for information that might help.

"We didn't have a funeral," Renate said, surprised by the heaviness of admitting that fact.

"No funeral!?" AC responded with a burst of exasperation, his voice raising at the end. "No funeral? He a human being, ain't he? I'm figurin' from all this he wasn't a good daddy. But he was a human being, and all human beings need a funeral, especially being your daddy, even if he wasn't a good one."

Renate felt that weight. She paused and said, "I just couldn't. No one would come. And I couldn't do it alone. I couldn't be the only one there. I'm just not okay right now. I'm working on it! But right now, I'm not okay and I couldn't be the only one there."

"Ah," AC said with wide, compassionate eyes, "I get that. You not supposed to be okay. But that man needs a funeral. It might help."

■ ■ ■ ■

When her father died, Renate became addicted to social media. She went on a major bender. Truth be told, she was already addicted, looking at her phone constantly. She excused herself by reminding herself it was part of her job. But it got really bad after she posted about her dad's death. The reactions and comments felt so important. It felt like they connected her to others. She desperately needed this sense of connection. Her soul thirsted for it. She soaked up every small consolation, reading them over and over. It felt good to watch the interaction numbers increase. In those first four hours Renate felt cared for. She wished for a call or a visit. But there was something buoyant, even reassuring, about the large number of people reacting to her sad news.

And then it was over.

The flood of reactions dwindled to a trickle after the four-hour mark. By the twelfth hour it all but dried up. Yet her grief only intensified. The speed of these online interactions was outpacing her sorrow. She needed to feel like someone truly saw her situation. She needed more consolation.

The next day, almost without thinking but aware she was looking for some reaction that would assure her of some connection, she posted again. She had no new news. He was still dead, and she was still grieving him.

The post read, "He's been gone twenty-four hours and I'm so sad. How can I miss a man I barely knew?"

The interactions were less than a quarter of the first post. The comments were shorter. They said things like "Hang in there" and "I hope you're okay," with a lot of sad faces and broken hearts.

Renate posted again the next day and again the next. She knew she was fishing for reactions, but she felt increasingly disconnected and alone. Each post returned fewer interactions. Far fewer than that of her friend who posted a video of her golden retriever eating ice cream or a former coworker who posted pictures of a meal she made from scratch. Now, on top of everything, Renate felt like an annoying failure. She could see it in the numbers. Those numbers haunted her, making the silence sting. Renate was getting direct feedback, paid in silence, on how little people cared.

Being a writer, and partly thirsty for interactions as well as wanting to honor her father, she wrote a personal obituary to post. The funeral home that picked up her dad's body asked if the family wanted to place an obituary in the local paper and online. Renate and her siblings declined. They didn't know what to say. The funeral director said he could submit a very basic obituary. Now Renate was ready to write her own. She knew it had to be honest and heartfelt to get the reactions she needed to feel some sense of connection and care, to win some consolation among the noise of ice cream cones, golden retrievers, and cooking. She also had genuine feelings she needed to get out. It was all twisted up inside her.

She posted her obituary. It received a lot of reactions, mostly in sad and teary faces. But almost no comments. None of the comments had any substance that could bear the weight of consolation. There were no direct messages or calls. However, one comment contained some substance but in the form of unwanted negativity and the very opposite of consolation. It was from some guy Renate didn't think she knew. And it was harsh.

It read: "Poorly written drivel. Full-on wah wah. I bet your dad is happy he's dead and doesn't have to read this. Plus, from your poor writing—so who knows—it seems like he was a jerk anyhow. Glad he's dead. Good day!"

It was a vicious punch in the solar plexus that took Renate's breath away. She didn't know how to respond or even whether she should. Luckily a few other people jumped in.

A former workout buddy responded, "This is not okay!"

A high school friend: "You're the jerk. Not okay, dude."

A cousin: "You're a troll. Don't be a jerk online. Renate, I hope you're okay. Sending love."

The comment from Renate's cousin got eighty likes. That was cold consolation. But at least it was consolation. Kind of. Still, no one called or texted. And despite the defending, Renate couldn't stop thinking about the cruel comment. As she intently watched the interaction numbers, needing them like air, she realized that indeed she was not okay.

During one of her online benders she saw an ad for eHelp.[1] eHelp is an online service that connects people with counselors and therapists. It promises convenience. The app allows individuals who are seeking help to connect with trained and certified therapists by text, voice or video call, or even (though rarely) in person.

As a side hustle, Renate once wrote the company's podcast ad. They advertise on hundreds of podcasts. She was always tickled to hear her writing being read back by a podcaster she admired.

The podcaster would read, "If you're busy like me, it's easy for stress to overtake your life. Has that ever happened to you? When I'm stressed, it's hard to feel okay. I easily lose myself or miss issues I could be addressing and problems I could be solving. I sometimes don't even know what's best for me. Sometimes we all need help. If you have a situation that's making you stressed or keeping you from being happy—or if you just know there is a better way to do things or see things and yet you can't quite get there— then the good people at eHelp can help. We're always evolving and life is stressful, especially when you're growing and changing. If you're feeling the stress, then give eHelp a try. It's easy and online. eHelp is an app that connects you to trained people who can help you solve your problems, deal with your stress, and find your happiness. Check it out today. eHelp *can* help."

Renate moved from independent contractor to customer, creating an eHelp account. She had to admit to herself that she wasn't okay. She wanted to be okay. She didn't want to feel so alone, and she didn't want to feel so stressed.

From Kidney Stones to Cut-Out Hearts to Math Genius

Michel de Montaigne wants us to truly live by way of seeking happiness. He wants us to loyally enjoy dancing and sleeping. For him, this is happiness. It is a style of living sincerely for immanent contentment. It's a style or way of life that refuses to lift its head to the heavens or bow its head in

---

1. A fictional company.

prayer. It wants nothing of the beyond, just more living. Monsieur Montaigne wants us to give attention to our own reflections, to our selves, to our gardens, to our cats. He wants us to test ourselves by reflecting with a friend on what it means to live (or absent a friend, putting pen to paper in self-reflection).

Our sincerity in reflection can produce the immanent contentment of happiness because it's done nonchalantly—in reflection we confess that we are each a self who reflects but comes to know nothing. We come to know that we don't know much at all. Nevertheless, this reflection changes us, drawing us into life, offering us the contentment of being ourselves. If we can sincerely embrace our lives, living inside immanent contentment, we can make a free society. A free society provides each individual the space and latitude to pursue happiness as their own immanent contentment inside their own sincere reflection on their own experience. (We've already seen how and why this backfires on us in late modernity, but it is nevertheless deeply within us.)

Montaigne died the good death in 1592. It was "good" because Montaigne experienced it fully. He embraced the pain of kidney stones and the anguish of dying—just like La Boétie did. The France that Montaigne left had settled into a delicate peace. Henry of Navarre had ended the civil war, calming the Catholic-Huguenot conflicts with the signing of the Edict of Nantes. But this fragile peace always risked being shattered.

In 1594, just two years after Montaigne's death, there was an attempt on Henry of Navarre's life. All evidence pointed to the Jesuits—they were the militant wing of the Catholic League at the time. The Jesuits were therefore expelled from the realm, kicked out of France. But ultimately this was a bad look for Henry of Navarre, who had supposedly converted to Catholicism. It didn't reflect well on the former Protestant but now Catholic king to expel a whole order.

In 1603 the Jesuits' time in the penalty box ended and Henry of Navarre allowed them back into France. It was a mistake that would cost Henry his life. The Jesuits were only allowed to form a handful of colleges and schools and do a little preaching. In 1607, René Descartes—who we thought was our daddy, to cite Pearl Jam again, but Toulmin convinced us otherwise—was a young student in one of those schools, the Jesuit Royal College at La Fléche. The land on which this school resided had connections back to Henry of Navarre himself. Three years into young

René's education, in 1610, a Jesuit named François Ravaillac jumped into Henry's royal carriage and stuck him fatally with a dagger. Another French king violently assassinated. The delicate peace between Catholics and Protestants shattered into a million pieces.

When this happened, young René was about fourteen years old and quite skilled at math. The death of Henry became the central event of René's youth. That isn't just speculation; we know it as fact. When the kings of France died, it was customary to have their bodies enshrined in one place and their heart in another. Henry of Navarre agreed that upon his death—which he imagined was far off in the future—his heart would be enshrined in the college chapel of the Jesuit college that young Descartes happened to be attending. It made sense. It would connect Henry with his ancestral lands of La Flèche and serve as a political concession, lowering the heat on the conflicts with the Jesuits. The second part didn't work.

With the king dead, the Jesuits claimed that Ravaillac was a lone stabber. Just a madman acting out of his own derangement. To show this, the Jesuits quickly claimed the king's heart and made arrangements for it to be led in procession from Paris to La Flèche in reverence. The whole school, young René Descartes included, would take part in the ceremony and liturgy that enshrined the king's heart in a silver chalice in the chapel. It was the biggest thing to ever happen to the school. Descartes was present for it all, watching and taking it all in as a talented, impressionable teenager.

While nothing could compare with the shock of Henry's assassination and the reverence of the enshrinement that followed, the school at La Flèche was also buzzing with word from Italy. Just months before Henry of Navarre's slaying, a math professor in Padua had published his observations of the moon and planets garnered by use of a new instrument called the telescope. The school was abuzz with his findings. "Galileo's reports were a shock, a thrill, or both, depending on the reader's temperament."[2]

The year 1610 was quite a time for the Jesuit Royal College at La Flèche and its students. A sonnet was written in commemoration of Henry of Navarre's death. It oddly brings together these two significant events. The sonnet speaks of Henry as a star and of planets and moons moving as Galileo reports. Inside the randomness of the king's death and the peril it meant for the delicate and fractured peace, there is the sure, dependable

---

2. Stephen Toulmin, *Cosmopolis: The Hidden Agenda of Modernity* (Chicago: University of Chicago Press, 1990), 59.

order of planets and moons. The universe is not dependent on the whims of madmen and the emotions of the religious but on the firm, never-changing laws of the natural order that can be deciphered by mathematics.

René's Mission

Along with many other factors in the other realms of Europe, the death of Henry of Navarre intensely stoked the coals that would set Europe ablaze with the Thirty Years' War. The war shaped the life of Descartes in many ways. Amid this war, he tried to do formally that which the sonnet pointed to. He sought a way to find order that could secure peace, an order that would be as sure as the movements of the planets.

As René was working out his theorems and theories, which, coupled with those of Isaac Newton and John Locke, would birth the cosmopolis, he was forced to leave France for Holland. The assumption by most biographers since the early nineteenth century was that Descartes needed a safe harbor in which to hide. It was assumed (which, if Toulmin is right, may be just propaganda coming to us from the seventeenth century) that free thinking was not welcomed in the Catholic or Protestant lands of Europe. This put mathematical rebels like Descartes at great risk. Amsterdam was one place that would welcome free thinking. The common belief was that René—like John Locke, whose ideas about the crown forced him to flee England—sought a Dutch haven in which to think and write.

More than likely, only part of this is true. René did much thinking and writing in Amsterdam, but there is some documentation (though it is foggy) that Descartes was also a spy.[3] You can take the boy out of the Jesuit school, but you can't take the Jesuit school out of the boy! Descartes may have been doing his part for France and Catholicism in the conflicts after all.

Spy or not, Amsterdam allowed Descartes the time and freedom to write. It does free the mind to be away from the lands of inquisition! Amsterdam was to Descartes what the château tower was to Montaigne, a place to reflect. Descartes reflected deeply on Montaigne. He came to see that Montaigne's skepticism was *mostly* right. The more you reflect,

3. See the biography by A. C. Grayling, *Descartes: The Life and Times of a Genius* (London: Pocket Books, 2005), 105–40.

testing yourself with essays, joining a friend in conversation on a topic, the more you must confess, "What do I know?" Until Galileo placed his eye on the telescope, we knew little about the movement of moons and planets. Montaigne asked "What do I know?" as someone who'd say it to a friend, as a statement of intellectual humility. It's an invitation to breathe and embrace life. Descartes, on the other hand, who had few friends, took it literally. "What do you actually know? What can be known at all?" ("What can be known?" was the primary question of the new science.)

Montaigne's attention on the self who reflects on its experience also shaped Descartes. He followed Montaigne that far. But then he turned the Montaigne art of conversation toward the rigidity of numbers. Unlike Montaigne, René was always much more comfortable with numbers than with people. René agreed that there was something important in the self, that indeed Montaigne was right that we are minds in reflection. And the mind can doubt all things. Skepticism is everywhere and encircles everyone. But it is not everything. What Descartes saw was that what cannot be doubted—what can indeed be known and therefore upend Montaigne's universal skepticism—is that the self is the one doing these reflections. The self is the one who doubts, who thinks. What cannot be doubted is that *I* am the one who doubts when I talk with my actual or imagined La Boétie.

The foundation to knowledge, then, is the self. It is not based in religious commitments but in order, not in confessions but in what numbers can testify to. Firm laws could now order society as they order the universe. This rationalism could free people from Europe's entrenched religious conflicts by getting religion itself out from the middle of the pursuit of knowledge. Those who followed Descartes tried to do this by building the cosmopolis.

This Cartesian story is not *just* self-indulgence on my part. Nor am I simply seeking to do due diligence in rounding out Toulmin's genealogy, linking Descartes and Montaigne in a narrative. Rather, it will play an important part as we clasp hands with someone just as intellectually gifted as Descartes who nevertheless sees things much differently: Blaise Pascal. To understand Pascal and the vision of evangelism he can lead us into, we must know something about his own two La Boéties—Michel de Montaigne and René Descartes. These interlocutors never left Pascal's imagination. Pascal, of course, never met Montaigne. But, as we'll see in the next section, Pascal knew many who were heralding Montaigne as their hero, reviving his memory. Those bringing forth a Montaigne rival were mainly middle-elite boys, sons of the civil servants of new wealth, who called themselves the Honest Dudes. It sounds better in French: *honnêtes hommes*, which means literally "honest men."

Pascal met Descartes when he was a young teen. He was introduced to Descartes as an able boy who showed signs of being a genius with numbers. Descartes sized up young Pascal and gave him the cold shoulder of French indifference. Descartes looked down his long nose at Pascal and basically responded with a meh.

Yet before I can explore Pascal and a vision of evangelism, more needs to be said about our sad times. We need to do more probing on how, ironically, Montaigne, who just wants us to be happy sleeping and petting cats, could create the conditions for sad times of full-on happiness-seekers. We need to deal with Renate's stress and our drives to just be okay. To do this we need to meet Pascal's friends, who—like Gen Zers discovering Dolly Parton for the first time—revived Montaigne's memory. To do this we need to return to France and its civil wars (there are so many of these civil wars!). This time we go to 1648, just over a year before René Descartes's death.

The Honest Dudes

You'd probably be paranoid too if you were a Bourbon boy taking the throne after Henry of Navarre and all the murdering. The fuel igniting most of these murders was coming not from outside the palace and its court but from within. Ravaillac, Henry of Navarre's assassin, couldn't have been a lone actor—how did he get such easy access to the royal carriage? Some nobleperson must have played a part. Since the reign of the Valois boys, the threats to the sovereign had come from the nobles. So it seemed only logical to strip power from all the nobles (and any other parts of society) and centralize that power solely in the crown. This particularly made sense to the mothers of these kings and kings to be. These mothers, because of their husbands' murders (or sicknesses), found themselves following in Catherine de' Medici's footsteps and being regents to their young sons as they began their rule.

When Henry of Navarre was murdered, his son Louis was crowned king at only nine years old. His mother Marie de' Medici—Catherine de' Medici's distant cousin—became regent. When Louis XIII came of age, he found himself deep inside the swirling conflicts of the Thirty Years' War and the possibility of further civil war breaking out in multiple fronts. To combat this, Louis XIII resigned himself to pulling in the reins, centralizing power in the crown. This would be accomplished only after his death. Louis XIII and Anne of Austria struggled to have children. It took them twenty-three years of stillbirths before Louis XIV—who'd come to be known as the Sun King and the builder of Versailles—finally arrived. But when the boy did arrive, Louis XIII was not long for the world.

The boy was not yet five years old when he was crowned king of France. He was everything to his mother. He was a miracle and a treasure. Anne would do anything to protect her little Louis. Named regent, Anne sought to push the centralizing processes further. She achieved the creation of an absolutism for the crown. It was the only way to keep her treasured five-year-old boy-king safe. Leaning on the cunning and cruelty of Cardinals Richelieu and Mazarin (who made the Guise brothers seem tame), the crown took on supreme and absolute power. When Louis XIV came of age, he proclaimed that he—his own person—was France itself. What Louis wanted was what France wanted. What was good for Louis was good for France. There was no division between the two. The will of the people was nothing; the will of Louis everything. Louis was the law; this was his divine right.

But before this all came to be, the nobility made one last great, willful push, seeking to topple this absolutism and stop the centralization of power into the crown. It brought forth a new kind of civil war. The Thirty Years' War had just ended with the Peace of Westphalia. It had been over thirty embattled years since Henry of Navarre had been stabbed in 1610, and a hundred years of civil conflicts (and blood) between Catholics and Protestants in France. Now that the threats of religious civil war were dissipating, a new front of civil conflict had arrived. This time, it was not over religion but the place of the nobles, princes, and law courts (remember that Montaigne served these courts almost a hundred years earlier before retiring to his château). Louis XIV was ten years old, Descartes a year from death, and Pascal twenty-five when the nobility revolted in what's called the Fronde.

The Fronde were a brutal five years of blood and savagery. Lives were lost, but also decorum and civility. The crown and the nobles were supposed to be responsible for upholding a cultured and proper way of being in the realm. But there was no room for any of that inside the all-out battles of the Fronde. Instead, "boorish behavior . . . associated with rough aristocratic heroism" became glorified.[4]

Inside this vacuum Damien Mitton—a son of new money, a writer, and a friend of Pascal—published a piece called "Description of the Honest Man." And with it the Honest Dudes, the *honnêtes hommes*, were born. An *honnête homme* was to be everything a noble could not be, especially inside the Fronde. An *honnête homme* indulgently embraced the joys of life, living with ease. An *honnête homme* was cool as a moral style. And an *honnête homme* was always humane and helpful, always "sensitive to the misfortune of others."[5]

An *honnête homme* sought "to be happy, but in a way that lets others be happy as well. His curiosity is boundless, but he is circumspect and modest; his conduct is relaxed, sometimes even negligent, and he has no fantasies about knights in shining armor."[6] Many across France took on the style. Their inspiration was none other than Montaigne. Montaigne the ultimate, the original, *honnête homme*. The *honnêtes hommes* brought forth a revival of Montaigne. Sixty years after his death (that thirty- and sixty-year cycle thing strikes again), Montaigne was hot again in Paris and across France. Montaigne was seen as the master of this moral style that the *honnêtes hommes* hoped would "replace the rough tastes of the moribund warrior aristocracy whose unwillingness to go gently into that good night makes for nothing but useless tumult."[7]

Why Happiness Is Soulless

Blaise Pascal tried on this moral style of happiness sought by the means of skeptical nonchalance. It didn't fit.[8] Pascal discovered that it wasn't just misfit for him but for the human soul itself. Indeed, the moral style of

---

4. Henry A. Grubbs, *Damien Mitton (1618–1690): Bourgeois Honnête Homme* (Princeton: Princeton University Press, 1932), 57.

5. Grubbs, *Damien Mitton*, 57.

6. Benjamin Storey and Jenna Silber Storey, *Why We Are Restless: On the Modern Quest for Contentment* (Princeton: Princeton University Press, 2021), 51.

7. Storey and Storey, *Why We Are Restless*, 51.

8. Voltaire, who in the eighteenth century took on this style and mixed it with the Enlightenment, hated Pascal, doing what Voltaire was known for, "making fun" of him. Voltaire conceded that Pascal was a brilliant writer, but Voltaire found it deplorable that Pascal thought Montaigne was wrong in his commitment to nothing beyond.

the *honnêtes hommes* looked like a comfortable and fashionable jogging suit. But Pascal realized it was really a cruel straitjacket, a torture device that could never deliver on its promises of happiness. It could never do so because it failed to truly see what it means to be human. Montaigne and his *honnêtes hommes* forgot that "out of the crooked timber of humanity, no straight thing has ever been made."[9] The *honnêtes hommes* overlooked something essential. The style of the *honnêtes hommes* and all their Montaigne-inspired happiness seeking failed to recognize that the human being is not only a self but also a soul.[10]

A self, if it were only just a self, might find happiness and be nurtured through happiness, which is Montaigne's great revolution. Yet such an outlook forgets all about the soul and the things beyond, and it therefore doubles down on the self.[11] An inflated self crowds out soul and spirit, making happiness our great (only) end.[12] Happiness hunting becomes the air that fills the self, inflating it like a balloon.[13] But unlike a balloon, the

9. Isaiah Berlin attributes this quote to Immanuel Kant—though no one has been able to find the reference in Kant. See Berlin, *The Crooked Timber of Humanity* (Princeton: Princeton University Press, 2013).

10. Mark Edmundson says, "The Self seems to hunger for such transcendence. There is an allure to the states of the Soul." Edmundson, *Self and Soul: A Defense of Ideals* (Cambridge, MA: Harvard University Press, 2015), 50. Terry Eagleton continues these thoughts, saying, "Ludwig Wittgenstein remarks in his *Philosophical Investigations* that if you want an image of the soul, you should take a look at the human body. He means . . . the body in action rather than the body as object. Practice constitutes the body rather in the sense that, for Wittgenstein, the meaning of a sign is its use. The human body is a project, a medium of signification, a point from which a world is organized. It is a mode of agency, a form of communion and interaction with others, a way of being with them rather than simply alongside them. Bodies are open-ended, unfinished, always capable of more activity than they may be manifesting right now. And all this is true of the human body as such, regardless of whether it is male or female, white or black, gay or straight, young or old. One can see, then, why this particular view of the body is not much in vogue with the fans of human difference and the apologists for the cultural constructedness of things." Eagleton, *Materialism* (New Haven: Yale University Press, 2016), 36.

11. Eagleton adds an interesting thought: "Imagine someone ringing you up and asking, 'Is George there?' It would make sense to reply, 'Yes, but he's asleep,' but it would sound odd to say, 'Yes, but he's dead.' To say that George is dead is to say that he is not there; and for Aristotle and Aquinas the reason why he is not there is because his body is not there, even if the remains of it are." Eagleton, *Materialism*, 38.

12. Don't read "self" as material and "soul" as disembodied. The distinction is that the human being has both an immanent existence (self) and a longing for the transcendent (soul/spirit). We need something outside us to fulfill or save us—this is what is meant by "soul/spirit."

13. Marilyn Harran offers another way to think about self and soul. She says, "For Luther, Christian life involves constant struggle—and thereby conversion as contrition. . . . This life is a struggle between the *homo carnalis* and the *homo spirituatis*." Harran, *Luther on Conversion: The Early Years* (Ithaca, NY: Cornell University Press, 1983), 105.

self without soul/spirit has no limit in its need for happiness.[14] For a self without soul who denies the beyond, happiness becomes insatiable. For the inflated self, happiness never comes to complete fruition. Happiness never allows itself to be obtained. There is always more of it to reach for and to want. Happiness is a fickle friend, even a fiend. Torturously so, complete happiness never arrives and surely never stays.

The arrival of complete, never-ending happiness never comes because a human being is not just a self but also a creature of soul/spirit.[15] Soul can never be found and nurtured by happiness. Happiness never brings out soul. Montaigne himself is sure of this, because soul/spirit always has a dynamic of the beyond to it.[16] This beyond makes for something more important than the self, something morally higher than happiness. Montaigne wants us to deny the beyond, to forget our soul, so that we might make our self the receiver of all life, happy with the ordinary leisures of sleeping and dancing—even dying—inside immanent contentment. The *honnêtes hommes* affirm that the self is found and fed by the chasing of happiness alone. Philosopher Pascal Bruckner says powerfully, "Pascal rightly described as insane man's will to seek in himself the remedy for all his ills."[17]

A soul, on the other hand, is not found through happiness. The more that happiness is elevated and the self inflated, the more that the soul is eclipsed and the spirit lost. Happiness is nice; we should all want it. But we should recognize that happiness cannot generate or nurture soul. Therefore, it will leave us always discontent (in angst, as Kierkegaard

14. Montaigne, of course, considered limits to be central to his thought. There were epistemological limits, limits to what we could know. But there was no limit to our contentment, no point where happiness was too much. Montaigne is really modernity's father in the sense of heightening epistemology and apotheosizing happiness.

15. Terry Eagleton pushes these thoughts deeper, saying, "We are at odds with ourselves not because body and soul are naturally at odds, but because of the temporal, creative, open-ended animals that we are. . . . To speak of the soul is to denote the kind of body that is capable of signifying; and because there is no end to signification, we are unfinished creatures perpetually in process and out ahead of ourselves. To call ourselves historical beings is to say that we are constitutively capable of self-transcendence, becoming at one with ourselves only in death. Besides, as creatures of desire, we are continually split between what we possess and what we aspire to, as well as between what we consciously imagine we desire and what we unconsciously do." Eagleton, *Materialism*, 24.

16. Think of the essential place of suffering in soul music or even soul food. For instance, it is the experiences of suffering in the South, under slavery and Jim Crow, that draws out the soul.

17. Pascal Bruckner, *Perpetual Euphoria: On the Duty to Be Happy* (Princeton: Princeton University Press, 2000), 35.

teaches us, building off Pascal). Immanent contentment is possible—as an all-encompassing way of being—only if we are just a self and not also a soul or spirit. What Pascal saw is that the depth and resonance of the soul or spirit is bound not in the pleasures of happiness but in the long-ing (call it the suffering) for something beyond. When we are seeking and encountering what is beyond, we are really alive. But to meet this beyond we must deny the idolatry of happiness. Soul cannot be embraced by the happiness of the self in immanent contentment. Soul is discovered only through sorrow.

Of course, a soul can be enraptured by joy. But joy does not come upon the soul, blessing the self, through skepticism and happiness hunting that keeps us from yearning for the beyond. Instead, joy is tasted when we en-counter what is beyond. Joy finds the self pulled into what is beyond and other. Joy comes when the soul finds communion, and deepest union, in what is broken and lost (the doorway into the beyond). Joy is the self's experience of discovering new possibility out of impossibility, wholeness through brokenness, life through death. When the self confesses its need for something beyond to come as soul/spirit and minister to the self, joy comes. It is in need, not in happiness, that we find soul. Sorrow—never happiness—calls out to spirit and produces soul. When *honnêtes hom-mes* drive for a complete happiness that eliminates sorrow, by eclipsing the beyond, they by default dismiss soul and spirit.

Pascal came to see that the only way to avoid overinflating the self and in turn find soul—to get in touch with the depth of spirit—is in the dark. The sacramental can be encountered only in dark waters and in what is broken and poured out. Every mystic, or reader of mystics,[18] knows this. Pascal returns to this mystical proclivity (thanks to his sister, as we'll see in the next chapter). He returns to sorrow even after master-ing the rationalism of the numbers of the Copernican Revolution. Pas-cal discovered in his night of fire that we find soul through sorrow. By encountering the living God of Abraham, Isaac, and Jacob (not the gods

18. Luther, who read Johannes Tauler and the *Theologia Germanica* and was immersed in the Psalms, placed sorrow and suffering at the center of his theological imagination. All of Luther's theology is built around the *theologia crucis*. What I'm trying to do in this project is construct a view of evangelism that addresses our late-modern context by starting and concluding with the theology of the cross. I want to view evangelism from the place of the *theologia crucis*. Evangelism will need to be critiqued. But it must be critiqued on this level, with acknowledg-ment of the centrality of the theology of the cross.

of the philosophers), we find salvation. This God of Abraham, Isaac, and Jacob does something that no first principle, no distant controller of the laws of nature, can. This God of the patriarchs and matriarchs arrives and encounters us with a personal name, meeting us as a minister of consolation, embracing our sorrow. "Blessed are those who mourn, for they will be comforted," Jesus says in Matthew 5:4. Into barren wombs (Gen. 11), abandonment (Matt. 27), and slavery (Exod. 20), God arrives with the consolation of God's name and the promise of God's presence. That is how we are transformed.

But the story of Pascal's night of fire must wait until the next chapter, where we'll see how evangelism invites the self into soul. Before the next chapter, we need to discuss how the self and the soul are bound in happiness and sorrow. This will allow me to make my final points on why our times are so sad and why an evangelism of consolation is necessary in late modernity. Going a step or two further in this direction will also reveal why Renate is so stressed and needs the aid of eHelp.

Happiness's Evil Twin: Depression

Pascal discovered that finding the soul does not happen through the pleasure of the nonchalant (nor, as we'll see at the end of this chapter, through the "chalant" of late-modern protectors of what is okay). Montaigne may help us embrace our self—that's not all bad. But by attending so intently to the self—by refusing to lift or bow our heads in reverent search for the beyond—the self takes on too much weight.[19] With soul/spirit minimized and therefore eclipsed, the full burden of significance, purpose, meaning, and ultimacy must be carried by the self. Like a skinny middle schooler doing the flex arm hang, trying to hold his body weight above a bar, the self carrying this weight shakes with fatigue. The burden and weariness placed on the self is something Montaigne couldn't have anticipated (but he should have, as both French and German mystics in the Rhineland in

---

19. For a similar argument, see Ross Douthat, *The Decadent Society: How We Became the Victims of Our Own Success* (New York: Avid Reader, 2020). To give him some of my language, Douthat's point is that we've become so concerned about happy selves that we as a society have spun in on ourselves. We're making no significant leaps or bounds in advancement other than in the areas of entertainment and identity broadcasting. Douthat claims that the way out of the decadent spiral is to look down and up: to return to prayer and space. To look beyond.

the thirteenth and fourteenth centuries did, as did Luther in Montaigne's own century).[20]

This fatigue ironically opens the self to happiness's true opposite. Let's be clear, *sorrow is not happiness's opposite*. That's completely wrong. Sorrow is a different genus from happiness. Sorrow is existential. It is bound in bare limit and finitude. Sorrow exposes being.[21] Happiness is circumstantial.[22] It is produced by my actions or others' actions. Happiness can never reach to the depth of sorrow, can never expose being. Happiness is too locked in action to reach being.

Inside the era of the inflated self, we ask happiness to do what it cannot do. We assume that happiness can somehow overcome limits and surpass the finite. We believe happiness (and getting more of it) can solve the sorrow of our souls. We come to believe that happiness can reach the existential. The *honnêtes hommes*, inspired by Montaigne, thought so. Pascal was sure they were wrong. Happiness is not built for such depth—it cracks and leaks like a cheap watch on a deep dive. Happiness can (over) feed a self but never nourish a soul. Happiness *cannot* overcome limits and finitude. But happiness can try to cover it, like a blanket that's too small, to switch analogies. Our obsession with happiness can distract us for a time from our limitation and finitude.[23] That's not all bad. No one can place their existential limits at the front of their mind at all times and still function.

20. I'm thinking particularly of those from the Rhineland, such as the Friends of God and Meister Eckhart.

21. At least Heidegger believes so. Those who've read my earlier project will know I agree with this Heideggerian point. See particularly Andrew Root, *The Children of Divorce* (Grand Rapids: Baker Academic, 2010), chap. 3; and Root, *The Church in an Age of Secular Mysticisms* (Grand Rapids: Baker Academic, 2023), chap. 4.

22. Happiness is indeed circumstantial, but part of what gives happiness so much purchase in modernity is the sense that happiness can be secured and therefore freed from happenstance. Modernity comes to believe it can make what is circumstantial dependable and controllable. But happiness is a circumstance that is almost entirely uncontrollable. Modernity wants to control all things and even believes it can control enough circumstances that it can make happiness so dependable that it can become our moral horizon and therefore our reason for living. Without seeking control—without placing such a high value on control—no one would consider happiness an end worth living for. Modernity's ability and desire to control happiness has given happiness an inflated significance.

23. At one time ritual allowed for this. Ritual centralized the soul but in a way that kept the self from being crushed by the existential. With the loss of ritual, happiness has become the medicine for our existential terror. For more on ritual, see Byung-Chul Han, *The Disappearance of Rituals: A Topology of the Present* (Malden, MA: Polity, 2020).

Happiness and sorrow, as difference genuses, are not bound in an either-or rivalry. They are not engaged in a tug-of-war. That means happiness is not an evil but something we should embrace and welcome when it comes (it's just not worth vigorously chasing, assuming we need it like air for the self to breathe). Because the two are bound to self and soul, respectively, *happiness and sorrow can cohabitate*. Sorrow is not happiness's opposite. Despondency or depression is happiness's opposite.

Depression is an ailment of the self, not of the soul. Social theorists such as Alain Ehrenberg, Byung-Chul Han, and Zygmunt Bauman have shown that depression is an outgrowth of the (too) high importance we put on the self.[24] Soul can know acedia,[25] but only a self can be stricken by depression. Depression is an outgrowth of the late-modern loss of soul. Depression is an epidemic of late modernity and the result of our neoliberal capitalist epoch meeting Montaigne (and Rousseau).[26] When the self becomes inflated by its pursuit of happiness, when it is asked to carry the weight of all significance and all meaning, the peril to the self is fatigue. Depression and anxiety come, these theorists believe, from the fatigue of being yourself (*la fatigue d'être soi*).[27] Anxiety is the self's need to secure its own happiness (through the actions of its own performance). Depression arrives

24. See Alain Ehrenberg, *The Weariness of the Self: Diagnosing the History of Depression in the Contemporary Age* (Montreal: McGill-Queen's University Press, 2016); Byung-Chul Han, *The Burnout Society* (Stanford, CA: Stanford Brief, 2015); and Zygmunt Bauman, *Making the Familiar Unfamiliar: A Conversation with Peter Haffner* (London: Polity, 2020).

25. Acedia is an apathy to pray. It starts in the passivity, in a disposition to receive. Acedia is an unwillingness or inability even inside passivity to be open to receive. Depression is birthed from a different mother. It has no connection to passivity. Depression is the exhaustion of the performance of the self. It is connected to the need to do and not receive, to act and not be. Therefore, though they sometimes look the same, they are very different. See Kathleen Norris, *Acedia and Me: A Marriage, Monks, and a Writer's Life* (New York: Riverhead Books, 2008).

26. For more on this, see Root, *Church in an Age of Secular Mysticisms*, chaps. 2–3.

27. Michael J. Thompson adds, "But this anxiety is not simply experienced in the same ways as in past phases of mass society. Today, as the public realm shrivels, anxiety has increasingly become experienced as an internal dynamic of the self. Increased inequality and hierarchical forms of life only make the individual less significant, driving us inward rather than outward to deal with the sources of the anxiety. Now, as the cybernetic society throws up a screen of a perfectly working social order, the problems one experiences become viewed as a property of one's own defects. As a result, the anxiety eats away at the inner core of the self, it dissolves the struts for ego strength that could otherwise serve as a fulcrum for focused, critical awareness. This new kind of anxiety is caused by the degradation of anabolic social relations, by the weakening of the ties to others that once permeated a more robust civic world." Thompson, *Twilight of the Self: The Decline of the Individual in Late Capitalism* (Stanford, CA: Stanford University Press, 2022), 210.

when we cannot, even with our best efforts, match Montaigne and dance when we dance and sleep when we sleep. Depression comes when we're just too tired, muscles shaking like the middle schooler, to hold the weight of our self.[28] We come to assume (especially as late moderns living inside the neoliberalism of the social media of the third decade of the twenty-first century) that there is a performative, winning way to dance and even to sleep.[29] We come to figure that dances are for the many eyes of TikTok and sleeping habits are to be tracked and analyzed by our smartwatch.

The depression falls on us when we find that there is no meaning even in petting our cat or working in our garden, when those things produce no connection. That's what happens when all meaning is bound to the self. Without soul/spirit, cats and gardens in themselves do not draw us into otherness; they have no ability to call out to us and connect with us. When we are locked in the self, cats and gardens have significance only through the performance of the self. When the self is left to carry all the weight of significance, purpose, meaning, and ultimacy, we can name no other ultimate purpose in petting cats and keeping gardens other than to make our self happy. Inside such purpose, nothing from outside us—be it a cat or a garden—comes back to us or meets us at the level of spirit or reminds us of the fragility of time and the vulnerability of what we care for. Even beauty can be found and determined only within us. Beauty becomes taste, something I personally like or don't like.

28. William Davies adds, "Perhaps it is no surprise, then, that a society such as America's, which privileges a competitive individual mindset at every moment in life, has been so thoroughly permeated by depressive disorders and demand for antidepressants. Today, around a third of adults in the United States and close to half in the UK believe that they occasionally suffer from depression, although the diagnosis rates are far lower than that. Psychologists have shown that individuals tend to be happiest if they credit themselves for their successes, but not for their failures. This might sound like a symptom of delusion, but it is arguably no more delusional than a competitive, depressive culture which attributes every success and every failure to individual ability and effort." Davies, *The Happiness Industry: How the Government and Big Business Sold Us Well-Being* (London: Verso, 2015), 143.

29. Pascal Bruckner takes us deeper, saying, "Capitalism has ceased to be a system of production based on saving and labor and become a system of consumption that assumes expenditure and waste. A new strategy, which includes pleasure instead of excluding it, does away with the antagonism between the economic machine and our drives and makes the latter the engine of development. But above all, the Western individual has extricated himself from the straitjacket of the collectivity, from the first, authoritarian phase of democracies, and acquired full autonomy. Now that he is free, he no longer has a choice: since the obstacles on the road to Eden have vanished, he is 'condemned' to be happy; or, to put it another way, he has only himself to blame if he isn't." Bruckner, *Perpetual Euphoria*, 40.

Inside this inflation of the self, little can feed the soul because the soul has been eclipsed by the self's drives for happiness. We can't just dance, pet our cats, or garden because we must do it *rightly*. We must do it in such a way that we extract happiness from it, like blood from a stone. (Petting a cat and gardening have become instrumentalized and therefore need to be controlled—spirit is lost completely as these acts are made a controllable instrument for our happiness. They are justified as stress relievers or good exercise: instruments to benefit the self.[30]) This need to extract happiness from life leads us to seek all sorts of digital exemplars.[31] We need to follow those who know how to extract happiness from activity,[32] those who are (or at least present themselves as) ever happy.

But by following these exemplars, we end up feeling guilty because they use their talent and overall magnificence to get much more than we do out of petting cats, gardening, and dancing. This ironically makes us feel bad about our self. We wish our self were as talented and heroic as those we follow. In the end, we need to do better and go harder so we too can extract happiness from our activities. (See where anxiety comes from?) When we can't, when we lack the energy to keep extracting, we tumble into depression. Depression is the opposite of happiness—its opposite but also its nemesis that it can't live without. Since almost everything that makes up the self is to be found through happiness, depression always threatens. One comes with the other.

Why We're Not Okay

We're depressed because we become too tired from chasing the happiness that is supposed to deliver—through our own actions—significance,

---

30. Echoing the diagnosis of Hartmut Rosa in *The Uncontrollability of the World* (London: Polity, 2020).

31. An exemplar is not to be confused with an expert. Expertise is dead, replaced by exemplars, celebrities, and influencers. The influencer is the happy self who is able to extract happiness at every turn from the things before them.

32. Mark Edmundson drives this deeper, saying, "When the goals of the Self are the only goals a culture makes available, men and women will address them with the energy that they would have applied to the aspirations of the Soul. The result is lives that are massively frustrating and not a little ridiculous. People become heroically dedicated to middle-class ends—getting a promotion, getting a raise, taking immeasurably interesting vacations, getting their children into the right colleges, finding the best spot, fattening their portfolios. Lives without courage, contemplation, compassion, and imagination are lives sapped of significant meaning. In such lives, the Self cannot transcend itself." Edmundson, *Self and Soul*, 50.

purpose, meaning, and ultimacy. We can't find the connection to the world that we're supposed to have by way of immanent contentment. So we're not content. Ironically, we're too tired to be content—Montaigne has boomeranged on us. We're too anxious that we're doing something wrong, being the wrong kind of self, to ever find a happiness that can secure us. We're too exhausted from chasing likes and striving for the right way to dance and sleep, to truly dance and sleep. We're depressed because we're too tired to be happy, too exhausted from bearing the weight of our self's need to be special enough to win its own happiness. These are indeed sad times.

Inside this anxious depression, where our own actions have failed us and the soul is ignored, we state that we're "not okay." When we say we're "not okay," we mean that we're anxious, our self is fatigued, and depression is threatening. We mean that we've found that *none* of our actions have made us happy. We can only imagine that we will be put right by some (new) action that brings happiness. And yet we have no energy for that.

When Renate says she's "not okay," she is anxious and uneasy. She needs to perform some action to feel happy, but these actions fail to meet or pacify her sorrow. When she says she's "not okay," she means that her self is not in a place to be competent enough to hold up all the weight of significance, purpose, and meaning. She knows that for her self to hold this weight she must be happy and that this happiness is achieved by her activity. But all her acting has made her too tired to do any of her actions in a winning or competent way. She therefore is "not okay" to act. Not okay to compete and perform. Which means her very self is not okay.

Because soul is ignored, sorrow threatens the performance of the self.[33] With the death of her father, Renate is forced to confront real sorrow, and she is therefore taken to the existential level that demands soul. No strategies of the self to win happiness by affirmation or recognition can reach her soul. But she keeps trying with post after post.

33. William Davies adds, "One of the last remaining checks on the neurochemical under-standing of depression was the exemption attached to people who were grieving; this, at the very least, was still considered a not unhealthy reason to be unhappy. But in the face of a new drug, Wellbutrin, promising to alleviate 'major depressive symptoms occurring shortly after the loss of a loved one,' the APA caved in and removed this exemption from the DSM-V. To be unhappy for more than two weeks after the death of another being can now be considered a medical illness. Psychiatrists now study bereavement in terms of its possible health 'risks,' without any psychoanalytic or common sense of why loss might be a painful experience." Davies, *Happiness Industry*, 178.

Renate is now caught and enclosed in her self. She is not okay with her self, and yet her self is all she has. She has no one to take her into soul to bear the sorrow of limitations and finitude—not until AC Williamson tells her that the personhood of her father, which is irreducibly self and soul, needs a funeral. The part of his being that is soul demands the funeral. Renate's father needs a funeral because, though as a self he was miserable and mean, he nevertheless was also a creature of soul. Renate needs this reminder in the funeral liturgy to escape her own self and face the existential depth of her own soul. For this reason, a celebration of life, as opposed to a funeral, is deficient—and pastors should avoid them. A celebration of life is one last performance of the self—it is self-centered. A celebration of life avoids sorrow and therefore loses the spirit of being. A funeral entails directly walking with a community into sorrow. A funeral proclaims that soul meets a self. The funeral invites Renate into sorrow to discover a sacramental reality that happiness is too flimsy to hold. But Renate's desire to be happy deceives her into thinking that a funeral is not necessary—it would be too much of a downer. Renate fears that a funeral will just be way too stressful.

All the Pressure and All the Anger

Inside these frantic loops of seeking to be okay by chasing happiness and running from depression, we experience stress. If happiness's opposite is depression and if depression comes from the exhaustion of our actions, then stress becomes the self's great adversary. Stress is the self's most frightful enemy. Stress, by definition, is a felt pressure, tension, or strain. A seawall, for instance, is stressed by the pressure of the rising surf. A leg has a stress fracture because of the strain of the constant pressure of a foot hitting the pavement. A self is stressed when circumstances produce mental or emotional pressure and therefore create strain. This kind of mental and emotional pressure that produces stress is ubiquitous in upwardly mobile late-modern contexts. In these contexts, even eight-year-olds talk of being stressed out. Eight-year-olds come to feel an acute pressure pinching their young selves.

The first three decades of the twenty-first century have been stressful times because we feel constant pressure on the self coming from the self. We feel the pressure to extract happiness from our actions and for such actions to win recognition from others that confirms that we are indeed happy (welcome to Instagram).[34] Feeling this pressure within us, we've also met an external environment, in these first three decades, that has exacerbated these tensions. There are circumstances and people with whom we disagree—*those* people from *those* states or *those* politicians or *that* coworker or *that* family member—keeping us from the immanent contentment that we assume will make us happy. We are morally outraged. We respond to the infusion of stress on top of stress with anger, even hateful rage. People often respond with violence when additional pressure is heaped onto a load of pressure. Stress itself, after all, is a violent reality. Think of the pressure on that seawall: if the pressure is not released, the wall will implode. Adding stress to stress has produced many violent acts across the West (it would be wise to disarm our stressed society, which believes its bold actions are the only way to secure the self).[35] When stress is compounded, people struggle to handle their anger—X (formerly Twitter) is proof.

We are a deeply sad society that is so angry because we are stressed in our attempts to be happy selves. We blame (resent)[36] others who add to our stress by not making our lives smooth and content—as the *honnêtes hommes* want it.[37] Increasingly, videos on social media capture the fits of

34. For a poignant discussion of this dynamic of needing to win recognition, see Thompson, *Twilight of the Self*, 202–5.

35. Hartmut Rosa adds, "My argument is, rather, that modern society as such has been propelled not only by a dynamic of progress but also by a dynamic of loss, and indeed that it is haunted by the fear, rage, and trauma caused by loss. This dynamic should thus occupy a central position in any analysis of modernity. Loss refers to the disappearance of conditions or phenomena in the social world that are not quickly forgotten, but rather remain in focus. Losses are typically regarded as negative because of the emotional connection (identification, possession, etc.) that we have to what has been lost. Grief, in the broadest sense, is the emotion most often associated with loss, but it can involve other feelings as well, such as fear, anger, or shame. The experience of loss can be related to specific events or states of affairs (the death of a loved one, the end of a friendship, the destruction of things), or it can be related to abstract conditions (the loss of status, power, meaning, community, or control). Positive expectations can also be thwarted (a future loss), and an imminent loss can be anticipated (the fear of loss). What is important is that something does not objectively (so to speak) become a loss by disappearing. Such a disappearance can only become a loss through its negative interpretation and effect—that is, via the subjective or social experience of loss." Reckwitz and Rosa, *Late Modernity in Crisis*, 55.

36. Even creating *ressentiment*. For much more on this, see Andrew Root, "Pastoral Leadership Lessons from Bonhoeffer: The Alt-Right, the Twitter Mob, and *Ressentiment*," *Dialog* 59, no. 2 (2020): 82–92. See also Eva Illouz, *The Emotional Life of Populism: How Fear, Disgust, Resentment, and Love Undermine Democracy* (Malden, MA: Polity, 2023), chap. 3.

37. For more on this, see Pankaj Mishra, *Age of Anger: A History of the Present* (New York: Picador, 2017).

outrage on planes and in stores as people crack under the stress of meeting unsmooth environments. The people we disagree with, who therefore add stress to our lives, are insufferable because they keep us from the immanent contentment that is happiness. If happiness is all we live for, then telling someone online that they should die isn't just hyperbole. We mean it—at least at some level. We want all the sources of stress eliminated and evaporated from our self. We want (even demand) this so that our energy can be turned completely to inflating our self by extracting happiness from our activities. Only then can our self handle the stress and keep holding the weight of significance and meaning. Sources of stress must be eliminated so the self can avoid the fatigue that brings happiness's opposite—depression.

Here Comes the Stress, There Goes the Devil

We are all coping (even battling) *not* with temptation but with the pressure of stress. Stress is our great adversary. Stress is our late-modern Voldemort, our great Darth Vader. But that's not quite right. In the absence of soul and the beyond and inside the inflation of the self, what torments us is no longer personified—that would all be too connected to soul/spirit. What threatens us is not an agent like Voldemort who tempts or menaces us. The attention on our own agency has cropped out all possible agency in the realm of soul or spirit. The lurking of the devil, for example, is a staple of an imagination that knows it is soul/spirit and therefore wrestles with temptation. As we'll see in the coming chapters, for Martin Luther this spiritual temptation, what he calls his *Anfechtung*, is connected deeply with sorrow.

But the personification of evil in the devil who tempts us makes little sense to an imagination that knows only an inflated self and the desire for immanent contentment. The devil and temptations disappear from such imaginations. The devil and his tempting have no place in Montaigne's château. Montaigne exorcises the devil from our imagination by turning our heads to the château. Descartes does so by showing us the numbers.

The devil and temptation are replaced by stress—an internal, psychological pressure that produces tension and strain, making it impossible for the self to be happy. Stress becomes our new nefarious enemy because it renders impossible the immanent contentment of dancing, sleeping, petting cats, and gardening. Stress makes even the château no happy place. Stress makes it impossible for the self to simply work harder to extract meaning, purpose, and ultimacy out of the self's own honest and content actions. And too much unmanaged stress will produce the arrival of happiness's evil twin, depression.

We must suffer through temptation so we can find the righteousness of union with the holiness of a great beyond. Stress, however, must be managed so we can be happy with our self alone. Stress is our late-modern enemy because it poisons the nonchalant contentment that the *honnêtes hommes* and Montaigne wish for us. Stress attacks the self (not the soul or spirit) and it must be managed by our constant attention and concern. When stress becomes acute, we manage it with a guide we call a therapist or counselor.[38] It becomes important to make it convenient to get the help of this management from a therapist or counselor. If a self needs to see a therapist because of stress, it's essential that that process not add to the stress (much different from the soul of a novice who enters the cloister or who is directed by a master, where discomfort is key). eHelp and other convenience-based counseling services make complete sense inside this reality of the self and its battles with stress.

When soul/spirit is eclipsed by a self that is threatened by stress, temptation is ignored and the pastoral is also ignored. When our being wrestles with spirit and confronts temptation, we need a pastor to lead us into spirit and minister to us. But when everything is eclipsed by a self that needs to manage stress in the realm of the immanent, we discard the pastoral and instead seek a therapist (our pastors need to act like therapists now). When stress is our greatest threat, we see everything through the prism of the psychological (not the arcane mystery of being, not through Word and sacrament). The therapist becomes necessary, and the pastor an odd hanger-on from an antiquated age. And this psychologizing of everything affects more than just pastors. Every part of our society—because it deals with selves who are threatened by stress and seeking happiness—takes on

38. "The therapist was not particularly interested in the substantive content of what was inside us, nor in the abstract question of whether the surrounding society was just or unjust. The therapist is simply interested in making his or her patients feel better about themselves, which required raising their sense of self-worth." Francis Fukuyama, *Identity: Contemporary Identity Politics and the Struggle for Recognition* (New York: Profile Books, 2019), 103.

a therapeutic tone.[39] Teachers, politicians, salespersons, bureaucrats, even rock stars and celebrities, all need to take on the shape of a therapist.[40] They need to justify the operations of their vocation psychologically.

Sin Disappears, Stress Makes You Sick

Because we ignore our souls and therefore seem impervious to temptation and yet are susceptible to stress, we're threatened by sickness—or, better, mental illness—rather than sin. A soul is tempted by and does battle with sin; a self is stressed by and does battle with mental illness. As inflated selves who ignore soul, we, like Renate, avoid sorrow at all costs. Sorrow attacks contentment. As such, it threatens to push us into an acute sickness. Sorrow, because of its resultant stress, isn't good for our mental health. And yet sorrow is inextricable from being, for we are living souls/spirits. We cannot live or love without stress and sorrow. No wonder the younger generation is afraid of both.[41]

39. Fukuyama states, "The rise of the therapeutic model midwifed the birth of modern identity politics in advanced democracies" (*Identity*, 103). Eva Moskowitz adds, "Today Americans turn to psychological cures as reflexively as they once turned to God." Moskowitz, *In Therapy We Trust: America's Obsession with Self-Fulfillment* (Baltimore: Johns Hopkins University Press, 2001), 1.

40. Eva Moskowitz provides a helpful overview of this therapeutic turn, saying, "This philosophy is not, however, merely a perspective, a means of understanding the world, but a faith, a program for individual and social development. There are three central tenets to this 'therapeutic gospel.' The first is that happiness should be our supreme goal. Wealth, public recognition, high moral character—each of these achievements is held valuable only to the extent that it makes us happy. Success, in the final analysis, must be measured with a psychological yardstick. . . . The second tenet of our therapeutic faith is the belief that our problems stem from psychological causes. Problems that were once considered political, economic, or educational are today found to be psychological. . . . The third and final tenet of the therapeutic gospel is the most important, but it is so universally accepted, so seemingly self-evident, that we hardly notice its existence. This tenet is that the psychological problems that underlie our failures and unhappiness are in fact treatable and that we can, indeed *should*, address these problems both individually and as a society. This is the essence of the therapeutic gospel. It is practiced in every conceivable institution, from professional sports to prisons, from businesses to schools." Moskowitz, *In Therapy We Trust*, 2–3.

41. William Davies states, "Stress can be viewed as a medical problem, or it can be viewed as a political one. Those who have studied it in its broader social context are well aware that it arises in circumstances where individuals have lost control over their working lives, which ought to throw the policy spotlight on precarious work and autarchic management, not on physical bodies or medical therapies. In 2014, John Ashton, the president of the UK Faculty of Public Health, argued that Britain should gradually move towards a four-day-week, to alleviate the combined problems of over-work and under-work, both of which are stress factors." Davies, *Happiness Industry*, 274.

It's not surprising that the language of "sin" and discussions about sin-
fulness have all but disappeared in the West, while concerns about mental·
health and the effects of stress are ever-present (in chapter 4 we looked at
the ubiquitous language of trauma). Stress-borne mental illness is a much
different moral framework from one bound in the temptation of sin. In
the moral framework of stress-borne mental illness, sin is incomprehen-
sible. The self's happiness becomes so all-encompassing that soul/spirit is
ignored. Therefore, discourses about, and imaginations for, sin disappear.
Sin is no longer considered a threat because we've forgotten that we're soul.
Sin is a reality that eats soul and damns spirit. Sin is devasting to spirit.
It presumes that there is an otherness, a beyond, that we can act against
and violate. Therefore, we can malform our self by giving our self to a
spirit that corrupts our soul. For sin to be coherent, we need to assume
that the human being is both self and soul. But sin is eclipsed when soul is
ignored. When we assume we are only a self, our imaginations of sin are
lost and any discourse on that subject is considered harsh and backward.

Premodern people wrestled daily with sin. They needed public prayers,
practices of meditation, and a confessor to receive *rest*oration. Returning
to discourses of sin might not only name the dynamic of the soul within
us but, in turn, give us direct ways, outside ourselves, to bring forgiveness
and *rest*oration to the self. The *rest* in *rest*oration is not possible for an
inflated self that has eclipsed soul/spirit. We supposedly advanced late-
modern people have little imagination for sin, but we nevertheless sense
we're in a great battle. Our battle no longer takes place in the realm of
soul and spirit but is completely locked within the self. What menaces us
is not sin but stress. Montaigne fails us here.

If the self were not inflated to the point of eclipsing soul/spirit, stress
could be received as a gift, even an invitation into prayers and confession
of the beyond. Stress warns us that the wall or leg is about to give way—
and violently so. It must be shored up or rested. The wall or leg has met
its limit. But a self without soul/spirit is assumed to have no limit.[42] The
self is its own god. There is nothing beyond that limits the self. We will
tell an eight-year-old that if she works hard there are no limits to her
success and happiness. Once these words hit her being, she is baptized
into an enclosed immanent world of stress. The self must keep constantly

---

42. This discourse of limit points to Dietrich Bonhoeffer's discussion of sin in *Creation and
Fall: A Theological Exposition on Genesis 1–3* (Minneapolis: Fortress, 1997), 85–90.

extracting its own purpose, meaning, and ultimacy from its own actions of performance to create significance for itself. Stress can be a sign that you need to stop or rest, but if you can never stop pursuing happiness, stress can never be a welcome (if painful) message.

Stress is inevitable, and it is a great warning for the self. A self who must extract happiness from all its activities, absent spirit, will inevitably feel the tensions and strains of the demands of winning this happiness. Achieved happiness—and it is an achievement—cannot escape the strains and tensions of performance. This achievement substantiates the self. Stress is inevitable because the self is so weighty, and by its own power, the self must hold its chin above the bar of happiness. Eventually, the stress of holding that weight above the bar will create a piercing fatigue. There is no way around this. All performers feel the stress of competition and review. Stress is a warning. If you bear too much stress, you'll be injured. Therefore, as selves in a late-modern world, we are always watching out for stress, even policing those who push selves into stress.

The Stress Police with Their Badges of "Not Okay"

Stress's effects on mental health have become our (sole) moral framework. It tends to be a moral framework without the beyond of soul. All moral frameworks must shape our imaginations and be practiced (they shape our imaginations by being practiced). And because a moral framework is always practiced in a social context, it must be policed, either firmly or lightly. Like inquisitors in the fifteenth or seventeenth centuries—who believed they were protecting Europe from sin—a class of late-modern examiners has arisen, mostly online, who police the moral framework of stress-borne mental illness.

These high-minded police are the *honnêtes hommes* of the twenty-first century. Their power rests in their chalance, the intensity of their earnest sincerity. Inside this earnest and sincere chalance—never nonchalance— they do their dogged policing of this moral framework in two ways.

First, they oppose all stigmas. Never stigmatize anyone. The mission of this class of moral police, these elite *honnêtes hommes*, is to tear down all stigmas. No self can be happy or escape the threat of stress if the self must confront stigmatization. If stress threatens us all, and if stress is the source of mental strife, then no one should be looked down on for being sick. There is no shame in sickness. You wouldn't blame someone for getting cancer. In the same way, you shouldn't blame someone for being anxious or depressed. (The assumption here is that sin entails blame, while sickness is blameless—though we never live this out purely.)[43] Anxiety and depression might be bound in the actions of the self's pursuit of happiness, but what makes a self sick is stress.

Even Will, the CEO who fired Renate, recognizes this axiom. Will demands that the HR department help manage his employees' stress, giving him and the company a moral high ground. Will combats mental strife with wellness. The company will not stigmatize mental illness. But Will can't stomach the sorrow of spirit that has no medication or interventions to fix it.[44] Sickness has treatment plans; sorrow, being soulful/spiritual, calls for the noninstrumental companionship of friendship (of ministry). Responding to sorrow is so counterlogical that Mary Ann wonders whether she's breaking HR protocol when she invites Renate into this friendship by offering to walk with her.

If all moral shortcomings are bound to sickness, as opposed to sin, then no one can judge—other than a therapist or the many pseudotherapists who diagnose constantly (meaning, we judge all the time through rapid armchair diagnoses that avoid stigma but allow for acute judgment). Having a diagnosis can even be empowering. You're not a jerk; instead, you just have an anxiety disorder and are on the spectrum. If it were sin, that would demand that you find restoration with the wounded and

43. We try to make sickness blameless and we think it is. But we can't help blaming people for their chosen actions. After all, the self is made happy by the self's own actions. So while the self should not be shamed for getting sick, a self could have made better choices, such as exercising or managing stress with meditation apps. We know we should not stigmatize, but we nonetheless heap guilt onto the one stressed. We can't avoid it because it's embedded within this anthropology of being happy selves who get this happiness by way of action. In the end, if the self doesn't have happiness, it's nobody's fault but the self.

44. Davies explains, "The science of stress was of the utmost importance for managers worrying about the depletion of their workforce. It became one of the main preoccupations of the human resources profession, who sought out rudimentary wisdom on a wide panoply of 'bio-psycho-social' complaints. The sheer breadth of contributory factors to stress—some tangible, others intangible—made it extremely difficult to achieve any control over it. This is in addition to the graver psychosomatic risks faced by those in precarious jobs, who move in and out of work, without even managers to support them from one month to the next. One conclusion to draw from this would be, as per the occupational health studies of the 1960s, that the fundamental politics of work had grown dysfunctional and needed a more wholesale transformation, and not simply piecemeal medical treatment. But would this be the lesson that was learnt?" Davies, *Happiness Industry*, 134.

seek forgiveness. But no, it's the wounded who need to apologize to you, because you are the one with a diagnosis that they aggravated. Because all selves battle stress and because stress causes mental illness, no mental illness should be stigmatized. In the end, no action that the self takes to be happy, as long as it really makes the self happy, should be looked down upon or stigmatized.

This class of police of the new *honnêtes hommes* will watch people's language very closely, because stigmatization lives in words and labels. A stigma is itself a language game. There is no forgiveness or restoration inside such violations, only punishment. These are the great inquisitors after all. Getting retribution for a violation is an amazingly effective stress reliever.

Second, these new *honnêtes hommes* police this moral framework by calling out actions, situations, and occurrences in individuals and institutions that cause or add to the stress on a self. It's "not okay" for an institution or individual to take an action that adds to a self's stress, for the self is perceived to be vulnerable. Even welcomed policy changes that may take time to work out are ruled "not okay." Progress is not celebrated if it even remotely causes some stress to a self. Eliminate all stress now! Stress places a franticness on our *right now*. Someone must be fired because of the stress this is causing particular selves. Forget due diligence, for the stress bearing down on vulnerable selves must be relieved immediately. A lecturer must be canceled and expunged from all communication, because even the *thought* that this lecturer will be on campus (even with each self's freedom and choice to attend the lecture or not) is too much stress, creating an unsafe environment for immanent contentment. There is urgency because otherwise the stress may dissipate and the moral high ground disappear. If we don't do something *now* and condemn whatever is adding stress, then we risk thrusting a stressed self into a dangerous illness. That illness may attack a self such that the self will become a threat to itself (e.g., suicide risk, self-harm). These twenty-first-century *honnêtes hommes*, who police this moral framework of stress, speak out not for themselves (though they do, of course—for their audience) but for all vulnerable and stressed identities that they determine to be in danger.

"Not okay" becomes a moral rebuke to those who add stress to a vulnerable self, because stress can bring mental illness and render someone so unhappy that they become miserable. So miserable that they come to hate their self. Nothing could be more dangerous in a world without soul than for you to hate your self. It would mean that you could find no purpose or meaning. You would tumble into a depression that could lead the self to despise its own self and take on a terrible action.

Such rebuke from these new *honnêtes hommes* indicates that a person's or institution's actions are wrong because they attack another self's ability to dance and sleep, to find immanent contentment, to be happy. The actions are deemed violations ("not okay") not because they are sinful but because they impose stress (rebuttals to the new *honnêtes hommes* consider this to be weakness—consider the pejorative "snowflake").[45] Stress threatens a self—even with annihilation. Policing stress now holds significant cultural power and importance.

Pascal and the New *Honnêtes Hommes*: A Summary

This new class of twenty-first-century *honnêtes hommes* are Montaigne's children: they glorify the self and yearn for the château. But they feel themselves to be at war (they serve as shock troops in the culture war). Because of that, they have no nonchalance. There can be no contentment in their immanence. In the absence of soul, the self carries too much weight to ever be as cool or content as Montaigne wants or as *honnêtes hommes* desire.

Pascal finds the original *honnêtes hommes* to be soulless because they have no way to deal with sorrow and sadness other than to go to war against sorrow and sadness. Ironically, a society full of *honnêtes hommes*, seeking their happiness in the moral style of Montaigne's immanent contentment, comes to be deeply and existentially sad. They come to fear the dark, even deny their finitude. Their attention is so fully fixed on dancing and sleeping, and getting affirmation for it, that they're unable to meet the real demands of living. Ultimately, their living, even their dancing and sleeping, Pascal believes, becomes too flat and soulless to be true and beautiful. Too flat and soulless to be sacramental.

The first three decades of the twenty-first century have delivered the return, in late-modern form, of the *honnêtes hommes*. Since the end of the 1990s and early 2000s we've moved headlong into the moral style

45. This has helped birth the neo-Nietzscheans. For more on this, see Andrew Root, *The Church in an Age of Secular Mysticisms* (Grand Rapids: Baker Academic, 2023), chaps. 6–7.

of *honnêtes hommes* and the immanent contentment of being all-out beyonder-denying happiness-seekers. Renate is one example.

Renate was a successful *honnête homme*. Will excitedly hired her because she was a gatekeeper. She platformed the style in her writing and Instagram reels. But now she stands alone in her sorrow. The other *honnêtes hommes* have no imagination for joining her sorrow because they have no visions inside their moral policing for such actions that enter the dark for the sake of living in the dark (there is no soul or spirit to find there).

When things get bumpy and the self is in need, the moral style of late-modern *honnêtes hommes* seems to produce not communion but only stress. Stress is the crisis the self bears when it has lost its soul and when happiness as immanent contentment becomes its only end. Being *okay*, as opposed to being *transformed*, becomes the highest good. Therapy becomes the spirituality of immanent contentment that assists the self in coping with the stress to become okay enough to be happy.

It's important to say that, like other forms of medical intervention, therapy is necessary and good. My above comments shouldn't be read otherwise. But if, over the course of a decade or two, cardiologists were proliferating, starting apps that allowed consumers to quickly and conveniently relieve stress on their hearts, we would wonder what in our environment is putting people at risk. We wouldn't just reframe heart disease as a good, pushing back at people for stigmatizing it. We would ask where all this risk is coming from. Are the diagnostics and interpretations of this risk correct? Or is there something else going on?

For the late-modern *honnêtes hommes*, if you're not okay, you are under stress. Being under stress means you have poor or at-risk mental health. Will's athletic apparel company's mission affirms that a self needs to be healthy. A healthy self can be a happy self because it is dealing with, overcoming, stress. A soulless self becomes obsessed with health because there is nothing beyond the self to be concerned with other than being fit enough to ward off all darkness and running fast enough to reach the contentment of achievement.

To Evangelism and the Pivot of This Project

To follow Pascal as we have (and will continue to do in the next chapter) leads us to ask some important questions about evangelism. For instance, is evangelism an invitation to find a religion that helps a self manage its stress and therefore be happy? Is this called "being saved"? Or is evangelism, at its core, the invitation into soul/spirit? Does evangelism speak the language of the self and its happiness? Or should evangelism speak the language of the soul and its sorrow? Ultimately, can transformation, inaugurated by the Holy Spirit, happen without soul?

Many Protestant forms of evangelism have conceded to the *honnêtes hommes* and the happiness-hunters. These forms of evangelism have fallen into the trap of a soulless self. Therefore, the sacramental dynamic of the infinite encountering the finite has been lost in sales pitches and strategies of influence. The temptation in these sad and stressful times is to mold evangelism in the shape of the market. We're tempted to claim that the Christian story can produce true happiness and freedom from stress (both mainliners and evangelicals make this claim). Being a Christian, going to church, or believing certain doctrinal propositions can solve the problem of sadness. But this risks an evangelism that strips away the Christian confession of soul/spirit. To keep soul/spirit and therefore to enter the sacramental, sorrow must be embraced. Particularly in our time, where rituals and symbols have lost the enchantment of spirit, sorrow remains the open door into soul and the spirit of the sacramental.[46]

Pascal has helped us take our final steps in understanding our sad times, and he will help us take our first new steps in this project. He has helped us claim that our time is indeed sad (and stressful). Pascal has shown us that the ways of *honnêtes hommes* are too bound to an inflated, and thus weighted, self. The weight of having to continually act to be happy has made us stressed, opening us to acute anxiety and depression. Our late-modern, chalant *honnêtes hommes* are bound to be deeply sad as they work so hard to be happy fighting against stress. They are bound to be sad because they live without soul.

This is our first step forward, and it will take us directly into Pascal's story. The only way into soul is through sorrow. A sacramental evangelism that brings people before a living God, and not just a form of religion, will need to follow the way of the cross, not the markets of the self. We will need to follow this way into Mary's own sorrow (John 19) and Jesus's

---

46. Pascal Bruckner says powerfully, "In short, Western societies dared to rebel against their own traditions by responding to pain not with the consolations of the beyond but with the improvement of this world." Bruckner, *Perpetual Euphoria*, 30.

cries from the cross (Matt. 27).[47] Here in this fire, Pascal believes, we can find the spirit of life, the very soul of salvation.

We turn now from descriptions of sadness and the need for consolation to the topic of sorrow and the sacramental world that consolation opens for the human being to encounter the divine. Evangelism seeks to invite the world into this real encounter with the Spirit of Christ ministering to our soul.

■ ■ ■ ■

"This was a bad idea," Renate thought to herself as she sat in an empty VFW hall. The room smelled. A musty oldness covered with a pink perfume mixed with a faint whiff of stale beer. The odor made her slightly nauseous. Or was the cause of the nausea the fact that no one had come? It was just Renate, an urn of her father's ashes, AC Williamson, and Pastor Manta. Two minutes before the funeral, only the people taking part in the service were present.

Renate's anxiety spiked as she thought about what it meant that no one was coming. She knew this would happen. She knew she wasn't okay enough to deal with the stress of failing at her father's funeral. She even became angry at AC for talking her into it. "That man needs a funeral," she annoyingly replayed in her mind, rolling her eyes as she remembered his words. Because of AC she decided to have her father's funeral in San Diego, with the promise that Pastor Manta would officiate. AC and Myrtle Halverson had promised that "the church will show up." Renate had no idea what that meant. But sitting in an empty hall, she was so sad she was angry.

"I don't even believe any of this garbage!" Renate thought to herself in frustration. She was like her father. At eighteen, Renate's dad left for

47. "Whence the inevitable attraction to pain in Protestant, Orthodox, and Catholic Christianity, a very real concern for the suffering that is accompanied by an attraction to unhappiness. 'Christ taught us to do good by suffering and to do good to those who suffer.' This explains the need to seize upon the suffering of others, as if one's own were not enough (thus the Polish clergy's attempt to transform Auschwitz into a modern Golgotha, or the solicitation for souls in which, according to some journalists, Mother Teresa engaged in her hospices in Calcutta, however great her merits may be in other respects). Or again the pronounced taste for martyrdom, dismembered bodies, and the obsession with carrion and decay in a certain kind of Christian art, the accent being put on the body's excremental nature, and finally the aesthetics of torture and blood in the mystics. Few religions have emphasized human filth as much as this one or shown such a 'sadism of piety.'" Bruckner, *Perpetual Euphoria*, 22.

Desert Storm, a twice-a-week church choirboy going to war. He returned wounded six months later, never again darkening the door of any church. Renate wanted to honor that reality by having the funeral at the VFW. But now she regretted that too. She regretted it all, thinking to herself, "This was so stupid. I knew, I just knew, this was a bad idea."

6

The Math Savant and the Fire

Pascal and the Promise of Our Sad Souls

Mary Ann and about twenty people streamed in just as the funeral was about to start. A stoplight had gone out, Mary Ann announced, causing traffic to move to a crawl. When the opening hymn started, there were about thirty people in the room. Renate's frustration melted into gratitude as she experienced something she'd never felt before: a deep sense of being carried.

Glancing around the room, Renate noticed no one from work—except Mary Ann, of course. No one from any of her wellness networks. None of her supposed friends. She had posted the funeral details on her socials, but no one came. Not even her sister or brother made it. The thirty attendees were mostly strangers from the church with a sprinkling of familiar faces. These strangers and slightly familiar faces were here because, as AC said to Renate, "We follow Jesus into sorrow. Where there's sorrow, we go. That's what we do." The faces Renate did recognize were connected to the Bible study or the Swedish Death Cleaning Team. Renate waved to Hazel Curran and Myrtle Halverson.

Seeing Myrtle made Renate cry. Such warmth came into Renate's body that she couldn't help it. The tears just appeared and flowed. Myrtle oversaw the Swedish Death Cleaning Team. She was everything Renate wasn't. Myrtle personified something Renate was trying to keep her readers from becoming. Myrtle was a late-fifties, rural-living, fast-food-eating, Walmart-shopping red voter in a blue state who had never been on a plane or seen a yoga mat. Myrtle wasn't into wellness, but she had soul.

Amid organizing and moving Renate's dad's stuff, Renate and Myrtle had many long conversations. About what specifically, Renate can't remember. Not because these conversations weren't important, but because they just were so natural, so in the moment, so meaningful. Myrtle never gave advice or tried to teach Renate something. She was just with her. In those moments of being truly present with Myrtle, Renate felt for the first time like she could really mourn. When she did, Myrtle comforted her with just her presence. Myrtle accompanied Renate through all the big and small decisions around her father's stuff. Pastor Manta always considered this caring, this entering sorrow, to be evangelism. Such caring made a case for faith by giving a direct experience of the ministry that is the faith. Renate did not realize how deeply it had touched something within her until she saw Myrtle again. Myrtle smiled at Renate from across the room, and she felt something reach for her, reminding her of the companionship she'd felt and the invitation she experienced to mourn and to be held and known.

As Renate turned to the front to hear AC read Scripture, she began to cry. She cried throughout the rest of the service. For the first time in a long time, Renate did not stop herself or try to stand outside of herself and look at herself to ask, "Am I doing it right? Is this what I'm supposed to be doing? Do I look stupid?" All the anxious sense of being watched, needing to perform, disappeared. Renate just cried, feeling held by these people. By Myrtle. By Hazel. By Mary Ann. By AC.

Renate allowed her being to slide into her sadness. As she did, she felt a sense of being bound, connected like a rock climber to a belayer. Renate was bound to these people who had entered her sorrow. She had an odd sensation that they were now tied together, that she was inside a greater story, some good news embodied by these people. Renate barely knew them, but something now beautifully entangled them. Renate felt like she could let go and spill into that sorrow, knowing she was upheld. For the first time, Renate felt like she had been opened to seek what might meet her in the sorrow. She no longer feared the dark. Was there something beyond her that could encounter her in this sorrow? She was open to see. As she slid into this sorrow, a presence met her and loved her. She met Jesus Christ. This was an event of evangelism. But the point was never to crassly evangelize Renate, giving a transfusion of one's interests to another, winning her attention and commitment. The point was to share in her sorrow. Inside this shared sorrow, the sacrament of Jesus's ministering presence was encountered, drawing her through the community's ministering practices to the presence of Jesus Christ.

Pastor Manta named this presence. He preached from the text that AC had read, Matthew 5:3–13:

> Blessed are the poor in spirit, for theirs is the kingdom of heaven.
> Blessed are those who mourn, for they shall be comforted.
> Blessed are the meek, for they shall inherit the earth.
> Blessed are those who hunger and thirst for righteousness, for they
>   shall be satisfied.
> Blessed are the merciful, for they shall obtain mercy.
> Blessed are the pure in heart, for they shall see God.
> Blessed are the peacemakers, for they shall be called sons of God.
> Blessed are those who are persecuted for righteousness' sake, for
>   theirs is the kingdom of heaven.
> Blessed are you when men revile you and persecute you and utter
>   all kinds of evil against you falsely on my account. Rejoice
>   and be glad, for your reward is great in heaven, for so men
>   persecuted the prophets who were before you.
> You are the salt of the earth; but if salt has lost its taste, how shall
>   its saltness be restored? It is no longer good for anything except
>   to be thrown out and trodden under foot by men.

That made no sense to Renate. She'd never read the Bible. She couldn't remember ever hearing even one verse—other than reading memes on social media that used the Bible to support some position Renate despised. As AC read the verses, it was all lost on Renate. She actually didn't even know it was a reading from the Bible. When they planned the service, AC and Pastor Manta had told Renate that there'd be a reading from Matthew. She thought it was a book of poems or something. If Renate had known, she would have refused. The last thing she wanted was her father's funeral—that she was reluctant to have in the first place—to become some weird religious crusade for the purpose of conversion.

But Pastor Manta would never have allowed that. To do so would be to instrumentalize someone's grief. It would turn sorrow into a device, not something sacramental. Pastor Manta considered sorrow too sacred for it to be used for anything other than the ministry of the Spirit who brings comfort and new life.

Pastor Manta preached on being "blessed." "What does it mean to be blessed? Usually we think of hashtag #blessed on social media," he said.

This caught Renate's attention. She was one of the first media people to write about the hashtag. She even used it before it became cool, and then no longer cool, to do so. If you looked back through Renate's socials, you'd see the hashtag after posts about her cruising on a yacht, vacationing in the Florida Keys, or dining at one of New York's top restaurants. It was humblebrag for sure.

Pastor Manta continued, "When we use #blessed we often mean all the good things that have come from our hard work. It's the spoils of what our talent has earned, like a quarterback or musical artist who thanks God after winning the Super Bowl or a Grammy. But that's not what Jesus means here. Look at who Jesus calls blessed. The poor, the meek, the merciful, the peacemakers, the persecuted. These aren't people who *do* something but people who stop and *receive* something. They are blessed because they're given a gift, and like Jacob who wrestled with God in Genesis 32, they are blessed with the gift of God's real presence."

Pastor Manta paused. Then, looking at Renate, he continued, "We're here today because 'Blessed are those who mourn, for they shall be comforted.' Let me say that again, 'Blessed are those who mourn, for they shall *be* comforted.' By whom? Who is going to do this blessing of comforting? By us in this room? No. None of us in this room have the power to bless. I don't. Even as a pastor I don't have the power in myself to bless anyone. No, all of us are mourners here. We mourn with you, Renate. You're not alone. Renate mourns a great loss. We, the people of God, mourn with her because she mourns. Because we too have known great mourning."

Pastor Manta turned toward the urn that held Renate's father's ashes and said, "And we know that Mr. Medlam mourned. Like all of us, he had hurts and wounds. Pain from war and life afterward. He loved—it was hard for him, but he loved—and therefore he mourned. He gave and he lost; he loved and he hurt. And Jesus saw it all. Today Jesus calls him blessed, for though it was so hard for him in this life to find comfort, Jesus promises to give him just that. We remember his mourning. In memory, we embrace his life today and mourn its loss. We all know what it is to mourn, don't we?"

Pastor Manta paused again and bent his knees a bit as he always did right as he came to a point of proclamation in a sermon. "But we know that Renate and Mr. Medlam are blessed—by Jesus himself—when they mourn, because we know something else, don't we? We know that Jesus is the great comforter. His comfort changes us all. The mourning of God in the death of Jesus becomes the very place where all sorrow is turned into a feast. We are salt because we join sorrow and believe there is a blessing there—God's presence. This is not the blessing of a new car, not the blessing of rewards, but the blessing of God's name, of God's presence, of Jesus's comfort. We are the salt that preserves sorrow and grief from the decay of abandonment and isolation. We enter sorrow because those who mourn, like Renate, are blessed. They are near to God. We don't bless them, we hold them, so that they can enter sorrow and be met by the One who cares for them and blesses them. We're just salt protecting sorrow from rot. We are the salt that joins sorrow because we know—from our own sorrow—that God is with the brokenhearted. We know that today God is with Renate. That Mr. Medlam's sorrow has brought him into the arms of Jesus. Amen!"

Pastor Manta paused one last time and said, "This is our great peace. Now, like salt at a table, let's pass it. Let's pass this peace. Peace not as a pause from our sorrow but as the reminder that we are present with one another, with Renate, in this sorrow. May the peace of God's presence in sorrow come to all who mourn. May it be for you, Renate. May the peace of Christ be with you all."

"And also with you," the room responded in unison.

Everyone stood and offered each other peace. They came one by one to Renate, passing her the peace of Christ, who blesses all who mourn. Each person touched Renate's elbow or grabbed her hand, looked her in the eye, and said, "The peace of Christ *is* with you." It was a form of care and an encounter with something that Renate had never known. She was sure, for the first time in her life, of God's presence, God's embrace, and Jesus's nearness. Maybe it was just collective effervescence or a psychological longing or the voodoo of the liturgy. Maybe. But Renate experienced something true and beautiful, something that ministered to her. This funeral that she'd resisted was the manifestation of these people's embrace. Inside this salty embrace she found something transcendent and redemptive in the sorrow. She was inside the good news. The darkness was indeed dark, but there was a presence of peace within that called her name.

■ ■ ■ ■

The last person to approach Renate leaned in awkwardly, not knowing the words everyone else was using, and said, "Renate, I'm so sorry."

When Renate saw her face, she did a double take. "Cynthia?" she said, astonished.

Cynthia was one of Renate's close friends in high school. They'd lost track of each other almost immediately after high school. Renate hadn't even thought about Cynthia for a decade. Renate couldn't believe she even recognized her. Especially because Cynthia was pregnant.

"I hope it's okay I came," Cynthia said with a cringe of unease.

"Of course," Renate said.

"I saw your post. I live in Orange County now. Husband, with a baby on the way," Cynthia added, pointing to her ballooned stomach.

Renate smiled back, as if the baby on the way wasn't obvious. Renate was shocked but happy.

"This was really beautiful. I'm glad I was here," Cynthia added. "I remember your dad from sleepovers and our senior trip. I just felt like I should come."

"Thank you," Renate said with a deep sense of appreciation. Her dad chaperoned that senior trip and used to make cookies for her friends at sleepovers. She'd forgotten all that. She'd forgotten he was more than a miserable man in a recliner, using his anger to keep him from mourning. She'd forgotten that right after her mom left, her dad was very involved, doing everything for her and her siblings. He'd dropped her older sister off at college, coached her younger brother's basketball team, and helped her prepare for her driving test. Inside the two decades of his decline into misery, she'd never thought about how hard it was for him to raise three teenagers suddenly by himself. Renate's mom left the day after her sister's high school graduation. Pastor Manta was right. He was in mourning! Renate was thankful that Cynthia reminded her of all that her dad had carried.

The Mozart of Math

Étienne Pascal, Blaise's father, carried a weight of tragedy similar to that of Renate's father. When Blaise was just three years old, his mother died. It was not unusual for mothers (or anyone really) to die at that time in France. But its regularity didn't minimize the pain. When Antoinette Begon Pascal died, she left Étienne to care for little Blaise and his older and younger sisters on his own. Étienne never slid into being one of *les misérables* (the miserable ones), but it wasn't easy.

Étienne centralized everything in the family, as Louis XIII did with the crown at the time. The family became its own kingdom with high walls, and Étienne himself set the rules and ethos. Even so, Étienne was not so much Louis XIII or Louis XIV as he was Henry of Navarre. Étienne centralized things in his family like the two Louis did the crown, but Étienne ruled with the benevolent spirit of Henry, taking on a perspective that resembled Montaigne's.

When the family moved to Paris, Étienne took control of his children's, particularly Blaise's, education. He was convinced that the best way to educate young Blaise and his sisters was in an open, child-centered manner. He allowed Blaise's own interests to direct his learning. As Benjamin Storey and Jenna Silber Storey point out, such an approach reflected that of Montaigne's essay "Of the Education of Children."[1] Education should feel like an exploration of the self in the château. But ultimately Étienne was a man of the new science (the new philosophy, as it was called) more than that of the Renaissance humanism of Montaigne. Étienne was very into math. Moving the family to Paris, Étienne connected with the cutting-edge minds of the new philosophy. He was even invited into their conversations.

But though Étienne himself may have moved past the Renaissance humanism of Montaigne, he still thought it was the best curriculum for his homeschooling of Blaise. Therefore, math was outlawed, at least until an appropriate age. Math was verboten until Latin and Greek had been mastered. Étienne himself was drawn to the new philosophy of Descartes and his numbers, but his son would first be made in the image of Erasmus

1. Michel de Montaigne, "Of the Education of Children" (1580), trans. Charles Cotton, ed. Patrick Madden, *Quotidiana*, accessed April 24, 2024, http://essays.quotidiana.org/montaigne/education_of_children.

before exposing the boy to any theorems—let alone Descartes and the new science.

But it's hard to keep true genius in its bounds. And Blaise Pascal was the Mozart of math. That kind of pure genius cannot be caged.

At about the same age that Blaise was when he moved to Paris, Wolfgang Amadeus Mozart was being taken from his Salzburg home to play his violin for royalty across Europe. Little Mozart was even taken to Paris to play for King Louis XV of France. Mozart's father, Leopold, was both similar to and starkly different from Étienne Pascal. Like Étienne, Leopold took responsibility for his son's training and education. But unlike Étienne's approach, when Wolfgang's gifts were spotted, he was taken to the world to perform his talent for European crowns in concert halls. Étienne instead kept Blaise always close, always inside the family. Mozart was one of the first child superstars. Blaise was never really given that chance. But where music came as an almost natural reflex to Mozart, so did math to Blaise Pascal.

The math of the new philosophy surrounded Blaise, but he wasn't allowed to listen and was forbidden to play it. Latin lessons took precedence. Frustrated and annoyed at the age of eleven, and having picked up the slightest murmurs of conversations on the topic, Blaise went to his room and figured it all out for himself. With no training and not one lesson, eleven-year-old Pascal did advanced geometry. He derived Euclid's thirty-second proposition from pure intuition. Not even Mozart could learn like that. Even Mozart had to be taught where to put his fingers on the piano and how to move the bow on the violin. Blaise could do the new philosophy by sheer instinct. His was pure genius, a divine bestowing.

What followed for Blaise was not royal palaces and concert halls but a coming out nonetheless. Marin Mersenne was the unofficial Parisian dean of the new philosophy. Mersenne created gatherings for discussions of the new ideas born from the new science of mathematics. Étienne was a member of the Mersenne club. After discovering Blaise's unusual erudition, Étienne did two things. First, he allowed direct instruction in math to join the Latin and Greek lessons. Étienne himself would teach the boy this new math. Second, he took Blaise to the gatherings of the proprietors of the new science. Étienne needed confirmation that Blaise indeed was gifted, and Blaise needed to engage with Paris's top minds of this new science.

Blaise impressed them all. All but René Descartes. Descartes was the aloof star of this new science. He was too self-assured to go to most of the meetings. When he did go, he acted as if he was too big for it all. Descartes was told that the homeschool boy was a savant. He was even given one of Blaise's papers. Descartes balked, sure that Étienne had written it himself. When Mersenne convinced Descartes that it was the work of the boy alone, the graduate of the elite Jesuit Royal College at La Flèche, like a prep-school villain in a 1980s teen movie, gave his disparaging meh.

Maybe Descartes, the always loyal (or at least never disparaging) son of Jesuit teachers, knew what was to come. Maybe Descartes knew that the young math savant would eventually lift his pen and become the greatest of all Jesuit critics to ever write in French. Blaise would come to land blow after blow against the Jesuits in his *Provincial Letters* (now considered some of the greatest writing ever to be written in the French language).

But before that could happen, young Pascal needed to master the new philosophy, invent the calculator, and revolutionize gambling. That's right, without Blaise Pascal there'd be no Silicon Valley or Las Vegas. That smarmy René Descartes can put that in his cosmopolis-shaped pipe and smoke it!

You Live by the Numbers, You Die by the Numbers

Math is a fickle thing. While math can uncover the firm laws of the universe, using it to predict the value of stocks and bonds is dangerous. It can turn on you quickly. Étienne painfully discovered this in 1638. Étienne was overleveraged in government bonds. The bonds were created by Cardinal Richelieu, who was the very blunt and vicious instrument of Louis XIII and Louis XIV's centralizing objectives. Cardinal Richelieu provided the muscle to bring all French power under the crown. The cardinal was part Tony Soprano, part Bernie Madoff, and all Niccolo Machiavelli. All wrapped up together in one red rope.

To finance this absolutist centralization, Cardinal Richelieu created bonds. Étienne bought them. They made him wealthy and allowed him to move the family to Paris, where he spent most of his time educating his children and doing math. But in 1638 Cardinal Richelieu decided to default on those bonds. Étienne's fortune was lost, as were the fortunes of many others. Étienne, with these others, spoke out against Cardinal Richelieu's deceit. But to cross Cardinal Richelieu in any way was to bring out his inner Tony Soprano. Therefore, these middle-elite investors had to flee to save their lives. Étienne stashed the children with a neighbor and sought safe harbor to wait out the violent storm of Cardinal Richelieu's temper.

This neighbor was Madame Sainctot. She was elegant and beautiful. She hosted in her home the most esteemed and intellectual salon in all of Paris. Blaise now was exposed not only to the Mersenne math club but also to the Madame Sainctot salon. Her true impact on the family came more through Jacqueline, Blaise's younger sister. Jacqueline too was beautiful and gregarious, and Madame Sainctot got her involved in children's theater. In a scene reminiscent of Herodias's daughter dancing in Matthew 14, winning her the favor of Herod and therefore the loss of John the Baptist's head, Jacqueline (though far less scandalously) performed for Cardinal Richelieu.[2] The cardinal was so moved that he promised young Jacqueline anything she wished. She wished for her father to be forgiven and welcomed back into the cardinal's, and therefore the king's, good graces. Cardinal Richelieu agreed and welcomed Étienne back, appointing him as the king's commissioner of taxes in Rouen.

It wasn't quite a full restoration. Étienne was not made whole financially. His life was secure, and neither he nor his children would starve. But Étienne's new post meant a departure from Paris. And worse than leaving Paris was working in Rouen. Being tax commissioner in this city proved a great challenge. The people had been revolting against taxation, making the streets and the books chaos. And for Étienne, being a tax commissioner in this challenging milieu meant there was little time for teaching his children or exploring the theorems of the new science. He was just too busy for that.

Blaise missed this time with his father. So at the age of nineteen, Blaise decided to help his father by making a calculating machine. Blaise hoped it would allow his father to return to the ease of teaching him math. The

2. Ben Rogers gives us some context: "After appearing in 1639 in a private performance laid on for Richelieu, she introduced herself to the cardinal, charmed him and made representation on behalf of her father, who was forgiven. The episode reminds us that the Pascals were connected not just to Paris's leading scientific circles, but also to its social ones—Jacqueline, at least, was a not infrequent visitor to the royal court. But it also reminds us that even a good loyalist like Étienne could find himself on the wrong side of the state. Pascal's life would illustrate the point again and again." Rogers, "Pascal's Life and Times," in Nicholas Hammond, *The Cambridge Companion to Pascal* (Cambridge: Cambridge University Press, 2003), 7.

invention of the first calculator would lay the ground of the eventual creation of computer engineering. Blaise built fifty of these calculating machines and sold them all—mostly to the extravagantly wealthy, who used them as a status symbol. The calculating machine indeed helped Étienne, saving him time.

But then an accident happened.

A Bad Slip That Brings New Thoughts

If you live in Minnesota, you know that a slip and fall on the ice is deadly. Ice kills! Mainly old people. When you slip on ice on a road or sidewalk you don't necessarily hit your head but instead tweak your back and jam your hip. If you're old, that fall can break bones. And a broken hip, wrist, or ribs can lead to a quick decline in an old person. The seemingly healthy elder after a fall—not on their head but their hip—will never be the same. There are so many stories in the upper Midwest that go just like this. Since the fall, grandma declined, and six months later she was in hospice. Snowbirds who leave the cold north are, of course, looking for warmer weather. But not necessarily for the sake of a tan and a pool. Those warm environments are without ice, and ice kills!

In winter 1646, Étienne, now fifty-eight—a relatively old man for that time in France—slipped on an icy walk in Rouen. He fell hard and broke his hip. Such an accident is dangerous in the twenty-first century. It was close to a death sentence in the seventeenth. Rouen was known not only for its tax angst but also its physicians. Rouen was the Mayo Clinic of seventeenth-century France. Or at least two of France's best physicians were citizens of the city.

Étienne demanded that only La Bouteillerie and Deslandes, these two great physicians, care for him. It worked. Not only did Étienne not die from his injury but he recovered full motion in the leg, walking just as before. But the recovery required over three months of treatment, forcing La Bouteillerie and Deslandes to spend a great deal of time with the Pascals. These two physicians became almost family.

The Pascals came to realize there was something unusual about these doctors. Both were followers of a priest named Jean Guillebert and called themselves Jansenists. Guillebert lead a group, inspired by the thought of a man named Cornelius Jansen, that was challenging the Catholic establishment—particularly the Jesuits. The group saw itself as Catholic, but even more so, as the true heirs of Augustine. Jansen's writings explored Augustine's position on sin, free will, human goodness, and grace. Guillebert and his followers came to believe that the Catholic establishment in France was not faithful to these positions. The establishment had, at best, diluted Augustine.

The accusations flew and conflict rose. The Jesuits had no patience for these Jansenists. Catholic or not, these Jansenists sounded far too close to Protestants. The Jesuits, as the pointy end of the spear, had been fighting such ideas in France for generations. They saw Jansenism as a great danger. The Jansenist view sounded too Lutheran: the human will stuck in sin and unable to do good outside of God's gracious working within the human agent. (And it should have, as Luther was an Augustinian monk deeply shaped by Johann von Staupitz's reading of Augustine—a story we'll pick up in a few chapters.)

Cue the smear campaign. The Jesuits painted the Jansenists as crazed. The rhetoric would intensify, heating to a boil in the 1650s, but in the mid-1640s, with Étienne's hip healing, it was just starting to simmer.

As the physicians tended to Étienne, changing bandages and working on range of motion, they talked with young Blaise. They gave Blaise some of Jansen's and Guillebert's writings. As he did with all intellectual endeavors, Blaise devoured them. He was moved by their position. He started to think about theological and spiritual matters, even penning a few essays. But for the moment, young Blaise considered it not for him.

Instead he explored gambling.

The Gambler and the Nun

By young adulthood, Blaise had already published groundbreaking mathematical papers, invented the first calculator, and read much of the Jansenist corpus. What he hadn't done was party. So he returned to Paris to give it a try. Partying consisted mainly of going to some of the most infamous salons. The Parisian salon was the dance club of the seventeenth century. But instead of dance beats, shots of Patrón, and hookups, the objective was to make new friends, hear new intellectual ideas, and gamble. Blaise jumped in with both feet. He met and became friends with the *honnêtes hommes*, heard discussion of Montaigne and Descartes, and brought his mathematical brain to the games of chance.

Both from playing and watching games of chance, Pascal developed his probability theory. This mathematical theory is still used today by insurance companies and casinos. The insulated homeschooler, let loose in the salons of Paris, made both Geico and Vegas possible. Not bad for an odd boy.

Yet right in the middle of the partying came a great sorrow. Étienne died. And salon life was wearing on Blaise. He wasn't quite ready to give it up, though. He had come to double down on it, but it nonetheless was not what he'd hoped. With Étienne's death, salon life felt particularly stale. Blaise's older sister was married with growing children, leaving only Blaise and Jacqueline under their father's care. Étienne left all his inheritance to Blaise and Jacqueline. It was enough to secure them a good life in Paris. Enough for Blaise to keep up the salon life and Jacqueline to have a good dowry.

But then the bombshell came. It shook Blaise even more than the news of the death of Étienne. Jacqueline announced that she planned to join the Jansenist convent of Port-Royal.

For a long time, Blaise had suffered from bad health and loneliness. He hid it well, but the suffering of ill health worsened. Jacqueline gives us the harrowing details in a letter, saying, "My brother, among other infirmities, could not swallow any liquids that were not warm, and even then he could only take them a drop at a time. But since he had all sorts of other maladies—dreadful headaches and severe indigestion among them—the physicians ordered that he purge himself every other day for three months." She continues, "The upshot was that he had to swallow medicines, heated, drop by drop. All this resulted in a condition painful in the extreme."[3]

Jacqueline contends that it was the suffering and sorrow of illness that began the shift in Blaise. Because of the sorrow of illness, Blaise became less interested in the numbers and theorems of the new science. He instead began concerning himself more directly with questions of spirit. But there was still a long way to go before he would be enveloped by the fire of the living God.

3. Quoted in Marvin R. O'Connell, *Blaise Pascal: Reasons of the Heart* (Grand Rapids: Eerdmans, 1997), 83.

Blaise kept a stiff upper lip amid the sorrows of his illness. But the thought of losing his sister to the convent was too much for him to face. He begged her to change her mind, but she wouldn't. He needed her care, and even more her friendship. But Jacqueline would not relent. Desperate, Blaise threatened to withhold her inheritance if she stepped one foot into Port-Royal. She didn't care. Blaise's sadness got all mixed up with the money. The sorrow was now acute, and it came in waves of three. The loss of Étienne, the debilitating illness, and the departure of Jacqueline—who was the only one who truly knew him and loved him—each sorrow crashed on Blaise one after another.

Finally, a truce was brokered by their older sister Gilberte, and Jacqueline departed. Blaise went to his room and wept. He was alone. The sorrow threatened to drown him, its wave unrelenting, mercilessly keeping him from air. For the next three years Blaise tried to buoy himself in the rough seas of the pain of sorrow by diving even deeper into the salon life of a free bachelor. His sisters called this "his worldly period."[4] In the end, that life was too vapid and isolating. The sorrows were always at the surface to meet him.

Sad and lonely, Blaise started to visit Jacqueline and his nieces, the Périer girls. The Périer girls had been sent to Port-Royal by their mother, Gilberte, to be educated.[5] In October 1654, Blaise moved apartments, leaving behind the Right Bank and its party scene. He took a new address on the Left Bank, on Rue Monsieur-le-Prince, near the Luxembourg Palace. Not coincidentally, this new address was only a stone's throw from his childhood home. To my mind, that signals two things. First, Blaise was finished running away from his sorrow. He was instead ready to enter that sorrow. Second, he knew he could enter it only through the embrace of others. Those others who joined him in his sorrow were always his sisters. He was ready to see what might meet him when his sorrow was truly shared with Jacqueline and his heart warmed in connection to his nieces. He needed to receive the friendship of Jacqueline's pastoral presence and to playfully care for his nieces (as we'll see, the dynamic of evangelism that can bear this sacramental personalism always has a dynamic of receiving and giving ministry). Only then could Blaise enter his sorrow.

4. O'Connell, *Blaise Pascal*, 92.
5. The Périer girls are the daughters of Gilberte, Blaise's oldest sister.

No one can enter their sorrow alone. The self can do many things alone. The self can actualize itself by the power of itself. When you follow Montaigne and seek to be only a self, all you need is you. Montaigne departs to the château to find not soul but self by the self alone. Finding the self by the self makes the self appear magnificent and (supposedly) happy. But soul, which is always discovered in sorrow, needs others. You can't find soul without others. Soul comes through confession and surrender. It is a ministerial reality. Soul comes by the gift of the Spirit received through the personal act of ministry—by the encounter of a name to a name.

Pascal meets his sorrow by walking from Rue Monsieur-le-Prince alongside the Luxembourg Gardens to the Port-Royal de Paris convent. (It's just south of the gardens and still stands today, though it is now a medical center, in an interesting callback to La Bouteillerie and Deslandes and Pascal's own sorrow of ill health.) As biographer Marvin R. O'Connell says, "What attracted [Pascal] to [the new apartment] was its proximity to the convent of Port-Royal de Paris, where, after a ten-minute walk . . . he could expect to come into the *consoling* presence of Soeur Jacqueline . . . and of the beloved Périer nieces."[6] Let's consider that "consoling presence."

Blaise became a regular visitor, sitting often with his sister, teasing his nieces, and talking with the other Jansenists about theology. Blaise told his sister that the bachelor life of gambling was wearing thin. Its vapidness was becoming torture. It gave no relief to his sorrow. He couldn't continue. The sadness of his loneliness, coupled with poor health, was overtaking him. Even with his incredible mind, Blaise couldn't just think his way out of it.

He needed Jacqueline's consolation. But to receive consolation, you need a confession. The two are bound. The event of evangelism always calls for a confession.[7] Blaise needed Jacqueline to join him in his sorrow as he confessed that sorrow. Blaise ultimately needed Jacqueline to walk with him and see what might meet him inside his sorrow. Confession invites another to come and minister to us by joining us in our sorrow or shame, walking with us to see what might be met in this sorrow. This is the heart of evangelism as consolation.

6. O'Connell, *Blaise Pascal*, 93 (emphasis added).
7. I'm trying to show that this confession is of sorrow, not the rationalized formula like in a tract, like the Four Spiritual Laws.

In a letter to Gilberte, Jacqueline tells of these discussions. Jacqueline explains to her sister, "[Blaise] comes to me and opens his heart to me so poignantly that I cannot but [commiserate with] him." This is the confession of sorrow. She continues, "He acknowledges that in the midst of his grand occupations and of all those activities that can contribute to making him love the world . . . he really wants to leave all this behind him. . . . And yet he feels no attraction toward the God he has abandoned. . . . He also believed himself capable of accomplishing everything on his own." And yet here is the further confession: there is no way—even feeling so capable—for him to square this circle and find something full and meaningful inside the sorrow that accompanies him in the world. Blaise is lost. But now through confession, he is not alone. His sorrow is shared by the act of confession. Jacqueline concludes her letter to Gilberte by saying, "This confession surprised me as much as it gave me joy. And ever since he confided it to me, I have conceived a hope that I never had before. I think it my duty to inform you of it and so obligate you to pray to God in our brother's behalf."[8]

Gilberte did pray. In prayer she joined Blaise's sorrow. Prayer is the central practice of consoling communion. Through that sharing, the fire came. From sharing in sorrow, the fire of the God of names—not of theorems—came as a great embrace of consolation and mercy.

The Fire of Spirit, the Igniting of a Pen

When the fire came, it came as an experience beyond rationality, an experience that outstripped any of the conceptions of the new philosophy. It was a revelation that made the moral endeavors of the *honnêtes hommes* seem insipid and misdirected. Both Descartes and Montaigne were but straw next to this fire that came upon Pascal.

I deliberately use "straw" here to hark back to Thomas Aquinas, who in December 1273, after celebrating the Mass, had an encounter much like Pascal's. Aquinas was a resident of Paris in the mid-thirteenth century, living not far from where Blaise experienced the fire more than 350 years later. Aquinas, one of the indisputable greatest minds of the church (*the* greatest mind of the Western medieval period), had a mystical experience

8. O'Connell, *Blaise Pascal*, 94.

in Naples that December night that revealed to him that his great theology was but straw. After this mystical experience Aquinas never wrote again. He died six months later. Blaise did the opposite. He started really living and writing. Whereas the fire incinerated Aquinas's pen to cold ash, the fire lit a rocket fuse in Pascal's pen.

The writing started immediately. At the end of November 1654, late in the night, with Blaise in deep sorrow—but that sorrow now shared by the pastoral care of Jacqueline and the prayers of Gilberte—the mystical fell again on a great mind of Paris.[9] As Pascal leaned into his sorrow and was encountered by this mystical reality, he grabbed his pen and wrote, "Fire. God of Abraham, God of Isaac, God of Jacob, not of the philosophers and the scholars." Pascal then wrote out Psalm 119:16, "I will not forget your word . . ."[10] This is all we have by way of description of what occurred.

The Word had come upon him. It had met Blaise's sorrow and given him consolation. The consolation had come not as ideas or styles but as relational connection to the one who judges and renews like fire. This God who met Pascal in fire was a great consolation of personal encounter. This God of names and words (who is the Word) came to care for persons. God met Abraham, Isaac, and Jacob, blessing and consoling them as they lived and yearned. This God therefore cannot be known or captured by the concepts of the philosophers—whether those philosophers were skeptical or rational—for these philosophers cared little for the encounters that come in sorrow. They seek what is true *not* in the dark but in the château or inside the theorems.

The light of fire revealed that there was no capacity inside Blaise himself—maybe the most capable person Europe ever produced—to encounter this God of Abraham. This God of Abraham was a fire that revealed that all human capacities are ash. This God burns like a bush aflame but unconsumed, speaking names (Exod. 3). This God becomes

9. Leszek Kolakowski adds, "Whether or not the conversion of November 1654 may be properly called a mystical experience, Pascal was not a mystic. Certainly he did not think that the world had been abandoned by God. But he was not a mystic in the sense of a man whose immersion into the divine reaches such a depth that he really achieves total or nearly total indifference to the world, whom God shelters uninterruptedly from fear, who sees death as moving from one to another and doesn't care about 'infinite spaces.' While he believed that 'all things are veils that cover God' and that 'Christians ought to recognize him in everything,' he painfully experienced the absence of God in nature." Kolakowski, *God Owes Us Nothing: A Brief Remark on Pascal's Religion and on the Spirit of Jansenism* (Chicago: University of Chicago Press, 1995), 138.

10. O'Connell, *Blaise Pascal*, 129.

known to the fools (1 Cor. 3) who suffer (2 Cor. 1). This God is not revealed
to Mersenne's club or in the salons filled with *honnêtes hommes*. God is
made known to the one who yearns for care and mercy.

This God of Abraham cares little for human capacities and capabili-
ties. God comes to Abraham because he has no capacities (not even the
ability to have a child). Abraham, even out of his incapacities, holds tight
to the capacities of God, who meets him and calls him by name (Gen.
17). God's Word is a promise that Abraham, inside his own sorrow, will
hold to. Holding to the promise is the only thing that makes Abraham
righteous (Rom. 4). He is righteous because he holds to God's promises,
trusting those promises most deeply inside sorrow (Rom. 4:3–5). Abraham
discovers that the promise itself consoles—not because the promise is a
warm idea but because the promise is bound inside the relationship with
the one who arrives and speaks to Abraham, with a name, becoming his
companion and ministering to him in his toil and disappointment. The
promise comes from the one who consoles those in sorrow. The promise
is given to the sorrowful. "Blessed are those who mourn, for they shall be
comforted" (Matt. 5:4). They will be comforted by the very fire of God's
name.

Set ablaze by this fire, Blaise wrote his two most famous works, *The
Provincial Letters* and *Pensées*. Both are considered to be among the greatest works ever written in French. The writing and thinking inside each is
mesmerizing, which is ironic for two texts that claim the human being is
stuck, unable in style or thinking to find happiness.

Pascal's pen begins with the failure of the style of Montaigne and his
honnêtes hommes. But instead of targeting Montaigne and the *honnêtes
hommes* directly, Pascal takes his shots at the Jesuits. He's not necessarily
looking for a fight. The Jesuits had swung first by disparaging Port-Royal
and the Jansenist theological commitments, calling Port-Royal unhinged
and heretical. Pascal won't directly swing back, but he will defend Port-
Royal. Not with force or violence of words but with comedy.

The Provincial Letters

It's a bit like the Blue Collar Comedy Tour. Jeff Foxworthy, for those
who remember him from the early 2000s, played the part of a backwoods
average Joe. His stand-up comedy was just observational. But it worked
(kind of) because Foxworthy was a simple blue-collar guy with no fancy

degrees and a lot of down-home common sense. From this location his observations could be penetrating, particularly toward coastal elites. Foxworthy unmasked the absurdity of the coastal elites by taking the listener out of New York or Los Angeles and dropping them in Alabama or Missouri. It was Pascal who practically invented this form of comedy.

To understand how, we need a bit of context.

A year or so after the night of fire, the Jesuits landed a staggering blow right in Pascal's neighborhood in the battles running throughout France. Young Louis XIV was finding the diversity of religious expressions in France off-putting and troublesome for his absolutist ambitions. Since the Fronde, the battle of the elites against the crown, the nobles had been made to come to heel. But this subjugation was less successful with France's different religious groups. Their unwillingness to cede put a particularly hot spotlight on the Jansenists and Port-Royal, a spotlight that the Jesuits were heroically happy to walk into. The Jesuits were always willing to play the part of the protectors of the realm and the crown in France. They saw themselves as France's true religious guardians. For a hundred years the Jesuits had been the masters of mayhem when it came to eliminating rivals. They always won. But they had not yet met Blaise Pascal.

The Sorbonne and its Jesuit-heavy theology faculty—which was about halfway down the street on the left from Blaise's flat to the convent of Port-Royal—was tapped to investigate the Jansenists. The Sorbonne's ruling was decisive and divisive. They shouted heresy, declaring Jansenism and Port-Royal out of bounds. The Sorbonne took immediate action, dismissing Professor Antoine Arnauld from the faculty. Arnauld was a leading Jansenist theologian and a friend of Pascal's.

Blaise decided that the bullies needed to be confronted and the Jansenists and Port-Royal defended. After all, how could Port-Royal be out of bounds if they had ministered to Blaise, walking with him into his sorrow and standing beside him in his distress as he encountered the God of Abraham who comes as fire. Port-Royal had evangelized Blaise, walking him into the good news that the God of Abraham is a God who saves by consoling. The ministry of Port-Royal needed to be protected. It became a conflict between forms of evangelism.

But Blaise knew that this kind of bully could not be confronted head-on. Not even Henry of Navarre, the first Bourbon king, could confront the Jesuits directly. Henry of Navarre had tried and ended up with two dagger holes in his chest, bleeding out in his royal carriage. The only way to confront this kind of bully was to go all Blue Collar Comedy Tour.

Pascal played the part far better than Jeff Foxworthy did. He wrote eighteen open letters, penned from the hand of his pseudonym Louis de Montalte. Like Foxworthy, Louis de Montalte was just a rube from flyover country who'd found himself in the big city. The big-city ways made no sense to this down-home, provincial guy. In writing home to his fictitious friends, Louis de Montalte tries to explain what is going on in the big city Paris, relaying to them the details of the conflicts between the Jesuits and Jansenists. With deep humor and cutting precision in argumentation, Louis de Montalte explains the absurdity of the Jesuit position.

When the first letter dropped, people couldn't get enough of it. They found the letter hilarious and delicious, its content and style sidesplitting. As with a new Taylor Swift song, people couldn't wait for the next one to drop. "The salons eat it up, and delight in the game of trying to guess the identity of the *Provincials'* author—a game that sometimes takes place in Pascal's presence."[11] The mystery of the author intoxicated Paris. The arguments against the Jesuits were celebrated beyond the great city. "Outside Paris . . . country priests began reading them aloud from their pulpits. [The letters] appealed to everyone who had been burned by the Jesuits' power game or simply enjoyed seeing overweening priests mocked. That turns out to be a lot of people."[12]

Pascal's Jeff Foxworthy, Louis de Montalte, sought to point out, in his backward ways, the capitulation of the Jesuits. The Jesuits hated the Jansenists, striking at them as they did, because Port-Royal's very presence convicted the Jesuits of their hypocrisy. The Jesuits were deeply grated by the Jansenists' Augustinism—the impossibility of humans to save themselves is always an offense to those who refuse to enter their own sorrow or embrace others' sorrow. The Jesuits were annoyed and angered by all the talk of human inadequacy and the confession of sin, because such talk didn't play well in Paris's salons or Louis's court. And those locations were right where the Jesuits wanted to be. What better place to evangelize? They tied evangelism to cultural influence. The Jesuits downplayed sin and humanity's incapacity to save itself for the sake of an evangelistic strategy.

11. Benjamin Storey and Jenna Silber Storey, *Why We Are Restless: On the Modern Quest for Contentment* (Princeton: Princeton University Press, 2021), 59.
12. Storey and Storey, *Why We Are Restless*, 59.

That approach made them permissive, believing they were a resource to help a self seek happiness. The Jesuits were willing to become the religious wing of both the *honnêtes hommes* and the king, framing Christian faith as a tool for happiness and power.

The seventeenth-century French Jesuit evangelistic strategy did not target the lost, sorrowful soul but a self looking for happiness (sounds a lot like contemporary American Protestantism). These Jesuits conceded that we are no more than just a self, rendering their view of evangelism soulless. As only selves, our highest good could only be our own happiness. French Jesuit religion contended that it could help with that pursuit of happiness. But as Pascal points out in the voice of Louis de Montalte, when happiness is our highest good, then power (and the political) becomes an insatiable desire. We long for power and political control so we can secure happiness and be our truest self. Evangelism becomes triumphalist, having no place for sorrow and therefore losing a sacramental personalism. Storey and Storey summarize this poignantly: "The enduring appeal of *The Provincial Letters* derives from their forceful suggestion that the modern alliance of permissiveness and power does not succeed in making men happy."[13] Evangelism in this shape, Pascal warns us, will never transform us, for it loses the sacramental that soul demands.

In the end *The Provincial Letters* did not allow Pascal to offer an alternative. Like any cultural sensation, the *Letters* began to take on a life of their own, a life outside what Pascal desired for them. *The Provincial Letters* did their job: they confronted a bully. They allowed France to see the hypocrisy. But amid the humor and sarcasm, Pascal's larger point had been eclipsed. People held onto the zingers against powerful priests. For example, a few generations later, Voltaire—who hated Pascal with a passion for all his commitments to human inadequacy and the living God of Abraham—gleefully relished the *Letters'* attacks on priests.[14] The cutting

13. Storey and Storey, *Why We Are Restless*, 61.

14. Sissela Bok states, "By the eighteenth century, Enlightenment thinkers increasingly rejected Pascal's views about the wretchedness of earthly life and the importance of thinking, above all, of true happiness as achievable only, if at all, in the afterlife. In 1734, Voltaire challenged Pascal in an essay that, while praising his genius, conjectured that he would surely have corrected his stern pronouncements, had he lived longer." Bok, *Exploring Happiness: From Aristotle to Brain Science* (New Haven: Yale University Press, 2010), 79. Peter Kreeft adds, "Voltaire joked that medieval French peasants knew more about the geography of Heaven than about the geography of France. Pascal would not see this as a joke but as a privilege." Kreeft, *Christianity for Modern Pagans: Pascal's "Pensées"* (San Francisco: Ignatius, 1966), 144.

humor fed Voltaire's disdain. Voltaire used the *Letters* to teach himself how to argue with humor and force. But Pascal's deeper point—an alternative view of evangelism not directed toward happiness but entering unhappiness to find life (for its here that we find the God of Abraham who consoles as fire)—was missed. Therefore, Pascal dropped the comedy tour and started a new project. It would become one of the most important works of the modern era.

Pensées

The point of this new project was to confront the duplicity of some priests and to shake the ground on which the children of Montaigne stood, also showing that the stepparenting of Descartes was also of little help. Both Montaigne and Descartes gave us modern conceptions of our humanity that do not, and could not, face the truth. Montaigne keeps us from truly looking at ourselves by means of constant diversion. Descartes uses reason. Pascal exposes the problems with both. Ultimately, Pascal seeks in this new project to get his reader to truly examine (and therefore confess) what kind of creatures we all are. If we really examine our existence, Pascal contends, we'll come to recognize that we are miserably stuck in sorrow. To be human is to be a creature caught in sorrow, who fears the sorrow so intensely that we'll do anything to ignore the sorrow and therefore avoid admitting how stuck we are within it. (It's not hard to see Pascal's influence on Søren Kierkegaard when the latter read him two hundred years later.[15]) This sorrowful stuckness became the focus of the new project.

15. Simon Podmore takes us deeper, saying, "Kierkegaard's words of personal desolation are keenly reminiscent of the anxiety that Pascal expressed so evocatively in his posthumously published *Pensées*. Pascal speaks specifically there of a dread of the infinite rooted in 'man's loneliness in the macrocosm'—the felt nothingness of man before that which is capable of crushing him. In this sense, his oppression sometimes sounds like a kind of cosmological *Anfechtung*. He languishes in the grip of an onerous infinity. In contemplating a fathomless universe, he speaks of the space that infinitely transcends the imagination; and indeed, 'it is the greatest perceptible mark of God's omnipotence that our imagination should lose itself in that thought.' Yet after turning man toward the immensity of the universe, Pascal declares: 'I want to show him a new abyss.' And so Pascal redirects contemplation from the infinite to the infinitesimal: to 'all the conceivable immensity of nature in this miniature atom.' Unlike Kant's deliberately superficial 'eye of the poet' whose gaze can perceive the sublime, Pascal's melancholy meditation is consciously reflective of cosmological and scientific insights of the Enlightenment, and it is from this atomic perspective that the human body itself derives a newly discovered sublimity: 'Anyone who considers himself in this way will be terrified at himself, and, seeing his mass, as given him by nature, supporting him between two abysses of infinity and nothingness, will tremble at these marvels.'" Podmore, *Kierkegaard and the Self before God: Anatomy of the Abyss* (Bloomington: Indiana University Press, 2011), 115.

This new project was never completed. Pascal died before he could shape it for publication, leaving it in the form of fragments. It therefore became known as *Pensées* (Thoughts) of Blaise Pascal. These thoughts articulate what Pascal calls a Christianity for modern pagans—in other words, an alternative form of evangelism. Who are these modern pagans? Not the Wiccans and wookiees of our internet age, who look to return to spells and potions—their paganism is not modern but a throwback. The modern pagans are those who seek happiness and believe it possible to secure it. The modern pagans are happiness-hunters. They are the children of Montaigne and the *honnêtes hommes* and the disciples of the new science who glorify human reason and hover around Descartes.

These modern pagans are us. We are all modern pagans because we refuse to truly see ourselves. We've built systems and structures, even religious ones, to avoid this truth of our unavoidable sorrow and stuckness. Pascal claims that Christianity liberates us to truly see ourselves, to confess what we are. *And what we are is fundamentally unhappy.*[16] We are creatures of sorrow, grieved beings. There is no way around this. This fact tortures us late moderns because we continue to think there is some technology, some hack, some accomplishment, some achievement that can override this fundamental reality. Pascal wants us to see that there is no such cure. We are, and always will be, unhappy animals because we are always stuck. The modern pagan seeks the magic of happiness to overcome this truth. The Christian (or better, the follower of the crucified one[17]) confesses this stuckness and surrenders to this sorrow, believing (which is faith!) that in the dark sorrow that is inextricable to our being we find the being of

16. Storey and Storey add, "Our very awareness of the misery Pascal so powerfully describes is the first proof of our greatness. Man is great precisely insofar as 'he knows himself to be miserable. A tree does not know itself to be miserable.' The tree, though just as frail as we are, does not experience these things as miseries. We do. Our miseries are akin to 'the miseries of a great lord, the miseries of a deposed king.' We experience ourselves as living in humiliating privation of what seems to us our proper state. 'What is nature in animals is misery in man.' The desires, movements, and even the weariness of the body are an embarrassment for 'the beast with red cheeks,' in Nietzsche's phrase, but for no other beast." Storey and Storey, *Why We Are Restless*, 74.

17. Of course, this parenthetical is simply to make the assertion that Christianity can itself become a religious idea that promises happiness and uses the living Christ of sorrows. It should also be pointed out here that it doesn't take too much examination to see how theologians like Karl Barth and Dietrich Bonhoeffer (and the others who opposed religion in the twentieth century) were in line with Pascal. Religion can be idolatry and fundamentally pagan when it refuses to call a thing what it is (to quote Luther in the Heidelberg Disputation).

Christ himself. Christ comforts and saves us through the wounds of his own sorrow (Isa. 53:5). This is the great joy of salvation by resurrection.

Stop Having Thoughts!

With all this talk of stuckness and inescapable sorrow, perhaps you've joined team Voltaire. Maybe you're thinking, with Voltaire, that Pascal is a dour and dangerous boy. All this talk of stuckness and sorrow, linked to our very being, is off-putting. It sounds harsh to our ears because our late-modern ears are tuned to the frequency of Montaigne and the pitch of modern paganism. But we'd be wrong to understand Pascal as misanthropic. Pascal is the furthest thing from being a hater of humanity. Rather, he's a great lover, which is why he's telling us the truth.

When Pascal says we're miserable animals, he believes we human beings are wondrously and beautifully made. But being so produces a (particularly postlapsarian) problem. "Our very awareness of the misery . . . is the first proof of our greatness. Man is great precisely insofar as 'he knows himself to be miserable.'"[18] As Pascal says, "A tree does not know itself to be miserable."[19] By nature, we are a self. But not just a self. We are also spirit or soul (and any practice of evangelism must acknowledge this). We are fundamentally creatures but creatures who can uniquely commune with spirit and the transcendent. This makes us both great and miserable. Ultimately it gives us a sense of always being stuck. As Augustine taught us long ago in his *Confessions*, and Pascal is mining through Jansenism, we are miserably restless until we find our rest in God.

Montaigne-style modern pagans have learned, Pascal believes, to distract themselves from this restlessness and therefore never rest. Or we make even our rest a distraction from our fundamental restlessness—welcome to your beach cabana at your all-inclusive resort!

A meme on X (Twitter) humorously encapsulates Pascal's point. The meme feigns being a wikiHow article that seeks to give absurd advice on "How to Be Happy." Below a cheesy animated picture it says, "1. Stop having thoughts." This is exactly Pascal's point. As creatures who think, we don't first and foremost discover in this thinking that we are contented

---

18. Storey and Storey, *Why We Are Restless*, 74, quoting Pascal, *Pensées*, S146–149.
19. Pascal, *Pensées*, S146–149.

selves (as Montaigne wants) or rational minds of ordered laws (as Descartes contends). Instead, inside our thoughts about what we are, we discover that we're creatures whose spirits long for a great communion that exists outside the self and in which the self has no capacity (no reason) from within itself to produce.

We are creatures of sorrow—not because we can't desire what is good but rather because we long so deeply for the good but find that it is always beyond us. All of our actions to produce this good for our self fail us. The only option is to avoid this conundrum by underthinking (Montaigne's advice) or overthinking (Descartes's advice). On either path, it becomes important that we avoid the longings of our sorrowful soul, and it is this avoidance that makes us pagan. It's better to forget about soul and just try to make the self happy (for happiness is within grasp of a self, but what fulfills a soul is beyond and uncontrollable for a self).

Montaignesque Pagans

Montaigne has become our great teacher, the true father of modernity. He teaches us how to ignore a part of ourselves and become modern pagans. "Montaigne recommends a [heavy] dose of diversion and prides himself on his conversational art of leading sad or angry souls step by step away from thoughts of grief or vengeance."[20] Ironically, Montaigne teaches us how to stop having thoughts. (I know that's an odd criticism to levy against the inventor of the essay, but Pascal thinks it's true.) To say it differently, Montaigne restricts our thoughts to the immanence of the self. As we said in chapter 4, Montaigne wants us to never contemplate what is beyond because, as Pascal is showing, that will inevitably lead the self into sorrow. (Montaigne did not stay in the dark long enough to find something within it. Pascal, on the other hand, found right in the dark the blazing light of the fire of the God of ministry.[21])

20. Storey and Storey, *Why We Are Restless*, 64.

21. Donald Frame adds, "In Sainte-Beuve's phrase, Montaigne remains the fox in Pascal's bosom; or Pascal's 'misery of man' is Montaigne's 'human condition,' and no one can prove that we should not accept it gratefully instead of regarding it with horror. Pascal makes a powerful case, especially in locating boredom at the center of the soul; but within a century Voltaire takes Montaigne's side, and the debate still goes on." Frame, *Montaigne: A Biography* (San Francisco: North Point, 1984), 314.

Montaigne is the master of diversion who wants us to turn away from, not into, our sorrow—though not necessarily in a defeatist way. Montaigne is no coward. He directly faces La Boétie's and his own death. Rather, as the father of modern pagans, he believes that if we can really embrace life, enjoy dancing and sleeping, petting cats and gardening, then we don't have to think about the sorrow and the stuckness. We can even die bravely like La Boétie, distracted from death by examining it. Happiness anesthetizes the sorrow; it will keep our soul from facing its longings. We won't even notice these longings of the spirit because we'll be so happy in our self. When we feel the sorrow, Montaigne contends, we should double down on our hobbies and interests—just keep bingeing Netflix. Keep one foot in front of the other, seeking more pleasure. Keep scrolling and scrolling, and the sorrow will stay sequestered.

Pascal, who never saw a dog video on TikTok or had an algorithm to assist in the Montaigne strategy, admits that there is merit to seeking pleasure through distraction. It will feel good to the self, but it will ultimately fail because it deprives the soul. As much as modern paganism wants to reduce us to just selves, we are also souls. Pascal knows that Montaigne's counsel will not ultimately work because he's tried it himself as a high-rolling gambler.

As a gambler, Pascal admits, diversion can appease sorrow—somewhat. Anyone who's had to cope with a three-year-old who has tragically dropped an ice cream cone knows this. You can console the three-year-old by producing a diversion, like a balloon or a funny dance by grandpa. Anyone who's walked into a casino can see the intent focus of those distracting themselves from a deep sorrow by concentrating so hard on the cards and yearning to win. Time flies in casinos because the game is such an all-encompassing diversion from life. There is no time to be sad when your money is on your mind and your mind is on how to win with a pair of jacks.

The problem is that diversion and distraction operate in reduction. They must flatten us into only a self, ignoring or denying that we are also soul. If we were only self, it would be enough to ignore sorrow, allowing diversion to numb us with happiness. But as beings who are also soul, this is never enough. In the end, Montaigne's inherently flawed strategy of diversion as the escape from sorrow short-circuits itself. The diversion of happiness never reaches the depth we need. And because we're also soul, diversion becomes a kind of miserable torture. Therefore, diversion, as a turning away from our sorrow, comforts us warmly with one hand and slaps us violently with the other. Pascal doesn't want us to miss this second hand. It's hard to miss, because it hurts too much. But we do often miss that this second hand is really just the other side of the same yearning for happiness by way of diversion.

So how does all this work? How does one hand both comfort and injure? Pascal knew this one-two operation well because he was a high roller. Using the gambler as an example, he explains it like this: the objective of gambling is to win. You want to leave the table with a full purse. You want to rest with your winnings. You tell yourself how happy you'll be if you win. You'll be able to pay off the car. Take away the stakes of winning and losing, and playing is no longer a potent enough diversion. Playing poker for potato chips sucks. You need the thrill of the chase, the highs of winning next to the lows of losing real money. The real money is worth chasing because it promises the contentment of rest and happiness. To have a few cold, hard Gs in your pocket will make your life better, your self happy.

But something strange happens when you win. You don't rest in this happiness. Rather, you feel compelled to play again. It never satisfies you to win and walk away. You must risk the rest that you have won, either today or tomorrow. You belly up again to the table and enter the activity of diversion. Inside diversion and the aims of happiness, rest has no consoling ability, because once your winning allows you to rest, you start facing the yearning of your soul and the unhappiness that drove you to the table in the first place. It pulls you back into the game. Once you have rest, you must face your discontent. Happiness can be achieved only by never resting, because when you rest you see the thinness of happiness. You see that it cannot hold your soul, which strikes you with a deep sorrow.

To avoid this sorrow, you must throw yourself back into activity. Diversion needs constant activity, with the goal being a rest you'll never accept. Therefore, diversion can never fulfill. It can never really make you happy. But it can distract you from the sorrow of your soul. You need the stakes of winning or losing to make the playing a worthy diversion. Yet that winning, while absorbing your attention and becoming your singular focus, will never truly satisfy. All you have is the chasing of wins that can never pay out at the depth of soul. You're stuck. That's Pascal's point.[22] All of

---

22. Pascal says, "The only thing which consoles us from our miseries is diversion, and yet this is the greatest of our miseries. For it is this which principally hinders us from reflecting

us are this brand of gambler. When we come to this knowledge, it "brings us not sanity and equilibrium but anguish."[23]

Montaigne's children double down on diversion, feeding the slot machine. We use diversion and distraction to avoid the thoughts that we are creatures who yearn for the communion of spirit. Being such creatures who must die and yet can imagine eternity makes us fundamentally restless. We are hunters for happiness whose souls are too restless to ever allow that happiness to satisfy us. Our souls long for rest, but that rest is haunted by a sorrow of soul that keeps us hyperactive.[24] Storey and Storey helpfully add, "Effective diversion must include both the hunt and the kill, for neither satisfies alone. Put the [self] at rest, and it longs for activity; put the [self] in motion, and it longs for rest. In neither does it find contentment."[25]

Pascal shows that Montaigne's ways of avoiding sorrow can never work, because we are compelled, as self and soul, to long for something beyond. We're forced to suffer this longing, to carry the weight of its anguish. Our soul reaches for something beyond that comes from outside the self. We can reach what is outside the self that could save and console the self only by turning into our sorrow, not away from it. As creatures who are self and soul we can never deny sorrow but must allow our being to fall into sorrow, discovering right inside sorrow whether there is something that (or, better, someone who) can console and therefore save our soul.

This leads to what Pascal thinks is the second way to be a modern pagan and avoid what is true about being human.

Descartesesque Pagans

As we said in chapter 5, there is much about Montaigne that Descartes appreciates—which is why Pascal rejects them both. Montaigne teaches Descartes to focus on the self and forget about soul. And why not? Math

---

upon ourselves, and which makes us insensibly ruin ourselves. Without this we should be in a state of weariness, and this weariness would spur us to seek a more solid means of escaping from it. But diversion amuses us, and leads us unconsciously to death." Pascal, *Pensées* (Garden City, NY: Dover, 2018), 49.

23. Storey and Storey, *Why We Are Restless*, 77.

24. Pascal links up with my work in dialogue with Hartmut Rosa. See Andrew Root, *The Congregation in a Secular Age* (Grand Rapids: Baker Academic, 2021); and Root, *Church and the Crisis of Decline* (Grand Rapids: Baker Academic, 2022).

25. Storey and Storey, *Why We Are Restless*, 64–65.

needs the mind of a self, not a soul that longs for what is beyond. The problem with spirit/soul is that it yearns for what is beyond the self and beyond physical nature. Descartes is not interested in anything beyond the natural. Those who follow him come to absolutely oppose the metaphysical. Metaphysics will become a dead topic in philosophy for centuries, replaced by epistemology.[26]

Like Montaigne, Descartes holds to a soulless self. But unlike Montaigne, Descartes is uninterested in the happy diversions of the château. Descartes seeks to investigate reason, a task worthy of human attention. The Cartesianesque modern pagan contends that it's inside such reasoned investigations that we discover that the human being is not miserably sad but amazingly clever. Just look at his equations. If human beings are sad or miserable, there must be a way for reason to fix it. Everything has been turned into a mathematical problem with a solution (this births our instrumental cosmopolis). There must be some medicine that science can provide to solve sorrow.

Pascal took those pills. Both metaphorically and literally. He was a gambler, trying on Montaigne's style of diversion with the other *honnêtes hommes*, but he also took the drops of warm medicine. Those drops saved his life but did nothing for his soul. The boy who mastered reason as a teenager came to see that the "heart [the soul] has its reasons, which reason does not know."[27]

We often miss the true meaning of this famous quote from *Pensées*. We read it through our modern pagan views of the self, taking it to mean that the self has wants and desires that make little sense to others who

---

26. Pascal says, "I cannot forgive Descartes. In all his philosophy he would have been quite willing to dispense with God. But he had to make Him give a fillip to set the world in motion; beyond this, he has no further need of God." Pascal, *Pensées*, 23. Thomas Hibbs adds to this, saying, "Pascal was aware of the deist option from his reading of Descartes. Pascal aligns Descartes' idea of divinity with deism, which, according to Pascal, is almost as distant from Christianity as is atheism, because neither conceives of God as personal and active in history. Sometimes it is assumed that the only alternative to a deistic and utterly impersonal conception of God is a voluntarist one, in which the principal attribute of God is his omnipotence. This God is present in Descartes in the form of the evil genius whose arbitrary will threatens our hold on any claims to knowledge of the world." Hibbs, *Wagering on an Ironic God: Pascal on Faith and Philosophy* (Waco: Baylor University Press, 2017), 177.

27. Here is Pascal in his own words: "The heart has its reasons, which reason does not know. We feel it in a thousand things. I say that the heart naturally loves the Universal Being, and also itself naturally, according as it gives itself to them; and it hardens itself against one or the other at its will. You have rejected the one, and kept the other. Is it by reason that you love yourself?" Pascal, *Pensées*, 78.

are not our own self (e.g., we romantically love whom we romantically love). But that is not what Pascal means. He intends to shift from the ground of the self to the ground of the soul. On this ground of soul, reason abruptly reaches its limit. Its theorems and patterns of investigation, its solutions and fixes, have no currency in the realm of soul. Reason is too full of hubris, too puffed in the chest, too mesmerized by its own abilities, to recognize that it knows nothing about soul. And we are souls as much as selves. Scientific reason has no answer for our misery.

Pascal points out that God is beyond all the investigative apparatuses of reason.[28] The God who arrives as fire, who encounters our person with God's own person, is beyond reason—far beyond the syllogism of the philosopher. Such syllogisms or methods are melted to liquid wax next to the fire of the God of Abraham. The soul is fundamentally in sorrow because what can save the soul is completely outside the self, so very beyond. The self has no way of reaching what it deeply needs.[29] The self can reach the philosophical methods of reason in its own mind. But because we are also soul/spirit, what we desire, what the heart longs for most, the self cannot produce. That can only be received. The self must become a passive receiver as the soul searches its sorrow. "The heart has its reasons, which reason does not know." Reason cannot know the God who is wholly other but comes near in love and consolation, ministering new life.[30]

28. Pascal's apophaticism inspires Kierkegaard and his assertions of the qualitative distinction between time and eternity.

29. Mark Edmundson says, "And what precisely does the Savior save one from? He saves you from Self. He delivers you from the horrible illusion that you are alone in the world and that no one can ever care for you and love you and sustain you. That crowd, through sharing, becomes a node of universal being and the people in it are finally, if temporarily, free. Some of them, perhaps, will spend their lives seeking this feeling in which Self melts away and the Soul becomes ascendant. They will do so by following Jesus, not in the literal sense of trooping after but in the deeper sense of trying to do as he would do, trying to be compassionate, trying to be kind." Edmundson, *Self and Soul: A Defense of Ideals* (Cambridge, MA: Harvard University Press, 2015), 74.

30. Daniel Garber explains, "One way of convincing someone to be a Christian would be to give that person reasons, arguments, rational motivation for adopting the position under consideration. But, Pascal claims, reason and experience can never lead us to real belief. Pascal is deeply pessimistic about the ability of reason taken by itself to lead us to any real understanding of the way the world is." Garber, *What Happens after Pascal's Wager? Living Faith and Rational Belief* (Milwaukee: Marquette University Press, 2009), 11.

The Wager and a Different Form of Evangelism

It should be said: Pascal never retreated into irrationality. Nor did he abandon the pursuits and disposition of science. Haters of Pascal like to accuse him of fideism (the idea that everything can be answered by faith), assuming Port-Royal had corrupted his amazing mathematical mind. That doesn't seem fair, and it's not true to his writings.

True, the whiz kid math star who mastered reason in his teens had a mystical experience that no equation can explain. But Pascal still held to the new science's drive for investigation. The whole of *Pensées*, as we've unpacked it, is infused with a vibe of investigation. Pascal wants us to test and to explore. *This is right where his alternate view of evangelism comes in.* The Jesuits wanted to shape the gospel for the salon and the court. They wanted an evangelism that could attract a self. Pascal investigated this approach and found it misguided because it could not square the circle of the misery of the human spirit. Our American Protestant forms of evangelism have often followed this seventeenth-century French Jesuit approach. Especially in a time of hyper self-interest, evident in our wrestling and fighting about identities, it seems only logical for us to form an evangelism for the self (alone). But Pascal would advise against that.

Instead of an evangelism that makes the gospel relevant to the cultural ethos of selves, Pascal contends that evangelism is instead an invitation into investigation. Pastor Manta does something similar with his sermon, and we'll see that this leads Cynthia, and particularly her husband, into that space. Evangelism explores who and what we human beings really are, which is why it focuses first on consolation, believing that the task for faith is made at this sacramental level of personhood. Evangelism unmasks our miserable sorrow. Inside this discovery that we are miserably sorrowful, Pascal offers the other most famous fragment of *Pensées*: the wager.

As with the "heart has its reasons" quote, we often mistake what Pascal means by his wager. That misunderstanding is a detriment to our views of evangelism. We haven't been able to shake off our modern paganism enough to see Pascal's real point. Most often the wager has been interpreted like this: "There is a fifty-fifty play. Either God exists or God doesn't; either there is heaven and hell or there is not. So what should you believe? Or, not really believe, but what should you *bet on*. If you bet on no God but find out after death that there is a God, you are fully screwed. Better to bet on there being a God, then even if you lose the bet, what do you really lose? Nothing. See, this is a good bet! All upside! No real downside—except perhaps the loss of free-range pleasure. So, come forward and follow Jesus! Come make your wager; it's a good bet. Evangelism is the opening of betting; it's a sportsbook. You can then, after making your bet, move on and distract yourself, using even religion as a tool to get and keep you happy." Pascal, as much as Marx, thinks this brand of religion is an opiate. And deeply poisonous.[31]

This kind of wager is *not* what Pascal means. Because such a wager cannot face who we really are as both self and soul. To read Pascal this way will flatten (and has flattened) our practices of evangelism. There can be no sacramental personalism in such a perspective. Pascal is not interested in us escaping the misery of unhappiness—whether now or in eternity. He has already informed us that there is *no way* out of sorrow. Stop looking for one—particularly in religion! We are the creatures that must suffer being selves and souls. To think a bet can win us escape is to have missed everything Pascal has sought. No belief, no diversion, no method of reasoning will free us—ever!—from the sorrow of being creatures of soul. There is no fifty-fifty here. You are 100 percent restless, sorrowfully searching for what your self does not and cannot possess.

But it is right here that the wager comes! You can either deny the sorrow and remain a modern pagan, chasing diversion and obsessing over reason, or you can turn and investigate your sorrow. You can walk right into the sorrow. You can let your soul that yearns search for what it does not and cannot possess within itself. If you investigate the sorrow, Pascal wagers, you will find the fire of consolation. You will find the God of Abraham, Isaac, and Jacob who brings new life through and within sorrow. The wager is a kind of unapologetic apologetic. It admits that there is no way within the human agent to solve our misery. There is no way for a human being to reason themselves to God and solve the restlessness of their soul.[32]

---

31. "Remember, it is not an argument for the existence of God but an argument for faith. Its conclusion is not 'Therefore God exists' but 'Therefore you should believe.'" Kreeft, *Christianity for Modern Pagans*, 303.

32. Andrew Prevot, drawing from the work of other mystics and writers on mysticism, adds, "Oneness with Christ may mean . . . willingly entering into the hells that others suffer, offering one's body as a vessel for their healing, accepting torment if this means that others are set free." Prevot, *The Mysticism of Ordinary Life: Theology, Philosophy, and Feminism* (New York: Oxford University Press, 2023), 138.

But if you surrender to sorrow and confess your unhappiness, you will find the God of Israel who redeems all.[33] Investigating our sorrow is the very opposite of fatalistically giving in to sorrow and allowing the sorrow to become demonic.

Blaise Pascal gives us a form of evangelism that invites us not into proofs for God, religious diversions, or culture accommodations, but instead falls into unhappiness to investigate what we might find there. The congregation and Pastor Manta are leading Renate to this place, taking her into an event of evangelism. This form of evangelism enters sorrow, wagering that the God who met Pascal in the night of fire will be found right inside the sorrow, giving to the self the communion of soul it so longs for.

Evangelism names our shared sorrow and invites our neighbors to stop running from their sorrow but instead to directly enter it. Evangelism is the invitation into this kind of Pascaline investigation, which is always done with others, in communion, by being carried. But importantly, it is not an investigation of the self (how does this religion or belief work for me?) but of the soul (I'm restless and longing, I'm hurt and broken, I'm alone and in need, and where are you O Lord?—Ps. 130). It is evangelism in the cadence of the psalmist. The church is the community that joins the world in its sorrow, proclaiming the good news that when sorrow is shared in mutual investigation, a fire of transformation comes and renews.

Moving Forward

Such a view of evangelism has deep resonance and great possibility inside the sad times of the first three decades of the twenty-first century. Blaise takes us far, but there is something significant he never mentions in *Pensées*. And it's a shame. He never mentions, and therefore neglects to investigate, the pastoral presence of Jacqueline and the prayers of Gilberte. Blaise

---

33. Kierkegaard adds, "And now, if we could say that obedience followed as a matter of course from suffering, then we might expect to find a man with the courage to choose suffering, one who, when suffering befell, had the courage to reckon he was fortunate. Ah, but it is not thus; learning does not come about so easily. Suffering itself is, from a human point of view, the first danger, but the second danger, which is still more terrible, is that we should not learn obedience. Suffering is a lesson full of danger; for, if we do not learn obedience—ah, then it is as terrible as if the most efficacious of medicines had the wrong kind of effect. In such danger man needs help: he needs the help of God; else he learns not obedience." Søren Kierkegaard, *Gospel of Suffering* (Cambridge: James Clarke, 2015), 55.

fails to see that soul needs communion. It is impossible to investigate the sorrow of the soul without another joining and caring for us. You cannot be consoled without others.

In the end, though Blaise takes us far, his attention to investigation and use of the language of gambling is too individualistic. He misses, at least in his descriptions, the vital presence of his sisters and their pastoral presence and practice. Therefore, Pascal, while essential to our reshaping of evangelism for our sad times, is too much of an arguer, too much of a shock comic writer, to take us into a fully reshaped practice of evangelism as consolation. As Blaise's own story shows, an evangelism of consolation needs at its core not a defender but a pastor. Pascal invites us to investigate our sorrow but doesn't see that we will need the accompaniment of a minister to join us as we do.

To find these kinds of pastors in the tradition who can help us as we build off Pascal, we must do a little looking. Our looking will take us back before Pascal to the ministries of Macrina, Gregory of Nyssa, Jean Gerson, Johann von Staupitz, and Martin Luther. In the next three chapters, we'll follow Pascal into sorrow, examining how, in this sorrow, we meet the God who joins and redeems sorrow. We'll see the shape of this redemption through the pastoral theologies of Macrina, Gregory, Gerson, Staupitz, and Luther. Each will help us see how consolation becomes the sacramental embodiment that takes us into Christ. *Evangelism in these sad times is ultimately the confession that God meets us in our human sorrow and through our sorrow takes our person into Jesus's own person.* This is good news! Through the art of shared sorrow we participate in the being of God and bring the good news to the world. Macrina, Gregory, Gerson, Staupitz, and Luther will show us this art.

■ ■ ■ ■

A short reception followed the funeral. It consisted mostly of people drinking coffee and getting the flowers to Renate's car. But everyone who stayed also gave Renate another word of peace and consolation. These people, some of whom she didn't know, all saw her sorrow and stepped right into it with her. Renate felt so sad and yet held in that sadness.

The room eventually cleared out, and only Renate, Pastor Manta, and AC remained. Cynthia had disappeared right after the service. Renate was disappointed not to catch up with her. It still shocked Renate that Cynthia had come at all. As Renate was thinking about Cynthia's appearance and disappearance, AC asked, "You good with how it all went? I know you were scared of doin' this."

AC's directness caught Renate off guard. She found herself answering without thinking, "It was hard. It was as hard as I thought. But different. It was the first time I really grieved."

"And what happened when you did?" Pastor Manta asked, entering the conversation, as he walked toward Renate.

"I hadn't really grieved because I was scared. I mean I've been sad, and sad that I'm sad, and worried and anxious that I wasn't doing any of my sadness right. Wasn't mourning the way I was supposed to. And that if I really did let go and mourn I'd break into a million pieces and never be put back together."

"Did any of that happen?" Pastor Manta asked.

"No. I'm not sure how to say this, but when I really mourned today, I did feel like I broke into a million pieces. But I felt held together. I've never felt this before. I think I was right to be frightened that I'd break into a million pieces, because no one was there to hold me together. Not until today. This time, the church was there—AC, Myrtle, Hazel, and Mary Ann. I knew they were holding me together so that I could just mourn. When you said in your speech about blessed are those who mourn, I just let go. When you said that my dad mourned, I just let go and cried for him. For his life, for his loss. And I don't how to say it, but I experienced something. A presence or a nearness. It was a spiritual experience for sure, but one like I'd never known. I mean, I've been really into spirituality for a long time. But this was different. Maybe I was imagining something, but I felt like someone, maybe Jesus—does that sound weird?—was with me. Blessing me, I guess. It was beautiful and pretty scary. But a different kind of scary than I was expecting."

Pastor Manta just nodded, acknowledging the event of evangelism and even moving into the response of discipleship, saying, "You've got to explore that. I think God has something for you in this sorrow. Walk into it, see if it was really Jesus. Keep going, keep letting go and leaning into the sorrow. But remember you can't do that kind of thing alone."

"We can walk with you," AC added with his direct flair.

Renate smiled and said, "Thanks!"

And that was the last time anyone at the church heard from Renate. She disappeared into the fog of time. But two weeks after the funeral a strange message was left on the church's voicemail.

7

Sisters as Pastors

Leaning into Sorrow and the Promises of Consolation

The message came from a man whose voice was filled with anxiety and desperation. "I've been trying to figure out what church it was, so I'm not sure if it was this one. But my wife is in trouble. We both are. I'm worried about her. She keeps talking about this church thing she went to or something. I don't know. She said it was up by Ramona . . . maybe. I'm wondering if that's you, can you help? I mean, honestly, if you're the church she's thinking of or whatever, we really, really need your help. Maybe you're not. But maybe . . . anyhow, my number is 867–5309. Okay bye . . . sorry . . . bye."

The church secretary, Judy, Pastor Manta, and Hazel listened to the message a half dozen times, trying to decipher what this man was referring to. They couldn't figure it out. They all decided he was looking for a different church. They agreed on that. But then Hazel said, "But we follow Jesus into sorrow, right Pastor?" and began dialing. She left her own voicemail with her number. When she hung up, all three shrugged their shoulders and figured it would come to nothing.

The next day, when Hazel had forgotten all about it, she got a call. It was the guy from the message. His voice had the same urgency of the voicemail. Hazel's first thought as the man talked was that he was intense and he must be exhausted.

"Thanks for calling me back," he said. "So, are you the church?"

"Um, I don't know," Hazel said. "I'm not sure, but first what is your name?"

"Oh man, did I not say it in the message? How stupid. Sorry, I'm Nate."

"Hi Nate, what's going on? I know you're in trouble or something, but what is it?"

"It's my wife. She was pregnant and we lost the baby. She's taking it so hard. It's our fourth miscarriage and this one was late. The latest. We thought . . . well, it's been hard. She hasn't gotten up from the couch since she came home from the hospital. The others were really hard on her too. But this one is scaring me. She's so heartbroken. I've never seen her like this. This was our last chance and, well, I think she's just given up. She didn't even talk for the first few days. When she did, she just kept talking about this church she randomly went to. Something to do with a friend from high school. She won't say more. She's mentioned it a half dozen times but won't say more. She doesn't say much of anything. She just keeps crying and it's freaking me out. Like majorly. So, is that you guys? Are you that church?"

"A thing for a friend?" Hazel asked. She was confused. This didn't sound like anything their church did. "When was it?" she asked.

"What? The thing?" Nate responded. "Two weeks ago or something. Hold on, I can look at our shared calendar. I don't know why I didn't think of that."

There was a pause as Nate looked. Then he said, "Oh maybe it wasn't a church thing. It says it was at the VFW. It says 'Mr. Medlam's funeral.'"

"Renate!" Hazel said. She knew right away that it was Cynthia. She hadn't met Cynthia at the funeral but remembered seeing her. She was hard to miss, as far along in her pregnancy as she was.

"Oh no. Okay," Hazel said as it all came together. "We'll come down and see her. What is your address?"

A few hours later Hazel, Myrtle, and a younger woman named Jackie arrived at Cynthia and Nate's. Nate welcomed them in. Hazel and Jackie sat with Cynthia. Myrtle had brought groceries and some prepared food, and after talking with Nate, she began tidying the kitchen and readying dinner. Hazel and Jackie told Cynthia that they were from the church. Cynthia said, "Yes, I know. I remember her." She pointed at Myrtle. "I saw you hug Renate. When I lost my baby, I thought 'I need a hug like that.'"

Myrtle came over and hugged Cynthia. Hazel and Jackie then just sat with Cynthia. They didn't say a word.[1] They ate what Myrtle had prepared as Cynthia lay on the couch. Then they sat longer, as Myrtle filled their fridge with labeled meals in Tupperware. The three women then left, promising to return tomorrow. Myrtle said, "I'll clean the bathrooms and whatever else needs doing. Hazel and Jackie, or our friend Wilma, will sit with you again. Is that okay?"

Cynthia nodded and whispered, "Please. Thank you."

The next day Myrtle, Hazel, and Mary Ann came back. Mary Ann was taking some time off work. Since Mr. Medlam's funeral she'd felt so fatigued. It had been a busy time dealing with Will and the launch of a new partnership with a fitness app. She figured she just needed a few days of rest. After almost three days of straight sleep, sitting with Cynthia felt right.

Nate and Cynthia's home was a place of juxtaposition. It was decorated warmly. The colors of the walls were bright. The natural light streamed in from big windows and an oversized sliding glass door. Pillows of all sorts and sizes were everywhere. Mary Ann thought to herself, as the three women entered, "Oh, these are pillow people." The juxtaposition was how deeply the once warm space was now filled with sadness and anxiety. Cynthia was still lying on the couch, right where Myrtle and Hazel had left her. She was wrapped in a turquoise blanket and pink robe.

Myrtle scrubbed the bathrooms, vacuumed the hallway, and heated up some food for everyone. Cynthia had refused to eat the day before. She hadn't eaten much of anything since she'd lost the baby. "Let's eat," Hazel said. And to everyone's surprise, Cynthia got up and sat at the table. There were a few comments about the food and the need to pass this or that. But for the most part, they all sat in silence. Even Nate, who was always anxiously filling the silence with some statement and couldn't sit quietly, was still as they ate. They all just rested in each other's presence.

Hazel broke the silence and told a story about her new dog, a rescue retriever mix.

"I love dogs," Cynthia said. "I grew up with them. We were going to get one for—" Cynthia stopped herself as the sorrow grabbed for her.

---

1. Robert Gregg says, "Gregory of Nyssa remarks that silence is an excellent medicine for the bereaved. Speech, if it comes while the soul is still inflamed, will cause the wound of grief." Gregg, *Consolation Philosophy: Greek and Christian Paideia in Basil and the Two Gregories* (Philadelphia: Philadelphia Patristics Foundation, 1975), 138.

Nate looked away, the sorrow reaching right for his soul.

"Well," Hazel said, "this guy needs *a lot* of walking. I'm walking every day now. Mary Ann and I used to walk Monday, Wednesday, and Friday. Now I'm every day!"

"Not me," Mary Ann jumped in. "I'm still Monday, Wednesday, Friday." But Mary Ann hadn't walked in a few weeks. She'd just been too tired.

Everyone laughed at the thought of Hazel being walked by the dog against her will.

"I guess it's good for me," Hazel added. "You can join us any time, Cynthia. I'm sure Trevor the Tormenter would love you."

Everyone smiled. Cynthia nodded. And then the silence returned. This time Cynthia broke it. She said, "I want a funeral for my Maddy."

Nate was taken aback. "We hadn't settled on a name. And a funeral?" he said.

Cynthia ignored his question. She asked the women, "Can you all do a funeral for her? Like with Mr. Medlam?"

"We can talk to Pastor Manta," Myrtle said. "I'm sure we can."

■ ■ ■ ■

Pastor Manta agreed. Cynthia and Nate decided that they'd baptize and bury Maddy at the same time. Cynthia insisted on it. The baby's remains had been waiting at the morgue, but it had been too painful and confusing to respond to the voicemails yet about what they wanted done.

Cynthia had been to church only a few times in the last ten years. She'd been present when her older sister had her children baptized. Cynthia hated how judgmental going to church had made her sister. "She became so rigid," Cynthia described it. It made Cynthia stay away from church for her whole adult life. Even so, the baptisms were meaningful and beautiful. She wanted that for Maddy. Pastor Manta was uneasy at first with the thought of baptizing a deceased baby. But eventually he agreed.

Cynthia wanted a baptism and a funeral. Nate wanted to talk.

After the funeral, Nate invited Pastor Manta for a beer and poured out his questions and thoughts. Pastor Manta recognized immediately that the questions, which in the end weren't really questions but statements, were Nate's way of grieving. Nate needed a confessor. Pastor Manta listened in silence. Nate wanted to know why God did this, but then said he didn't believe there was a God. Then he said he didn't know how he could love someone he never met, missing this child he never got to know. He wondered what is love and what is their future. Did the God he didn't believe in care about that future? How could God know we're all so sad and not do something about it? And what about Cynthia? Why couldn't Nate protect her? Why couldn't God? Would she be okay? It all came rushing out.

Pastor Manta finished his soda (he'd passed on the beer) and said, "I get it. First, there was nothing you or Cynthia did wrong. There was no way you could have kept this from happening. And it hurts like hell. I know that. I lost my older brother. We were pastoring together. I was his associate. It was my first years as a pastor. I'd admired him my whole life. He was the first Latino pastor in our denomination. I became a pastor because he did. He was the most important person in my world. He led me to Jesus. I wanted to be just like him. Then he died in a terrible car accident. I mean terrible. I had to do his funeral, closed casket—my first funeral!—with all these same questions you have." Pastor Manta paused and let the sorrow of his lost brother hit him again.

He continued, "Having experienced it, what is God doing about it? It's hard . . . but I think, *something*. Something very hard to recognize at first but very wonderful when you do. To see it you need to really lean into the sorrow of it. Then you experience it—what God is doing with it. And believe me, I know that's very hard. But you do have to lean into all the sorrow. And you can't do that leaning in alone or you'll fall into a dangerous place. If you're interested in leaning in, we have a group that meets Tuesday nights to do just that. We'll hold you. I'm still needing that holding, still needing the encouragement to lean in. At first I didn't, I was too mad. So mad I started sneaking drinks. That's why no beer for me. But that's another story. Even twenty years after losing my brother, I'm still needing that holding. We'll lean in with you and Cynthia." Pastor Manta's views of evangelism were infused with a community of disciples who journey into sorrow.

The Dead Pastor

There are two late-modern critiques of Christianity often echoed by certain late-modern Protestants. Such critiques affect our confidence in evangelism. The first critique is that Christianity is far too concerned with heaven and therefore lacks the empathy for this-world struggles. The second is that Christianity is toxically patriarchal. These critiques exist because there are more than a few examples of such realities. That cannot be denied. There have been more than a few expressions of Christian faith that have sought to escape the world. To the point of telling mothers of dead children not to grieve for their dead children for they are now in heaven. They're in a better place, or God needed them more than we did, or they are now angels looking down. And in our own day there have been a plethora of structures and behaviors that have been toxically patriarchal. These examples cannot be ignored. But to assume that the whole of the tradition lacks compassion and is toxically patriarchal is anachronistic.[2] For example, we have Gregory of Nyssa, one of the greatest pastoral theologians of the tradition.

Gregory's story is not unlike Pastor Manta's (with a resonance to Pascal's own story). Gregory, born around 335, entered a family that became Christian under persecution. His grandparents and parents lived in the time of the martyrs. The martyrs' stories were still fresh and forming. His brothers Naucratius, Peter, and Basil were all leaders and venerated as saints. Basil particularly made a mark not only with his defense of Nicaean Christology and articulations of the Trinity but in his reorganization of monastic life and his overall leadership as a bishop of Caesarea. As able as Basil was as a thinker, he was even more skilled as an administrator. As Gregory's older brother, Basil was the gravitational force that set the motion of Gregory's own life. Gregory was happy to be a rhetoric teacher, spending his days in his books, when Basil came and convinced him to become the bishop of Nyssa.

Basil was a pastor to many people. The church, into our day, owes him a debt. But ironically, Basil was *not* Gregory's pastor. Gregory's pastor,

---

2. Henry Adams adds to this, saying, "The Church itself never liked to be dragged too far under feminine influence, although the moment it discarded feminine influence it lost nearly everything of any value to it or to the world, except its philosophy." Adams, *Mont Saint Michel and Chartres* (New York: Penguin, 1986), 260. The great Peter Brown adds, "For women in the ancient world, the cemetery areas had always been a zone of 'low gravity,' where their movements and choice of company were less subject to male scrutiny and the control of the family. The new shrines, when not crowded on days of festival, were oases of peace and beauty, with flowing water, rustling trees, filled with the cooing of white doves. In the shrine of Saint Stephen at Uzalis, we can see how the vast tranquility of a shrine could engulf and heal a woman caught in the rigidities of her urban setting." Brown, *The Cult of the Saints: Its Rise and Function in Latin Christianity* (Chicago: University of Chicago Press, 2015), 44.

as it was with Pascal, was his sister, Macrina. Jacqueline is a sort of seventeenth-century descendant of Macrina. What we know about Macrina comes directly from Gregory's pen. It comes because she died, and Gregory was *deeply* grieved. Very deeply. Basil—who too had died—may have been the one who moved Gregory into ministry. But it was Macrina who showed Gregory what it meant to be a pastor. Her loss throbs within him. Gregory writes to enter the sorrow.

The Life of Macrina

Like many of the other consolation writings that follow Gregory's, this one takes the form of a letter. Consolation can never be just theoretical.[3] It must be fundamentally practiced. It is always pastoral. Consolation is one of the tradition's deepest forms of doing theology, and it is *never* disconnected from the practice of ministry. Consolation is the heart of pastoral theology. It knows nothing of a theory-practice split—so much so that it can't even bear a self-soul split.[4]

Gregory is in sorrow. In sorrow, he takes a journey as a pilgrim to the Holy Land. Gregory believes all of life is a journey and he has vowed to visit Jerusalem. The Christian life is a pilgrim's life. On this journey Gregory reconnects with a monk named Olympus in Antioch. As they talk,

3. Mary Melchior Beyenka, drawing from Augustine, pushes us deeper, saying, "Consolation is defined as 'the alleviation of misery or distress of mind or spirit.' Words of sympathy have always been among the means employed by friends to comfort those who grieve over the loss of their dear ones in death. Yet the unpractised words of friends are sometimes halting and so the ancient Greeks and Romans had the custom of calling in philosophers at a time of grief, for they professed to be healers of moral pain. They had ready certain remarks which, like moral medicines, fitted the particular ills of their fellow men. When the universal need for consolation was recognized by the schools of rhetoric in antiquity, there developed a well-defined literary genre, the *consolatio mortis.*" Beyenka, *Consolation in St. Augustine* (Washington, DC: Catholic University of America Press, 1950), 1.

4. Robert Gregg adds, "The Cappadocian Fathers belong to that company of early Christians in the East who refused, however ascetic their practice of the faith, to disavow the world to which they preached, and who refused, despite the strictures of their fellow believers, to renounce their loyalty to the very culture they labored to convert and reform. The result was a posture which might seem to moderns paradoxical: advocates of detachment from the world are unwilling to surrender their attachments to the cultural heritage of the Hellenists. In this the Cappadocians, like the Alexandrians before them, were simply advancing and elaborating the thesis of the early Apologists: their Christ revealed . . . that wisdom and virtue towards which the entire pilgrimage of Greek poets and philosophers had been straining through the centuries." Gregg, *Consolation Philosophy*, 125.

Olympus takes an interest in Macrina's story. He particularly wants to hear how she died. Olympus is not concerned about the details necessarily but *the way* she faced death, the way her spirit or soul encountered it.

Monks, particularly in the fourth century, meditated often on dying. So too did people like Montaigne. They wanted to explore *the way* to face death and to die well. We late moderns are not so interested in how to face death as much as how people die—the latter being what news stories and sometimes obituaries tell us. We're more interested in the details of what killed someone than in how that someone prepared for death and faced it well. We want to know: Was it an accident? Cancer? The person's fault? Or some bad luck? For us late-modern Westerns living in consumer societies, contemplating death to prepare to die is abhorrent. We like to forget we're going to die at all.[5]

Not so with Olympus or Gregory. Olympus wants to contemplate death. And Gregory takes a pilgrimage to prepare for his own death.[6] Gregory is walking to face the sorrow of losing his sister and brothers. Gregory decides, with his letter, to write a biography of Macrina for Olympus. The point is to give Olympus more than just information about Macrina's

5. Michel Foucault gives a long but insightful quote: "I think that we can see a concrete manifestation of this power in the famous gradual disqualification of death, which sociologists and historians have discussed so often. Everyone knows, thanks in particular to a certain number of recent studies, that the great public ritualization of death gradually began to disappear, or at least to fade away, in the late eighteenth century and that it is still doing so today. So much so that death—which has ceased to be one of those spectacular ceremonies in which individuals, the family, the group, and practically the whole of society took part—has become, in contrast, something to be hidden away. It has become the most private and shameful thing of all (and ultimately, it is now not so much sex as death that is the object of a taboo). Now I think that the reason why death had become something to be hidden away is not that anxiety has somehow been displaced or that repressive mechanisms have been modified. What once (and until the end of the eighteenth century) made death so spectacular and ritualized it so much was the fact that it was a manifestation of a transition from one power to another. Death was the moment when we made the transition from one power—that of the sovereign of this world—to another—that of the sovereign of the next world. We went from one court of law to another, from a civil or public right over life and death to a right to either eternal life or eternal damnation. A transition from one power to another. Death also meant the transmission of the power of the dying, and that power was transmitted to those who survived him: last words, last recommendations, last wills and testaments, and so on. All these phenomena of power were ritualized." Foucault, *Society Must Be Defended: Lectures at the Collège de France 1975–1976* (New York: Picador, 1997), 248.

6. Peter Brown adds, "At death, the crevasse came to open wide. No one could be secure at that awful moment. Macrina, sitting upright in her bed facing the east, prayed the long, somber prayer of the dying, which put into ancient words a sense of perilous uncertainty: 'Place beside me an angel of light, to lead me by the hand . . . and may the Envious One not stand against me on my way.'" Brown, *Cult of the Saints*, 67.

life. The letter becomes a *vita* of a saint (it's common to record the life of a saintly person, keeping the résumé of God's work through them for future generations). But Gregory's letter is also more than that. It's a biography of consolation. It takes the form of a *vita*, but it is an example of what a few hundred years later will become known as the consolation of philosophy. Even in Gregory's time, across the Mediterranean world, early elements of the consolation of philosophy were popping up.[7] As Gregory tells Olympus, Macrina was a skilled philosopher.

The point of the consolation of philosophy was to help people deal with the fear and pain of loss. How to best face this loss was debated. Was it best to face this fear and loss as an Epicurean or a Stoic? Was it better to face it with flowing passions of mourning or reserved and re-signed rationality? (We've already seen how this debate raged on into the sixteenth and seventeenth centuries, Montaigne affirming the passions and Descartes rationality, Pascal calling both pagan and, like Gregory, finding a way beyond both.) Particularly in Gregory's time, the live question was, How should a Christian face loss?[8]

The New Job and the List of Sorrows

Gregory answers by examining the pastoral life of his sister. How did the great Macrina deal with loss? To answer, Gregory must first establish that she knew much loss. Sorrow was a deep part of Macrina's life. Gregory tells Olympus that Macrina was not only a great pastor but a new Job. Gregory uses the example of Job in many of his other pastoral consolation letters, and in the middle of *The Life of St. Macrina* he links his sister's life with the life of Job. Very high veneration. The book of Job is the original consolation literature, and Gregory believes that Macrina embodies it in her own holy life.

7. For a discussion of this background, see Paul A. Holloway, *Consolation in Philippians: Philosophical Sources and Rhetorical Strategy* (New York: Cambridge University Press, 2001), 55–60.

8. "The Cappadocian consolation letters and sermons provide a most interesting model. . . . They typically start by expressing the situation, and sometimes the author's own grief. But then there is a reverse movement. Although we must not be free of emotion, we must be moderate. Standard consolations are drawn from the pagans, but reinforced by the Christian hope of resurrection." Richard Sorabji, *Emotion and Peace of Mind: From Stoic Agitation to Christian Temptation* (New York: Oxford University Press, 2010), 394.

Gregory tells of Macrina's many sorrows. They started before she was born.[9] Macrina was the oldest child of a great Cappadocian family of the church. Her mother was married off to her father only after her mother's parents were killed as martyrs. Macrina is a child born out of this sorrow. The loss of her grandparents brings her into the world. Her own holiness is inseparable from what is found in sorrow. The birth of Macrina was also difficult. In deep labor pains, her mother slid into unconsciousness. As she woke, an angel addressed the little one, giving Macrina a secret name.

The indelible sorrow that transformed Macrina happened when she herself came to the age of marriage. Macrina was betrothed to someone for whom she had a deep affection—perhaps unusual for the time. She anticipated a life just like her mother's, managing a household as a mother to children. Then sorrow struck. Her fiancé died and she was deeply grieved. As she leaned into the sorrow, the Spirit came upon her and transformed her.

Macrina chose—or, better, was called—to never marry. Gregory says, "She strongly insisted that the young man who had been joined to her in accordance with her parents' decision was not dead, but that, in her judgment, he was living in God because of the hope of the resurrection."[10] Her fiancé was on a great journey, she explained to her parents. Therefore, instead of remarrying, she'd give her life to the contemplations of God's presence in sorrow. Gregory tells us that she becomes Thecla—the true teacher—revealing this as the secret name given to her at birth by an angel or even Thecla herself.[11] In the early Byzantine church Thecla was

9. Robert Gregg adds to this connection to Job, saying, "The treatments of Job in the Cappadocian writings are not uniform. Basil's epistolary references are abbreviated, but they contain the core ingredients of this particular consolatory argument-by-example. He writes of this man whose life was a lesson in bearing misfortune." Gregg, *Consolation Philosophy*, 186. *

10. Gregory of Nyssa, *The Life of Saint Macrina*, ed. Kevin Corrigan (Eugene, OR: Wipf & Stock, 2001), 25.

11. Brown gives us further texture: "If we turn to Gregory of Nyssa's life of his sister Macrina, we can see what this could mean in a cultivated Christian family. Macrina, Gregory writes, was only her public name; she had a true, secret name, revealed in a vision. For when her mother was giving birth to her, she dreamed three times that she was holding her child while a majestic figure, the virgin martyr Thecla, gave her the name of Thecla. She was really giving birth to a second Thecla. The dream was crucial for Macrina's mother, a young woman, who had married unwillingly, merely to gain the protection of a husband when her parents had died, and for whom this was the first experience of childbirth: the labor became easy, and Macrina was born with her identity secured. The sadness of physical birth had been redeemed. Macrina would soon be joined by a succession of formidable brothers. But with her identity reinforced and a trifle overshadowed by her mysterious link to the exemplary virgin Thecla, Macrina always

known from a second-century apocryphal text called the Acts of Paul and Thecla. The Thecla of that text was a noble woman who, after meeting Paul, became a disciple, leaving her fiancé to follow the gospel. Macrina doesn't leave her fiancé but finds in the loss of her fiancé the presence of Jesus Christ meeting her in sorrow. Macrina becomes the new Thecla not *only* by renunciation but, like Job, by embracing sorrow, leaning into it, and finding that God moves inside it. This mystical encounter in sorrow is what Macrina teaches, making her, at least to her brothers (and mother), the great Thecla who teaches them Paul's theology of the cross. Her students, Basil and Gregory, became the most imaginative theologians of church history, helping us conceive of how the divine and human commune. Macrina knew this experience inside her sorrow and embodied it as a pastor to her brothers and to the poor to whom she was called.

It became clear, after this sorrow, that Macrina was solely God's servant, faithful in all ways. She was the great teacher Thecla. When the righteousness is spotted, the storms of sorrow come, as they did for Job. Her father, Basil the Elder, was struck ill and died. His death shook them all.[12] But what happened a few years later was far heavier.

Macrina's brother Naucratius, who had given his life to caring for the poor and elderly, and his friend are killed in a hunting accident. His death also shakes the family. Already in sorrow with the loss of Basil the Elder, they are shaken to the core. Macrina's mother is overwhelmed with grief. Basil the younger (Macrina's brother), who was in Athens becoming friends with the other Gregory, Gregory of Nazianzus, comes home. Gregory of Nyssa tells us that Basil the younger returns home puffed with importance, insufferably self-assured and even arrogant. Basil's education has made him proud and self-important. Macrina rebukes him and leads him back to humility, showing him the true philosophy.[13] Thecla forms the great Basil, becoming his great teacher,

---

remained different. As a child, she had lived 'as if she was still in her mother's womb'; as head of a convent, her life trembled on the invisible frontier between the human and the angelic." Brown, *Cult of the Saints*, 58.

12. There is some debate about when Basil the Elder died. In the introduction to Kevin Corrigan's translation of *The Life of Saint Macrina*, he says she was twelve when he died. Gregory seems to put the death after her betrothed is dead. Maybe that is right around the age of twelve, yet for our purposes I've placed the event securely after the death of her fiancé.

13. Georges Duby says this about humility: "According to the mysticism of an author like Tauler, humility allows man to draw so close to God that he becomes 'divine.' Such proximity of a God embodied in the attitudes and sufferings of his creatures obviously implied a victory

outstripping even the minds of Greece. She was wiser than any Athenian philosopher.

Macrina and her mother grieve for Naucratius. The sorrow envelops her mother. Macrina knows that there is something that meets you in such grief. She encountered it herself with the loss of her fiancé. Macrina leads her mother into sorrow (an act of evangelism). Like Macrina before her, her mother experiences the transforming work of the ministering Spirit of Jesus Christ. She follows Macrina into the mystical life of contemplation and service. Macrina becomes her mother's teacher. Macrina then turns the family estate into a monastery and takes over the care of her youngest brother, Peter—who himself becomes a saint, learning too from the great Thecla.

Macrina was teaching the arcane mysticism of sorrow, overseeing the monastery, and teaching Peter when Basil, her brother, became ill. The eldest brother, who led and loved like thunder, died from that illness. When word came to Macrina about Basil's death, she again faced the sorrow. Gregory is shaken, the sorrow overwhelming him. He watches Macrina intently—she is his teacher after all. Gregory says about her, listing her litany of sorrows like Job's, "The high quality of her thinking was thoroughly tested by successive attacks of painful grief to reveal the . . . undebased nature of her soul, first by the death of her other brother, Naucratios, after this by the separation from her mother [who too died] and third when Basil, the common honour of our family, departed from human life." Gregory lets the sorrow hit him and he says, "So she stood her ground like an undefeated athlete, who does not cringe at any point before the onslaught of misfortune."[14]

Gregory tells Olympus that in the midst of all this sorrow, he decided he needed to go and see his sister. It had been too long. The demands of his own bishopric kept him from his great teacher. On the way to the monastery, Gregory had a dream that alarmed him. When he arrives, he's told that his premonition is true. Macrina is bedridden and ill. She is suffering and dying. Macrina is fighting for her own life. The pain and sorrow of her illness overwhelms Gregory. The pain she suffers is intense.

---

over a number of taboos, over ecclesiastical indictments of human virtues and pleasures." Duby, *The Age of the Cathedrals: Art and Society, 980–1420* (Chicago: University of Chicago Press, 1981), 219.

14. Gregory of Nyssa, *Life of Saint Macrina*, 33.

He sits with her, prays for her, and receives her prayers for him. Macrina bears her illness holding to the promise of God's love and mercy. She faces her death in assurance of God's nearness, inside the great hope of resurrection. Macrina is sure she is met in her sorrow and suffering. But as she has known, death is a great thief.

Death, Satan, and the Resurrection

Gregory tells Olympus, drawing again from Job, that death viciously snatches. Death is no friend; there is nothing noble in it (this is different from what Platonists or Stoics believe). Gregory tells the monk that death is the attack of Satan.[15] To Gregory, the body and soul are fused. This makes death a great enemy, and resurrection our only hope. Gregory is the great theologian of resurrection—learning this from his sister. Resurrection promises a great transformation where death is defeated and our being is recreated in the full and complete image of God.[16] Gregory is the theologian of resurrection only because he suffers in great sorrow, knowing the cross.

Gregory watches Macrina intently as his teacher, as a great master of spirit. When sorrow comes, is she an Epicurean or a Stoic? Which philosophy consoles her? Is she overcome by passions of mourning or firm rationality? Macrina grieves, but the passions don't overtake her. She stands up like an athlete amid the sorrow, more rational than Gregory could ever be. She can do this because the passions of mourning, the pain of sorrow, are freed from being locked in the self. Faced with sorrow, neither the Epicurean ways of passions nor the Stoic ways of rationality will lead beyond the self, and both will imprison it. But if we follow the sorrow, leaning into it, seeing it as an invitation into a journey—a pilgrimage—we will discover that it is a passion that exists on the borderline of the self. Thus, sorrow takes us out of our self and moves us into the land of soul. If we follow the sorrow, we will find the Spirit of ministry caring for us in the embrace of Jesus Christ himself.

15. There is a place for dying in the goodness of nature, but death is the snatching of life that imposes a great sorrow. Karl Barth draws a distinction between death and dying. See Barth, *Church Dogmatics* III/2, *The Doctrine of Creation*, trans. Geoffrey Bromiley, ed. T. F. Torrance (Edinburgh: T&T Clark, 1958), sections 40–48.

16. For a discussion of this sense of resurrection as transformation, see Gregg, *Consolation Philosophy*, 205–7.

Sorrows of death and illness are demonic (and unredeemable) only when they are locked in a self. But when they take us into soul, we meet someone—we meet the presence of Jesus Christ, who invites us to grieve but in the assurance and embrace of the ministry of the Spirit.[17] Here we feed on the sacrament of the resurrection. Macrina, like her own great teacher Paul (remember, she is Thecla), is "afflicted in every way, but not crushed, . . . struck down, but not destroyed" (2 Cor. 4:8–9), because she is met in her sorrow at the level of soul. Her life and death take the shape of the cross and resurrection.

Her response takes her beyond Epicureanism and Stoicism because sorrow becomes the doorway into resurrection. As Pascal taught us, resurrection is a reality the philosophers cannot know. It is pure fire. As it did with Job, sorrow is a doorway that takes the great Macrina to God.[18] It transforms her, clothing her in the resurrection. It gives her assurance that all sorrow shares in the being of God, who ministers life out of death. To underline this point, Gregory ends his story of Macrina by time-jumping back from her death to her healing of a little girl's eye. Gregory ends his letter this way to highlight one last time for Olympus how Macrina, through her sorrow (the cross), feeds on the sacrament of resurrection. Healing is the sign of the resurrection's coming.

Gregory doesn't want Olympus to miss that the resurrection comes only by way of the cross. Inside sorrow is a great resurrection reality. To encounter this resurrection reality of soul, sorrow must be entered as what it is—true, heartbreaking suffering. Gregory gives us a picture of Macrina standing like an oak against the winds of sorrow.[19] But the

17. Drawing on Augustine, Mary Melchior Beyenka says, "Augustine calls God a consoler in grief, for God either teaches men to bear grief or He heals that which is burdensome. Christ suffered in order to console us by his example; the Paraclete is sent to the sad—a Comforter, God is likened to a doctor, healing the pain of grief by the promise of another life and by His words recorded in Scripture. Grief has a purpose which is taught by Scripture." Beyenka, *Consolation in St. Augustine*, 50.

18. "To suffer means to give oneself over to God and his story, which through Jesus has already been revealed to be precisely that suffering. One's suffering must be part of that story if it is not to be an act of inventing our own story." Hans Ulrich, *Transfigured Not Conformed: Christian Ethics in a Hermeneutic Key* (Edinburgh: T&T Clark, 2023), 78.

19. Mary Melchior Beyenka adds, "Augustine had pondered the words of Scripture which urge the Christian to 'weep with those who weep.' In his compassion the consoler must feel the sorrow of another, yet he must also be free from all painful emotion when he assists those in need of consolation. His acts should be characterized by tranquility of mind, for he acts not from the stimulus of painful feeling, but from motives of benevolence. Thus Augustine does not set aside the words of Scripture, but qualifies the compassion of the consoler, who by

picture he gives of himself is much different. Gregory is a weeping willow, bent to the ground by the winds of loss. Gregory becomes a mess when Basil dies. He breaks down in the text itself as he talks of his sister, and he tells Olympus that he threw himself down on Macrina's grave in grief.[20] Gregory wants to show Olympus that what he learned from his sister is to enter the sorrow. Gregory has become that pilgrim. But it hurts and it humbles. Unlike Macrina, Gregory is not an undefeated athlete. Nevertheless, Macrina assures Gregory by her life that in the sorrow that hurts (and calls for humility) there is a great transformation.

Transformation through sorrow is the *evangel*, the good news. To evangelize is to invite the one who hears to enter the presence of the living God by being joined in their sorrow, which draws sorrow into soul. In this joining we taste resurrection and are saved. To evangelize is to teach and preach, like Macrina, that in sorrow is the one who ministers new life. To evangelize is not to convert people's interests (making them into religious adherents) but to invite them to find the ministry of the Spirit in their sorrow. The act of evangelism gives consolation, as Gregory does to Olympus by telling the story of Macrina. Telling her story consoles

---

first grieving with the one in distress can then refresh him with consolatory words." Beyenka, *Consolation in St. Augustine*, 44.

20. Caroline Walker Bynum says, "Gregory, like other writers of the mid-fourth century, felt horror at decay. 'Mortal remains [except those of the martyrs] are to most people an object of disgust,' he wrote, 'and no one passes near a tomb with pleasure; if despite all our care, we find an open grave and cast our eyes on the horror of the body that lies therein, we are filled with disgust and groan loudly that human nature should come to this.' When the grave of his parents was opened to receive Macrina's body, he panicked. Horrified (as Basil and Gregory Nazianzus were also) at the prospect of disturbing a putrefying corpse or of mingling bones from several bodies, Gregory sexualized what he feared by describing it with a reference from Leviticus that actually concerns incest . . . : 'How, I ask myself, will I be spared . . . condemnation if I look at the common shame of human nature in the bodies of my parents, which are certainly decomposed, disintegrated, and transformed into an appearance unformed, hideous, and repulsive?' Behind Gregory's hope of resurrection lies a desperate desire that neither his parents nor his siblings will really decay, whatever is to happen to their flesh. When he discusses the parable of Lazarus and the rich man (frequently problematic for patristic exegetes), it is very important to him to explain that a soul between death and resurrection can still have a finger in potential—that Lazarus's finger still 'exists' while decomposed. But if decay can be transcended, this must be accomplished by the particular Macrina or Basil who began to transcend it in life. To Gregory (as to Origen, Aphrahat, and Ephraim), the body of the ascetic begins already on earth to live the life beyond procreation and nutrition it will have in heaven. Here on earth we have many needs, writes Gregory, we are seduced by material things, buried (as it were) under the rubble of an earthquake. But we must begin the journey toward the purity of heaven, shaking off uncleanness." Bynum, *The Resurrection of the Body in Western Christianity, 200–1336* (New York: Columbia University Press, 1995), 84.

Gregory as well. In these acts of consolation, they share in the being of God, who is known through God's acts of ministry and care.

■ ■ ■ ■

Nate started coming to the Tuesday night Bible study. He had a note-book filled with his *why* questions. (Why does God allow babies to die? Why do people like you even believe there is a God? Why did God allow this to happen to Cynthia and me?) Pastor Manta told him that those questions were important. He told Nate that these *whys* were important and that he believed Nate would have them answered. But the Bible study wasn't really about *whys*. In Pastor Manta's mind, the Christian life itself wasn't about solving *whys* but discovering a *who* inside a *what*.

"That's what I learned from reading the book of Job. *Whys* are not as important as who God is and what God is doing in the world. I read the book of Job a lot after I lost my brother. And I read it over and over when I was in treatment for my drinking. I told you, Nate, I was sneaking drinks to deal with the pain. Well, one or two turned into fifteen or twenty. I was the drunk pastor."

AC jumped in, "We should read Job. We ain't read it since I been comin' to study."

So they read Job—slowly, and twice through, for the next four months. Nate came every week. In those six months he never came on a Sunday. But he did join the church's slow-pitch softball team. He was a power hitter with quite a potty mouth. Nate swore every time he made an out. It annoyed AC, but it made Pastor Manta laugh.[21]

Cynthia started walking with Hazel and Mary Ann, though eventually Mary Ann found the walking to be too tiring and stopped going, saying things were just too busy at work. On these walks Cynthia never said a thing about God. Never hinted that she had her own *why* questions. She didn't mention the funeral and rarely said anything about the loss of Maddy. Hazel and Mary Ann knew she was carrying it. But they just walked, sometimes in silence but mostly talking and laughing at Trevor the Tormentor. Cynthia loved that dog. Hazel and Mary Ann were pretty sure Cynthia walked with them only to be with Trevor. She always greeted him

21. For an important piece that contributes to my thoughts here and a rich articulation of what it means to welcome newcomers to the church, see Jessicah Duckworth, *Wide Welcome: How the Unsettling Presence of Newcomers Can Save the Church* (Minneapolis: Fortress, 2013).

enthusiastically before saying anything to Hazel or Mary Ann. Cynthia started bringing Trevor homemade dog treats from recipes she'd found online.

So it came as a shock to Hazel when Cynthia dropped some news about four months after the funeral. About halfway into a walk, Cynthia said, "I think God is telling me to be one of those chaplains, like at the hospital." It was the first time Cynthia had ever said anything about God. "How do you become one of those?" she asked Hazel. Hazel was dumbfounded.

8

Goodbyes That Save

Great Sorrow and Consolation Evangelism

Cynthia was sure of it. Her most painful experience—a literal hell to her—had become an invitation. She felt a pull to live through that experience again and again with other people. This was a mystery of spirit (and the spiritual justification for evangelism). What broke Cynthia, she now wanted to see mended in others. Losing Maddy drove her to want to join other couples on that same journey. In that horrible experience Cynthia had found something she'd been reluctant to speak of. She didn't have the language for it. She needed to heal first. She needed to pet Trevor the marvelous, energetic Tormentor and walk with Hazel. Through those seemingly ordinary experiences of friendship, Cynthia became sure that this was what she wanted.

But not just what she wanted. She believed she needed to do this because Jesus wanted her to. She still didn't have the language to explain it. But inside the deafening sorrow of piercing silence and her own cacophonic cries, she heard Jesus speak. It happened twice. Both times it startled her. Cynthia explained to Pastor Manta that it first happened right after Hazel, Myrtle, and Jackie had first visited. When they left, Cynthia felt some peace for the first time since the loss. Even her sleep had been fitful. But after they left, she lay on the couch and found herself sliding into a restful sleep. When she awoke, she heard him. She's certain she was awake. She

221

was sitting up when she heard Jesus say, "It's me, Jesus. Your little one is with me. Have Maddy baptized."

"It overwhelmed me," Cynthia said. "I'd never thought about Jesus in my life. I hadn't been to church since I was fourteen. I only went to Mr. Medlam's funeral because it was in the VFW. But I was sure that voice was Jesus—I mean, I think it was. Jesus knew my baby's name, and she was with him. What could I do? I had to have her baptized."

Pastor Manta nodded in wonder. "I had a similar experience," he said. "When Hazel told me you wanted Maddy baptized, my first thought was 'No. We don't do that.' I was going to tell you that, but I was wrestling with some unease about it. The next day I was down at the mission we support, and a homeless man said to me out of the blue, 'Pastor Manta, bring the little ones to him. Especially the littlest, bruh. Got it, do it, bruh.' At first, I dismissed it. You hear a lot of random things in the soup kitchen line. But then it hit me. I knew it was about you. I knew I had to baptize Maddy. It was a word from God."

They sat in silence, taking it all in.

"And the second time?" Pastor Manta asked.

"It was similar," Cynthia said. "Mary Ann had stopped joining me and Hazel for our walks. I was worried it would be too weird for it to be just me and Hazel. I was scared she'd ask me about how I felt. I thought about not going anymore. But then I had this dream where Mary Ann was drowning in a pond and Trevor was racing out to save her. When he came back to shore—and I know this is weird—he had a tag on his collar that said 'Chaplain.' I never saw Mary Ann come out. I woke up and heard that same voice, the one I knew was Jesus. The voice said, 'Take the badge and follow.' That's when I told Hazel I think I'm supposed to be a chaplain."

"I hated our chaplain," Nate inserted. Nate had been sitting there the whole time, overwhelmed. He'd never heard any of these stories. These things really disturbed him. Nate mentally added a few more *whys* to his list. *Why* was Jesus talking to his wife? *Why* was God messing with their life? *Why* was Pastor Manta taking these weird psychological manifestations seriously? And deep down, Nate wanted to know, *Why*, if this really was Jesus—which he doubted—did Jesus not speak *to him*?

Cynthia picked up on Nate's unease. "I know, I know. I don't even know what to make of it."

"Neither do I," Pastor Manta said. "Especially the second one. Maybe Jesus is calling you to be a chaplain. Maybe. I think Jesus calls us into sorrow. I think we find Jesus there. I have, and so many others have in this church. But we'll have to test this second word."

"Test it?" Nate asked, a bit flabbergasted. "Why? I mean, how? No, I do mean why? What do you mean test it?"

Dying Well in Rome

Macrina and her brothers—Gregory of Nyssa and Basil of Caesarea—and their friend, Gregory of Nazianzus, were drawing together the philosophy of the time with the biblical narrative to explore what it meant for a follower of Jesus Christ to mourn.[1] How do those who anticipate the resurrection grieve loss? No part of this exercise was simply theoretical for them. Basil and the two Gregorys were writing letters of consolation to those across their bishoprics, giving their people a philosophy of consolation. But these were just hummed melodies, far from a full symphony of consolation. Such a work had not yet been written.

That work would appear in the year 524. The man to pen it was a Christian in Rome named Boethius. His book became a Latin classic, read by all Western theologians of the medieval period. The book, *The Consolation of Philosophy*, was considered the last great piece of writing of the classical period and a staple of medieval education.[2]

The book itself is all Bonhoeffer, long before Bonhoeffer. Boethius's text is one of the original prison texts (coming after the four letters Paul wrote in prison[3] and long before Martin Luther King Jr.'s "Letter from Birmingham Jail"). Like Paul, Boethius was a prisoner in Rome. But unlike

1. Articulating and describing this is the objective of Robert Gregg's book, *Consolation Philosophy: Greek and Christian Paideia in Basil and the Two Gregories* (Philadelphia: Philadelphia Patristics Foundation, 1975), esp. chaps. 1–3.

2. Richard Kieckhefer adds, "The consolation literature of the Middle Ages, directly or indirectly inspired by Boethius's *Consolation of Philosophy*, remained popular in the fourteenth century, and authors such as Meister Eckhart contributed new specimens of such consolatory reflections. It has been suggested that this literature draws more from Stoic indifference than from religious conceptions of patience, yet the border was surely a weak one, and Eckhart was able to use the genre to express ascetic-mystical notions of suffering." Kieckhefer, *Unquiet Soul: Fourteenth-Century Saints and Their Religious Milieu* (Chicago: University of Chicago Press, 1984), 76.

3. These letters are Ephesians, Philippians, Colossians, and Philemon.

Paul, Boethius was an important Roman governmental figure who had fallen. He had been falsely accused of treason and jailed for a year, awaiting a ruling on his execution. Boethius knew his demise was inevitable. He would soon be killed. Therefore, he wrestles in this text with what it means to live knowing you're going to imminently die. How do we do that before God? How do we find consolation?

Boethius frames his thoughts as a Christian but ultimately uses Neoplatonism to support his ideas of consolation. He writes not simply as a Christian but as a Roman philosopher. In the book, he finds himself in dialogue with a woman who is philosophy itself (Lady Wisdom, as found in Proverbs 8). Philosophy teaches him to die well. It is philosophy that comforts and consoles him. Hence the title *The Consolation of Philosophy*. Philosophy draws Boethius into the wisdom of Neoplatonism. The use of Neoplatonism was not unusual for the time. Across the East and West, from the Gregorys to Augustine (and, powerfully, the great foundational writer of Eastern and Western mysticism, Pseudo-Dionysius), theologians were drawing from Neoplatonism as a resource for their Christian contemplations. Boethius died embraced by the wisdom and reason of philosophy. Philosophy taught Boethius to die not in concern for his outward circumstances but with attention to his inner life. All three of our French moderns—Montaigne, Descartes, and even Pascal—could affirm this. In many ways they all write and think inside the legacy of such an imagination.

With his attention on his inner life, Boethius dies in Rome. Some eight hundred years later, Rome itself seemed about to die. It was threatened to be executed by the political maneuvering of French kings.

Back to Those French Kings

The Eternal City was not seeming all that eternal when, in 1309, the pope refused to reside in Rome. Pope Clement V took his pointy pope hat and moved to France, residing in Avignon.[4] Clement was happy to move, but it was the French King Philip IV who made it happen. Turns out, French kings are ambitious, never more so than when they're fighting with England.

---

4. For a history of this period, see Joëlle Rollo-Koster, *Avignon and Its Papacy, 1309–1417: Popes, Institutions, and Society* (Lanham, MD: Rowman & Littlefield, 2015).

Philip intended to use some church coin to fund his battles against his English enemies. Pope Boniface VIII refused to allow it. Entrenched quarreling ensued. Boniface made it clear that the pope ruled on *all* matters. Philip's rebuttal: not in France, he doesn't. Philip was essentially calling Boniface arrogant, addressing his rebuttal to "Your Venerable Conceitedness." Both dug in. Ultimately Philip won, stalemating the vote for the next pope until he got his man: Clement V, who, four years after becoming pope, moved the curia to French soil in Avignon.

The papacy stayed in Avignon for the next 120 years. This was a shame for Christendom. But it was never worse—and never more theologically and pastorally problematic—than between 1378 and 1417. During this period the church was divided between two popes: one in Rome and one in Avignon. The Western church split and became confused. The horrible impact of having two popes is lost on most of us because of the shadows of the Protestant Reformation that came a hundred years later. But at the time, the crisis of having two popes was beyond calamity. It created a great embarrassment and deep shame, leaving the common people in a pastoral crisis. For a generation of theologians, having popes in both Avignon and Rome was *the* issue. The whole situation was called "the Babylonian captivity of the church" (Luther would mobilize the title for his own writings of reform in 1520).[5]

The most important university, with the top theology faculty in the fourteenth century, was in Paris. Just down toward the Seine from the apartment where Blaise Pascal would have his night of fire some two hundred years later, priests and theologians were wrestling with the crisis of the two popes. No one was more concerned than the chancellor of the university, Jean Gerson. Gerson considered the existence of two popes to be an existential crisis. He prodded professors and students to address it. He pleaded with the kings and dauphins of France who followed Philip IV to intervene and resolve it. But there was no easy solution, and Gerson suffered under this reality.

5. G. H. M. Posthumus Meyjes adds texture: "Thus the Church will never lack leadership, for Christ himself stands as guarantor of the regular exercise of the hierarchical functions. It is he, and not the Pope, who gives the Church life in the hierarchical sense. The background to this thesis is the idea that all offices in the Church receive their inspiration directly from Christ; and that as such the assembled Church is sufficiently endowed with the power to lead Christendom." Posthumus Meyjes, *Jean Gerson—Apostle of Unity: His Church Politics and Ecclesiology* (Leiden: Brill, 1999), 151.

Gerson suffered under many realities. These sufferings gave him the nickname "doctor of consolation," and he became the teacher of Luther's great pastor who helped form the *theologia crucis* into not just a theoretical idea but a pastoral reality, moving an imagination for consolation to the deepest level of divine and human action.

Gerson and His Sad Times

The Gerson family were the French medieval version of Macrina's family—with one important difference. Unlike the great Cappadocian family, the Gersons had no noble connections. They were peasants with no real wealth. And yet their oldest child became chancellor of the university and the greatest pastoral theologian of his generation.

Like the great Cappadocian family, however, the Gersons were large (five boys and seven girls). Just as Macrina's parents were faithful laypeople, so too were the Gersons. The Gerson father was a farmer, and their mother was a devout woman of prayer, lavishly loving her children. (She's remembered as the second Monica, in reference to Augustine's mother.)[6]

From inside this great love, many of the children ended up giving their lives in service to the church. Both the Cappadocian and Gerson families were led by the oldest child. Macrina was the great teacher of her siblings. Jean was the leading pastoral voice for his brothers' education and their (and four of his sisters') entrance into monastic life. The Gersons, not counting Jean the eldest, sent seven of their children into a life of prayer (Jean gave his life to the church at the university and spent his later years in exile in a monastery but never as a monk). Two of those brothers who entered the monastery as monks were also named Jean. The Gersons had three sons named Jean (cue the old *Newhart* show bit, "This is my brother Darryl and my other brother Darryl"). No one is sure why all the Jeans. (Were the other boys named after their able older brother, or did the Gersons just lack creativity, misplacing the baby name book?)

6. Brian McGuire adds, "Like so many boys who joined the clergy or became monks, Jean Gerson seems to have been especially attached to his mother. Elisabeth la Chardeniere came from a leading family in the district and may not have considered herself to be a peasant at all. She was devoted to her children, as she indicates in a letter to Jean's younger brothers when they were living with him in Paris." McGuire, *Jean Gerson and the Last Medieval Reformation* (Philadelphia: Pennsylvania State University Press, 2005), 2.

More than creativity, the eldest Jean had an iron will and an open heart. The peasant boy somehow made it to Paris to study. He was an able student with deep wisdom. His teacher, the great Pierre d'Ailly, took notice and invited Gerson to join him and other delegates of the university on a trip to Avignon. They traveled there to discuss the doctrine of the immaculate conception with the curia. The experience moved Gerson deeply. He left Avignon convinced that the papal schism needed to end and in turn that the spirituality of the clergy needed to be renewed. The university needed to serve the church in doing both.[7]

Gerson received his chance to move the university in this direction when Pierre d'Ailly was appointed bishop of Puy. The chancellorship opened, and Gerson, at the tender age of thirty-two, was elected.[8] But some things never change. Gerson found himself drowning in the frustration of academic administration, annoyed by it all. The church needed reforms, and the faculty was caught in petty ego battles. These problems pushed Gerson into a deep depression. So deep that he left his position for a time.

The late fourteenth century itself was depressing. These were very sad times indeed—maybe the saddest the West has ever known. Europe was still recovering from the horrors of plague.[9] Death and loss were striking

7. "The voice of the University spoke against the *Voie de Fait* more explicitly than lightning and thunder. In a stupendous twelve-hour sermon preached before the King and court on January 6, 1391, Jean a young scholar already famed as a preacher, expressed the opposition. Twenty-seven years old and two years short of his doctor in theology, Gerson was a protégé of the Chancellor Pierre d'Ailly. . . . As the struggle over the schism intensified, he was to become the foremost advocate of the supremacy of a Church Council over the Pope, and the most memorable French theologian of his age." Barbara W. Tuchman, *A Distant Mirror: The Calamitous Fourteenth Century* (New York: Ballantine, 1978), 479.

8. D. Catherine Brown takes us deeper, saying, "In 1395 Gerson succeeded d'Ailly, now a bishop, as chancellor of the university. He held this office until his death and raised its formerly modest prestige to an entirely new level by his activities and strong personality. Its stature grew with Gerson's. As chancellor, Gerson inevitably became more heavily involved in the initiatives of the university to end the schism, now almost twenty years old. Although a partisan of the *via cessionis* (way of resignation), Gerson opposed the growing movement in the university for withdrawal of obedience, because he feared that such action would merely enlarge the schism." Brown, *Pastor and Laity in the Theology of Jean Gerson* (London: Cambridge University Press, 1987), 6.

9. Barbara Tuchman, having written the best book on the fourteenth century, says, "In October 1347, two months after the fall of Calais, Genoese trading ships put into the harbor of Messina in Sicily with dead and dying men at the oars. The ships had come from the Black Sea port of Caffa (now Feodosiya) in the Crimea, where the Genoese maintained a trading post. The diseased sailors showed strange black swellings about the size of an egg or an apple in the armpits and groin. The swellings oozed blood and pus and were followed by spreading boils and black blotches on the skin from internal bleeding. The sick suffered severe pain and died

Europe in ways hard to imagine. Over a third of the continent's population was lost. Whole villages had been decimated, every person in them dying. France was hit particularly hard.[10] Despair was ripe.[11]

Coupled with this, France was in the middle of a hundred-year war with England. Raids and conscriptions abounded.[12] When the nobles weren't fighting the English, they were fighting one another. House Orleans and House Burgundy were at each other's throat—literally. The Duke of Orleans was murdered by the Duke of Burgundy. One of Gerson's own theologians at the university, Jean Petit, wrote a book justifying the Duke of Burgundy's act. Gerson had to oppose him. The church censored Petit. Such scandals kept the people from getting pastoral attention when they needed it most.[13] Instead, the church (and the court) was divided and ob-

---

quickly within five days of the first symptoms. As the disease spread, other symptoms of continuous fever and spitting of blood appeared instead of the swellings or buboes. These victims coughed and sweated heavily and died even more quickly, within three days or less, sometimes in 24 hours. In both types everything that issued from the body—breath, sweat, blood from the buboes and lungs, bloody urine, and blood-blackened excrement—smelled foul. Depression and despair accompanied the physical symptoms." Tuchman, *Distant Mirror*, 92. She continues, "The plague accelerated discontent with the Church at the very moment when people felt a greater need of spiritual reassurance. There had to be some meaning in the terrorizing experience God had inflicted. If the purpose had been to shake man from his sinful ways, it had failed. Human conduct was found to be 'wickeder than before,' more avaricious and grasping, more litigious, more bellicose, and this was nowhere more apparent than in the Church itself" (123).

10. See David Herlihy, *The Black Death and the Transformation of the West* (Cambridge, MA: Harvard University Press, 1997). Robert Knecht adds, "Destructive as it was, the Black Death was not the only cause of demographic decline in fourteenth-century France. Regional studies have revealed a dip in the years leading up to the Black Death. This can be blamed on poor harvests in Flanders and northern France in 1315 to 1317." Knecht, *The Valois: Kings of France 1328–1589* (London: Continuum, 2007), 5.

11. Mark Burrows says, "As an era in which 'a melancholy weighs on people's souls,' to recall Huizinga's view of the later Middle Ages, the fifteenth century appears as a time of the decay of 'an overripe form of civilization,' a gloomy era which leaves the reader of its surviving documents with 'the same impression of immense sadness.' 'Always and everywhere in the literature of [this] age,' Huizinga concludes, 'we find a confessed pessimism.'" Burrows, *Jean Gerson and De Consolatione Theologiae (1418): The Consolation of a Biblical and Reforming Theology for a Disordered Age* (Tübingen: Mohr Siebeck, 1991), 63, quoting Huizinga, *The Waning of the Middle Ages: A Study of the Forms of Life, Thought, and Art in France and the Netherlands in the Fourteenth and Fifteenth Centuries* (Garden City, NY: Doubleday, 1954), 31.

12. With one sentence, Lauren Johnson tells us how brutal the war was: "More men had been killed in this century of war, it was claimed, than were alive [in the fifteenth century] in both realms [France and England]." Johnson, *Shadow King: The Life and Death of Henry VI* (London: Head of Zeus, 2019), 165.

13. Brown adds, "For Gerson 'No salvation outside the church' might well have been rendered 'No salvation without the pastor.' He would have been in full agreement with an anonymous English preacher's remark that without priests 'there is no help to any Christian man.'" Brown, *Pastor and Laity in the Theology of Jean Gerson*, 36.

sessed with its own infighting. The schism, and overall confusion of the clergy, was leaving the people without the care and direction they needed.

Gerson felt a deep responsibility to respond to these sad times by preparing clergy to minister to peasants like his parents. As the head of the university, he became quite unusual in his love for the laity (particularly children)[14] and the secular clergy (the pastors not in the cloister but toiling with farmers and merchants). The university had not had much concern for such people. Gerson wanted to change that.

But it was much easier said than done. Not only the university but the whole Latin church needed reform. The Petit incident, sanctioning murder, was a sign. The schism and utter stubbornness of the two popes was proof. Gerson preached and wrote against them all. Finally, a council was called at Constance. It was an eventful and historical gathering. Gerson took center stage. But quickly the spotlight burned.

From Constance to Exile

The council started out with what seemed like a win for Gerson (though not by the measure of posterity). Gerson opposed the Bohemian professor, Jan Hus. Gerson's mission was to hold the church together.[15] And Hus

14. In the introduction to Gerson's work, Brian Patrick McGuire says, "[Gerson] insists . . . that uneducated lay people can have direct experience of God, even more so than overeducated clerics, and yet he can be scathingly critical of the language used by those who try to describe their immediate perceptions of God." McGuire, introduction to Jean Gerson, *Early Works* (New York: Paulist Press, 1998), 4. James Connolly adds, "Though [Gerson] was Chancellor of the University he did not think it beneath his duty to take upon himself the training of little children. Men of his own day looked at this work as a folly of his; in our time such devotion would be considered remarkable despite all the stress that we put on child-welfare. His project was to train the character of youth so that when temptations of any sort came to them they would be strong to resist." Connolly, *John Gerson: Reformer and Mystic* (1928; repr., Eugene, OR: Wipf & Stock, 2023), 86.

15. Brown takes us into the council, saying, "The obvious bankruptcy of the *via cessionis* turned Gerson into a committed supporter of the *via concilii*. In 1409 the dissident cardinals of both papal courts convoked the Council of Pisa, and Gerson wrote several treatises defending this action. Although he did not attend the council himself, he at once adhered to the new pope, Alexander V, elected there. This did not, however, end the schism as neither of the other two popes would resign. Eventually the Pisan pope, now John XXIII, had to yield to the pressure exerted by the Emperor Sigismund, and convoke the Council of Constance to resolve the situation. In February of 1415 Gerson left Paris for Constance as a delegate of the king, the university and the ecclesiastical province of Sens. His leading role in the council is well known. It was his sermon, *Ambulate*, that was instrumental in calming the anxiety and confusion caused by John XXIII's sudden departure from the council in March 1415. Gerson urged the members

was not helping. Gerson shared Hus's calls for reform, but *not* with the deep cuts into church order that Hus was pushing. The council's condemnation of Hus was a win for Gerson (though a loss in hindsight).[16] The Council of Constance held only one more tainted win and then a great loss for Gerson.

Coming into the council, Gerson had believed that the issue of the two popes would be resolved if the now three people asserting that they had a right to the papacy abdicated and a new election was called. This resolution required a great deal of patience, but it happened. The schism ended when Martin V was elected in 1417. But the horse trading and political maneuvering of the whole process was exhausting. The result was a relief but not the complete success that Gerson had hoped. The change didn't come with an overwhelmingly renewed spirit of reform and faithfulness, which can be seen clearly in the grand loss that Gerson experienced next. With this loss a great danger dawned for him.

Regarding Petit and his tract, the council decided that the justification of murder fell under opinion and not doctrine. Only one of Petit's theses regarding the Duke of Burgundy's murder of the Duke of Orleans was condemned. The new pope, to Gerson's shock, even lifted Petit's censure. This put Gerson in significant danger. It was clear that the Duke of Burgundy was behind all this. Gerson had written directly against the vicious duke. Gerson had been protected by the church and the church's censoring of Petit. But now that protection was gone. Gerson was exposed and couldn't return to France. Now exiled, Gerson was held up in Constance for a time before escaping into the southern German-speaking lands.

---

to remain in session and produced arguments to justify the legitimacy of the council despite the absence of the pope. His arguments were accepted and eventually the council succeeded in getting rid of the three popes and elected Martin V. Gerson also played an important role in the condemnation of Wyclif and Hus, serving as a member of the commission that interrogated the latter." Brown, *Pastor and Laity in the Theology of Jean Gerson*, 8.

16. James Connolly adds, "Against the heresy of John Hus he waged a bitter contest, and was one of the most persistent opponents of the Czech as we have seen. When, after the condemnation and the death of Hus, the heresy did not subside but grew to greater and more fearful proportions, the assistance of Gerson was enlisted again and he was asked to compose a tract to contradict the errors that were winning many adherents in Prague. This was the occasion for the *Tract against the Heresy of the Communion under both Species, for Laypeople*. The tract reiterates the stand which Gerson had taken at an earlier date against the teaching of Hus. He urged charity in dealing with the heretics, but at the same time advocated that appeal be made to the Emperor as the defender of orthodoxy, if the heretics did not desist in their error." Connolly, *John Gerson*, 181.

In a monastery there, Gerson felt like Boethius. Gerson's beloved teacher Pierre d'Ailly exposed him to Boethius's text. Like Boethius, Gerson now believed he was imprisoned and awaiting his death. More than any jailer, his own sorrow served as his prison's four walls. He became so sad. Plagues, deaths, war, murders, schisms, devious dukes, and power-hungry popes made Gerson's times so sad and filled his life with so much sorrow. He had become lost, an exile far from the lands he loved.

Inside these walls of sorrow Gerson decided to pen his own Boethius-inspired tract. Instead of calling it *The Consolation of Philosophy*, Gerson called his piece *De consolatione theologiae* (*The Consolation of Theology*). The shift in title signaled a change in perspective that has huge ramifications for us. The shift from "philosophy" to "theology" signals that Gerson's consolations will have an evangelistic focus. He contends that the sorrowful don't need reason or rightly ordered passions as much as they need the *evangel*. They need a word of salvation. Gerson believes consolation—while impossible to instrumentalize—can reform. It can save because we meet God inside consolation. Consolation possesses the weight to convert and transform us inside our sorrow, taking us from death into life. These consolations do more than just give the sufferer perspective or buoy them in the sorrowful sea of death. Rather, consolation can transform a self by the hidden cruciform power of soul.

The Doctor of Consolation Is Born: *ad Deum*

Gerson begins *De consolatione theologiae* in a similar vein as Gregory of Nyssa. He reminds us that we are on a pilgrimage. All human lives are lived as a journey. The medieval person walked a pilgrimage; that is what it meant to live. The late-modern life follows this in the sense of us always seeing ourselves as on the way. The difference is that late moderns are never sure what we're on the way *to*. The pilgrim is always aimed toward the sacred on this journey.[17] She is headed *ad Deum*, "to God." We late

17. Georges Duby takes us into the world of the pilgrim, saying, "A pilgrimage was three things at once. First of all, it was an act of penance. The bishop imposed it, as an instrument of purification, on individuals who publicly confessed to exceptional misdeeds. Next, it was a symbol. By traveling, a pilgrim acted out the procession of God's people toward the promised land and drew nearer to God's Kingdom. And finally, a pilgrimage was a pleasure. At this period there was considered to be no more attractive type of amusement than traveling—particularly when one traveled with friends, as pilgrims generally did." Duby, *The Age of the Cathedrals:*

moderns journey for fulfillment and purpose to capture our dreams, but we never really do so *ad Deum*. We have even come to see evangelism as a way to include church in late-modern people's activities. We struggle to see evangelism as an invitation to walk *ad Deum*, to God. Evangelism is pilgrimage. It is the moment, which continues again and again, of turning to God by turning to our sorrows, trusting that inside these sorrows we will be met and we will be *ad Deum*. Evangelism is the first step of the journey. Evangelism and discipleship meld as we walk and invite others to walk with us. Evangelism is the invitation to walk with people on the journey to God.

We struggle with seeing evangelism this way because there is another element to *ad Deum* that we resist as late moderns—particularly as sad people seeking the therapeutic. In Gerson's time, *ad Deum* was also an idiom for "goodbye" (adios, adieu, etc.). When Gerson sadly left Constance, he had to say *ad Deum* to a return to France. To go to God on a pilgrimage is to walk near death, bidding farewell to what was—to this life—and surrendering to God alone. In pilgrimage we find God in the sorrow of the goodbye. God is met on the trail *ad Deum* because all journeys of pilgrimage cause the sorrows of goodbye, and inside these sorrows God draws near, ministering to us. The trail is a path of sorrows where God meets us.

To journey without the sorrow of *ad Deum* turns us from a pilgrim to a tourist. The tourist journeys but never *ad Deum*. The tourist rarely aims toward God and *never* says goodbye. The tourist departs, knowing they will return. It wouldn't be a holiday if it wasn't a break, and then they return to a life similar or the same to their life before the trip. Tourism

---

Art and Society, 980–1420 (Chicago: University of Chicago Press, 1981), 50. Peter Brown adds, "The pilgrim committed himself or herself to the 'therapy of distance' by recognizing that what he or she wished for was not to be had in the immediate environment. Distance could symbolize needs unsatisfied, so that, as Dupront continues, 'Le pelerinage demeure essentiellement depart': pilgrimage remains essentially the act of leaving. But distance is there to be overcome; the experience of pilgrimage activates a yearning for intimate closeness. For the pilgrims who arrived after the obvious 'therapy of distance' involved in long travel found themselves subjected to the same therapy by the nature of the shrine itself. The effect of 'inverted magnitudes' sharpened the sense of distance and yearning by playing out the long delays of pilgrimage in miniature. For the art of the shrine in late antiquity is an art of closed surfaces. Behind these surfaces, the holy lay, either totally hidden or glimpsed through narrow apertures. The opacity of the surfaces heightened an awareness of the ultimate unattainability in this life of the person they had traveled over such wide spaces to touch." Brown, *The Cult of the Saints: Its Rise and Function in Latin Christianity* (Chicago: University of Chicago Press, 2015), 87.

constitutes a break from stress and monotony to relax and return to what was left. Tourism is about happiness or immanent contentment and never sorrow. Without the goodbye, there is no capacity to transform. To journey without ever saying goodbye is to resist sorrow and therefore follow a trail that is not *ad Deum*, to God, but to the self. But to walk the journey or path and accept the sorrow is to be *ad Deum*, to be moved to God.

Both Cynthia and Nate, in their own distinct ways, are walking the incredibly painful journey of losing a child. They are saying goodbye to Maddy and to their hopes and dreams for what their future and family were going to be. Importantly, they are now walking this journey with the *sanctorum communio*, with Pastor Manta's church. They are walking it *ad Deum*, to God. To accompany another in their journey of sorrowful goodbye is to evangelize (without instrumentalization), because in walking with the sorrowful we're directed *ad Deum* in and through the goodbye. The church is called not to fix the sorrow but to journey with the one who bears it.[18]

If we lose this sense of pilgrimage, evangelism becomes grossly instrumentalized. Evangelism becomes an instrument by which to convince people of new ideas or sell them on new religious interests and involvements. Evangelism becomes something other than pilgrims joining pilgrims in saying goodbye, trusting that God meets and transforms us inside the sorrow of goodbyes. In joining the sorrowful journey of the human spirit in saying goodbye, we encounter the divine being who arrives to minister to us. Cynthia and Nate are led to God, *ad Deum*, by Hazel, Myrtle, Jackie, Mary Ann, and Pastor Manta journeying with them. The church's calling is to walk with others and console them as they say goodbye, repeatedly reminding them that to say goodbye is to be *ad Deum*.

Inspired by Gerson, we can say that evangelism is a pilgrim's way. Evangelism journeys with those in sorrow who are forced to say goodbye, witnessing to them that in saying goodbye we are near to God, we

---

18. Mark Burrows elaborates: "The way to a merciful God, as Gerson here perceives it, is not through meritorious works set within the penitential system but through *tentationes*, the *Anfechtungen* which lead us first to desperation and only then to a confidence in God's mercy. *Theologia* and above all the biblical promises of grace per *Jesum Christum*, rather than the sacrament of penance, establish the signposts leading *viatores* toward hope in Deum. In this regard we find at least the essential structure of Luther's later insight that we must 'spring over' from our sins to Christ's righteousness, finding our righteousness not in our own works but in Christ who is himself the sacrament of our reconciliation." Burrows, *Jean Gerson and De Consolatione Theologiae*, 72.

are ministered to by this God, and our very being is taken into God's own being.[19] We are *ad Deum*. The only thing evangelism can do is direct people *to God*. Gerson wants us to see that the path to God is always a trail of sorrowful goodbyes.

A New Lady

When Boethius was imprisoned awaiting his execution, he was met (in his literary imagination) by a woman named Philosophy. Philosophy gave Boethius the wisdom to die well, to die like a Christian version of Plato's teacher Socrates.

Gerson has no wish to be like Socrates, who took his hemlock happily. Gerson is too heartbroken for that. He's too firmly on the pilgrim's path of goodbyes. Gerson sees himself not as Socrates but as Jeremiah, a man of deep sorrows now in exile. "Gerson himself is *advena* [the immigrant, the foreigner], the pilgrim interpreted according to biblical models whose fate it was to wander in exile from his native land."[20] He cannot return to his beloved France. But Gerson explains that while being in the pain of exile, he is also Mary. Though he mourns, he rejoices amid the sorrow, like Mary who "magnified God through her spirit,"[21] because God is doing something in and through the sorrow. God has met him inside the sorrow. Gerson rejoices because, like Mary, his sorrows have been seen by God (like Hagar in Gen. 16). The sorrows have become the location of God's act and being. Therefore, joy has met Gerson inside the heavy sorrow.

Gerson has no interest in Boethius's Lady Philosophy. She can keep her rose. In his exile, Gerson finds that she doesn't return his calls. Rather, Gerson has eyes only for Lady Theology. It is *not* philosophy that consoles, Gerson believes, but theology. What consoles is *not* necessarily learning to cope with grief by balancing passions with reason. Gerson knows poignantly, now in exile, that facing sorrow is not just about fortifying the inner life. It isn't primarily an internal operation. Rather, on this pilgrim's

---

19. "Nonetheless, God seemed to attach more weight to love manifested in suffering than to love displayed in other ways. Suffering was the means par excellence for demonstrating love: this was the rule for Christ, and consequently for his saints as well. The devotion to which this outlook led might be brutal, yet it seemed to follow inexorably from the logic—of Christian belief." Kieckhefer, *Unquiet Souls*, 89.

20. Burrows, *Jean Gerson and De Consolatione Theologiae*, 30.

21. Burrows, *Jean Gerson and De Consolatione Theologiae*, 30.

path of sorrowful goodbyes, Gerson wants to know who meets him. If this is a journey to God, *ad Deum*, how will God draw near?

Lady Theology, using the narratives of Scripture, whispers how God draws near. She gives Gerson visions of God's acts inside sorrow, proclaiming how God journeys with the heartbroken, blessing those who mourn. Lady Theology is the great teacher. But she is much more than a Socrates. She does something different from what Lady Philosophy does. Lady Theology is a consoling companion on the pilgrimage path. She comes near only on this path, inside the journey. She is no disconnected teacher but a pastor who teaches and consoles by drawing near in the sorrows of goodbyes. Theology is for living on the path of goodbyes. As Luther will say, theology must be a theology of the cross; it calls sorrow sorrow and seeks God's very being in that sorrow.[22]

Lady Theology is anything but theoretical. Theology, for Gerson—especially being in exile—is not academic but always pastoral. Before the Council of Constance, he had wanted to turn the whole University of Paris in the direction of the practical. But he failed. Now in exile, depressed and filled with sorrow, Gerson discovers that theology can indeed minister and that theology is always pastoral. Theology only appears, the lady only draws close, when you are right on the path. Lady Theology appears when and where the goodbyes impinge and the road is hard. She comes with her much different (cruciform) kind of wisdom. Only then does theology help us see, even proclaim, the nearness of the God of Israel, showing us that this God is a minister. Theology reveals that what cannot be God—the crucified body of Jesus—is indeed the fullness of God. Theology gives us visions, inside life's pains and trials, of a God who finds what is lost, heals what is broken, and redeems all—by suffering all.

Lady Theology invites us out of our self to encounter what is beyond us, coming to us as the arriving, ministering God. The pilgrim's path contains arrivals from inside goodbyes. Lady Theology is not interested in

22. This is to paraphrase the Heidelberg Disputation. Simeon Zahl adds, "Luther developed his theology of justification by faith through a process of reciprocal interpretation between exegesis and experience, and argued that 'experience alone makes the theologian.' But, following encounter with theological appeals to subjective experience in the arguments of radical reformers like Andreas Karlstadt in the 1520s, Luther altered course. He began to qualify the role of experience substantially, arguing that in matters of salvation 'you must judge solely by the Word, regardless of what you feel or see.'" Zahl, *The Holy Spirit and Christian Experience* (New York: Oxford University Press, 2020), 11.

stiff propositions of theology as a system (Gerson even takes a step away from thinking that theology is speculative, as the Scholastics believed, which Luther will pick up and develop further). Rather, Lady Theology is about the theological necessity of life on the path of sorrowful goodbyes. God ministers life out of death by dying. Ultimately, Gerson believes that it is in seeing how God meets us in our sorrow—not how the self should stand up under sorrow—that we are consoled and united with God's being.

The Lady of Low Anthropology

For Gerson, theology is a way of seeing amid seeking on the path of goodbyes.[23] Theology allows us to recognize (understand) that we are being sought by the Spirit in our sorrow. Because it is a way of seeking inside the journey of sorrowful goodbyes, it never starts in the inner life of riches but only in the poverty of the self (to Paul's point in 2 Cor. 12:10: "For the sake of Christ, then, I am content with weaknesses, insults, hardships, persecutions, and calamities; for when I am weak, then I am strong").

Lady Philosophy seeks to deposit riches in Boethius, giving him the inner resources to face his demise (Montaigne, and Rousseau who follows him, shifted this, claiming that the deposit of riches is already in our self, and we just need to excavate it). Lady Theology, on the other hand, has no riches to give. She believes that all that glitters is not gold. After all, gold itself offers little help inside the deep goodbyes of the pilgrim's path. Lady Philosophy turns us into our self, but Lady Theology leads us to seek and see what is beyond and outside of us. Lady Theology appears only on the path, when we are *viatores* (travelers), poor wayfarers and wanderers.

Lady Philosophy gives Boethius and his readers the works of the self that can console the self. But Lady Philosophy cannot get to soul. Gerson claims that the self is only and always in poverty. (We see here how *De consolatione theologiae* sows the earliest seeds of what, through Staupitz and then Luther, will grow into the *theologia crucis*.[24]) The self has no works to console itself or save itself from the pains of the goodbyes.

---

23. Charles Taylor believes such seeking is called for in our kind of secular age. See Taylor, *A Secular Age* (Cambridge, MA: Belknap, 2007), part 5.

24. A larger theological point I'm hoping to make in these discussions is to show that Luther's *theologia crucis* comes from Gerson and Staupitz. In the DNA of Gerson's *De consolatione theologiae*, and then Staupitz, we can spot that Luther's *theologia crucis* is fundamentally a pastoral assertion about how God meets those in temptation and despair rather than a forensic or formal assertion about a system of thought.

The self is always stuck in impossibility, wrestling with temptations to turn away from this poverty of sorrow and seeking a contented happiness somewhere other than the path of the *viatores*.

For Gerson, unlike Boethius, there are no works that can console or save the self, not even the learned ones of Lady Philosophy. The self needs something foreign to it, outside of it. The self must meet something on the path of goodbyes. The sorrow is too deep for any other cure. No works from Lady Philosophy or anyone else will heal it. All the *viatores* have is their utter desperation. All they have is the poverty of their goodbyes.

But when, out of this poverty, the self in its desperation cries out to God, the pilgrim finds the consolation of God's arrival. Because that consolation comes from the very being of God, it saves (more on this in the next section). Lady Philosophy gives the self works as a way of attending to sorrow. Lady Theology offers grace and new life coming out of the cries of sorrow. The only work that Lady Theology needs is the cry of the psalmist. Theology begins and ends for the human agent in this cry. Lady Theology describes what we find in this cry; she attends to the events of God's arriving to bless those who mourn. Mark Stephen Burrows states this well: "As a 'theology of seeking,' . . . Gerson refuses to place any confidence in human works . . . ; the [pilgrim] seeks God through an utter desperation in self . . . and a corresponding trust in divine righteousness—as [Gerson] later summarizes, *per desperationem ad spem*, through desperation (in self) to hope (in God)."[25]

A dialectical movement stands at the heart of Gerson's thought. The pilgrim lives out of this dialectic. The desperation in the self, when confessed, leads to hope in God. It moves the pilgrim of sorrowful goodbyes to a disposition of receiving God's very presence. When the self cries out,

---

25. Burrows, *Jean Gerson and De Consolatione Theologiae*, 49. Burrows continues, "Here we find that Gerson interprets the familiar *imitatio Christi* theme not in ethical terms, but in the more abstract psychological terms of *conformitas voluntatis*: that is, we are to conform our wills to God's, just as Jesus conformed the highest part of his human will to the divine. He quickly concedes, however, that all human effort in this regard is ultimately futile, and this because of the power sin—original, actual, and habitual—holds upon *viatores*. *Imitatio Christi*, yes, but Gerson insists that the incapacity which sin inflicts upon us requires more than natural effort: in the final analysis we are to cry out with the apostle, 'Unhappy man that I am! Who will deliver me from this body of death?,' whereupon let us answer. 'The grace of God through Jesus Christ our Lord (Rom. 7, 24–25).' Ethics and soteriology meet upon the common ground of his Christology, a doctrinal merger which Gerson locates not in a speculative discussion *de providentio Dei* but within the horizon of the peculiar divine covenants of scripture." Burrows, *Jean Gerson and De Consolatione Theologiae*, 50.

God comes and consoles as Spirit to soul. The human agent is drawn to God inside sorrow. Sorrow is the very ground where conversion and transformation occur.

Burrows helpfully adds, "In . . . [a] passage which bears unmistakable Pauline echoes (i.e., to 1 Cor. 1.21 ff.), Gerson defines 'the method and approach of theology' as a journey 'to wisdom . . . through foolishness,' contending that *theologia* brings us 'through the greatest despair about humanity and leads us through inestimable and intolerable desolation,' only in order to 'lead us upward to the highest hope in God . . . and to the firm consolation above.'" Burrows continues, "Desolation and despair, then, become the ineradicable context of human life, fulfilling the biblical dictum [in Job] that 'man is indeed born to labor.'"[26]

Evangelism entails not so much giving riches to another (whether religious or therapeutic) but rather joining others in their sorrow of goodbyes on the path. Evangelism invites others to take the first step (and many more steps) of pilgrimage. Evangelism ministers to the one in sorrow as the concrete manifestation of God's very presence. To evangelize is to join our neighbor in their sorrows, inviting our neighbor to do something quite odd (and foolish!). We invite them not to turn away from their sorrows but to journey into those sorrows, becoming one of the *viatores*, accepting that they are a traveler (but not alone!), and to see what they find in these sorrows. Lady Theology helps us see this mystery of God bringing life and hope to what is dead and lost. Evangelism is the wager, à la Pascal, that if we lean into our sorrow, if we begin the journey, the crucified and now living Christ will meet us, uniting our soul with the Spirit.

Hazel, Myrtle, and Pastor Manta are living out this way of evangelism with Cynthia and Nate. Evangelism that takes the shape of the *theologia crucis* is a ministry of inviting our neighbor to cry out to God (not just committing their interests to something). In this crying out to God we find that Lady Theology serves us by giving us biblical visions of God's joining us and ministering to us on this path of goodbyes. Reading Job becomes an important piece of the community ministering to Nate and Cynthia. Gerson believes that in crying out as *viatores*, our neighbor will indeed find salvation.

---

26. Burrows, *Jean Gerson and De Consolatione Theologiae*, 65, quoting *Oeuvres complètes de Jean Gerson*, vol. 9, ed. Palémon Glorieux (Paris: Desclée, 1972), 198. Gerson's quote of Job 5:7 comes from 9:227.

What Saves?

In our late-modern Protestant discussions of evangelism, we have engaged in an odd kind of editing. Inside our narratives of decline, Protestants have wondered whether a new attention to evangelism might be needed. But oddly, even accepting the necessity of evangelism, we've been uneasy with evangelism's attention to salvation in and through Jesus Christ. Attention to salvation seems to violate our late-modern concerns for tolerance and pluralism. We even come to worry that it's wrong or fundamentalist to be people yearning for heaven. We seem to want to edit out salvation from evangelism. Such editing only reveals that we are more concerned about selves in châteaus than souls on a pilgrim's path. We believe the château might be an immanent heaven before death, without death, and without the pain of goodbye. Whether explicitly or implicitly, we've contended that the problem with evangelism is not that we are seeking to leverage a market but that people need to be saved. (Only a Protestantism enveloped in imaginaries of late-stage capitalism could assume that seeking a market is necessary or neutral, while seeking physical and metaphysical salvation is wrong and off-putting.)

But scratching out salvation can be maintained only if we keep sorrow forever at bay and live not on a path as *viatores*, wayfarers, but only in Montaigne's château, constantly petting our cat. We are uneasy with claims of salvation and assertions of the need to be saved because we are Montaigne's children—he wants us yearning for nothing beyond. We journey only to get to the château to find immanent contentment, thinking that such contentment can last forevermore.

But Pascal taught us that resting in contentment forever is not achievable —not in this life. To be human is to say goodbye. To be human is to suffer, just as to love is to know the pain of separation. We should not forget Montaigne's pain of saying goodbye to La Boétie. You cannot live a human life without saying goodbye. Suffering goodbyes shows us that we are as much soul as self. We are the creatures of soul because we suffer all sorts of goodbyes. These goodbyes force us into being *viatores*, wanderers as exiles. As *viatores* we seek a home for our soul to be saved from the deep sorrow and despair of goodbyes. Such saving—differing from how Montaigne has trained us—will have to come from outside of us. For there is nothing within us, Gerson contends, that can achieve the salvation we need. We are too bound to the path, our goodbyes are too heavy, to ever save ourselves in a way that could give rest to our souls.

There are no human actions or efforts that can shield us from the sorrow of goodbyes. There is too much poverty of sorrow in the self, as Gerson has shown, for it to be otherwise. Gerson once thought that human action could participate in its own salvation. Gerson thought there were certain practices (particularly of penance) that could save us by our own effort. But deep in his own exile, Gerson came to be an Augustinian.[27] No human efforts, only confessions of sorrow, can participate in our salvation. We need something beyond the self to come and save the self by embracing the suffering of our soul. When we are on the path and crying out to God, none of our own actions can save us from our sorrow. But as creatures of soul, we are in sorrow and therefore need saving. On the pathway of goodbyes, we are all seekers of salvation. Suffering goodbyes, we are creatures who need a salvation we cannot produce ourselves. Because we are both self and soul, we are beings who need to be saved—this is what the fire taught Pascal as he broke up forever with Lady Philosophy and found Lady Theology.[28] Therefore, a commitment to soteriology allows evangelism to do more than just convince a self to participate in something; it can point a soul *ad Deum*.

But late-modern Protestants are justifiably concerned that evangelism will be used to instrumentalize "being saved." Conservative Protestants have tended to do just that. When this instrumentalization happens, theology becomes no longer a lady who meets us on the path of sorrows but a brute who demands loyalty to propositions. Salvation becomes an operation of mental consent. Theology becomes a religious mark used for brand loyalty, no longer a path by which to guide and comfort. Being saved becomes a rational operation (echoing Descartes) and loses the suffering soul (of Pascal). Ultimately, being saved loses personhood inside the drives for instrumentality.

27. This shift makes Gerson an important resource for the great Augustinian monk and master Johann von Staupitz.

28. "Gerson anticipated Luther's sola gratia: grace alone brings salvation. But the individual could be prepared for the reception of grace. Gerson was poised between the old monastic theology, beautiful in form but elitist in its view of the world, and the new protestant theology, radical and at times rabid in its rejection of human effort." McGuire, *Jean Gerson*, 119.

Gerson is also worried about instrumentality, causing him to return to Augustine.[29] Gerson contends that Lady Theology plays an important part in leading the *viatores* to salvation. In claiming that Lady Theology leads to salvation (as Macrina does to her brothers), Gerson is making a significant claim. In turning to Lady Theology as consolation, Gerson turns away from the operations of the sacramental system. Burrows explains, "It is striking to note that Gerson . . . identifies the guiding and consoling role of *theologia* in terms that he had earlier reserved following medieval practice for the sacrament of penance. As he establishes [now], it is theology and not the sacraments which lead us through life, for she 'gives herself as companion . . . on the pilgrimage.' . . . Theology, rather than these sacramental acts, . . . fulfills the central role in consoling *viatores* by leading them *ad Deum*."[30]

But Gerson is not antisacramental. Yet, in line with our arguments above, he wants to release the sacramental from the rigid systems of control that the hierarchy wielded against the *viatores*. The sacramental system, Gerson believed, became instrumentalized and therefore could not deal with the sorrowful cries of the goodbyes of *viatores*. Gerson recognizes that the sacramental—the real presence of Christ—comes to persons on the path. The bread (and wine) is essential.[31] But it is a humble meal for the wanderer, feeding the pilgrim. The real presence of Christ comes in the ministry to the sorrowful.[32] Lady Theology leads us to see God's acts of ministry to us, teaching us to recognize the absurdly beautiful mystery that in sorrow and suffering God works to bring life out of death.[33]

29. Here is Gerson in his own words: "For some people, any sound whatsoever is harmful, whether of a person or of a bird, of song or of speech. But for others, hearing church chant often helps them to concentrate on what they want to think about. Saint Augustine confesses about himself that, soon after his conversion, when he heard the psalms or hymns being sung in church, he would weep, and the truth would penetrate into his heart, and he would experience a great good." Gerson, *Early Works*, 97.

30. Burrows, *Jean Gerson and De Consolatione Theologiae*, 68.

31. The wine is in parentheses because only priests could take the wine. The common person was not allowed to partake.

32. Echoing both Luther's and Bonhoeffer's conceptions of *Stellvertretung*.

33. This kind of thinking came to impact Luther through Staupitz. Luther was no disciple of Gerson—he argued with him as much as he was inspired by him. But the DNA of his theological imagination can be seen clearly here, which Burrows highlights very well. Discussing Gerson, he says, "Human achievement, even in terms of the sacrament of penance apparently cannot lead us out of this spiral of despair. On the contrary, knowing that our sins are 'a great abyss and darkness beyond measure, more numerous than the sands of the sea,' we are to collapse in complete desperation of [our] own defense, taking the part as if in a trial not

What saves is the sacramental sharing of the pastoral, the joining in sorrow, the finding of the soul joined to the Spirit in the poverty of the self. The sacramental apparatuses of the priest must give ground to the pastor who invites the pilgrim to tell their sorrowful story through the lens of Lady Theology's articulation of God's acts of ministry in Scripture. The ministry of God saves by coming to the poverty of the self, bringing the self into glory through the backwardness of the cross. Here we find the real presence of Christ. We are not saved by religious apparatuses but by an encounter with the living Christ who comes near in sorrow, bringing us new life by blessing those who mourn (developed further in the next chapter).

The sacramental, for Gerson, is bound in the shared life of sorrows. Gerson wants his priests to be not managers of the apparatuses but pastors of pilgrims who journey with the sorrows of great goodbyes—just like the congregation does with Cynthia. Gerson believes that such an approach can usher us into salvation, for here the soul of the self is ministered to and taken into a new life of faith, hope, and love. It is on the path of sorrows that our being—our soul—is bound to the being of Christ. We are, through our sorrow, now *in* Christ. We have Jesus's very life as our own, which death and all sorrowful goodbyes cannot overcome, for he himself has overcome all death (1 Cor. 15). As Jesus shares in our sorrows, bearing our stories of goodbyes, we no longer live but he lives in us (Gal. 2), becoming our story and our identity, for he has turned our sorrow into the joy of sharing in his life. Consolation is a sacramental reality that brings the real presence of Christ that saves.

And Then There Is Joan

Gerson could never go home. But he was eventually allowed to return to France, for large parts of France were now under English rule. Gerson grieved this great loss. With his enemies now occupied with other threats, he had the opportunity to return to France. Amid the English domination, a return to Paris was not an option. Taking the opportunity, Gerson moved to Lyon to take up residence at the Celestine monastery where his

---

of the defendant but rather that of accuser, witness, and judge against ourselves, and thus 'exaggerating [the charges against us] as much as we are able.'" Burrows, *Jean Gerson and De Consolatione Theologiae*, 69.

brother was prior. Even back in France, Gerson could see himself only as a wanderer. He would be one of the *viatores* for the rest of his life. His sad times were intensified by the English domination.

In the year before Gerson's death something strange happened. An eccentric teenage girl, connected to house Orleans, asked for an audience with the beleaguered French King Charles VII, who was now a vassal of England. This girl told Charles that she had had visions in which she was called by God to save France from the grip of England. The seventeen-year-old Joan was convinced that God had spoken directly to her. Charles saw an opportunity. He commissioned her—a young woman!—to lead men into battle (shocking in itself for the early fifteenth century). With Joan's presence came victories.[34] But was this God's doing? Were her visions true?

At the University of Paris, Gerson's old home, they thought not. Stoked by the defenders of house Burgundy—who murderously hated house Orleans—the university faculty accused Joan of sorcery (and, perhaps worse, wearing men's clothes!). In May 1429—just two months before his death—Gerson came to Joan's defense. He wrote a treatise call *De puella aurelianensi*, which a few years later would be read at Joan's trial but would fail to save her life. The fire came and (contrary to the experience of Blaise Pascal, who also spent time in Rouen) the fire consumed to ash her mortal life. But this time, unlike when he criticized Jan Hus, posterity was Gerson's friend. Joan's memory came to feed the church and France itself.

Gerson's defense played its part. Not surprisingly, Gerson's greatest concern, even regarding Joan, was pastoral. As a pastor, he wanted to

34. Robert Knecht adds, "One day in 1425, the year in which the Burgundians attacked Domremy, her native village in Lorraine, Joan heard voices of saints ordering her to go to the king and save the kingdom. She approached Robert de Baudricourt, the captain of the neighbouring town of Vaucouleurs, but it was only in 1429, after it had been besieged, that he took her seriously and provided her with an armed escort. She reached Chinon on 4 March where she was received by Charles VII, who had been forewarned of her coming. Not everyone at court was well disposed towards her. The chancellor, Regnaut de Chartres, archbishop of Reims, was suspicious of visionaries and prophets, especially if they were women. The church at the time was wary of mystics who claimed that they had a direct line to the Almighty. Joan was not alone of her kind. . . . She was examined by matrons who pronounced her to be a virgin (and therefore not in league with the devil) and by theologians who vouched for her orthodoxy. The Maid (or *La Pucelle*) was then given a suit of armour, horses, an armed escort and a white banner bearing the device 'Jesus Maria.' In addition to 'fans' who had followed her from Lorraine, she won the support of various captains and young noblemen, including the duc d'Alençon." Knecht, *Valois*, 68.

defend her by speaking for what was just, but he also wanted to discern the Spirit. Were Joan's visions from God? From the devil? From her own subconscious? Or maybe from some other psychological longing?

Joan's accusers said that surely her visions were from the devil and her actions from hell! Gerson insisted that Joan's accusers were wrong. He built his own assurance on a few points of discernment. The first is the most dubious. Gerson explained that Joan could not be doing the devil's work because her cause was just. It was right to free France from England, because the shape of God's natural order demanded that French lands be ruled by a French king—not an English king! Looking back in time, it's fair to look askance at this point and conclude that Gerson was clouded by his own patriotism.

But from here Gerson gets more grounded and helpful. He asserts that Joan never "resort[ed] to superstitious practices forbidden by the church."[35] In other words, Joan's experiences have a place in the tradition. The biblical witness points to similar experiences of visions and visitations. Joan is standing inside practices and dispositions that Lady Theology has used to give wisdom, drawing the soul into the Spirit. Important for Gerson, Joan is trying to unite, not divide, the church (his same concern in not supporting Hus).

But Gerson's final point is the most important and is interconnected with his consolation theology. D. Catherine Brown, writing on Gerson and women, states this final and most important point well, explaining that Gerson contended that Joan "is not trying to further her own interests . . . and the Maid constantly urges men to righteousness."[36] Humility as the shape of the pastoral is central to Gerson. Even in his earlier writings humility is central to his vision.[37] The one who walks the pilgrim's path and meets the living God in sorrows will function in the world as a humble servant. The one joined in the sorrow of goodbyes, experiencing the encounter of ministry, will in humility become a minister, seeking to meet other *viatores*

35. Brown, *Pastor and Laity*, 224.
36. Brown, *Pastor and Laity*, 224.
37. Mark Burrows says, "The inner dynamic of his 'pastoral' theology depends upon a humility toward oneself—'*humiliet se homo quantum potuerit, sibi vilescat, se deficiat*'—and, at the same time, a trust and hope in God. . . . This does not directly render the content of Luther's later *simul iustus et peccator*, but the soteriological context of this theme as well as its broad theological structure certainly anticipates the function of this Reformation insight." Burrows, *Gerson and De Consolatione Theologiae*, 188.

on the path, consoling them, urging them toward righteousness by inviting them to lean into sorrow and search it. This searching of sorrow can be done only in humility, for the one who leads is but a *viator* too. Gerson sees this same disposition in Joan. She is a strong leader but not for her own gain. She leads *men* to righteousness in the humility of claiming not her own genius or heroism but God's action of mercy and righteousness. Of course, it's all mixed up with late-medieval battles, knights, and intrigue. But for Gerson, ultimately, we can discern the Spirit if the call leads the called one into humility, if the called one is ushered deeper onto the path of the pilgrim, and ultimately if the call leads one into being a consoler of humanity by the embrace of the humility of Jesus.[38]

Encountering the consolation of those who minister to her, Cynthia experiences a distinct call to live on the path of the *viatores*. Living here, she is called to join others. Having received consolation as the work of the Spirit, she is called to participate now in consoling others, participating herself in the event of evangelism, inside another's own great and grating goodbyes. Cynthia is called to help them encounter this same Spirit. She is shaped by a humility that Gerson would recognize and proclaim as the work of the Spirit.

■ ■ ■ ■

The next day Pastor Manta called Cynthia. "I'm still not sure what to make of your vision. But I think we need to follow it. I think we need to see if this is God's call." Pastor Manta connected Cynthia with a friend who was a spiritual director and a chaplain at the local hospital. Three months later Cynthia was taking her first seminary class. Two weeks after that first class Cynthia and Nate joined the church. They had become disciples. When were they evangelized? Converted? It's hard to say. But it started with *persons* from the church joining Cynthia and Nate, giving consolation as the action of ministry.

They both told the church council that membership meant little to them. What did matter was committing to a community that walked with

38. Matthew Wilcoxen develops humility as a theological category, saying, "Divine humility is the concept I propose for expressing the fact that God's perfect being is always and already oriented toward his creature. Humility serves to express the interrelation between the attributes of God's intrinsic being and his actions *ad extra*." Wilcoxen, *Divine Humility: God's Morally Perfect Being* (Waco: Baylor University Press, 2019), 4.

them in their sorrow. This community was helping them figure out where and how God was calling to them, from within that sorrow, to join the world's sorrow. To also go into the world as witness to the presence of Christ in sorrow. They were choosing to join these people, this community, in walking this path of sorrows as a communion of *viatores*. Nate still wasn't sure he believed any of it. He still had a lot of unanswered *why* questions. Cynthia knew only that she had met Jesus and he had spoken to her in her sorrow. They were both on the path and committed to it. Even with their doubts, they were pilgrims. They had been evangelized, the *evangel* arriving in their lives with the good news that Jesus comes in sorrow. And they called it good. They had met Jesus in sorrow and were now ministering to the world out of that sorrow. They were disciples.

■ ■ ■ ■

The week that Cynthia and Nate stood in front of the congregation and made their commitment to journey the path with this community, Mary Ann offered a prayer request. The congregation was small enough in its Sunday gatherings to allow people to share their prayer concerns with the entire congregation. Mary Ann stood before the table that held the bread and wine that the community would feed on after their prayers and said, "I've been very tired for the last six months. I thought it was just the stress of work. But I just couldn't kick it. I had blood drawn and something seems wrong. I have scans Tuesday. I'm pretty scared. God, please be with me. I'm worried. . . . I'm scared."

The congregation said in unison, "Lord, hear our prayer."

An email went out the next Friday. Mary Ann had stage 4 lung cancer. It had spread everywhere.

9

When Temptation Is Good

And God Is Full of Sorrow

Mary Ann's pilgrimage took a new turn. She'd been on this path since Valentina had joined her sorrow, following Jesus into sorrow and giving Mary Ann consolation by being a friend. Mary Ann had felt claimed by the *evangel*. She joined Valentina on her path of illness. Mary Ann was now on that same trail. She underwent terrible treatments. The chemo started immediately. She had her first dose the Tuesday after the diagnosis. It hit Mary Ann like a freight train. She was so sick. But she had promised Will, the founder and CEO of the apparel company, that she'd be back to work by the end of the week.

To his credit, Will was moved when Mary Ann told him she was sick. He wanted to be as helpful as possible. They'd been through battles before, and Will wanted to be there for this one. It was Mary Ann, not Will, who pushed to get back to work. She didn't want to be one of those people who just sat around feeling sorry for herself. She didn't want the diagnosis to end her life. She wanted to keep things as normal as possible. She planned to beat this, after all. Her son had just had a child, and Mary Ann planned to watch her little granddaughter grow up.

Will was determined to help. When Mary Ann lost her hair, Will convinced the executives to shave their heads in solidarity. Of course, they posted everything on social media with hashtags like #fight #battle

#nevergiveup #MaryAnnStrong. Will also put his money where his mouth was. He connected Mary Ann to a top nutritionist and gave her access to spas and other health and wellness professionals. It all helped, particularly with the side effects of the chemo. Mary Ann had more energy to be with her granddaughter. That was a gift. However, over three months it didn't shrink the tumors. Not even the chemo seemed to be making a dent.

Mary Ann's doctors tried a stronger drug. But that chemo too was rebuffed by the cancer. The stronger drug knocked Mary Ann off her feet. In response, Will upped the interventions, giving Mary Ann access to daily massages and a music therapist and hypnotist who claimed to be able to convince the immune system to fight cancer. Will claimed that this therapist had ways to get the body to fight the cancer that the medical industry and Big Pharma feared. He also ordered a particular fruit from South America for Mary Ann that he said showed signs of supercharging the immune system. Will had been taking it himself for years. He claimed he hadn't had so much as a cold since taking it each morning. Mary Ann took some of the fruit in a smoothie. She had a "Super Will Smoothie" every day for a month. It tasted disgusting. Mary Ann fought to get it down and keep it down. But nothing helped. Not the therapist, massages, or gross fruit could shrink the tumors.

After four months Mary Ann was getting sicker and sicker. She made it to the office only once a week. She could only manage to spend one afternoon a week with her granddaughter. That hurt more than the cancer ravaging her body. She grieved this loss deeply. Hazel, Myrtle, AC, and Wilma took turns being with Mary Ann most nights. They sat with Mary Ann in this grief. The sitters sat and cared for her. Almost every evening, Hazel watched home improvement shows with Mary Ann and drove her to all her appointments. Hazel even asked Cynthia to take care of Trevor the Tormentor. The dog needed more walks than Hazel could give him. Hazel needed to be with Mary Ann. Plus, Hazel sensed that Cynthia needed Trevor in her life more than she did. Trevor still had a ministry to do with Cynthia.

One day Hazel was sitting next to Mary Ann at an appointment. New scans had been taken. Mary Ann didn't want to hear the results alone. Maybe she sensed that they wouldn't be good. She was right. Not only had the tumor not shrunk; it had grown. There were even new spots. It was the worst news possible. The doctor admitted as much and then launched into further treatment options. The doctor talked about an exploratory radiation treatment done in Reno. When Will heard the news, like the doctor, he jumped into overdrive, offering the option of a spa in Denmark where cold plunges, raw fish, and chants at the moon were used as a miracle cure. "I bet your doctor didn't tell you about the Denmark group," Will said. "They're scared of these groups because they'd totally destroy the medical-industrial complex. I can help you get there. I know some people who can give you a good travel deal. And I know a guy who runs the group. They don't let just anyone in, but I can pull some strings."

There was now a franticness to the whole situation. Mary Ann was reminded again and again to never give up. She wasn't sure what to do. Should she go to Reno or Denmark? Her doctor was clear that they had come to the end of treatments at their disposal. But there were other options, the doctor kept saying.

Mary Ann did what she'd done for years when faced with a hard decision. She took it to the Bible study. It had been hard to get to gatherings the last few months. Mary Ann had been too sick. But this Tuesday she laid it all out. What was better, Reno or Denmark? They all sat in silence. Then AC said the one thing that no doctor or wellness professional would: "I think we'd better face the facts, Mary Ann: you gonna die. It makes me sad, but living and dying in God is what we do as human beings. And it seems it's your time to die. It hurts me to say it, but honey, you gonna die."

It took the air out of the room. Everyone was now in tears. No one had said these words to Mary Ann. No one said, "You are going to die." No one told Mary Ann the truth. No one but her church. Neither the doctors nor Will could say it. There was always another option, a moon shot to keep them from admitting the truth that all pilgrims' paths end with a great goodbye to life. This goodbye is painful and full of suffering—it's never not—but even in this painful goodbye Jesus comes to us, taking us through our sorrow into life forevermore in him. AC's words hit Mary Ann like a truck. But they also liberated her, connecting her to the group and sacramentally binding her to Jesus's own suffering. All that consoled her.

They sat a long time in silence, with only the sound of sniffling and tears. Finally, Mary Ann broke the silence. "I am. I'm going to die," she said with tears streaming down her cheeks. She looked at each face around the circle and said, "You're my friends, my family of faith. Help me die well. Please, *please*, help me die well." The whole group was now sobbing.

"We will," said Pastor Manta.

"We will," said Hazel.

"We will," said Nate, his face overwhelmed and puffy with tears.

The Cross of Consolation of Theology

In the Heidelberg Disputation of 1518, written about ninety years after Gerson's death, Martin Luther says that a "theologian of the cross calls a thing what it is."[1] But what is the thing? The thing is sorrow. Sorrow is sorrow. Evil is evil. Despair is despair. A theologian of glory fails to call things what they are. A theologian of glory, instead, calls good evil and evil good, calls sorrow a distraction or an opportunity for personal betterment, calls despair a loser's lament. To connect Luther's words with Gerson, a theologian of glory spends all their time with Lady Philosophy. A theologian of glory believes that human beings can exist outside the sorrow of goodbyes, outside the ever-present temptation to escape goodbyes. A theologian of glory believes God can be found (*ad Deum*) without sorrow.

A theologian of glory believes the self—in itself—is rich and therefore able to constitute the self's own being of happiness. A theologian of the cross instead reminds us that we are human creatures, always pilgrims, and therefore we must be constantly saying goodbye. We are the creatures who are dying and tempted to deny all our sorrow. But it's inside this sorrow, and by wrestling with this temptation, that we find ourselves in the real presence of Jesus Christ. In wrestling with sorrow, the foreign (to the self) righteousness of God comes to us, redeeming us with Jesus's own life that ministers to us.

AC is a great theologian of the cross because he calls a thing what it is. Mary Ann is going to die. There is both pain and peace in his proclamation. The pain comes because the anesthesia of denial is gone. But peace also comes, because facing this truth opens the suffering soul to meet consolation. Mary Ann is coming to a great goodbye—one we all must journey toward. AC refuses to avoid this reality. The temptation is to hide from this reality, taking shelter from this truth in our own self-imposed châteaus. To give the ministry of consolation, it is necessary to call a thing what it is.

---

1. Martin Luther, *The Essential Luther* (Indianapolis: Hackett, 2018), 27–28.

The theology of the cross is a theology born from Lady Theology. Luther follows Gerson in seeing theology as a consoling and ministering reality. The theology of the cross grows from the soil—out of the ground[2]—of the theology of consolation.[3] Luther, like Gerson, believes that a theology that attends to our sufferings ministers by naming our sorrows and drawing us into visions of God's nearness.[4] The *theologia crucis* is a *consolatione theologiae*.[5] It is not primarily a theology of forensic atonement, bound in the speculations of the faculty. Instead, it is first and foremost a pastoral theology that seeks to name how God is present in sorrow, doing God's good work of bringing life out of death inside our most real human experiences of loss and sorrow. Luther, as we'll see below, uses this consolation theology in the theology of the cross to talk in the deepest terms about who God is and how God acts in the world.

2. Rhineland mystics such as Meister Eckhart and Johannes Tauler use the idea of ground often. They ask us to get to the ground in our pilgrimages. Their mysticism reaches not up but down into the ground of sorrow and the suffering of human impossibility.

3. Michael Massing offers an example of how Luther's theology was a theology of consolation, saying, "'If God help me,' Albrecht Dürer wrote to George Spalatin, 'I will go to Dr. Martin Luther and make his likeness in copper for a lasting memorial of the Christian man who has helped me out of great anguish. I beg your Honor if Dr. Luther writes anything more in German, please send it to me at my expense.' The Nuremberg master never would get a chance to meet Luther, but, as his comment to Spalatin suggested, he had recently undergone a deep emotional crisis, and his study of Lutheran doctrines had helped him overcome it. Luther's teaching that man is justified by faith would work such a powerful effect on Dürer that he would abandon secular subjects for religious ones and give up his former exuberant style for an intensely austere one." Massing, *Fatal Discord: Erasmus, Luther, and the Fight for the Western Mind* (New York: Harper, 2018), 386.

4. Thomas Kaufmann discusses the rise of pastoral theology and Gerson's and Staupitz's places within it, pointing to how this impacted Luther. See Kaufmann, *The Saved and the Damned: A History of the Reformation* (New York: Oxford University Press, 2023), 41–43. Werner Packull pushes us deeper, saying, "It has even been argued that Tauler and Gerson were Luther's 'earliest major conscious opponents.' His definition of the *homo spirituolis* as the man of faith as early as 1516 fundamentally threatened the entire medieval system. These claims may exaggerate Luther's reformed theological consciousness for 1516. For Luther will use mystical vocabulary after 1516 to argue against traditional assumptions concerning the nature of sin, grace, and sacramentalism. Moreover, Luther's perception of the externalness of the 'righteousness of God' may in fact have been influenced by mystical conclusions." Packull, *Mysticism and the Early South German-Austrian Anabaptist Movement 1525–1531* (Eugene, OR: Wipf & Stock, 1977), 28.

5. "If, then, consolation is Luther's central message, and although it remains as a prominent feature of pastoral recommendation in the longer Reformation era, Luther's successors will characteristically add another: the pressing obligation to repent, not simply as a state of mind, but to demonstrate that mood in the betterment of one's outer life." Susan C. Karant-Nunn, *The Reformation of Feeling: Shaping the Religious Emotions in Early Modern Germany* (New York: Oxford University Press, 2010), 98.

Therefore, through the theology of the cross, the theology of consolation rises to the level of the revelation of God's being.

To make this connection between the *theologia crucis* and *consolatione theologiae*—to claim that the theology of the cross is a consolation theology (moving to the deepest level of God's own being)—we need to spend some time with the linchpin between Gerson and Luther: Johann von Staupitz.

Luther himself always remained a bit lukewarm about Gerson. Gerson was too French, too papal, and too focused on human capacities for Luther's liking.[6] But Luther's pastor and theological mentor, the man who consoled Luther by introducing him to Lady Theology, Johann von Staupitz, always deeply admired Gerson. Staupitz particularly loved *consolatione theologiae*.

Staupitz was the kind of theologian that Gerson always wanted the University of Paris to produce, a theologian who never turned from the pastoral because he never turned from concerns of how the human being finds redemption. As David Steinmetz says so poignantly, "Johannes von Staupitz was not a speculative theologian. The fine points of metaphysics and epistemology, which fascinated many theologians in the later middle ages, excited little interest in him. His theological reflections were devoted almost exclusively to the explication of the drama of human redemption." What interested Staupitz was "the dialogue between heaven and earth, between the self-giving *misericordia* [mercy] of God and the dire *miseria* [misery] of man."[7] The dialectic between mercy and misery is central and fertile to Staupitz's pastoral theology. Luther learned this dialectic from Staupitz, and it is embedded in Luther's own *theologia crucis*.

---

6. James Connolly adds, "Drawn by the prestige that clung to the name of Gerson, Luther approached him in an hour of need, and found, by his own declaration, great solace. Later in life he was to refer to him as his great comforter, and declare that 'he more than any other had the gift of calming consciences.' It was to those writings of the Chancellor that were calculated to counteract abnormal spiritual conditions that the reformer of the sixteenth century betook himself, and it was principally from these works that he drew his opinions. He esteemed Gerson to be of greater help than such Saints as Jerome, Augustine, Ambrose, Bernard or Thomas of Aquin, because he, more than they, paid heed to temptations that were of a spiritual nature. For this reason, Gerson had been the means of saving many souls from despair, and that, said Luther, 'was the reason why the Pope condemned him.'" Connolly, *John Gerson: Reformer and Mystic* (1928; repr., Eugene, OR: Wipf & Stock, 2023), 357.

7. David Curtis Steinmetz, *Misericordia Dei: The Theology of Johannes von Staupitz in Its Late Medieval Setting* (Leiden: Brill, 1986), 1.

Staupitz was always seeking first to comfort the souls of the *viatores* rather than to win arguments. Through the motifs of mercy and misery, Staupitz pushed Gerson's pastoral thoughts into the deeper waters of who God is and how God acts in consolation. Staupitz—inspired by Gerson— asserts that a consolation of theology needs a God of love, grace, and mercy who can be known only through Jesus Christ. He drives the consolation of theology onto more significant theological and christological grounds. Luther learns this from Staupitz. Luther's education came most directly by the consoling and pastoral heart of Staupitz. Staupitz taught Luther these ways by being his minister. Luther's sorrows were shared by the consoling embrace of Staupitz. As Luther says, Staupitz was "a preacher of grace and of the cross."[8] Luther knew this from the inside.[9] Luther followed Staupitz—in his own unique way—making grace and the cross, mercy and misery, all for the sake of the ministry of consolation, central to his own imagination.

Who Is Staupitz? Misery's Business Is Mercy

When Gerson was forced into exile from France, he escaped to the German-speaking lands. In those lands, Gerson wrote *De consolatione theologiae*. A generation later, in those same lands, Johann von Staupitz was born. Unlike Gerson (and Luther after him), Staupitz came from nobility. He grew up as childhood friends with Frederick, who became known as Frederick the Wise. Frederick the Wise became elector of Saxony and played a major part in keeping Luther alive in the early days of the Reformation. There is little doubt that Staupitz's love for Luther and Frederick's love for Staupitz was more than advantageous. Staupitz did a lot of protecting of Luther in the 1520s. Staupitz's noble upbringing gave him a cooler temperament and more patient disposition to the orders of the day than the red-hot Luther could muster. While Luther swung from emotional pole to pole, Staupitz remained more baseline and balanced.

8. Steinmetz, *Misericordia Dei*, 1. Luther says this in a letter from February 9, 1526. It can be found in Luther's Works (*Weimarer Ausgabe*), 2:264.

9. "Luther once claimed in his characteristically expansive fashion that he had 'revived everything from Staupitz' and acknowledged his old friend to be the originator of evangelical doctrine. Staupitz, for his part, in his last letter to Luther dated April 1, 1524, referred to himself as Luther's brother and pupil." Steinmetz, *Misericordia Dei*, 2, citing Heinrich Boehmer, *Martin Luther: Road to Reformation* (New York: Meridian, 1960), 105.

Both knighthood and the monastery were open to Staupitz as a child of nobility. He chose the church and took vows in the Augustinian order in the cloister of Munich. A familiar Augustinian convent near his family home perhaps drew him to the order. But the order was also growing in its theological reputation. Giles of Rome and Gregory of Rimini had represented the order at Gerson's own great University of Paris. Staupitz himself never studied in Paris. He took his degrees at Cologne, Leipzig, and finally Tübingen. Particularly through sermons, Staupitz showed himself in Tübingen to be an able (if a little dry) theologian. But he was an even more able pastor.

The next years of Staupitz's life were spent as a prior caring for monks, teaching them to pray and read the Bible. This work of ministry solidified Staupitz's unique theological voice. It also brought him into contact with Luther, introducing Luther to Lady Theology. As Staupitz cared for monks—ministering to ministers—he came to emphasize three theological motifs. Staupitz's pastoral theology revolved around these three foci that are bound in the practice of consolation.

Focus One

The first of these three foci is the necessity of temptation. Temptation sets in motion the generative dialectic of misery and mercy. No one wishes for temptation, but no pilgrim can avoid it. The goodbyes are too acute, too pained, to avoid it. Entering those goodbyes, Staupitz believes, is necessary. In so doing, the pilgrim is taught not to trust in one's own self and ability to will its own happiness. Staupitz has little confidence in the will of the human agent (more on that in the second focus).

Staupitz sees our great temptation as believing that our self has the ability to escape the sorrow of goodbyes and will our own happiness. This temptation is ever-present in late modernity. Both Mary Ann's doctor and Will, in their own ways, seek to heroically or ingeniously avoid or conquer all the goodbyes of sickness.

Ultimately, the temptation, Staupitz believes, is to deny that we are creatures and therefore finite. This primal temptation goes back to Genesis 3: we believe we can be a creator who can exist beyond goodbyes, contending that our self is not a creature. We are tempted, like Adam and Eve with the tree of the knowledge of good and evil, to believe that our will (our own word!) can save us. We're tempted to assume that happiness is our own creation, brought forth by us: we are our own great creator, able to make a château of unending happiness.

This temptation, Staupitz contends, always remains nearby. We are always tempted to think too highly of our wills. But our response to this temptation should not be self-hatred. Staupitz is no fan of self-mutilation in any form. He leads Luther to a kind of penance that is neither physically nor psychologically bound in punishing the self and wounding the soul. For Staupitz, temptation is not a shame but a gift. It invites the pilgrim "to flee to the mercy of God."[10] The misery of the temptation is that it puffs the self to the point that the self believes it can be protected from all goodbyes. This effort will inevitably fail, leaving the self in deep sorrow. But this sorrow produces the further temptation to double down on the self and work harder and harder to win happiness by the will of the self. This burden to create your own self-maintained happiness becomes a weight of misery. And it's why our own times are such sad ones. So many late-modern people are miserable because they believe their own wills can create their own eternal happiness (eternal because they never think of their own finitude). Inside this misery, only the mercy of God, coming in the consoling presence of Jesus Christ and his Spirit of ministry, can save.

Staupitz believes that this temptation—this misery—is met directly by the mercy of God. This mercy is seen in the crucified body of Jesus Christ, who wills only the will of his father (John 14). This love meets temptation and frees the self to receive the love and mercy of God, ministering to our soul. God is full of mercy. God is pure mercy, Staupitz proclaims. The bodily and cosmic life of Jesus Christ reveals this truth. Inside the temptation, and the sorrow and misery it produces, we experience the presence of Jesus Christ drawing near. Staupitz consoles by telling the sorrowful to think not of their own will and action but only of Jesus Christ himself.

Focus Two

This leads us to the second focus of Staupitz's pastoral theology. The same year that Staupitz arrived at Tübingen, the great Gabriel Biel died. When a great theologian dies, their school often spends the next year or so in remembrance, auditing their work. When I started my doctoral work at Princeton Theological Seminary, James Loder had just died, and

---

10. Steinmetz, *Misericordia Dei*, 20.

I observed this kind of remembering and auditing in full effect. To arrive as a student the year after a great theologian dies gives you an interesting and in-depth education on the deceased scholar.

Biel was known as the great German theologian of the time. All late-medieval German theology students read him; Biel was on everyone's syllabus. Luther himself was raised on Biel.[11] Important to Biel's theological system was predestination, which he contended was "based on foreseen merit."[12] Like an algorithm that can predict future purchases by examining past ones, the idea was that God foresaw future merit based on your past and present willing of virtuous works. Predestination was therefore glued to foreseen merit.

Staupitz followed Biel, at least in part. Staupitz agreed that God is an electing God who makes covenants. Staupitz's biblical commitments convinced him of this. But this electing, this choosing that God does, Staupitz believed, is based not on merit but on mercy alone. There is no human merit involved at all in God's election (here Staupitz shows his Augustinian colors). God acts with and for humanity out of pure mercy. God is "motivated by His gracious lovingkindness alone and not a reaction on His part to the prior activity of His creatures."[13] Staupitz was taking a big step away from Biel and most late-medieval thinking. He was placing grace as divine action, not virtue as human action, as the very lifeblood of election. But grace can be grace, and escape sentimentality, only if it is understood inside the dialectic.

Staupitz acknowledges the dialectic here as well. God does not elect in the way of a benign kindergarten teacher who just likes everyone the same. That is not grace! That has no correlation with the Word that elects. Treating everyone the same cannot be grace, for God's mercy is always a response to human misery—God comes to Israel while they are enslaved in Egypt (Exod. 20). God elects and blesses not those who are worthy but those who are in sorrow. God's being is revealed in acts of ministry. God *is* a minister. Therefore, God chooses to be with and for those who are

---

11. Marilyn Harran adds, "We do know that Luther prepared for the priesthood by working his way through the *Canonis misse expositio* of Gabriel Biel. We know that Luther was acquainted with the works of Jean Gerson and Johannes Tauler, both of whom employ the term 'conversion' in their mystical writings but understand it quite differently." Harran, *Luther on Conversion: The Early Years* (Ithaca, NY: Cornell University Press, 1983), 44.

12. Steinmetz, *Misericordia Dei*, 20.

13. Steinmetz, *Misericordia Dei*, 21.

in sorrow, consoling them, saving them—giving them life out of death. God's mercy is concretely encountered as God's ministry.

To console the sorrowful is to attend to those whom God has predestined and elected to care for by being present with them. God elects to be God for those who suffer great goodbyes, not those who perform good works. The church evangelizes by witnessing to this electing truth. Evangelism and election cannot be disconnected, and neither can evangelism and consolation. Evangelism proclaims God's work of election, God's choosing. This work is witnessed to by the church and Jesus's disciples consoling those in sorrow ("Blessed are those who mourn," Matt. 5:4). Those who mourn are elect by God, given God's presence inside their suffering.

Staupitz helps us see that it is those in sorrow (misery) whom God chooses to be with and for, giving them God's own presence on their paths of goodbyes. We discover or experience our election not by our great works but by our humble surrender to our suffering. By leaning into it we find that the living God made known in Jesus Christ ministers to us there and then sends us to those who are in sorrow to minister to them as the way to share in God's very being. Like temptation, for Staupitz, predestination is bound inside the dialectic of misery and mercy.

Focus Three

In the second focus Staupitz breaks with common medieval thought. Yet in the third focus Staupitz reminds us that he is still a medieval man. The third focus of his pastoral theology revolves around penance. Penance—maybe unfortunately—has fallen out of favor in the modern era. When we leave the pilgrim's path for the château there is little reason for penance. After all, the self puts the self right. And happiness rights all wrongs. Montaigne doesn't think much of penance. He calls us instead to enjoy our gardens and cats, our dancing and sleeping. Penance assumes a path beyond the happiness of the château, a path in which Montaigne is utterly uninterested.

Yet, as with election, Staupitz both affirms and denies the commonly held theological position regarding penance, especially as it comes from Biel. As a pastoral practice penance was wrapped up with a nominalism that put a "strong emphasis on the ability of the natural powers of man, unaided by grace, to do the will of God."[14] Penance was a work of the

14. Steinmetz, *Misericordia Dei*, 21.

self, empowered by the self to will the self to act rightly. Penance was the willingness of the self to put itself in line with the will of God. Hence the reason for flagellating the body or mind.

This kind of penance, Staupitz believed, was all misery and no mercy. Penance was a willed act of misery that lost the dialectic, forgetting the mercy. This version of penance locked action so deeply inside the will of the self that grace was lost. Without the mercy of grace, penance became masochistic. Luther jumped right into this form of penance when he entered the monastery at Erfurt. He discovered, thanks to Staupitz's care, that such penance without mercy became an insatiable, self-imposed misery. The self became a vicious warden. Such penance produced the belief that you could escape misery by taking a small (self-imposed) dose of misery. You took this little shot of misery to not have to face the sorrow of the goodbyes of the soul.[15]

That form of penance, Staupitz believed, cuts God out of the whole process. The human will takes on its own penance, forgiving itself by its own power. Repentance becomes dependent on human actions alone and not the love and mercy of God. The dialectic is lost.

Inside this way of thinking, misery is malformed, locking it within the self. Misery becomes something other than a condition of the soul and part of the pilgrim's path *ad Deum*. Rather, misery is considered to be self-controlled and therefore self-conquered. Locking misery in the will of the self has the worse effect of losing an imagination for a merciful and loving God. God is not joining our misery but instead demanding we impose acts of misery on our self to satisfy God. Lost is the mercy of God's ministry to come and deliver, blessing us in our miserable goodbyes.

To escape all this, Staupitz contended instead that penance was a practice that moved the human being to *stop*! Penance was a call *to stop and receive*, not *to act and will*. Inside this stopping and receiving, the self confesses the sorrow of its soul, placing its being on the path of the pilgrim who receives God's mercy. Penance is the confession of sorrow. Penance gives over our sorrow of goodbyes—that which has happened to us or which we've caused for others—to God. Penance involves stopping our

15. There are important connections here to self-mutilation, which has been our pervasive epidemic in the late-modern West. It's no surprise that once the self becomes apotheosized—containing only the will, and happiness being the only measure of the good life (and goodbyes denied)—the self hurts itself.

own willing and only walking the path to receive God's mercies, receiving God's ministry of love. Penance is the return *ad Deum*, to being, by joining with others and saying goodbye, finding God's mercy inside the goodbyes. Penance is not what the self wills. Penance is how the soul surrenders.

When Lightning Strikes

Penance pushed Martin Luther into the monastery. The story is well known (and maybe overblown). In early July 1502, Luther was returning to the University of Erfurt, where he studied law, when a lighting bolt nearly struck him dead. As the thunderstorm rolled over Luther without cover, and fear enveloped him, he cried out to Saint Anne, saying that if God saved him, he'd enter the monastery. Luther may have already been pondering this entrance. But on surviving, and to his father's disappointment, he entered the Augustinian monastery at Erfurt. There Luther fed on Biel's theology and nominal philosophy. He became a tortured master of penance, forcing his body and will into miseries, without mercy, to please a distant God.

When not diving headlong into self-willed acts of penance, Luther was devouring the Bible, becoming a skilled interpreter of the sacred texts. Luther explains that he was devouring the biblical text because the drives of self-will were torturing him. He was trapped in his own will, imprisoned in the self, tempted to overcome and therefore deny all his goodbyes. Luther says, "When I was a young master in Erfurt, I continually wandered about sadly because of the *Anfechtung* of arrows, so I devoted myself to much reading of the Bible."[16] The text proved to be a mercy.

In the same year that the lightning struck and Luther entered the monastery, Staupitz's childhood friend Frederick the Wise decided to form a university in the town of Wittenberg. Frederick wanted his new university to rival Leipzig. Frederick trusted only one man with this ambition: his lifelong friend Johann von Staupitz. In 1502 Staupitz was named professor of Bible and dean of the faculty at Frederick's new university.

But poor Staupitz was never able to settle into academic life. Just when he started, in 1503, Staupitz was elected vicar-general of the German

16. Quoted in Martin Brecht, *Martin Luther: His Road to Reformation 1483–1521* (Minneapolis: Fortress, 1985), 47.

observants of the hermits of St. Augustine. This responsibility required that Staupitz become familiar with all the young monks in his charge, putting him in direct contact with brother Martin in Erfurt.

The Meeting and the Arrows

When Staupitz met Luther, he was both impressed and intrigued by the brother. He was impressed by the young monk's passion for the Bible and skill in interpreting it. Such attention to the text was not always present with monks at the end of the medieval period. Few monks even had access to a Bible—rarely having one of their own. When Luther got his hands on a Bible in the Erfurt library, he never let it go. As a Bible professor, Staupitz spotted Luther's unique abilities. Game knows game, as the kids say.

But Staupitz was also intrigued, even perplexed. This young, able monk was tortured. He was torturing himself. Brother Martin spent as much time in confession as he did reading the Bible. Luther tells us, "Once I confessed for six hours."[17] Six hours is a long time, even for people whose minds haven't been warped by streaming services, clickbait, and sound bites. Luther read the Bible not as an academic exercise but to keep his misery, his *Anfechtung*, from overtaking him. The Bible consoled his soul. The rumors were swirling that brother Martin was wearing out his confessors. (Six-hour confession sessions will do that.) Luther's confessions were so demanding that for a time the vicar-general became his confessor. Staupitz stood in the breach, hearing Luther's confessions.

Staupitz became Luther's pastor.[18] Luther's confessions were somewhat unusual and at times annoying. Luther didn't (often) confess direct sins. In a line that shows the difficulties that most monks felt holding faithfully to their vows of celibacy, Luther says that when he confessed to Staupitz it wasn't "about women, but about the real knots."[19] By "the real knots"

17. Quoted in Brecht, *Martin Luther*, 68.
18. "'If Christ is to help you,' Staupitz said, 'you must keep a list of real honest-to-goodness sins and not go hobbling around nursing toy ones, imagining you commit a sin every time you fart!' (This was Luther's colorful phrasing of Staupitz's statement, which was no doubt more demure.)" Massing, *Fatal Discord*, 171. He continues, "Staupitz tried to expose [Luther] to a different image of the Almighty—that of a benevolent father who cares for his children and desires their love in return. He spoke of God's compassionate readiness to confer his grace on man and of the sanctified path that the sacraments offered to attain it." Massing, *Fatal Discord*, 171.
19. Quoted in Brecht, *Martin Luther*, 69.

Luther means the misery of trying to please God in and through his own will. This inability to get the self to will for itself was an experience that Luther could only describe as his *Anfechtung* (plural *Anfechtungen*). The more he trusted in his self to seek piety and do good, the more the *Anfechtung* fell upon him, attacking him. The young Luther sought to run from the *Anfechtung*. The six-hour confessions and sweating of the will were ways of avoiding the *Anfechtung*.

But what does Luther mean when he uses this strange German word? What is the *Anfechtung*? This word—not original to Luther—is connected to the sorrows of the soul and the goodbyes of the pilgrim.[20]

Luther speaks of *Anfechtung* as temptation. But he does so only after Staupitz ministers to him. Remember, for Staupitz temptation is good, for it draws us into the mercy of God. Staupitz never wants us to stress about our temptations but to see them as an invitation to turn to a loving God full of mercy. Young Luther knew little of mercy when Staupitz first met him.

Luther will experience *Anfechtung* for the rest of his life. *Anfechtung* cannot be instrumentalized; it can't be solved and finished. It is inextricable from the one living before God. The pilgrim will meet *Anfechtung*; there is no avoiding it, for the pilgrim *must* say goodbye. For Luther, *Anfechtung* becomes the central experience that engenders his theology of the cross (as we'll see). The mature Luther trusts only theologians who have some sense of the *Anfechtung* in their theological visions.[21] Only those who know this sorrow, Luther believes, can understand the consolation of theology. And theology is for consolation, for the goodbyes of dying and

20. Dennis Ngien explains, "*Anfechtung*, the term which Luther borrowed from the German mystic Tauler, was theocentric and therefore must be distinguished from that which is anthropocentric. *Anfechtung* is sometimes translated as 'temptation.' Its root means 'assail,' 'combat,' or 'bodily struggle.'" Ngien, *The Suffering of God according to Martin Luther's Theologia Crucis* (Vancouver: Regent College Publishing, 1995), 32.

21. "In the spring of 1516, while Luther was still lecturing on Romans, a fellow monk (Johannes Lang) gave him a copy of Tauler's sermons. Luther was immediately taken by the mystic's emphasis on suffering, self-denial, and passivity in the Christian life." Ronald Rittgers, *The Reformation of Suffering: Pastoral Theology and Lay Piety in Late Medieval and Early Modern Germany* (New York: Oxford University Press, 2012), 98. Martin Brecht explains that Luther was drawn to Tauler because he saw within him an *Anfechtung*. Luther saw a consolation theology at play. Brecht says, "Tauler becomes a witness to the hellish experience of *Anfechtungen*, unknown to the scholastic theologians. In Tauler Luther found more solid and true theology than one can find in the dogmatic textbooks of all the scholastic doctors of all the universities." Brecht, *Martin Luther*, 139.

being damned, to paraphrase Luther's famous saying. Luther's coming theological breakthrough in the theology of the cross meets the human experience of *Anfechtung*, speaking to this great sorrow by consoling us with God's mercies. And these mercies are deep!

Anfechtung is a concrete and central human reality. It makes the theology of the cross a consolation theology. There is no theology of the cross without the experience of sorrowful *Anfechtung*. Because of this reality, the theology of the cross must be seen as a consolation theology. The theology of the cross becomes ossified in stiff doctrine—and moved away from the pastoral—when *Anfechtung* is ignored.[22]

For Luther the *Anfechtung* falls as a deep depression. Seemingly early in Luther's life it pushes him into frantic actions, to confess for six hours and to sleep on a hard bed. Later in life *Anfechtung* pins Luther to his bed, covering him in a heavy despondency. The *Anfechtung* is never cured.

Anfechtung represents something more than a psychological state, though no doubt it is a psychological burden for Luther. Rather, in his mind *Anfechtung* is a malaise of the soul, not a sickness of the self. To be specific (which is hard because Luther never defines it clearly), *Anfechtung* can be understood as a nullifying, a pushing into the void. The soul must face this great negation. *Anfechtung* is the great terror of goodbye. It's a haunting of nothingness.[23] It's the misery of coming to realize that all your efforts to will the self into piety or happiness are impotent and pointless. There is no way out of your sadness, no way for your actions to substantiate your self or put your self in a place beyond the sorrows of all the goodbyes that threaten your being.

22. Dennis Ngien adds, "The solution to the absolute hiddenness of God, for Luther as for Staupitz, is not theoretical but practical, that is, by way of the proclamation of the gospel apart from which 'God and Satan are virtually indistinguishable.'" Ngien, *Suffering of God*, 131.

23. Simon Podmore nicely connects Kierkegaard with Luther's *Anfechtung*. Podmore contends that Kierkegaard updates and reworks the concept. The astute reader will notice that I'm doing the same. I'm even updating Kierkegaard, placing *Anfechtung* within the reach of the late-modern person. Podmore says, "Although there are thematic affinities between Kierkegaard's *Anfægtelse* and Luther's *Anfechtungen*, however, I maintain that Kierkegaard's dialectic of *spiritual trial* not only inherits but partially divests itself of its Lutheran inheritance. In fact, Kierkegaard is not only rehabilitating the Lutheran term but critiquing, refining, and reenergizing the notion of spiritual trial for a generation that is oblivious and desensitized to its significance." Podmore, *Kierkegaard and the Self before God: Anatomy of the Abyss* (Bloomington: Indiana University Press, 2011), 123.

The *Anfechtung* is like arrows of sadness.[24] The *Anfechtung* leads to the temptation to give in to the misery. To lose faith. To contend that God is a misery, a devil who has no mercy. To depend on the self, to do more, and to do better only pacifies the *Anfechtung* for a brief spell before it comes back with a double force and more arrows.[25]

To put all this inside the motif we've been using, and to give *Anfechtung* a late-modern patina, *Anfechtung* is the temptation to abandon the pilgrim's way and refuse to say goodbye. It's to try to live outside goodbyes, to create a life where you never need to say goodbye, for the will of your self is so magnificent that it becomes its own god.[26] *Anfechtung* is the temptation to claim that the self has no need for goodbyes because the self can will itself out of all its sorrows (it just needs a few therapeutic hacks that now come conveniently via an app). *Anfechtung* is the temptation to believe that God is not a good and loving minister, nor are you a being who needs ministering to. The self is its own god.

Staupitz has taught Luther to lean into temptation, seeing what can be found there. Because of his own reading of the Bible as prayer, Staupitz is betting that the merciful love of God will reach back to embrace. Confessing *Anfechtung* entails crying out of sorrow. By crying out, which Luther sees in the psalmists (Luther wears out the Psalms in his devouring

24. Ronald Rittgers adds, "Luther says that he knows by experience what it is to be cooked by God in the pot of Moab and to have one's soul enlarged through divinely imposed suffering. For Luther, these assaults especially took the form of despair over his salvation as he contemplated the seemingly impossible demands of God—to love God and neighbor with no hint of self-interest—and the likelihood that he was not among the elect." Rittgers, *Reformation of Suffering*, 93.

25. Dennis Ngien pushes us deeper, saying, "In contrast to the mystics, Luther argues that the union with Christ does not come about through the discipline of a complete submission or self-denial. Rather it happens in the *Anfechtungen* which are laid upon men by God himself. . . . *Anfechtung*, says Luther, is the attack of God upon a person, 'God's embrace.' It is God who performs an alien work of leading the sinner to hell in order to bring him back as His proper work of justification. Encounter with the dialectic of the alien and proper work was through his reading of Tauler's sermons as he acknowledged in his marginalia. Luther took over Tauler's terminology, giving it a specific content that is in accordance with his *theologia crucis*. The concepts—*Anfechtung, tribulatio, tentutio, compunction*—reveal a deeper understanding of Luther's *theologia crucis*: it is the *opus alienum* of God because God meets us in suffering as He suffers with us. Luther learned that the *Anfechtung* had stripped him of any soteriological resources or causal power within himself to save himself, and thus he had no claim upon God. The temptations force the believer to a humility." Ngien, *Suffering of God*, 32.

26. No one in Luther's time could think this, but all of us after Montaigne and Rousseau can.

of the Bible[27]), we properly respond to *Anfechtung*.[28] We should cry out to God—in sorrow, anger, even wonder—and plead with God to meet us inside the *Anfechtung*. *Anfechtung* demands that we recognize the primary actor in the drama of redemption as God, not the self.

Wittenberg and Good, Sweet Staupitz

As Staupitz was finding a balance between the work of professor, dean, and vicar-general, political conflicts arose between the Augustinian order and Rome that necessitated Staupitz's attention. The balancing of professor, dean, and vicar-general roles taxed him, but it was possible with the help of trusted colleagues. Staupitz found Luther peculiar but captivating. Staupitz had a real love for the young man, finding his mind and passions to be compelling. Luther, in turn, saw Staupitz as his minister and mentor. So "in 1508 Luther [was] appointed at Staupitz's behest to the University of Wittenberg to fill the Augustinian chair of moral philosophy in the faculty of arts."[29]

27. Martin Brecht gives us some interesting detail on Luther's use of Psalms, saying, "When Luther received the sad news of his father's death, he took his Psalter, withdrawing to his bedroom, gave vent to his grief, and cried himself out. He recalled the love he had received from his father, whom he thanked for 'what I am and have.' He comforted himself in the knowledge that Hans Luther had seen the true light and had fallen asleep in Christ; nevertheless, in this event he experienced a bit of his own death. Now he was the eldest in the family, and he would have to follow his father through death to Christ. It was several days before he got over the loss." Brecht, *Martin Luther: Shaping and Defining the Reformation 1521–1532* (Minneapolis: Fortress, 1994), 378. Brecht also writes, "Luther recognized that the Psalms speak about those who undergo *Anfechtungen*, and they are the ones who are especially capable of understanding and praying the Psalms. On this basis the *Anfechtungen* could be affirmed. The biblical text confirmed Luther's own experience, that a man always falls short of God's demand, always remains a sinner, or—even worse—that he does not acknowledge his situation before God, and rather what he wants to offer God is precisely his own pious acts. But this makes everything even worse—man makes God, with his verdict over him, into a liar. This is the real sin, not recognizing that one is a sinner. Putting forward one's own righteousness, trusting one's own power, not recognizing one's own unworthiness even in the monasteries. The theology teachers are accused of not making man's situation clear to him, and so of spreading poison." Brecht, *Martin Luther: His Road to Reformation 1483–1521*, 132.

28. Ronald Rittgers says, "Between the summer of 1513 and the fall of 1515, Luther gave a series of lectures on the Psalms (*Dictata super Psalterium*) in which he spoke frequently of suffering in the Christian life. . . . In his early lectures on the Psalms, Luther begins to articulate a new soteriology that contains a very different and much broader understanding of faith. For the Luther of the *Dictata*, faith includes *intellectus* and *affectus*, along with humility and hope." Rittgers, *Reformation of Suffering*, 88.

29. Steinmetz, *Misericordia Dei*, 9.

Being together in little Wittenberg gave Staupitz and Luther more time with one another. Staupitz became close to Luther's sorrows and struggles, hearing his confessions and speaking into them, as Staupitz began to care more deeply for the young professor.[30]

Inside this pastoral relationship, Staupitz encouraged Luther to pursue his doctorate. Luther resisted. Staupitz insisted. In October 1512 the degree was bestowed, and Luther was made professor of Bible, taking over Staupitz's chair. The political conflicts facing the order had become too much for Staupitz. He had been called away too often from Wittenberg, spending long stretches in Munich. Balancing the demands of professor and vicar-general was no longer possible. But Staupitz had promised Frederick the Wise that his new university would make an impact. Staupitz felt obliged to fill his open chair with someone he trusted who could make the impact that Frederick wished. Martin Luther certainly did that. Just not in the way that Frederick, or anyone in Christendom, could have imagined. Luther's hammering of paper to Frederick's castle church door shook the world.

Before Staupitz left his chair vacant for Luther to fill, departing frequently for Wittenberg, Staupitz left an indelible mark on brother Martin. It was a mark of love, coming as a ministry of consolation. It converted and evangelized Luther. It turned Luther into an evangelical, a proclaimer of God's mercy and good news of God's consolation.

Just as in Erfurt, Luther was tortured in Wittenberg by his *Anfechtung*. Staupitz had taught him not to fear the temptation and sorrow but to lean into it, finding God's acts of mercy. But Luther couldn't shake Biel's nominalist thoughts on predestination. Staupitz taught Luther through his consolation that the way of the psalmist was the way of faithfulness. Mercy indeed met misery inside the embrace of the minister. And the penance that Staupitz led Luther into was not the battering of the will but a surrender of the will to stop and receive God's merciful goodness as a gift.[31] Penance

30. Gordon Rupp gives us more texture, saying, "Luther . . . recalled the comfort he had received from Staupitz. 'If I didn't praise Staupitz, I should be a damnable, ungrateful, papistical ass . . . for he was my first father in this teaching, and he bore me in Christ. If Staupitz had not helped me out, I should have been swallowed up and left in hell.'" Rupp, *Luther's Progress to the Diet of Worms* (New York: Harper Torchbooks, 1964), 31.

31. John Barclay provides us a nice discussion of Luther and gift: "Luther's theology is centrally gift—the gift (grace) of God expressed definitively and once-for-all in death, and resurrection of Christ, and the gift/generosity of Christ on to others in free Christian service. Against a long-established tradition Luther reconfigured the Mass as the reception of grace in Word and not as a sacrifice offered to God in the hope of obtaining benefits (for oneself or

was an act of confession that moved the human being into a stance that opened them to receive God's free gift of mercy.[32]

But predestination haunted Luther. He couldn't shake it. Even with the reworking of temptation and penance inside the experience of Staupitz's ministry, predestination tortured Luther. How could he trust that God would meet him as minister? How could he trust that God would respond to his *Anfechtung* with grace and not damnation? Was his sorrow a sign of God's abandonment? Was his suffering, and even sadness, proof that God had predestined him for damnation? Luther just couldn't shake these questions.

With a bit of frustration, Staupitz told Luther (as Luther reports it), "One must keep one's eyes fixed on that man who is called Christ."[33] Staupitz tells Luther to focus on the crucified Christ to understand how God acts and therefore predestines.[34] Predestination cannot be abstracted from the life and death of Jesus.[35] As Luther introduces these words, he says

---

for others) from God. God, in other words, gives freely with no strings attached, and believers are to do likewise. Luther places much on imitation of Christ or, better, participation in the dynamic or the Christ-event: believers are to be (as he puts it) 'Christs' to one another, passing on the unconditional love of Christ to others. It is essential for him that this love is practiced for no reward or calculation of return: it is not an interested or instrumental love. The believer 'lives only for others and not for himself, . . . considering nothing except the need and advantage of the neighbor.' The spirit of this self-giving is also crucial: service must not be grudging or obliged, but given cheerfully, willingly, and freely. Gift-giving is, in other words, a pure, gratuitous act, liberated from the need to gain anything by the fact that Christ has given all things already, and freed from a self-seeking attitude by pure concern for the other." Barclay, *Paul and the Gift* (Grand Rapids: Eerdmans, 2015), 57.

32. "If there is reciprocity in this relationship, it is for Luther entirely free of instrumental ends: we love and obey God only *because*, not *in order that*. Putting all the stress on the single, once-for-all, completed gift of God, Luther seeks to take the gift-relationship with God out of a pattern of repeated circularity." Barclay, *Paul and the Gift*, 113.

33. Quoted in Rudolf Markwald, *A Mystic's Passion: The Spirituality of Johannes von Staupitz in His 1520 Lenten Sermons* (New York: Peter Lang, 1990), 120.

34. Markwald adds to this: "With this reply Staupitz gives us an insight into his understanding of God's grace. Under the shadow of the cross it is not human action or reaction that counts but the Father's self-revelation who receives and gives satisfaction in His dear Son's love. Staupitz places his unique interpretation of grace right into the center of the crucifixion event with the words 'my Son, in whom I am pleasing myself,' he means that Christ's willing obedience unto death on the cross is a key element in God's pleasing and pleasure." Markwald, *Mystic's Passion*, 120.

35. Karl Barth (whether directly or indirectly) takes Staupitz's advice, developing the richest theology of election that Protestantism has ever seen. See Barth, *Church Dogmatics* II/2, *The Doctrine of God*, trans. Geoffrey Bromiley, ed. T. F. Torrance (Edinburgh: T&T Clark, 1957). Barth does just as Staupitz advises, fixing his eyes on Jesus, thinking of a theology of election through Christ. Jesus is both the man elect and the man damned.

with tenderness "my good Staupitz said."[36] Luther's loving minister, who walked with him in sorrow, consoling his battered soul, said to Luther that when he fears God's hiddenness and worries about God's anger, he should look to Jesus, for the only God we can know is the man of sorrows who is consoled by his mother, who gives us his body as salvation by consolation. Through consolation the Spirit takes us into new life.

The christological lens that births the Reformation theology of justification is born from a ministry of consolation. The theology of the cross is a theology of consolation. The pastoral act is to walk the pilgrim's path of sorrows. In sorrow, Staupitz tells Luther not to hide from the sadness but to lean into it, for the God made known in Jesus Christ, who knows all sorrows, will be found there. (This sacramental reality claims that God resides in sorrow and suffering.) What God predestines is to care for the one in sorrow and suffering. Sorrow is not a sign of God's abandonment but of God's election. *Anfechtung* is an outward sign of God's predestination. Staupitz tells Luther to never let his sorrow lead him away from God, for sorrow is a sign of God's electing love. Staupitz wants Luther to know that God, in and through Luther's sorrow, has chosen him, destined him to receive God's presence as the ministry of life out of death. This same proclamation is made by the disciple and the church to the late-modern, sad happiness-seeker. By giving the ministry of consolation we invite our neighbor to recognize that they are elect, and this event of recognition is evangelism. As those who console, we remind our neighbor that God has said yes to them and that God is moving in this very moment inside their sorrow to bring life out of it.[37]

36. Markwald, *Mystic's Passion*, 45.

37. Dennis Ngien adds, "Just as an infant is born through a narrow and dark birth canal to new life, we too are born through the narrow and dark passage of death to new life. To illustrate the journey of death, Luther quoted Jesus' own words in John 16:21: 'When a woman is in travail she has sorrow; but when she has recovered, she no longer remembers the anguish, since a child is born by her into the world.' This road through the dark valley, though painful and frightening beyond words, may be traveled safely when we are assured of its end. Our faith does not demand that the pain of grief and the death be denied. On the contrary, it is the very harsh reality of death that makes the heavenly mansion so desirable, and so gloriously exuberant. Luther wrote, 'So it is that in dying we must bear this anguish and know that a large mansion and joy will follow (John 14:2).' Only in the light of this immeasurable joy of new heavenly life can we celebrate our death as our 'feast day,' the day of our birth into the life beyond." Ngien, *Luther as a Spiritual Adviser: The Interface of Theology and Piety in Luther's Devotional Writings* (Eugene, OR: Wipf & Stock, 2007), 31, quoting *Luther's Works*, vol. 42, ed. Jaroslav Pelikan and Helmut T. Lehmann (St. Louis: Concordia, 1965), 99–100.

In 1533, when Luther says "my good Staupitz," he claims that Staupitz was the one who started the Reformation teaching on justification as
the word of a suffering God.[38] Staupitz, from within the ministry of the
theology of consolation, inspires the Reformation vision that God is a God
who comes to the sorrowful. God gives faith so that we might trust that
God justifies sinners by God's love and mercy made manifest in the body
of Jesus Christ. In Luther's telling, Staupitz's ministry of consolation—his
practice—births the *theologia crucis.*

When in his sorrow Luther fixes his eyes on the man called Christ, what
he sees is that the one suffering, the one who bears all forms of *Anfechtung,*
turns all the sorrows of dying into the joys of new life. When he fixes his
eyes on the cross, Luther discovers that God suffers. We can thereby be sure
that our sorrow is a sign of our election. Luther comes to understand that
consolation, as the joining of sorrows, invites the world to fix its eyes on
Jesus. Through this evangelistic task of the church, the world is drawn into
the being of God by the ministry of consolation. By linking evangelism
with the ministry of consolation, evangelism becomes always embodied.
The gospel must be proclaimed by bodies that minister in consolation.

Our goodbyes are the place where God chooses to work, electing us
for life. Our sorrowful goodbyes are the only sign that we are chosen and
therefore predestined for salvation by God. Those who must say goodbye—
which, of course, is all humanity—are those whom God promises to be
for by being with. "For Luther, . . . the real significance of Christ for faith
does not lie in the imitation of Christ's sufferings [a work of the will of the
self] but rather in the believer's participation by faith in His suffering as a
sacrament for us."[39] For this participation to be sacramental—a sharing
in God's real presence—God must console us by knowing and bearing the
sorrow in God's own being. For our sorrows to be a sign of our election,
God's own being must have its life around sorrow too. Luther sees this when
he fixes his eyes on Jesus Christ and him crucified, as Staupitz encourages.

Luther can see no other way: God must suffer. The cross is the suffering
of the Son *and* the Father in the Spirit. The God of Israel, known in the

---

38. Ngien gives the full quote and context: "Luther said in 1533 that all his Christocentric
thinking stemmed from that of his confessor, Staupitz: 'However my good Staupitz said, "One
must keep one's eyes fixed on that man who is called Christ." Staupitz is the one who started
(our) teaching (namely, on justification).'" Ngien, *Suffering of God,* 39.

39. Ngien, *Suffering of God,* 36.

cross of Christ, is the great God of consolation, because the divine being both gives and receives consolation from Godself. Luther uniquely sees that God consoles in the deepest of ways, taking us into God's being not through our wills but by our impossibilities of sorrowful goodbyes—by the cross which is a great (the greatest) goodbye that God must bear. God consoles by choosing (predestining) *Godself* to suffer, taking on all the sorrows of the world. Sorrow, and the weak but profound act of consolation, draws us into God's being. For God (not just Jesus's bodily life) suffers. The Trinity consoles itself because the Godhead truly suffers. Consolation can transform the human being, giving us Jesus's own being (Gal. 2:20) without any works, because God has suffered and now acts for Godself and the world as the great consoler.

But we need to say it again. The profundity of this claim that God is a consoler is bound in the confession that God suffers. The theology of the cross, as a consolation theology, has its sacramental (even mystical) depth in the claim that God consoles the world, meeting the pilgrim in their goodbyes, because God's own life is built around consolation. God's life is a life of consolation because God, in God's own being, knows suffering and sorrow. God experiences a great goodbye in the cross of Christ. God overcomes sin by consoling the sinner. This consolation is a judgment (and a harsh one for those who refuse the confession of their sorrow) that brings grace and mercy.

Communication of the Passible

This emphasis on divine suffering is Luther's unique offering to the tradition, and one with great pastoral (and evangelistic) importance. It is controversial, however. Luther's claim that the essence of God suffers (*Deus passibilis*) is provocative. To claim that God suffers is to depart from the Neoplatonist thought that goes back to most of the patristic fathers (including Gregory and Macrina).[40] These fathers claimed, building off

40. Gordon Rupp adds, "Luther has discarded the psychological teaching of Aristotle of a *habitus* within the soul, and in its place is a new anthropology of the person, the whole man. It breaks with the Platonic and neo-Platonic division between soul and body and returns to the biblical division between 'flesh' and 'spirit,' the conception of man as a sinner confronted in all his personal existence by the person of the living God." Rupp, *Luther's Progress to the Diet of Worms*, 40.

Greek philosophy, that God could not suffer, for God was impassible. But as a professor of moral philosophy before becoming professor of Bible, Luther has deeply studied Aristotle, even teaching Aristotle. Luther gives his first lectures as professor of Bible on the Psalms. These studies make Luther dubious of Aristotle and other Greek philosophers. Aristotle seems to have a conception of human works, and human drives for excellence, that ignores goodbyes and the temptations of *Anfechtung*. Luther sees no impassible commitments in the psalmists. The psalmists don't seem to view God as unmovable.

What Luther can see in the psalmists are the sorrows echoed in the cry of the cross and the claims that God consoles the brokenhearted (Ps. 147). Fixing his eyes on Jesus and him crucified, even as he reads the Psalms, Luther can see it no other way. "For Luther, Christ's humanity is no curtain behind which an impersonal and immobile God hides, but rather it actually expresses God's heart, the innermost essence of God Himself."[41]

For Luther, God suffers because the divine nature as well as the human nature of Jesus suffer. The human nature of Jesus communicates— drawing—the divine nature (through *communicatio idiomatum*) into the concrete experience of loss and the goodbyes of sorrow. The Godhead suffers, experiencing sorrow. Jesus's suffering on the cross is communicated directly and fully to the inner life of the Trinity. Luther sees no break in communication between the human and divine natures of Jesus. What Jesus knows on the cross is what God in Godself bears. Hence, when Luther looks on the cross, he can say "the crucified God."

From this event of the cross, the trinitarian life becomes a life of consolation. God consoles Godself—this is the passion. This passion of consolation is so deep that death itself is no match for it. From the consolation of God, experienced in the death of Jesus, God consoles the dead body of Jesus, bringing Jesus's body back to life out of God's own suffering of the goodbye. This goodbye is truly suffered, both Jesus's own loss and the Father's loss of a Son. All who experience goodbyes are invited into (elected for) participation in God's own life, a life that is full of the consolations of mercy as acts of ministry.

Consolation itself, received by humanity through the humanity of Jesus (the humanity of God, as Karl Barth says[42]), participates in the transformation

---

41. Ngien, *Suffering of God*, 67.
42. Karl Barth, *The Humanity of God* (Richmond: John Knox, 1960).

of death into new life. The divine being can minister new life to our sorrows (coming right into our sorrows), because the divine being knows sorrow and bears its own goodbyes. We can share in God's being by way of sorrow. Sorrow is part of God's story, bound in God's being. Through the doorway of our sorrow we are invited into union, into a real sharing in God's being. The distinct but shared sorrows of the human and the divine (and how they are communicated between them in the person of Jesus Christ) allow us to participate in the divine life. For through the consolation of our sorrows we are "in Christ," as Paul repeatedly says in his epistles. Our sorrows are in Christ and shared by Christ, who communicates them fully and completely to the Father.

Sorrow (alone) becomes the place where the human shares in the divine. We participate in God's life. Through the *communicatio idiomatum*—essentially the modem that communicates the signal between human and divine that exists within Jesus Christ—his own suffering is brought into God's own being. We participate in God's life not by works or virtues but by our sorrow. Consolation reveals that this union is salvation, for consolation gives the being of God to humanity through sorrow. Our sorrow calls out to God, and God's consolation reaches toward us. Salvation, this union of sharing in the divine being, comes by way of God's consolation to the sorrowful human soul. Consolation is sacramental, taking the human into the divine because God is moved by our sorrow, because of the *Deus passibilis* of the *communicatio idiomatum*. When Luther takes Staupitz's advice and looks upon Jesus Christ, he sees a *Deus passibilis*, a suffering of God through the *communicatio idiomatum*, the communication of the divine and human natures of Christ.[43]

---

43. Dennis Ngien pushes further these thoughts, saying, "The 'hypostatic union,' for Luther, means that the Logos always exists in union with the flesh, thus he resists any attempt to separate the eternal Word from humanity, as occurs in the case of the *extra-Calvinisticum*. The hypostatic union is an event in history, but from all eternity Christ's divinity must not be conceived apart from His humanity and vice versa." Ngien, *Suffering of God*, 66. He continues, "This means for Luther that God's passibility is not established by the *communicatio idiomatum* but this rather is a theological means to realize or articulate that God, in Christ, did suffer and die. Luther does not start from the doctrine of the *communicatio idiomatum*; rather he starts from the identity of the person of Christ in its unity as depicted in the New Testament. Jesus Christ, as one concrete and living person, is the ground from which Luther is operating. More precisely, the declaration of impassibility goes off the track for the simple reason that Christ did suffer and we are not allowed to separate God and man in Christ as the Nestorians did. If Christ is one with God and one with man, he must be so as a whole person so that suffering is not only predicated of the human nature but also of the entire person. In and through this

Consolation stands at the heart of God's own being. God the minister consoles the world by sharing our sorrow. When this sorrow is shared by the trinitarian life—as happens profoundly and ultimately in the death of the Son—sorrow becomes the seedbed of new life. The theology of the cross makes the whole of the Christian confession a proclamation of divine-to-human consolation.

Evangelism simply but profoundly invites the sorrowful to receive the ministry of Jesus Christ by means of the community of ministers (the church) entering their sorrow. This reception of the ministry of consolation takes them into the life of God. They participate in the divine being as the divine being participates in human sorrow. The good news, the *evangel*, is that God is so for us (electing us) that God meets us in our goodbyes, embracing us in mercy, promising us new life out of our deaths.

In 1512, Staupitz left Wittenberg. He would return from time to time, but never for long. Munich, the Netherlands, and finally Salzburg called for his attention. Luther missed Staupitz. But Luther's great teacher and pastor had done his formational work with Luther.

It's interesting to wonder whether Luther would have published the Ninety-Five Theses, which exploded into such an argumentative blaze, if Staupitz and his levelheaded comfort had been close by in those pivotal years. Who can know? From 1517 onward, Martin Luther was known as one of the West's greatest polemists. His writings are fiery hot, humorous with insult, and unrelenting. Without discretion, he swings on princes, popes, and cardinals. We admire him because he could "do no other." Luther's polemical flare has become admired and imitated for the last five hundred years. Theologians and politicians copy his direct, bare-knuckle passion for a position.

These traits are part of who Martin Luther was, but they are not the whole of Luther. We can see a different Luther through his relationship with Staupitz. Luther took certain ideas from Staupitz—developing them for himself—but more so, Luther took on Staupitz's way of being. Thanks to Staupitz, Luther understood the role of the theologian to be always a pastor, and the pastor as one who always gives the theology of consolation.

---

person God Himself suffered. Therefore the doctrine of the *communicatio idiomatum* is not the starting point for the affirmation of divine passibility, but rather is the means by which Luther develops the conclusion he has drawn from the Bible" (69).

Luther's polemical writings of the 1520s (which are brilliant and necessary) have the unfortunate side effect of eclipsing the consoling Luther of his devotional writings.[44] In those writings, Dennis Ngien has shown, the polemical bar fighter disappears, and the sensitive and compassionate pastor who concretely addresses sorrows and enters people's great goodbyes becomes present.[45] In these writings Luther is more consoler to those suffering goodbyes than raiding Reformer.

Protestantism would do well to take a break from the heroic, polemical Luther and remember (even emulate) the Luther of pastoral consolation. A world like ours—filled with sad happiness-seekers in misery who are stuck in their self-imposed châteaus of fragile authenticity—needs evangelism and ministry not as polemics but as consolation, not as arguments but as visions of how sorrow itself is shared by God and brings peace and mercy. What is needed is a theology of consolation as the pastoral shape of evangelism.

■ ■ ■ ■

In the weeks since Mary Ann asked the Bible study to help her die well, the church sprang into action. The sitters continued to sit, and others worked to get Mary Ann's space as she wanted it when she died. A hospital bed was moved into a room that overlooked the mountains. Mary Ann loved the view. She drank coffee every morning looking out that window. She had bought the house because of the view; she wanted to die looking out that window. Others made it so that Mary Ann could spend as much time as possible with her granddaughter, helping with rides and arrangements. At times it hurt so much. The thought of leaving that little girl behind, the tragedy of not seeing her grow, of missing her graduation and wedding and so much more, hurt tremendously. At times, the sorrow suffocated Mary Ann so much that she was tempted to hide from it. For a week, Mary Ann decided not to see her granddaughter. But Hazel confronted her and told her to go into the sorrow, to lean in. Hazel told Mary Ann to not fear the sorrow and its pain but know that God bears

44. Ronald Rittgers adds, "In the minds of his contemporaries, at least those who were sympathetic to him, Luther was first and foremost a pastor who was deeply committed to the care of souls." Rittgers, *Reformation of Suffering*, 113.

45. See Ngien, *Suffering of God*, 19–54. For more on Luther as consoler and not polemist, see Neil Leroux, *Martin Luther as Comforter: Writings on Death* (Leiden: Brill, 2007), 229.

it with her. Entering the sorrow, Mary Ann found that it hurt, but even so, every hour with her granddaughter was experienced as a gift. Those hours with the little girl ministered to Mary Ann as she prepared to take her last breaths.

Three weeks before those last breaths, the church had a goodbye service for Mary Ann. No one was sure where the idea came from, but they decided it was right to say a proper goodbye to Mary Ann as she proceeded ahead of them on the pilgrim's path.[46] They needed the *ad Deum* of saying goodbye, and Mary Ann needed the church's proclamation that her journey was indeed *ad Deum*, to God. Invitations and announcements went out. Will was much less helpful now that Mary Ann had decided to die well instead of continuing to fight. He just didn't understand it. "You never give up," he told coworkers. "I'd fight to the last breath, flying to every alt treatment I could find." When Mary Ann invited Will to the goodbye service, he flat out said no, explaining with an affectless look, "It would be too much of bummer." Will pulled away. He couldn't call a thing what it is. He couldn't give consolation.

The congregation blessed Mary Ann and prepared for this goodbye, praying over her, anointing her with oil, and blessing her with words of honor. Everyone was given a sheet of paper with the words, "Mary Ann is . . ." People took turns sharing their answers.

Hazel said, "Mary Ann is . . . my friend, my companion, my sweet walking partner."

Myrtle said, "Mary Ann is . . . the one who helped me through my depression. She was used by God."

AC said, "Mary Ann is . . . loved and never forgotten."

And then to everyone's surprise and shock, Renate came forward. No one had noticed her in the back. She was wearing dark glasses and had been crying. She walked to the front with her sheet and said, "Mary Ann is . . ."

---

46. For a discussion and example of this, see Kara Root, *The Deepest Belonging: A Story about Discovering Where God Meets Us* (Minneapolis: Fortress, 2020). The service below echoes what was done with Marty in that book.

Epilogue

To the End

"... someone who helped me." Holding it up in front of the congregation, Renate elaborated, "Mary Ann is someone who cared for me when she didn't need to. Someone who showed me that God cares. Now I want to care for her."

There wasn't a dry eye in the room. Mary Ann stood up and hugged Renate. She was so moved that Renate had showed up. For a long moment, almost awkwardly long, Mary Ann just couldn't let go of Renate's hands. It was all such a gift.

After the service, Renate explained that following her father's funeral, she knew something important had happened, that God had met her in some way, that she was put on a pathway. But then the pulls of a new job came and she got busy. She lost touch with what had met her in those sorrowful days of saying goodbye to her father, and for no particular reason, she drifted away from the path. When an old coworker forwarded the announcement for Mary Ann's goodbye service, something came over Renate. She felt a call, a distinct push, to go and be with Mary Ann, to console her as she had consoled Renate. Renate was at the goodbye service to join Mary Ann on the path just as Mary Ann had joined Renate.

After the service, Renate joined the sitters. When Mary Ann was moved into hospice, Renate remained, even spending nights at Mary Ann's house to care for her by being there. Renate didn't want Mary Ann to die alone like her father. Something larger than Renate—something she was sure was God—was calling her to be there. In the final weeks, Mary Ann asked Renate to read her the Gospels and the Psalms. Reading Scripture to Mary Ann moved Renate. She had never read the Bible before. She didn't know any of the stories. She even started to read passages when Mary Ann had fallen asleep. Ever since, she has read the Psalms and Gospels. They move her. What particularly stirred her was how they comforted Mary Ann.

In the final days, when even medication could not blunt the pain and Mary Ann felt tremors of fear, she'd say out loud, "I've been baptized. I've been baptized. Though I walk through the valley of the shadow of death I will not fear. I've been baptized."

Renate was dumbstruck witnessing it all. She thought to herself, "I'm watching someone who has lived with and for God, die with that God." She wasn't sure what to make of it. But it moved her, it assured Renate, as much as Mary Ann, that this was all happening—this dying—inside a much bigger story. Renate knew she herself didn't have such a story, but she knew she needed it. She needed to walk the path.

The next Tuesday, at 3:07 p.m., Mary Ann died. The sun was peeking out from a cloud as the afternoon shadows landed on the mountain. It was quiet. It was heavy.

Two weeks after Mary Ann's funeral service—in which Renate read two psalms and a passage from the Gospel of Mark, texts she'd read over and over to Mary Ann—Renate asked Pastor Manta to baptize her.

A month later Renate, Nate, and a baby named Marvin (the child of two other members of the church) were baptized. Pastor Manta spoke of the beauty and pain of the moment. On this Sunday, Nate (and Cynthia standing with him) was claiming that in all of life's goodbyes his only hope was in the man who is called Christ. His hope could be found in entering these waters of death to receive his life. It was appropriate but also sorrowful, Pastor Manta said, that on this day that Nate was being baptized, Nate and Cynthia would have to watch a baby in the church, baby Marvin, be baptized. It would be a reminder to Nate and Cynthia of their loss of baby Maddy, and they would again grieve what they had lost.[1] But by going into these waters, they were proclaiming that it is in the deepest sorrows that Jesus meets us. In the consolation of these

1. John Barclay says, "The Christian life is, for Luther, a continuous return to baptism: 'a Christian life is nothing else than a daily Baptism, once begun and ever continued. For we must keep at it incessantly, always purging out whatever pertains to the old Adam, so that whatever

sorrows, we are free to celebrate God's work in the life of little Marvin. But they were also committing—because Marvin too is entering these same waters—to give his little soul the consolation as his pilgrim's path begins, with all its goodbyes. Nate and Cynthia, and the whole congregation, will need, as part of the community of faith, to remind Marvin of that. Renate, too, is standing here as both consoled and consoler—this is the depth of the Christian life: we are evangelized (justified) by receiving consolation; we are made disciples (sanctified) by giving consolation. Renate, and the whole community, will need to remind Marvin and one another that life is filled with sorrows, but blessed are those who mourn, for theirs is the very consolation of Jesus Christ who takes us into the life of God. We shout to the world that we have been baptized, that in the dark waters of sorrow and loss, we have found new life. For the consolation of the Father to the Son in the Spirit now reaches us.

Renate's sorrow, shared with others, is the sacrament that saves her. Renate now becomes part of this story. In this baptism she enacts what she has experienced: in the giving and receiving of consolation in the cold waters of loss, there is a birth into new life.

■ ■ ■ ■

The next Tuesday the email came. The subject was ominous. It came from the district headquarters. It read "Charges against You for Heretical Actions." Pastor Manta had been given a heads-up that it was coming, but it was still disconcerting when it came. Word had gotten out that Pastor Manta had baptized Maddy's body. The email said, "We don't baptize the dead," accusing him of misusing the sacrament. But there were other concerns laced with the charges. Pastor Manta was told, confidentially, that these other concerns moved the Maddy incident from troublesome to disciplinary. He was being made an example of.

In a small denomination built on evangelistic mission, where evangelism is core, some felt that Pastor Manta had ignored this commitment. He didn't seem zealous to preach for conversion, they said. Pastor Manta was asked to answer two questions, both carrying the weight of discipline: (1) Why did he baptize a dead infant? and (2) How does he evangelize,

---

belongs to the new man may come forth.'" Barclay, *Paul and the Gift*, 109, quoting Luther, *Large Catechism*, "Holy Baptism," sec. 65.

and what must someone do to enter the community of the elect? Who is welcome in his community as a true believer?

Responses to these two questions were to be given in writing by the end of the month. In four months' time, Pastor Manta would stand before the district national meeting and answer questions on these matters. After that time, a vote and a decision would be made on any discipline, including possibly revoking his ordination. This was serious. But Pastor Manta was at peace. He was given the advice to keep the written responses short. There were many contentious issues at play, and Pastor Manta was being used as a political football. He was told that the longer the responses, the more ammunition he'd be handing those of ill will.

After weeks in prayer, Pastor Manta wrote:

Dear Committee,

I first write with thanks. I'm thankful for the work of God in my life, the church, and most importantly, the world. I have been blessed to be included in God's ministry and humbled to work alongside so many of you doing such good work to proclaim God's grace and mercy. In that humility I write in response to your inquiries.

First, on the matter of the baptism. I will say that it was not without great wrestling and unease that I decided to baptize this infant who had died. The request came from the grieving mother. I did not in any way think this was a kind of pagan superstition. I did not think there was magic in the baptismal rite. But neither did I think the act meaningless or only symbolic, and therefore it did not matter whether the child was alive or dead. I knew the baptism would be a ministry to the grieving mother, but I did not simply do it as a therapeutic act. I did it because I felt called to by God. It was undertaken with great prayer and discernment. I believe that I heard God's command to do so, and I had this confirmed by the community. I also believe there was confirmation theologically. Baptism is not a human act but a divine one. To be baptized is to be taken into the death of Christ to receive, by his gift alone, his life. Baptism is a sure sign that God enters death to bring life out of it. In this child's death, I became assured that God was at work, that God particularly was moving in the deepest sorrow of these parents, blessing them as they mourned. I believe that can be confirmed by what has followed.

I can speak to this when standing before you. To say so now could be too utilitarian.

Rather, what I'd like to emphasize is my commitment that God is found in sorrow, that God—not us—works in sorrow, blessing and saving us by drawing us into life. Baptism is the giving over of the human to this reality. Baptism immerses the human in God's story of Jesus entering sorrow for the sake of salvation. All I did, in her death—a heart-wrenching reality—was immerse this little one in the story of Jesus Christ. Death is part of all our stories. And little Maddy's came too soon. But coming too soon does not mean her death can't be immersed in the story of Jesus. And baptizing her claimed that Jesus gives himself to all those in the sorrow of death. I baptized the child because I believe the child is sacred to God, and part of Jesus's story, in life and in death. She has a name. In asking for her to be baptized, the mother who named her asked, in her sorrow, for her little one to be immersed in the death and life of Jesus. Even with the concern that I could be guilty for doing it, I did it, because I believe it was the work of the Spirit. I believed I needed to care for this mother and father, and make a pronouncement about the child.

Which takes me to the second matter: "How do we evangelize? And who do we welcome?" I believe that evangelism is bringing people to recognize, like the disciples on the road to Emmaus (Luke 24), that Jesus is before us, attentive to our stories of loss and deep sorrow. I personally don't evangelize, but my community does. Evangelism is a communal reality. It's a way that the community is in the world. The way we evangelize is by following Jesus into sorrow. As most of you know, I have personally known sorrow—deep sorrow. And in that sorrow, I found that Jesus Christ was crucified and made alive for me. I found that in sorrow Jesus is at work. We evangelize together by entering sorrow and ministering to those in grief. Evangelism is witnessing to Christ. And we think Jesus is active in sorrow, doing God's good work. We believe we find Christ in sorrow.

Who do we welcome? We welcome *all* who know sorrow. All who know sorrow are welcome. But this is not an easy path. To say that we enter sorrow to welcome all who know sorrow is the invitation into a costly grace. What is costly is not our efforts. What is costly is that to truly enter sorrow you must lose yourself. We tell people to see themselves as loved but to not concern themselves with themselves. There can be no healing in sorrow when the self becomes everything. This is the temptation of sorrow. Instead, we tell (and show) people to focus on the sorrow, not on themselves. We join them in leaning into that sorrow. It's in this moment of leaning that evangelism happens. Then we invite them to focus on the sorrow of others, joining them in that sorrow as the act of love and worship. This is where evangelism meets discipleship (we believe evangelism is for discipleship). All are welcomed who know sorrow, and the consoled become the consolers. The sorrowful must attend to the sorrow of the world so that we can find ourselves in Christ, who is always with and for the sorrowful.

It is with deep humility and respect that I offer these answers.

Pastor Roberto Manta

■ ■ ■ ■

Two weeks before the national gathering, Pastor Manta's trial was taken off the docket. New, more pressing issues had come to the surface. Issues more financial and political. Pastor Manta was told that his letter assuaged concerns. He was both relieved and disappointed. He was relieved that the charges were dropped. Relieved that he didn't need to go through the trial. But disappointed that he was accused in the first place. Disappointed that he couldn't offer his theological visions for evangelism and discipleship. Disappointed that the denomination was like a dog chasing a car, ultimately not concerned about contemplating the possibilities that Jesus enters sorrow and calls us to join the sorrow of the world with consolation. They wouldn't get to hear the rest of the story.

But primarily, Pastor Manta was relieved that now he could focus again on leading his community to follow Jesus into sorrow.

Index

acedia, 149

Adams, Henry, 208n2

ad Deum, 231–34, 235, 240, 250, 258–59

Alexander V (pope), 229n15

algorithms, 93, 256

ambition, 36

Ananias, and conversion of Paul, 14

Anderson, Wes, 120n34

Anfechtung, 155, 188n15, 233n18, 259, 260–64, 265, 268, 270

angst, 145–46

anxiety, x, 30, 35, 80, 149, 152, 160

Aristotle, 107, 269n40, 270

Arnauld, Antoine, 185

Ashton, John, 157n41

Atlantis, 45

Augustine, 178, 190, 209n3, 216n17, 216n19, 224, 241n29

authenticity, 41, 60, 61, 67, 70–82, 91–95, 114

autonomy, 150n29

Avignon papacy, 224–25

baptism, 276–77

Barclay, John, 265n31, 266n32, 276n1

Barth, Karl, 189n17, 215n15, 266n35, 270

Basil, 208, 212n9, 213, 214, 217

Basil the Elder, 213

Bauman, Zygmunt, 149

beauty, becomes taste, 150

bereavement, as mental illness, 152n33

Berlin, Isaiah, 67n16, 144n9

Beyenka, Mary Melchior, 209n3, 216n17, 216n19

Biel, Gabriel, 255–56, 265

blessing, in sorrow, 24, 26, 170–71

Bloom, Allan, 68–71, 80, 83

Boersma, Hans, 21n10

Boethius, 223–24, 231, 234

Bok, Sissela, 187n14

Bonhoeffer, Dietrich, 12n3, 22n12, 23n15, 189n17, 223, 241n32

Boniface VIII (pope), 225

booster and knocker, 70–71, 73, 82

Brecht, Martin, 261n21, 264n27

Brown, D. Catherine, 227n8, 228n13, 229n15, 244

Brown, Peter, 208n2, 210n6, 212n11, 232n17

Bruckner, Pascal, 145, 150n29, 164n46, 165n47

Burge, Ryan P., 16n6

Burrows, Mark, 228n11, 233n18, 237–38, 241, 241n33, 244n37

Burton, Tara, 97n64, 123n39

Bynum, Caroline Walker, 217n20

calculating machine, 176–77

Cambridge University, 84–86, 89

Campbell, Colin, 65n12, 107n3
cannibalism, 108
capitalism, 150n29
Cappadocians, 209n4, 211n8, 212n9
Case, Anne, 40n4
Catherine de' Medici, 108–9, 141
cats, petting, 141, 150, 151, 156, 192, 239
chalant, 147
chalant sincerity, 124–25, 128
Charles IX (king of France), 109, 110–11
Christianity, late-modern critiques of, 207–8
Christian life
  and consolation, 277
  as return to baptism, 276n1
  as pilgrim's life, 209
church
  bankruptcy and renewal of, 50–54
  disappearance of, 42–43
  future of, 44–47
  mission of, 51
  renewed by the Holy Spirit, 49
Clement V (pope), 224–25
Coligny, Gaspard de, 110–11
Columbus, 108n5
communicatio idiomatum, 270, 271
conformitas voluntatis, 237n25
Connolly, James, 229n14, 252n6
consolation, ix–xi, 2, 54, 257
  Gregory of Nyssa on, 209
  as sacramental, 24–25
consolation of philosophy, 211, 223–24, 231
consolation of theology, 21–23, 231, 234,
  236, 250–53, 262, 269
Constantine, 52n16
consumerism, 17–19, 150n29
contentment, 116–17, 119
conversion experiences, 11–13, 14
"cool" (as a descriptor), 123
cosmopolis, 83–89, 92–93
Council of Constance, 229–30, 235
counselor, 156
Crary, Jonathan, 125n40
cross of Christ, 268–69, 270
culture war, 15, 80
cynicism, 30

d'Ailly, Pierre, 227, 231
dancing, 120, 121, 124, 136, 145, 151, 156,
  162, 192, 257
Davies, William, 150n38, 152n33, 157n41,
  160n44
da Vinci, Leonardo, 87
Davis, Walter A., 79n35
death, contemplating, 210–11
Deaton, Angus, 40n4
decay, 217n20
Declaration of Independence, 115
deism, 195n26
depression, 30, 126, 147–52, 156, 160, 262
  as opposite of happiness, 149, 151
Derrida, Jacques, 78
Desan, Philippe, 117n26
Descartes, René, 43–44, 83, 84, 86, 88,
  137–41, 173–75, 182, 188, 189, 191,
  194–97, 211
Deslandes, 177, 181
despair, 250
despondency. See depression
Deus passibilis, 271
devil, disappeared from imaginations, 155
discipleship, 2, 201
  by giving consolation, 277
diversion, 192–93, 194, 198
doubts, 140
Douthat, Ross, 147n19
drug overdose mortality, 40n4
Duby, Georges, 213n13, 231n17
Duckworth, Jessicah, 218n21
Dürer, Albrecht, 251n3
dying well, 118–19, 210, 234, 249

Eagleton, Terry, 144nn10–11, 145n15
Eckhart, Meister, 148n20, 251n2
Edict of Nantes, 112, 137
Edmundson, Mark, 144n10, 151n32,
  196n29
efficiency, 63
Ehrenberg, Alain, 149
Einstein, Albert, 105–6
election, 256–57, 266–67
Ellul, Jacques, 50n13

energy, 97n46
Enlightenment, 84, 86
Epicureanism, 215, 216
essay, 105–7
evangelism, x, 15–16
  as consolation, xi, 1–2, 22, 28, 30, 200, 217–18, 257, 273
  as context bound, 25
  as dying for the sake of others, 50–51
  and election, 257
  embraced pursuit of happiness, 129
  as entering sorrow, 168–69, 171, 199, 201, 207, 238, 272
  as immanent, 21–22
  and institutions, 43
  instrumentalization of, 233, 240–41
  Jesuit approach to, 197
  loss of the sacramental, 129
  as managing stress, 163–64
  as pilgrimage, 232–34
  as reviled, 16
  sacramental personalism of, 180
  as the "schmole," 19–20
  as theology of the cross, 2–3
  triumphalism of, 22, 187
evil, 250
exiled Protestants, 16–17, 19
exiles. See viatores
expertise, 91, 151n31
extra-Calvinisticum, 271n43

far right, 65, 75, 76, 78, 79
fatigue, 148, 149
Fauci, Anthony, 91
fideism, 197
Fontana, Biancamaria, 113n13
Foucault, Michel, 78n33, 210n5
Foxworthy, Jeff, 184–85, 186
Frame, Donald, 107n4, 121n36, 191n21
Francis II (king of France), 109
Frank, Thomas, 17n7
Frederick the Wise, 253, 259, 265
Fredriksen, Paula, 50n12
freedom, 45
  of the chateau, 68

and happiness, 98, 117
  loss of, 62–64, 95–98
Fronde, the, 142–43
Fukuyama, Francis, 62n4, 156n38, 157n39
fulfillment, as self-located, 69–70

Galileo, 138, 140
gambling, 175, 178, 181, 193–94, 200
Garber, Daniel, 196n30
gardening, 120, 150, 151, 156, 192
genealogy, 29
Gerson, Jean, xi, 23, 25, 26, 27, 28, 200, 225–38, 256n11
  effect on Staupitz, 251–53
  in exile, 230–31, 235
  influence on Luther, 241n33, 252n6
  and Joan, 242–45
  on salvation, 239–42
  on sorrow, 236–38
  theology of the cross, 236n24
Geuss, Raymond, 67n15
Giles of Rome, 254
God
  beyond all reason, 196
  impassibility of, 271n43
  meets us in our sorrow, 200
  suffering of, 268–72
good life, different versions of, 14–15
goodness, 14–15
Greek philosophy, 270
Gregg, Robert, 205n1, 209n4, 212n9
Gregory of Nazianzus, 213
Gregory of Nyssa, xi, 23, 25, 26, 27, 200, 208–15, 269
  on consolation, 209
  on the resurrection, 215–17
  on silence, 205n1
Gregory of Rimini, 254
grief, loss of places for, 97
Guillebert, Jean, 177–78
Guise brothers, 109–11, 142
Gunpowder Plot, 112

Hacker, Jacob, 64n9

Han, Byung Chul, 27n20, 93n44, 116n20,
    148n23, 150

happiness, 8, 15, 38–40, 95–98
    achieved by never resting, 193
    anesthetizes sorrow, 192
    cannot overcome limits and finitude, 148
    of the chateau, 68, 257
    as eliminating sorrow, 146
    as elusive and unfulfilling, 96
    and freedom, 98, 117
    idolatry of, 146
    of immanent contentment, 127–30
    obsession with, 27
    as only measure of good life, 258n15
    and people we disagree with, 155
    and power, 187
    pursuit of, 28, 95, 129
    and self-fulfillment, 53
    through health, 18

happiness hunters, x–xii, 164, 189, 194

Harran, Marilyn, 144n13, 256n11

Hartle, Ann, 115n19

Haybron, Daniel, 125n42

heart, has its reason which reason does not
    know, 195, 197

heaven, 24

hedonism, 70–71

Hegel, G. W. F, 44, 72

Heidegger, Martin, 72, 148n20

Heidelberg Disputation (Luther), 189n17,
    235n22, 250

Henry II (king of France), 108–9

Henry III (king of France), 108–9, 111

Henry of Navarre, 110, 111–15, 116, 137–38,
    139, 141, 142, 173, 185

hermits, 52–53

Hibbs, Thomas, 44n5, 119n29, 195n26

Hochschild, Arlie Russell, 26n18

honnêtes hommes, 143–45, 146, 148, 154,
    156, 164, 182, 184, 187, 189
    policing stress, 159–62

hope, 36

Howard, Ben, 24, 25

Huguenots, 109, 112

human beings, as moral animals, 36–37

humility, 213, 217, 244–45

Hus, Jan, 229–30, 230n15

hypostatic union, 271n43

identitarianism, 77n31

identity, 80

Ignatieff, Michael, 22n11, 23n16

imitation of Christ, 237n25

immanent contentment, 121–30, 136, 145–
    46, 152, 162, 239
    and therapy, 163

immanent over the transcendent, 118

individualism, 62–64, 67, 68–72, 80, 94, 96

influence, 151n31

Inglehart, Ronald, 65n10, 95n45

institutions, and fulfillment, 42

instrumentalism, 64, 88–89, 96

instrumentalizing grief, 170

instrumental reasoning, 62–64, 67, 72, 82,
    83, 84–85, 87, 94

irony, 121–23, 128

Isabel, Queen, 108n5

Jacob, blessing of, 26

Jansen, Cornelius, 177–78

Jansenists, 177–78, 181, 184, 186, 190

Jefferson, Thomas, 28, 98, 115, 116

Jesuit Royal College at La Fléche, 138, 139,
    175

Jesuits, 137–38, 178, 184, 185–86
    on evangelism, 197
    on happiness, 187

Jesus Christ
    blessed the world in its loss, 27
    imitation of, 237n25
    invites us to grieve, 216
    ministry to the sorrowful, 241
    nearness in sorrow, 171–72

Joan, 242–45

Job, 212n9, 214, 218, 238

Johnson, Lauren, 228n12

John XXIII (pope), 229n15

joy, 146

justice, eclipsed by power, 77–79, 80
justification, 267–68

Kant, Immanuel, 144n9
Karant-Numm, Susan C., 251n5
Karlstadt, Andreas, 235n22
Kaufmann, Thomas, 251n4
Kieckhefer, Richard, 223n2, 234n19
Kierkegaard, Søren, 22n13, 121, 129n52,
    145–46, 188n15, 196n28, 199n33, 262n23
King, Martin Luther, Jr., 223
Knecht, Robert, 109nn7–8, 110n9, 111nn10–
    11, 228n10, 243n34
knowledge, 13
Kolakowski, Leszek, 183n9
Kreeft, Peter, 187n14, 198n31

La Boétie, Étienne de, 105–6, 107, 115, 118,
    119, 137, 192, 239
La Bouteillerie, 177, 181
Lady Philosophy, 234, 236–37, 240
Lady Theology, 234–37, 238, 240, 241, 251,
    252, 254
Lasch, Christopher, 69n17, 70
Lazarus and rich man, parable of, 217n20
left, new, 75, 76, 78, 79
liberalism, lost ideals of, 75
lifestyle, 18
Lilla, Mark, 75n26, 77n31
Locke, John, 139
Loder, James, 255–56
loneliness, 30, 66, 67, 130
loss, 154n35
Louis XIII (king of France), 141–42, 173, 175
Louis XIV (king of France), 142, 173, 175,
    185
Louis XV (king of France), 174
Luther, Martin, xi, 23, 25, 26, 27, 146n18,
    148, 155, 189, 200, 225
    on Anfechtung, 259, 260–70
    Heidelberg Disputation, 235n22, 250
    pastoral consolation of, 273
    polemical writings, 272–73
    shaped by Staupitz, 178
    on Stellvertretung, 23n15, 241n32

on theology of the cross, 146n18, 250, 251,
    261, 263n25
use of psalms, 264n27, 270

Macrina, xi, 23, 25, 26, 200, 209–17, 226,
    269
mainline Protestantism, 16–17
Marie de' Medici, 141
marketing, 18
Markwald, Rudolf, 266n34
Martin V (pope), 230
martyrdom, 54, 165n47
martyrs, 52–53, 208
Mary (mother of Jesus), 234
Massing, Michael, 251n3, 260n18
math, 173–74, 175
McGuire, Brian Patrick, 226n6, 229n14
mental health, 126, 158
mercy, and misery, 252–53, 255
merit, 256
Merleau-Ponty, Maurice, 72
Mersenne, Marin, 174–75
Meyjes, G. H. M. Posthumus, 225n5
ministry of consolation, 267
misery, 189n16, 190, 258, 261
    met by mercy, 252–53, 255
    of pleasing God through one's own will, 261
missional theology, 51
Mitton, Damien, 143
modernity
    control of, 148n22
    malaise of, 61–62
moderns, on self-fulfillment, 36–38, 41–42
Monica, 226
monks, 53
    dying well, 210
Montaigne, Michel de, x, 28, 29, 30, 36, 38,
    40–41, 44n5, 67–68, 70, 86, 98, 104, 113,
    114, 125, 182, 190, 191–94, 236, 263n26
    death of, 137
    essays of, 106, 107–8, 116–17, 118
    on happiness, 136, 141, 144–45
    pain in death of La Boetie, 106, 107, 118,
        121n36, 192, 239
    Pascal on, 140–41, 188, 189, 191

revived in *honnêtes hommes*, 143
on sincerity, 120–25
skepticism of, 139–40
Montalte, Louis de (Pascal pseudonym),
    186–87
Moore's law, 45
Moskowitz, Eva, 157nn39–40
mourning, 170–71
Mozart, Wolfgang Amadeus, 174

narcissism, 69–71, 80
Naucratius (brother of Gregory of Nyssa),
    208, 213–14
Neiman, Susan, 65n11, 74–79, 91, 122
neoliberalism, 122
neo-Nietzscheans, 162n45
Neoplatonism, 224, 269
Nestorians, 271n43
Newbigin, Lesslie, 51n14
new left, 75, 76, 78, 79
new philosophy, 173–74, 182
Newton, Isaac, 44n6, 83, 84, 86, 89, 139
Ngien, Dennis, 261n20, 262n22, 263n25,
    267n37, 268n38, 271n43, 273
Nichols, Tom, 91
Ninety-Five Theses (Luther), 272
nominalism, 257, 265
nonchalant, 123–24, 147
Norris, Kathleen, 149n25
Norris, Pippa, 65n10, 95n45
"not okay," 151–52, 161–62, 163

O'Connell, Marvin R., 181
Olympus (monk), 209–11, 216
Osmer, Richard, 12n2, 13n4

paganism
    denies sorrow, 198
    as happiness-hunting, 189–91
pain, 165n47
Paltrow, Gwyneth, 12n1
parable of Lazarus and rich man, 217n20
Pascal, Blaise, x–xi, 28, 29, 30, 68, 140–41,
    143–44, 162

and Descartes, 141
entered sorrow, 180–81
on gambling, 193–94, 200
on happiness, 143–47
individualism of, 200
on the Jesuits, 184–86
on Montaigne, 140–41,188, 189, 191
night of fire, 146, 147, 183–84, 199, 225
on the resurrection, 216
on the soul, 196
wager, 197–99, 238
Pascal, Étienne, 173–76, 179
Pascal, Jacqueline, 176, 179–82, 183, 199,
    209
pastoral, addresses the soul, 156
Paul
    conversion of, 14
    prison letters, 223
Peace of Westphalia, 142
penance, 257–59
Pensées (Pascal), 188–89, 199
performance, 159
Périer, Gilberte, 180, 182, 183, 199
Peter (brother of Gregory of Nyssa), 208,
    214
Petit, Jean, 228–29, 230
petting cats, 141, 150, 151, 156, 192, 239
Philip IV (king of France), 224–25
philosophy, 234. *See also* consolation of
    philosophy
    consoles the self but not the soul, 236–37
Pierson, Paul, 64n9
pilgrims, pilgrimage, 53, 54, 209, 231–34,
    238, 250, 255, 261, 263
plague, 227–28
Plato, 45
Podmore, Simon, 188n15, 262n23
politics, must match identity, 54
populism, 95
Port-Royal, 179–81, 184–85, 186, 197
postmodernism, 80
power, eclipses justice, 77–79, 80
prayer, practice of consoling communion,
    182
predestination, 256, 265–67

Prevot, Andrew, 198n32
probability theory, 179
prosperity gospel, 129
Protestant Reformation, 225, 267, 268
Provincial Letters (Pascal), 184–88
psalms, Luther's use of, 264n27, 270
Pseudo-Dionysius, 224

Raphael, Rina, 12n1, 128n51
rationalism, 140, 146
rationalists, 87, 89
Ravaillac, François, 138, 141
Reckwitz, Andreas, 18n8, 76n30, 127n49
recognition, 72–73, 75, 76–77, 82
relativism, 69–71, 81
religion, as instrumental, 65
Renaissance, 43–44, 45, 51n13, 86–88, 90,
    92–93, 105, 173
ressentiment, 65n11, 154n36
restoration, 158
resurrection, 215–17
rhetoric, 87
Richelieu, Cardinal, 175–76
righteousness of God, 250
Rittgers, Ronald K., 27n19, 263n24, 264n28,
    273n44
ritual, 148n23
Rogers, Ben, 176n2
Rosa, Hartmut, 22n14, 63n6, 125n41,
    151n30, 154n35, 194n24
Rosenstock-Huessy, Eugen, 47–54
Rosenzweig, Franz, 50n12
Rossinow, Doug, 75n27
Roudinesco, Elisabeth, 77n31
Rousseau, Jean-Jacques, 38, 116n21, 120n35,
    236, 263n26
Rupp, Gordon, 265n30, 269n40

sacramental, cannot abide the instrumental,
    93
sacramental evangelism, 164
sacramental imagination, 93
sacramental ontology, 20–21, 22
sacramental system, 241–42

sadness, x, 39–40, 42, 81. *See also* sorrow
Sainctot, Madame, 176
St. Bartholomew's Day, 110
salvation
    edited out of modern evangelism, 239
    as happiness, 129–30
    instrumentalization of, 240
    as turning sorrows to God, 2, 239–42, 271
Schmitt, Carl, 76n28
"schmole," 19–20
Screech, M. A., 116n22
secular evangelicalism, 17–19
self, 38, 43
    desperation of, 237
    as foundation of knowledge, 140
    and happiness, 144–45, 146, 149, 151
    immanence of, 191
    inflation of, 148–51, 155, 158, 164
    meaning is bound to, 150
    Montaigne on, 119
    obsessed with health, 163
    as own god, 263
    and soul, 144–45, 158, 181, 236
self-fulfillment, 36–46, 47–48, 50–51, 53–54,
    63, 71, 96
self-mutilation, 255, 258n15
separation of church and state, 114
sickness
    as blameless, 160
    vs. sin, 160–61
silence, 205n1
Silicon Valley, 92–93
sin
    disappearance of, 157–59
    eclipsed when soul is ignored, 158
    vs. sickness, 160–61
sincerity, 120–25
skepticism, 108, 113–14, 116, 139–40
sleeping, 120–21, 124, 136, 141, 145, 156,
    162, 192, 237
Soave, Robby, 65n11
Socrates, 44n5, 87, 234
soft despotism, 64–66, 95
Sorabji, Richard, 211n8
Sorbonne, 185

sorrow, 2, 21, 23, 81, 197–99
  as doorway to resurrection, 216
  embracing of, 164
  flattened to unhappiness, 127
  of goodbyes, 233, 238, 239–40, 242, 244,
    250, 254, 258
  of illness, 179–80
  in the life of Macrina, 211–15
  loss of places for, 97
  not happiness's opposite, 148, 149
  as part of God's story, 271
  as a pilgrimage, 215
  as problem to be fixed, 130
  as sign of election, 267–68
  and transformation, 217
  as way to the soul, 146, 164
soul
  eclipsed by the self, 156, 158
  and happiness, 146
  needs communion, 200
  not found through happiness, 145–47
  Pascal on, 196
  and sorrow, 146, 164
Spaulding, Henry, 116n23
Staupitz, Johann von, xi, 23, 25, 27, 178,
    200, 240n27, 250–60
  foundational work on Luther, 272
  influence on Luther, 241n33, 263–64, 266
  theology of the cross, 236n24
Steinmetz, David, 252, 253n9
Stellvertretung, 23n15, 241n32
stigmatization, 159–62
Stoicism, 215, 216
Storey, Benjamin and Jenna Silber, 120, 173,
    187, 189n16, 194
stress, 153–62
  causes mental illness, 160–61
  as a gift, 158–59
  as "not okay," 161–63
  policing of, 159–62
Strong, Bryan, 12n2
suffering, under slavery, 145n16
suicide, 40n4

Tauler, Johannes, 146n18, 251n2, 256n11,
    261nn20–21, 263n25
Taylor, Charles, 29–30, 36, 41, 61–67, 70,
    71–74, 80–81, 89, 92, 94, 112, 114,
    114n16, 236n23
technology, 45
temptation, 156, 254–55, 261. See also
    Anfechtung
  disappeared from imaginations, 155
  as good, 261
Thecla, 212–13
theologia crucis. See theology of the cross
theologian of glory, 250
theology of consolation, 267–68, 272. See
    also consolation of theology
theology of seeking, 237
theology of the cross, xi, 2–3, 213, 238,
    250–53, 269, 272
  and Anfechtung, 261–62
  in Gerson, 226, 236n24, 251
  in Luther, 146n18, 250, 251, 261, 263n25
  in Staupitz, 236n24, 252–53
theology that tends to suffering, 251
therapist, therapy, 26n18, 126, 156–57, 160,
    163
Thirty Years' War, 139, 142
Thomas Aquinas, 182–83
Thompson, Michael J., 128n50, 149n27
Tocqueville, Alexis de, 64, 95
tolerance, 112, 113
Toulmin, Stephen, 29, 30, 43, 67, 68, 82–92,
    94, 98, 113, 114
tourist, 232–33
tragedy, 121–23, 128
transformation, 13n5, 164
trauma, as blockage to immanent content-
    ment, 127
Trevelyan, G. M., 112n12
tribalism, 76, 79
Trilling, Lionel, 120n35
Tuchman, Barbara W., 227n7, 227n9

Ulrich, Hans, 216n18
unhappiness. See sadness
universalism, 76–77

University of Chicago, 85–86
University of Erfurt, 259, 260, 265
University of Paris, 235, 243, 252, 254
University of Tübingen, 254, 255
University of Wittenberg, 259, 264–65, 272

viatores (travelers), 236–38, 239, 241, 243, 244–45, 246, 253
victimhood, 76–77, 79, 80, 127n47
violence, 92
virtue, 39
Voltaire, 143n8, 187–88, 190, 191n21

Wallace, David Foster, 121–22
Walls, Andrew, 51n14
Walsh, Sylvia, 22n13

wanderers. See *viatores*
wellness, 9, 128n51
Wilcoxen, Matthew, 245n38
Williams, Rowan, 126n46
winners and losers, 18, 26, 124
Wittgenstein, Ludwig, 29
Woodstock, 88, 89–91
world, uncontrollability of, 22n14
World War II, 47
worship, 114
Wyclif, John, 230n15

Yoder, John Howard, 52n16

Zahl, Simeon, 235n22